COACHING EXCELLENCE

Frank Pyke

Editor

Human Kinetics

Library of Congress Cataloging-in-Publication Data

Coaching excellence.
    p. cm.
  Includes bibliographical references and index.
  1. Coaching (Athletics)--Handbooks, manuals, etc.
  GV711.C616 2012
  796.07'7--dc23

                    2012025522

ISBN: 978-1-4504-2337-3 (print)

The web addresses cited in this text were current as of September 2012, unless otherwise noted.

Developmental Editor: Heather Healy; **Assistant Editor:** Claire Marty; **Copyeditor:** Patsy Fortney; **Indexer:** Nan N. Badgett; **Permissions Manager:** Dalene Reeder; **Graphic Designer:** Joe Buck; **Graphic Artist:** Tara Welsch; **Cover Designer:** Keith Blomberg; **Photograph (cover):** Ryan Pierse/Getty Images; **Photographs (interior):** Neil Bernstein, © Human Kinetics, unless otherwise noted; **Photo Asset Manager:** Laura Fitch; **Visual Production Assistant:** Joyce Brumfield; **Photo Production Manager:** Jason Allen; **Art Manager:** Kelly Hendren; **Associate Art Manager:** Alan L. Wilborn; **Illustrations:** © Human Kinetics, unless otherwise noted; **Printer:** Total Printing Systems

Human Kinetics books are available at special discounts for bulk purchase. Special editions or book excerpts can also be created to specification. For details, contact the Special Sales Manager at Human Kinetics.

Printed in the United States of America   10   9   8   7   6   5   4   3

The paper in this book is certified under a sustainable forestry program.

Human Kinetics
P.O. Box 5076
Champaign, IL 61825-5076
Website: www.HumanKinetics.com

In the United States, email info@hkusa.com or call 800-747-4457.
In Canada, email info@hkcanada.com.
In the United Kingdom/Europe, email hk@hkeurope.com.

For information about Human Kinetics' coverage in other areas of the world,
please visit our website: **www.HumanKinetics.com**

                                                                      E5633

COACHING
EXCELLENCE

CONTENTS

Preface   vii

Acknowledgements   ix

Introduction: The Modern Coaching Landscape   xi

PART I

BEING A COACH 1

1   Roles and Responsibilities of the Coach 3

2   Coaching Styles and Skills 13

3   Qualities of Respected Coaches 29

PART II

MANAGING THE PROGRAM. 43

4   Planning and Evaluating the Program. 45

5   Creating a Positive Team Culture 59

6   Relating to Others. 71

7   Managing Risk 87

PART III

DEVELOPING THE ATHLETE 97

8 Evaluating the Athlete 99

9 Designing a Training Program 111

10 Implementing Training Methods 125

11 Analysing Technique 147

12 Teaching Sport Skills 171

13 Sharpening Mental Skills 185

14 Advocating Appropriate Nutrition 201

15 Addressing Injuries and Illnesses 215

16 Nurturing Life Skills 229

Index   239

About the Editor   251

About the Contributors   253

PREFACE

This coaching text continues and builds upon a series of popular coaching manuals. The first, *Towards Better Coaching*, was published in 1980 followed by *Better Coaching* in 1991 and 2001. This book is titled *Coaching Excellence* to reflect the progress that has been made in the profession during the past thirty years and to indicate how expectations of coaches have increased during that time.

Our coaches must strive to become thoroughly informed and fully capable of addressing the significant challenges ahead of them. Surveys show that participation in sport is gradually declining as we succumb to a more sedentary life style, particularly among our children and adolescents. Additionally, more countries are now involved seriously in elite sport, which makes winning on the world stage increasingly difficult. So, whether coaches are involved in junior, recreational or high performance sport, meeting these challenges requires them to always aspire to be their best, both in their technical area and as people. These aspirations match the expectations coaches have for members of their squads.

Coaching Excellence is divided into three parts. Part I describes the ever-expanding role of the modern coach in delivering a high quality program. Emphasis is placed on the importance of social skills, self-awareness, knowledge, experience and a willingness to learn. The management, organisational and communication skills required to have a positive influence both on and off the field are detailed. The qualities of some of Australia's best coaches, past and present, are described, and this part includes valuable comments from some of these coaches and in some cases from those with whom they have had a close association.

Part II focuses on the principles underlying the conduct of a successful program. It emphasises the coach's role in encouraging everyone to work together. This involves creating a team-oriented culture within the program and then managing relationships with all the parties likely to have some influence on it. This section offers advice on how to manage the risks and ethical issues that confront a coach, which is an area that creates continuing problems in modern sport. Careful planning and critical evaluation of the program are also included as an essential part of ensuring that the best possible outcomes are achieved.

Part III demonstrates the application of Australia's highly regarded scientific approach to athlete development. It includes evaluating the demands of a wide range of different sports as well as the attributes of the athletes involved and then developing a training program that meets the mental and physical requirements of each individual. The section presents the most recent information available on specific mental, technical and tactical skill and fitness training programs and does so in a manner that is practical and readily usable by coaches. Chapters on life skill development, nutrition and injuries and illnesses also provide current and valuable knowledge from within each of these important areas of athlete health and welfare.

The best coaches are always searching for a better way. In elite sport, coaches are invariably motivated by a desire to help athletes and teams succeed. In school and recreational programs, the motivation is to enable more participants to enjoy sport and enhance their health, well-being and self-confidence. This book, by sharing the latest knowledge, research and applications of our best sport coaches, scientists and professionals, can play a key role toward achieving those objectives.

ACKNOWLEDGEMENTS

I would like to thank Chris Halbert from Human Kinetics for initiating this project and for her enthusiasm and dedication to its successful completion. In addition, the authors were prompt, committed and enthusiastic, and that was much appreciated.

I would also like to thank my wife, Janet, for her wonderful support throughout this project, as well as all the previous projects.

In particular I wish to acknowledge all the coaches and athletes I have had the privilege of working with and being inspired by during my career.

—*Frank Pyke*

INTRODUCTION: THE MODERN COACHING LANDSCAPE

OUR SPORT

During the past 30 years, the sporting landscape in Australia has changed markedly. Our population has become more culturally diverse, potentially making more sports available to more people. Although this has not necessarily resulted in an increase in the number of people participating in sport, in international competition we have continued to outperform many other countries with larger populations.

Participation and performance are closely linked. If there are large numbers playing a particular sport, the chances of producing champions are greater. The performances of these champions then encourage others to participate. Conversely, low participation rates have an adverse effect on the chances of generating outstanding performances within the sport and the subsequent involvement of others.

Participation in sport is now being seriously challenged by time spent in sedentary pursuits, many of which involve sitting in front of screens: televisions, computers, gaming systems and mobile devices. The modern lifestyle discourages physical activity and is one of the most significant factors leading to an increase in the number of overweight and obese individuals, particularly children and adolescents.

The situation is quite different in high-performance sport, in which more countries are now involved in the pursuit of excellence. Success on the international stage is seen as an important means of generating national pride and is accompanied by high public interest and expectation. This is fuelled by global television coverage and modern Internet communication that provide viewers with access to an ever-expanding range of major sporting events.

In the constant search for a winning formula, high-performance sport has become more commercial and professional. Consequently, many athletes, coaches and members of support services teams are now employed full-time in elite programs and are well remunerated to meet the commitments of hectic competition schedules. This has become possible as a result of the increased financial support provided by governments, the corporate sector and the public.

OUR COACHES

At the heart of our involvement in both recreational and high-performance sport are our coaches. There are substantial demands on them to ensure that, with the increased number of sports now available to our children and youth, a large enough talent pool is available and the people in that pool have a clear pathway through the sport and have the opportunity to maximise their potential. This process requires coaches, and their athletes and teams, to commit to a plan and be prepared to do the hard work necessary to fulfil its objectives. Once people become involved in school, recreational and high-performance programs, it is imperative that coaches maintain their interest and involvement and minimise participant dropout.

Coaches have the responsibility for ensuring that athletes enjoy participating and improve their skill and fitness while doing so. To fulfil this responsibility, the coach must understand the sport, know the athlete and be able to implement a program that will bring about the improvements required to reach the established performance goals. The coach must also be able to work cooperatively with others connected in the program, including sporting clubs and associations, schools, parents and particularly in elite programs, the personnel who provide specific services to athletes.

In high-performance sport, one of the greatest challenges for the coach is to ensure that all members of the athlete support team are working in consort. For example, when an athlete receives mixed messages from the coaching, physical conditioning and physical therapy staff about the best way forward with a particular injury, it creates confusion and uncertainty. It is the coach's role to bring the support team together on a regular basis to establish a unified view and communicate this to the athlete. Another continuing problem for coaches and management in modern sport is ensuring that their athletes are not involved with performance-enhancing drugs and any other illegal or unethical behaviours both within and outside sport.

The time commitment of coaches can become excessive. This not only includes planning and supervising the training and competition program of the athlete or the team, but also coordinating support staff and dealing with administrators, sponsors and the media. Furthermore, the degree of stress experienced is heightened by the public pressure to achieve good results. Coaches must learn to cope by delegating some responsibilities to others, putting their health and family foremost on their list of priorities and ensuring that they have a life outside sport.

OUR PROGRAMS

Sports science has grown noticeably within the Australian university system. What were formerly known as physical education and recreation courses are now commonly labelled as sports and exercise science or human movement. Several universities also now offer coaching science courses and use the textbooks of the national coaching accreditation program.

Several scientific disciplines form the biological and behavioural basis of sport performance. These include physiology, functional anatomy, biomechanics, motor learning and control and psychology. Among them, they define the fitness, technical and tactical skill and mental qualities required to achieve success. They also provide the scientific basis of athlete development programs through a better understanding of the physical and mental demands of the sport, the attributes of individual athletes and the suitability and effectiveness of a prescribed training regime.

Sports medicine, physiotherapy and nutrition specialists are also now valuable members of the support staff for high-performance teams. The prevention and treatment of injury and illness is of paramount importance, particularly in sports in which explosive movements and body contact are commonplace and competition schedules are heavy. Healthy, performance-enhancing diets accompanied by sufficient replacement fluids are essential for all athletes.

Coaches are now better educated, but creativity and innovation are also important to producing winning and breakthrough performances. New methods employed with success should undergo scientific scrutiny to be validated or refuted by solid research. This approach has served Australia's sports institute and sports academy network very well through the years and established the country's favourable international reputation in the application of science and technology in sport.

Finally, coaches at all levels of sport should strive to develop their athletes' life skills. There are many social benefits of participating in sport, including establishing a social network and having a sense of a community and, in the process, learning to be cooperative, disciplined and respectful of others. Ultimately, these are more important outcomes than a team or an individual winning a particular event. Coaches, with the help of parents, can encourage these growth opportunities for athletes and help instil in them a love for the spirit of sport that they can retain throughout their lives.

THIS BOOK

No single resource can contain or convey everything that a coach should know and do. So *Coaching Excellence* does the next best thing. It builds on the basics to provide serious and high-performance-level coaches a wealth of information to become more adept in their roles.

Expert contributors to this book were carefully selected to ensure the best knowledge, research and insights for coaches to take and apply in working with their athletes and teams. The content is divided into three interrelated parts that are important to coaches.

Part I examines the on- and off-field roles and responsibilities of a coach. This section provides examples of a number of successful coaches with very different personalities and skills. Reflective comments from athletes who have performed under their tutelage add an interesting perspective.

Part II covers planning and coordinating a high-quality program. In such programs, all those involved have agreed to a set of core values that are associated with success within the boundaries of fair play. As expected, this requires ongoing objective evaluations and a commitment to achieving long-term success regardless of any pitfalls encountered in the process.

Part III explores the applications of the sports sciences to enhance the fitness and the technical, tactical and mental skills of athletes. All the research findings in this book have very practical applications that coaches can use to take individual and team performances to new heights. Indeed, the contributors to this section show an equal appreciation of the health and well-being of both athletes and coaches. They also appreciate the challenges of coaching and advocate a balance between sport and life that will in turn benefit the athletes.

Clearly, the best coaches are those who know their sports, their athletes and themselves and are always searching for ways to improve their programs. In elite sport, this is invariably motivated by a desire to win. However, it never takes too long before any new method finds its way into school and recreational programs, enabling more participants to enjoy sport and thereby enhancing the health, fitness, well-being and confidence of the community.

PART I
BEING A COACH

BEING A COACH

CHAPTER 1

Roles and Responsibilities of the Coach

———— Cliff Mallett

Sport has the potential to change people's lives. Specifically, sport can be a vehicle for positive development because it prompts participants to learn, achieve and develop. Engagement in sport can foster personal growth, enabling young participants to become fully functioning adult citizens and make a contribution to broader society. Sport can promote well-being and academic achievement and transform people's lives, including those in positions of disadvantage. Conversely, negative sporting experiences can hinder development.

Experiences participants gain from journeying through sport influence their subsequent views of sport, the world and their place in it—such is the potential power of the sporting experience. Nonetheless, sport is not inherently good and does not inevitably lead to positive outcomes; learning in and through sport is contingent on quality experiences. In many instances, quality coaching is the key to quality participant experiences.

The coach is central to the potential of sport to contribute towards participants' positive development. In the sporting context, coaches, teachers and peers are the most influential people on youth. Coaches in particular are in a position to promote the importance of health, human rights, inclusion and engagement in a productive lifestyle. This promotion doesn't happen without explicit and deliberate guidance and an understanding of the power of sport. Coaches should be equipped to deliver on these expectations and potential.

Most people acknowledge the central role of the coach in the coach-athlete-performance relationship. In recent times, the key roles and responsibilities of the coach have increased and necessitated a commensurate program of development to produce quality coaching and subsequently contribute to the holistic development of participants. In response to the significant growth of sport in Australian society, the vocation of coaching has evolved, especially over the past three decades.

The advent of the Australian National Coach Accreditation Scheme (NCAS) and many sports taking responsibility for coach education and development has contributed to the evolution of sport coaching in Australia. Many coaches seek these formal and less formal learning opportunities to develop their craft. National and state institutes of sport, as well as academies within national sporting organisations, have also contributed to the development of coaching. Furthermore, coaching science researchers and scholars and formal coach education programs in the university sector have also contributed significantly to the professionalisation of coaching as a vocation.

COACHING AND THE COACHING PROCESS

Sport coach development programs designed to help coaches deliver positive sporting experiences are in their infancy compared with such programs in more established vocations within the performing arts, such as music, art and ballet. These fields have long-established programs for directing their development and professionalisation.

Sport coaching is a social activity and consequently involves the interactions of many people such as coaches, athletes, parents, officials and support personnel. As a result, coaches must be sensitive and responsive to differences in ability, race, religion and gender to get the best from people. People engage in sport for many reasons, and coaches must recognise the range of needs, goals and aspirations that produce different physical and psychosocial responses (e.g., motor skills, emotions).

Sport coaching is considered a systematic and integrated process rather than a series of unrelated training sessions or learning experiences. The coaching process refers to the purposeful engagement of coach and athlete over time to improve skilled performance, and the coach is responsible for leading this process.

Coaches are charged with the responsibility to influence (i.e., lead) in all sporting contexts (recreational to elite). This notion of sport leadership highlights the power of coaches in the coach-athlete-performance relationship. In leading the coaching process, coaches need to be conscious of the athletes' goals as well as their own goals for coaching.

PRIMARY AIM OF COACHING

Young people spend nearly half their time in leisure pursuits, and sport is a popular organised recreational activity with the potential to promote positive development. Although sport has been associated with positive experiences and outcomes, such as improved confidence and academic achievement, it has also been linked with negative experiences and outcomes, such as stress, burnout, dropout and low self-esteem.

As architects of the sporting environment, coaches are responsible for fostering participants' healthy development. Coaches are important role models for children and youth and, along with parents, are significant adult influences. How coaches interact with sport participants determines the outcomes of participation. Hence, coaches play a pivotal role in the contribution of sport to physical and psychosocial development.

Positive athlete outcomes from sport can be summarised in the four Cs, which come from the positive youth development literature:

- Competence
- Confidence
- Connection
- Character and caring

Competence is associated with a positive view of oneself in specific contexts, such as sport, academic, work and social environments. To feel competent is a fundamental psychological need for humans in all cultures. Sport participants (at all levels) who feel competent are more likely to be internally motivated to work hard, persevere and subsequently pursue and achieve excellence.

The sense of accomplishment that occurs when an athlete achieves a goal is a powerful force for internal motivation. Hence, the sporting context should foster a sense of competence in all participants, including those whose abilities are less developed compared with others of the same age. Obviously, the role of the coach is central to promoting a sense of competence. Contexts that hinder the perception of competence are associated with lower motivation, performance and well-being.

Confidence has to do with a sense of positive self-worth and self-efficacy. This global view of oneself influences motivation, the capacity to learn and subsequent performance. Confidence is initially developed during childhood and can be fragile, especially throughout adolescence. Helping children and youth to be curious, to show initiative and to be independent and autonomous fosters a sense of self-worth. Coaches who focus on self-referenced improvement promote internal motivation, a willingness to work hard and resilience. Furthermore, they create athletes who view themselves positively.

Connection is associated with a sense of belonging. We all like to belong to particular

Tony Marshall/EMPICS Sport/PA Photos

Coaches can help youth players develop competence in their sport and confidence in themselves.

groups, and a key reason for children's engagement in sport is to pursue friendships with their peers. It is also noteworthy that this need to belong continues throughout the human life span. Athletes at the elite level have the same need to belong that children do. Sport provides opportunities to develop a strong sense of belonging to teams and squads. These positive bonds among team members provide a warm and friendly environment in which to develop physical and social skills and to learn prosocial behaviours. Furthermore, positive connections with other adults (coaches) through constructive and encouraging feedback promote enjoyment and other positive outcomes, such as increased effort.

The development of *character* and *caring* has not always been associated with sport participation. Nonetheless, sport can contribute to the development of character and a sense of caring for others (compassion) if explicitly taught by the coach and other significant adults such as parents. Moral development and integrity are associated with this fourth C. The respect for societal rules and the demonstration of appropriate behaviours both on and off the field are central to the development of good moral character. Moreover, sportspeople with good moral character are sensitive to issues such as access for all and tolerance of differences.

Developing competence, confidence, connection, character and caring in athletes should be the charter of sport coaches. Hence, coaches should be mindful of how they behave and how they go about contributing to the holistic development of their athletes. Consideration of the four Cs in coaching practice will foster positive sporting experiences for all. A focus on holistic development will encourage athletes' continued engagement in sport, which is necessary to enable them to develop their sporting abilities.

FORMS OF COACHING

The term *coach* can mean different things to different people. In a broad sense, sport coaching is associated with helping others in the context of sport; however, not all coaches undertake the same type of work. The context in which coaches operate usually determines the form of coaching undertaken. Coaching scholars and educators have recognised four forms of coaching:

- Instructors or sport teachers (e.g., golf)
- Participation coaches (e.g., Little Athletics)
- Performance or development coaches (e.g., school, youth academies)
- High-performance coaches (e.g., institutes of sport and professional team coaches)

Instructors are sport leaders who provide basic instruction to beginners on how to play specific sports. Sport instructors or teachers are common in sports such as tennis, swimming and golf. Sport teachers introduce interested learners to the basics of how to play the sport, and generally the instructor and learner engage in a limited period of interaction. The key focus is to improve the performance within a short time frame. Instructors work with both young people and adults. People who engage with sport instructors do not participate in formal competition.

Participation coaches generally provide opportunities for people to engage in sport as a productive leisure pursuit. These coaches generally work in community contexts in which there is low-level competition. In these contexts, participation is emphasised over performance enhancement, and the focus is on enjoyment and health. Participation coaching predominately occurs in junior sport contexts, although there are some sports in which adult participation coaching occurs.

Development or performance coaching occurs in formal competitive environments such as schools and club sports and typically involves a stable relationship between a coach and athletes during a competitive season. The focus is on preparation to enhance performance, which requires an increased level of commitment in coaches and athletes compared with recreational contexts. The identification and development of sporting talent is consistent with the work of development coaches. It is noteworthy that although the focus is on performance enhancement, enjoyment is necessary to develop internal motivation to sustain engagement.

High-performance coaches work in elite sporting environments. Their work is typically highly organised and systematic but necessarily fluid and dynamic. They develop sophisticated plans for training and competition; however, they must be flexible and adaptable to adjust to a changing environment such as injury or poor performance. High-performance coaches focus on successful performance, including winning.

To produce successful performances, these coaches engage in highly complex tasks involving the extensive collection and monitoring of data to inform and regulate training and competition plans. Moreover, high-performance coaching necessitates interactions with a range of paraprofessionals (e.g., specialist coaches and sports science and sports medicine experts) and generally requires full-time employment (e.g., head coach in a professional national football league). Another form of high-performance coaching is representative team coaching (e.g., state or Olympic team coaching), which requires a slightly different skill set.

Importantly, all coaches should be valued for the individual and collective contributions they make in facilitating learning and development in and through sport for people of all ages. In recognition of the importance of all forms of coaching, coaches in all classifications have strong support in becoming more expert (e.g., higher levels of coach accreditation in participation coaching and youth coaching as well as high-performance coaching). Specialised accreditation opportunities reflect the various forms of sport leadership and the associated differences in the roles and responsibilities of the actors.

DEVELOPING A COACHING PHILOSOPHY

The development of a personal set of views on coaching (i.e., one's coaching philosophy) is an ongoing process derived from coaches' own life experiences, including their families and education experiences. Coaches' views on coaching are representative of their values—what they believe is important. These beliefs and principles are significant because they influence how and why coaches coach the way they do.

Coaching philosophies usually change over time. Initially, coaches might focus on performance enhancement and a win-at-all-cost attitude. However, over time coaches might shift their thinking about the purpose of their coaching to encompass a broader understanding of how sport participation contributes to the holistic development of participants. Articulating their coaching philosophies can be challenging for many coaches. Often, it is not until they take the time to reflect on their practice that they can have some clarity about their views on coaching.

Articulating a coaching philosophy requires coaches to be self-reflective and authentic. They should be true to themselves and be who they are instead of trying to be someone else. The evolution of a coaching philosophy takes time and self-reflection about what values are really important.

Often, coaches' real values emerge when they are faced with coaching dilemmas. For example, does a coach play the best player in an important match, after that player is badly injured? It is important that coaches' espoused values be reflected in their behaviours because athletes and parents judge what coaches value based on their behaviours.

The ethical bases of practice should frame coaching behaviors. As stated earlier, sport coaching is a social activity and, therefore, bound by unwritten rules for social behaviour—what is acceptable and appropriate in a given circumstance. Coaches are often asking themselves, What should I do? Although ethical codes for behaviour have been developed and appear to be black and white (i.e., one action is right and one action is wrong), the reality is that judgements about ethical behaviours are complex. Consideration of the context is critical when evaluating coaches' decisions.

Many coaches of professional and Olympic sports, in which performance outcomes are critical to future funding and employment, face dilemmas that challenge their values and beliefs and subsequently affect their behaviour. The link between performance and rewards such as money and status can move coaches, athletes and officials beyond acceptable and appropriate behaviour.

In performance sports, coaches and athletes are always looking for an advantage over their opponents. In pursuing this advantage, the boundaries between acceptable and unacceptable behaviour in some circumstances may become blurred. Coaches need to remember to replace emotional reactions with a considered and clear ethical understanding of practice. Moreover, they should be able to present reasons for their decisions and, in doing so, justify their actions.

Ethical issues do not arise only in performance sports; they can also be found in recreational sports in the form of harassment, discrimination and bullying. Hence, guidance regarding appropriate and acceptable behaviours in sport is needed. Codes of behaviour in sport, which are typically based on moral values, can help guide coaching practice, and they usually reflect coaches' responsibilities to uphold the trust placed in them as well as their duty to care for the athletes they work with.

Codes of behaviour address the rights of others, but how each coach implements them is a personal matter. The application of ethics in daily practice is where codes can fall short. Coaches must not only be aware of the ethics of coaching practice, but more important, they must understand them and apply them appropriately. An example is providing equal time for all players in a team.

Coaches need to think before acting. Reflecting on the potential consequences of specific actions enables them to be clear about the rationale for their decisions and to be prepared to explain that rationale.

The Australian Sports Commission has produced guidelines for appropriate behaviour for coaches, officials, parents and athletes. Following are some of the guidelines for coaches:

- Operate within the rules and spirit of your sport, promoting fair play over winning at any cost.
- Encourage and support opportunities for people to learn appropriate behaviours and skills.
- Support opportunities for participation in all aspects of the sport.
- Treat each person as an individual.
- Act with integrity and objectivity, and accept responsibility for your decisions and actions.
- Respect the rights and worth of every person regardless of their gender, ability, cultural background or religion.

Based on Australian Sports Commission. Available: http://www.coachingaus.org/ethics.htm#Code

These guidelines highlight the fact that coaches should accept responsibility for their actions and demonstrate trust, competence, respect, safety consciousness, honesty, professionalism, a belief in equity and good sporting behaviour. Nevertheless, a governing body such as a coaches' association should be responsible for monitoring and regulating the behaviours of coaches within the parameters of the sport. The governing body should also be responsible for imposing sanctions on coaches who digress from the code. Accountability, monitoring and regulation are needed to professionalise sport coaching.

PROFESSIONALISATION OF COACHING

Coaches develop specialised knowledge, undertake the requirements for accreditation and registration and adhere to a code of ethics, among other tasks associated with professional practice. Therefore, the professionalisation of coaching is associated with continuing development in becoming a knowledgeable, competent and ethical coach. This ongoing development requires coaches to be lifelong learners, which is consistent with many vocations and professions.

As previously stated, coaching has a strong influence on the quality of the sporting experience. Moreover, coach development is key to sustaining and improving the quality of sport coaching. Quality coaching is strongly linked to learning through a unique combination of formal (university education), informal (mentors, coaching work) and non-formal (seminars, workshops) learning opportunities. Coaches report several key sources of learning that include the following (in no particular order): coaching experience, playing experience, university study, personal reflection, observing other coaches, discussions with other coaches, working with other coaches, external consultants, professional reading, professional development courses, in-house programs, watching television, previous occupations and family and friends.

As coaches develop their craft, they usually seek and value many sources of learning and development. Nevertheless, continuing professional development is the responsibility of coaches themselves, who should seek support and opportunities from others such as govern-ing bodies and external organisations such as those in the university sector. Coaches should be assertive in seeking learning opportunities from a variety of formal, informal and non-formal learning contexts.

Given the various forms of coaching, coaches' learning needs are highly idiosyncratic. Coaches are likely to have a sense of what they know, what they don't know and what they want to know, which is typically governed by their coaching experiences and the athletes or teams they coach or have coached, as well as their formal educational background and other life experiences. Of course, the more one learns, the more one comes to realise how little one knows—such is the joy of learning!

SELF-EVALUATION

People often talk about reflection and its importance in developing the craft of coaching. Basically, when coaches reflect, they think about practice, including what they said and how they behaved. In thinking about their coaching practice, coaches typically consider reflective questions such as the following:

- Did the session go to plan? Were the goals of this week's training achieved?
- What went well? How do I know?
- What might I change for next time? What are the consequences of the proposed change?
- How are the athletes responding to the program? What do they like or dislike?
- How might I deliver the message another way?

Coaches often reflect during training and competitions, as well as at the end of a session, training week or training month, which explains why many people consider coaching a 24/7 job. Coaches are often thinking about the best ways to do their jobs—why they coach the way they do and perhaps why some coaching strategies worked and others did not. In this way they develop their coaching practice.

Self-reflection can be unguided or guided by others. Many coaches video their coaching sessions (an unguided option) so they can review them to determine what went well and what did not. Other coaches invite critical friends to observe their coaching practices and to provide some constructive feedback (a guided option) about their behaviours. This provides a different lens through which to view their coaching practice and can both affirm and challenge how coaches behave.

Self-reflection, over time, should move beyond mere descriptions of what happened. It should also consider the underlying reasons for the results and at times challenge taken-for-granted assumptions that underpin coaching practice. Quality reflection is shaped by inquiring questions and is a skill that requires regular practice.

Although it is important to focus on coaching, it is probably more important to reflect on how the athletes experience that coaching. The most important information about coaching comes from the athletes themselves. Many experience coaching at least three times per week over several months, making their feedback particularly useful. Although seeking feedback from athletes might feel somewhat threatening to coaches, the information is crucial in understanding how athletes view the coaching they are receiving. Knowing how athletes view and respond to coaching can stimulate coaches' self-reflection. Coaches can solicit feedback by asking athletes basic questions such as what they like and don't like about how they are being coached. (See the Feedback section later in this chapter for more information.)

To further their development, coaches need to consider why they coach the way they do. Many simply coach the way they were coached as athletes. Unfortunately, these practices might not be the way to get the best from athletes and promote their holistic development. Furthermore, generational changes in how young people view the world have been a catalyst for many changes to coaching practices. Reflective coaches challenge their cultural practices and respond to how their athletes prefer to be coached. This self-reflection is a central part of the professionalisation of coaching.

NETWORKING

Coaches primarily learn the craft of coaching, aside from their personal experiences, from others. Many learn about coaching practice from their experiences as players. In the early stages of their coaching careers, coaches initially draw on their playing experiences and how they were coached, and they typically replicate those practices. Over time they begin to experiment with different approaches after observing other coaches in action, and usually receive direct guidance from other coaches during coach education and development workshops and seminars. During these observations coaches are keen to learn specific drills and skills, but also how other coaches deliver and communicate their messages to enhance athlete learning and development.

Although coaches are encouraged to share their knowledge, many are reluctant to communicate 'sacred' knowledge. This reluctance does little to progress the professionalisation of coaching. More important than the content itself is using it appropriately in coaching practice, which is unique to each coaching context and dependent on the specific situation or circumstance.

FEEDBACK

Coaches' ongoing development requires feedback about their practice. As previously stated, athletes themselves are a key source of feedback. Although asking athletes about their experience of the coaching they are getting can be a little intimidating, coaches appreciate and benefit from their feedback. Asking for feedback also sends a message to the athletes that their opinions are valued. A simple way to collect this feedback is to ask athletes to write what they like and don't like about the coaching. Allowing them to respond anonymously is a good way to ensure that the feedback is honest. Asking the team manager or another person to collect the information might be a useful strategy. Coaches need to ask themselves: How can I improve my practice without receiving information from those who experience my coaching?

More formal measures (questionnaires) can also be used to collect data on coaching from athletes. The Coaching Behavior Scale for Sport (CBS-S) enables athletes to provide data about their coaches' behaviours that move beyond winning and losing percentages. This multidimensional questionnaire includes a range of coaching behaviours such as physical training and planning, goal setting, mental preparation, technical skills, personal rapport, negative personal rapport and competition strategies. Feedback from such a questionnaire can guide reflection and subsequent practice.

LIFE BALANCE

Coaching seems to be a 24/7 occupation in many cases. To promote quality coaching and longevity in the vocation, coaches require a balanced lifestyle to counteract the emotionally draining aspects of the job. Burnout in sport is often associated with athletes; however, coaches who do not find the appropriate balance between coaching and other life pursuits also risk burnout. Coaches who want to have an impact over a long period of time in their sport must strike an appropriate lifestyle balance. Finding time each day to chill and recover from the daily stresses of coaching is the key to longevity in coaching.

SUMMARY

- Coaches are the architects of the sporting context and as sport leaders have the power to create learning environments that contribute to positive athlete development.
- The four Cs are a helpful way to think about the holistic development of youth: competence, confidence, connection and character and caring. Consider how coaching explicitly contributes to the four C's for each athlete.
- Athletes who feel valued and are progressing in their physical and psychosocial development are more likely to remain in sport and benefit from their sustained engagement. Sport coaching occurs in a range of contexts, and the work of coaches in all contexts should be recognised and valued.
- Coaches at all levels need to develop their philosophies of coaching, which should be considered in conjunction with ethically based decisions regarding how to interact and behave in the sporting environment.
- The professionalisation of coaching requires an acceptable code of ethical behaviour and the continuing professional development of coaches in all domains.
- Coaches are personally responsible for their learning and development, including reflecting on their work both internally and with guidance from others.
- Ongoing engagement in sport requires that coaches find the appropriate balance between work and play and model this balance for their athletes. Life balance improves the quality of coaching and fosters longevity in the vocation.

REFERENCES AND RESOURCES

Australian Sports Commission. www.coachingaus.org/ethics.htm.

Bowes, I., & Jones, R.L. (2006). Working at the edge of chaos: Understanding coaching as a complex, interpersonal system. *The Sport Psychologist, 20,* 235-245.

Côté, J., Bruner, M., Erikson, K., Strachan, L., & Fraser-Thomas, J. (2010). Athlete development and coaching. In J. Lyle & C. Cushion (Eds.), *Sports coaching: Professionalisation and practice* (pp. 63-84). Edinburgh: Elsevier.

Cushion, C.J., Armour, K.M., & Jones, R.L. (2003). Coach education and continuing professional development: Experience and learning to coach, *Quest, 55,* 215-230.

Gilbert, W., & Trudel, P. (2001). Learning to coach through experience: Reflection in model youth sport coaches, *Journal of Teaching in Physical Education, 21,* 16-34.

Irwin, G., Hanton, S., & Kerwin, D.G. (2004). Reflective practice and the origins of elite coaching knowledge. *Reflective Practice, 5* (3), 425-442.

Jones, R., Armour, K., & Potrac, P. (2004). *Sports coaching cultures: From practice to theory.* London: Routledge.

Jones, R., & Wallace, M. (2005). Another bad day at the training ground: Coping with ambiguity in the coaching context. *Sport, Education, and Society 10* (1), 119-134.

Lerner, R.M., Fisher, C.B., & Weinberg, R.A. (2000). Toward a science for and of the people: Promoting civil society through the application of developmental science. *Child Development, 71,* 11-20.

Lyle, J. (2002). *Sports coaching concepts: A framework for coaches' behaviour.* New York: Routledge.

Lyle, J., & Cushion, C. (Eds.). (2010). *Sports coaching: Professionalisation and practice.* Edinburgh: Elsevier.

Mallett, C.J. (2010). Becoming a high-performance coach: Pathways and communities. In J. Lyle & C. Cushion (Eds.), *Sports coaching: Professionalisation and practice* (pp. 119-134). Edinburgh: Elsevier.

Mallett, C., & Côté, J. (2006). Beyond winning and losing: Guidelines for evaluating high performance coaches. *The Sport Psychologist, 20,* 213-221.

Mallett, C.J., Trudel, P., Lyle, J., & Rynne, S. (2009) Formal versus informal coach education. *International Journal of Sport Science and Coaching, 4,* 325-334.

Rynne, S.B., Mallett, C.J., & Tinning, R. (2010). Workplace learning of high-performance sports coaches. *Sport, Education and Society, 15,* 315-330.

CHAPTER 2

Coaching Styles and Skills

—— Brian Douge

Athletes acquire the ability to compete through their exposure to a variety of learning experiences. They learn by engaging in activities at more challenging levels, observing more accomplished athletes, being guided through well-structured development programs and acquiring and applying knowledge about how to perform and compete. Coaches are responsible for delivering a program that best facilitates their athletes' ability to develop and compete.

How well a coach achieves this is greatly determined by the coach's command of the coaching process. The coaching process involves the coordinated delivery and integration of the many key components of coaching, and it includes the productive engagement of the coach with the athlete. A successful process results in effective coaching and leads to optimal athlete development. Just as a chef produces a quality meal by cleverly contriving and mixing the ingredients of a recipe, a coach produces a quality athlete by cleverly choosing and integrating athlete learning experiences. For example, the ingredients for the coach might be equipment set-up, instructions about what to do and feedback. The cooking (the coaching process) might be the relationship of the equipment use to performance requirements in competition, a precise and motivating method of delivering instructions and what method (oral or written; public, private or internal) of delivering feedback is used. This chapter provides information about leadership and coaching styles and skills that create a successful coaching process and enhance the experiences and competitiveness of athletes.

LEADERSHIP STYLES

Coaching style, often described as the art of coaching, is the approach adopted by a coach to best respond to the needs of the athletes, the team or both. Advanced coaches combine their natural and nurtured personalities with those of successful coaches to construct an approach to the coaching act that best fits the situation. A coach's adoption of a particular leadership style is greatly determined by the specific situation confronting the coach and athlete(s) at any given time. It is also determined by the culture of the sporting community; the coach's inherent personality, disposition and past experiences; and the characteristics and expectations of the athlete(s).

The following categorisation of leadership into three styles (authoritarian, democratic and submissive) provides an understanding of three broadly accepted approaches to sport coaching. However, it is essential to recognise that no single leadership style is most suited for all circumstances. Adept coaches use a combination of coaching styles, and the best coaches do this in a way that results in optimal athlete learning and performance.

AUTHORITARIAN LEADERSHIP

The authoritarian style of coaching is autocratic and involves absolute rule by the coach. Athletes are told what to do by the coach and must adhere to a designated chain of command. In team sports, a number of people may report to the coach: assistant coaches, team leaders, specialist support staff and athletes.

In authoritarian regimes, all information and advice to the team or individual athletes must be referred through the coach for approval. The authoritarian coach typically applies external controls, both punitive and rewarding, to manage athlete commitment. An authoritarian approach is often needed when team strategies are undermined by selfish players or when the coach needs to act quickly to arrest an escalating problem.

For example, imagine that Professional Rugby League coach Chris, as part of his pre-game address, had discussed with the team the plan to play a less expansive game in the first 20 minutes by keeping the ball in the forwards to complete each set of six tackles followed by a kick down field. After 10 minutes of the game, the ball was lost in the second tackle of a set of six when it was passed wide to an unsuspecting winger. The player who prematurely passed the ball has a history of being selfish and undermining the team. Chris benched the offending player and at halftime reminded the team that in some situations he will take complete control and apply consequences to those who do not commit to the team plan.

The authoritarian style of leadership works best with athletes who lack the understanding, knowledge or experience to contribute effectively to their program. It works best when the situation requires a clearly defined approach to extinguish any opportunity for athlete confusion or misinterpretation of their responsibilities.

DEMOCRATIC LEADERSHIP

The democratic style of leadership involves give and take, collaboration with athletes and support staff, questioning techniques and cooperation. Asking athletes questions about their performance and training is an effective method of encouraging them to become skilled at identifying and solving their own problems

As an example, consider lawn bowls coach Gwen. She noticed that as her player, Julia, tried to give more weight to the bowl when driving at the head or attempting to take out an opponent's bowl, she tended to lose balance during the delivery. Gwen instructed Julia to perform some drives using her normal stride; then told her to try performing some drives using a slightly longer stride. Gwen asked Julia what felt different between the shorter- and longer-stride bowls. Julia commented that the longer stride seemed to create more momentum and required less effort to add weight to the bowl. Julia then practised using the longer stride for drives and the shorter stride to play draw shots. She found that she was much more stable for both shots.

The question that Gwen was asking was a higher-order question requiring considerable thought. Democratic coaches use more higher-order questions to empower their athletes to not only solve their own problems or enhance their performance outcomes but also to acknowledge that the athlete's opinion is important and highly respected. The athlete and coach work together making equal contributions to the program of development and performance. This approach works well when athletes show a keen interest in their development and have levels of understanding that allow them to make worthwhile contributions to the program.

Lower-order questions are another strategy democratic leaders use. Coaches use lower-order questions to encourage athletes to remember concepts and ideas. A concept in basketball would be the use of a zone defence. Players could be asked to remember their individual roles in the zone defence. In this situation the coach would speak to individuals and ask them to describe their roles, and the coach would then observe their ability to remember their roles while playing the game.

The democratic leadership style involves extensive consultation; all parties are prepared for a sharing of ideas, and consensus drives the adoption of an idea. The coach becomes a manager and ensures mutual respect among the individuals as well as respect for those with expertise in specific areas.

Consider the example of Noelene, coach of the state netball team, who was concerned about the superior defensive skills of the opposition, particularly the goal defence. Noelene decided to hold a team meeting. Her team's goal attack had competed against the player of concern many times and indicated that the opposition's goal defence was exceptional at intercepting the high ball because of this player's superior leap. The team decided to use bounce passes and low, direct passes to the goal attack. The outcome was a significant reduction in intercepts.

SUBMISSIVE LEADERSHIP

The submissive style of leadership involves giving control to the athlete. The coach becomes a resource whose credibility comes from leading by example, past experience, knowledge and a courteous and easygoing relationship with the athlete.

Submissive coaches focus on facilitating athlete development by creating an environment with quality role models and challenges that increase the athlete's desire to be competitive and improve. Rather than coercing athletes to be competitive or become more competitive, quality submissive coaches create situations that facilitate athletes' desire to change their approach. Ways to facilitate athlete development include providing opportunities to respond, setting realistic expectations, giving athletes time to adjust to changing situations, building step-by-step progressions into the program and ensuring that athletes experience the thrill of the skill.

Consider the example of Greg, a world-class golfer. His game became erratic and he lacked consistency. He contacted his coach, Charlie, a highly respected coach with outstanding credentials for producing good golfers, and asked him to analyse his swing. At Greg's request, Charlie watched Greg hit many practice balls. Charlie noticed that Greg was flattening the arc of his backswing as he became tired or when he strove for extra distance with the long irons or driver. Charlie offered a few solutions, and Greg chose to focus on a kinaesthetic feedback stimulus early in his backswing, which prompted the correct arc at the top of the backswing. It resulted in the improvement he was seeking.

A submissive style of coaching works best with experienced, mature and reasonably successful athletes. Provided the athlete does not, in any way, erode the coach's credibility by giving the impression that the athlete knows better, this approach can strengthen the bond between coach and athlete and enhance the inner cultural strength of a team.

COACHING DIFFERENT AGES

This section categorises players as children (0 to 12-year-olds), adolescents (13- to 17-year-olds) and adults (18 years old or older). Admittedly, there is no precise moment in time when children become adolescents and adolescents become adults. Some players in one age category display a level of maturity typical of those in another category. When an individual or team is observed to be mature or immature for their age, the coach may need to use a different approach. However, it is reasonable to use age to group athletes into developmental levels.

CHILDREN

The formative years are critical for developing correct movement patterns, self-efficacy and approach behaviours. With children age five and under, coaches should focus on basic movement patterns such as running, jumping, twisting, turning, catching, throwing, hitting, kicking and balancing. They should modify all aspects of the activity to ensure a pleasurable outcome, avoid any unnecessary trauma and use imagery and exploration as part of the movement experience.

With children 6 to 12 years old, coaches should focus on introducing and reinforcing specific sport movements. Modified rules and equipment should continue until the adult version of the sport can be adopted without detracting from the enjoyment and achievement experiences delivered in the modified environment. Imagery and exploration continue to be useful provided the pathway to acquiring correct automated technique is not compromised.

Most learning pathways are formed at this time, and coaches must be careful to teach technique correctly. Children at this age learn basic movement patterns more easily than at any other time in their development.

Children in this age group learn faster, better and more easily in a multi-sensory environment. Dynamic sound, colour, touch and kinaesthetics (sensations of the body) provide the essential stimulation to increase activity levels. Coaches need to vary their language and tone, seek out and create exciting environments and emphasise the feelings (tactile and kinaesthetic) that indicate good technique.

For an example of the use of imagery, consider how Graeme, a learn-to-swim coach, taught Justine the backstroke. Justine's father was curious as to how Graeme would teach his seven-year-old daughter the correct arm action. Graeme asked Justine to imagine that she was standing in front of an apple tree and that two juicy apples were just behind her that she could reach. One apple was on her left side and the other was on her right side. Graeme asked Justine if she could, without turning around, reach forwards and upwards with her right hand, keep her arm perfectly straight, reach behind to grab the apple on her right side and then throw it into an imaginary fruit basket that was next to and slightly behind her right leg. He then asked Justine to do the same with her left hand. Justine's father was amazed to see how Justine's arm movement resembled the backstroke arm action.

Individual focus and individual positive reinforcement strategies are essential when coaching children, especially in team sports. Coaches should strive to devote their attention to the correct aspects of a performance and provide positive comments in conjunction with feedback. Rather than, 'Don't do it that way!' the coach's approach should be, 'Try this.'

Whenever possible, all athletes in a squad should be able to hear the coach's positive movement-specific comments directed at individuals. When children hear these comments, they strive to imitate the movement so that they too can attract similar positive reinforcement comments from the coach. Over time the coach can reduce the frequency of these comments as the athletes become more internally motivated and mature.

ADOLESCENTS

Adolescents experience many life changes. Growth spurts, hormone adjustments, identity formation, self-consciousness, response to peer pressure, risk taking and questioning of traditional customs and laws are a few of the characteristics of adolescents that influence the style of coaching required to enhance athlete performance. A program that has consistent expectations and rules, provides the rationale for athlete development strategies, includes the athlete in the decision-making process, and provides opportunities for the athlete to be exposed to a range of roles and experiences will appeal to the adolescent.

In both individual and team sports, adolescents need opportunities to connect and participate with their peer group. Coaches can achieve this by encouraging them to practise with each other without coach involvement, arranging social activities, identifying friendships and providing opportunities for friends to compete and practise together, as well as supporting those who may at times be rejected by the peer group.

David, coach of the nation's youth track and field team, wanted his athletes to experience leadership and to take the focus away from individual performance. He held a meeting with three well-respected multiple-event team members. He asked them to speak to the team, both individually and as a group, about a campaign theme for the team to use at the upcoming national championships. The team decided to honour the contribution of the retiring team manager, Pat, who had voluntarily managed the team for the past 20 years. To emphasise the theme, the leaders had one of the athletes design a caricature of Pat to go on the back of the training singlet with the inscription 'This One's for Pat'. Pat was overwhelmed, and his response certainly created an enduring focal point for everyone during the championships.

Adolescents respond well to repetitive skill training and opportunities to acquire a broad range of techniques and experience a broad range of roles. In relation to athletic involvement, adolescents should not be type-cast or pigeon-holed as being a particular type of athlete. Throughout the program they should have the opportunity to experience all roles within a team and be exposed to the full range of movement experiences the sport has to offer.

Adolescents often demonstrate a lack of respect for authority because they are frustrated by a lack of opportunity or have been forced to foreclose on their identity. Many have an obsession with appearance. Coaches can significantly diminish the effect of this fixation by having compulsory training uniforms, travel uniforms and participation uniforms.

Adolescents also take risks both within their sport and socially, despite not having the cognitive maturity to manage those risks. They must be monitored at all times to ensure that they do not develop overuse conditions or offset feelings of failure and self-consciousness with inappropriate challenges of authority and succumb to unwise social temptations that often run parallel to a sport program. Adolescents are capable and ready for a respectful and collegial approach to their sport. However, the boundaries for such a relationship must be set and rigidly upheld.

ADULTS

Coaches of adults must be able to provide them with a comprehensive understanding of every aspect of performance including environmental, mental, strategic, technique, opposition and conditioning factors. Depending on the sport and the level of performance, the coach adopts varying levels of responsibility for these aspects of performance. In the current situation of sophisticated sport analysis, it is difficult for any adult coach to have total command of every aspect of performance. Coaches should limit their input to what they know and enlist the expertise of others when required, or work in collaboration with athletes to overcome any program knowledge and experience deficiencies.

Adult athletes must be encouraged to take responsibility for their own performances. The

Cynthia Lum/Icon SMI

Coaches for elite, adult athletes, such as Samantha Stosur, must enlist the help of other experts and work collaboratively with the athlete.

coach provides the program, monitors athletes' responses, provides justification for the program, analyses outcomes, delivers appropriate and accurate feedback and constantly re-evaluates and updates every aspect of the program.

As an example of providing feedback and updating a program, consider Geoff, the coach of a state men's squash team. At a postchampionship meeting, Geoff provided each player with a summary of his performance in each of the seven games the team played throughout the championships. The summary included the number of unforced errors; the number of forced errors; the percentage of drop shots, boasts, lobs and drives (down the wall and across court); which shots attracted the most errors; which shots resulted in winners; and the relationship between errors and the player's time in the match.

Geoff concluded that each player had an area of the game that needed improvement, and the area was different for each player. In addition to encouraging each player to work on his deficiency in his own time, Geoff set aside some time at team training for the players to focus on these areas. He designed an appropriate program for each player and decided to reassess all players' performances using video analysis in one month's time.

A critical role of the adult coach is to establish challenging and achievable expectations for all athletes and to guide the athletes through predetermined stages of development. These stages of development may not necessarily follow a continuum and will be disrupted by unexpected events such as injury, other personal trauma or changes to the profile of the opposition. For this reason it is often desirable for a coach to have been an athlete and have had personal experience dealing with the usual and unusual circumstances inherent in sport participation. However, this is not essential and can be overcome by being receptive to seeking advice from others and working through these circumstances in consultation with the athlete.

Most important is the coach's ability to relate to adult athletes and to command their respect. Although there may be situations in which the coach uses 'native cunning' and appears to be just one of the group yet continues to command respect, this should be the exception rather than the rule. Coaches of adults are advised to set high socially acceptable standards for themselves, and when in the sporting context, to limit their involvement to the athlete development and performance program.

GENDER DIFFERENCES

For the most part, male and female athletes respond differently to coaching and have different coaching needs. Some people have extreme male characteristics, others have extreme female characteristics and others have a mix of both. However, both male and female athletes need role models. Females generally need role models to promote the confidence they need to achieve, whereas males often need role models to reinforce how to act appropriately. The advice that follows refers to what is generally true for male and female athletes, but of course, differences exist. Coaches need to pay attention to the needs of their specific athletes.

COACHING FEMALES

Coaches of female athletes need to accept that their athletes, for the most part, are personable, sensitive, intuitive and empathetic. The female athlete appreciates hard work and direction but will seek out justification, explanation and quite often open discussion before totally committing to a coach's requirements. Developing a two-way relationship, which often goes beyond merely providing support in the sport environment, can provide the necessary personal connection female athletes need to build confidence and experience the extremely important feelings of belonging and being understood.

It is essential in both team and individual sports to get to know the individual. What are her goals, and what motivates her? Female athletes often tolerate being treated differently from other athletes, female or male, provided the motive and rationale for the behaviour of the coach is transparent and the athletes believe they are being afforded equal consideration. Coaches of female athletes need to be prepared to engage in frequent and sometimes in-depth verbal interactions. This helps the athlete to understand the rationale behind the actions of the coach as well as imparting a sincere desire to ensure that the athlete is comfortable with the situation, particularly in relation to the needs of the team. Coaches who make the effort to do this reap the benefits that come from managing a known rather than an unknown entity.

Anna, an Olympic downhill ski coach, realised that she had two very competitive and sensitive female athletes vying for one position on the Olympic team. She also knew that the athletes were close friends with different peer groups in the potential final chosen squad. Anna decided to have a meeting with the two athletes and explain the coaching approach she would adopt in the coming months to make a decision about who would represent the country at the Olympics. The approach included time trials, pressured practice sessions, observations by a panel of three independent experts and a full-scale competition immediately prior to the final team selection.

She asked the athletes for input about the proposed approach to selection, and once agreement was reached, confirmed their unquestioning commitment to the outcome. Together, Anna and the two athletes presented the strategy to the entire training squad and asked for their support during what was to be a very emotional time for the athletes. The camaraderie created in the squad and, in particular, between the two athletes not only alleviated unwanted stress and tension but also significantly enhanced the performance of both skiers.

COACHING MALES

Coaches of males should understand that their athletes are often objective, analytical, one dimensional and visual processors who apply a fact-based perspective to most situations. Feelings are rarely the focus of the coaching process with male athletes. The male athlete wants to know what has to be done and the associated objective rather than being concerned with his relationship with others.

The male athlete strives to gain ascendency, is very competitive and gains confidence

through being able to control a situation. The desire to be first prompts a systematic action-orientated and self-centred approach to performance. Feelings can distract male athletes and interfere with the successful performance of a task. Providing male athletes with ways to manage their aggressive temperament and overstimulated hyperactivity can improve their ability to analyse and mastermind a situation and respond appropriately. Constructing a simple, one-dimensional strategy with clearly stated goals and objectives accompanied by a logically associated action plan to realise the athlete's and the team's potential certainly appeals to the male athlete.

Pat, a tennis coach, became aware that his young player Bernard tended to lose concentration, become tense and overhit the ball at critical times in important games. He and Bernard

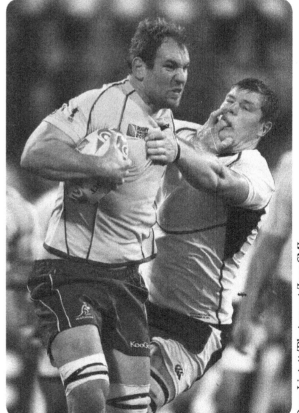

Dave Lintott/Photosport/Icon SMI

The desire of male athletes to achieve ascendancy leads them to be extremely competitive. Coaches must channel this energy through clearly stated goals.

analysed video of several critical situations in which Bernard had become overly aggressive and made errors in technique. Pat worked with Bernard to re-establish the skill routines for the specific affected strokes. He then arranged for Bernard to watch tapes of champions in similar critical situations and asked him to observe how they seemed to handle the pressure.

Pat then applied the logic that it is better to hit the ball in and make the opponent play a shot than go for a winner and hit it out. During subsequent competitions against lesser opponents, Pat required Bernard to set very challenging goals for each match that would put him under extreme pressure. Then, in these situations, Bernard had to focus on practised skill routines and aim to hit the ball in at all times. The combination of rigorous analysis, logic, visual role models and objective goals resulted in a significant reduction in unforced errors at critical times in the game.

LEARNING AND THINKING STYLES

Every athlete has a preferred learning style, and no one learning style is better than any other. Visual, auditory and kinaesthetic are the mediums (Gardner, 1993) used by athletes to learn, and these combined with different ways of thinking make up an athlete's learning style. The types of thinking an athlete might use include concrete sequential (an orderly approach), concrete random (organised after reflecting on personal experiences) and abstract sequential and random (thinking in concepts and ideas).

Visual learners are athletes who learn best by focusing on relevant visual cues and by analysing according to performance images in the brain. Providing images of good performances; using video analysis; and making visual comparisons of movement outcomes such as ball flight, the position of the body relative to space, stopwatch times and the distance from a competitor are examples of the approaches coaches can use with visual learners.

Auditory learners are athletes who learn best by focusing on relevant auditory cues. Coaches can facilitate learning in these athletes by providing concise oral descriptions of performance requirements; highlighting auditory cues that represent good performance such as the sound of a racing hull as it cuts through the water when the sails have been trimmed to perfection, or the sound of a speed ball being rhythmically 'rattled' against the timber by a boxer; ensuring that athletes can hear oral feedback being given to other athletes; and encouraging athletes to articulate relevant aspects of past, present and future performance.

Bodily, or kinaesthetic, learners are athletes who learn best by focusing on the relevant tactile, muscular and joint sensations that occur during movement. Coaches can facilitate learning in these athletes by emphasising the sensations that accompany a good performance (e.g., the feeling of pressure on the blade of a perfectly positioned rowing oar); pushing athletes through escalating stages of aerobic or anaerobic stress to highlight the internal sensations associated with fatigue and comfort; and feeling the optimal angle of joints to determine the ideal backswing position when playing various shots in golf or racquet sports.

Athletes have preferences for which medium (visual, auditory or kinaesthetic) to use to enhance their development. Astute coaches notice which learning style best describe each of their athletes and strive to use the perceptual medium each athlete prefers. However, when coaching teams or groups of athletes, coaches need to incorporate a variety of visual, auditory and kinaesthetic mediums into the coaching process to address variations within the group.

Not only do athletes have a preference for a particular medium, which can vary depending on the circumstances, but they also have preferences for the way information is delivered in conjunction with the medium. Some athletes prefer that coaches provide clearly defined sequential steps to achieve a given outcome, either in practice or in competition. These athletes adopt a very orderly approach to training and competition and are often described as concrete thinkers (Gregorc, 1982).

For example, Coach Heather was aware that, during a match, her talented young squash player, Brian was not able to analyse and respond to the strengths, weaknesses or game strategies of his opponents. Knowing that Brian was more comfortable with a structured game plan, Heather devoted practice time to help Brian learn specific sequences of shots to be played in response to specific plays by the opponent. For example, an opponent's drop shot was to be followed by a cross court lob from Brian. Once this sequence was perfected, Heather introduced the playing of a 'down the wall' drive in response to an opponent's drop shot. Brian became extremely confident about not only his ability to play the required shot but also his ability to choose when to play a lob or a drive.

Concrete random thinking (Gregorc, 1982) athletes absorb ideas and impressions and then organise the information using reflection and personalised experiences. Coaches of these athletes realise that, during a match, the athlete is capable of analysing the strengths and weaknesses of an opponent as well as reflecting on an opponent's response to competition situations. The athlete then randomly applies strategies developed during practice or acquired from personal experiences that have been successful in the past either for the athlete or for other athletes. Exposing these athletes to a variety of opponents and providing them with a variety of game-specific practice drills encourages them to use their ability to analyse and reflect during a competition.

Badminton player Tony complained to his coach, Margaret, that he felt limited by being coached to play specific sequences of shots in matches. He believed he was more competitive during a match when he could randomly select shots he believed would respond best to specific situations as well as his opponent's skill set and game sense. Margaret decided to take a more game-orientated approach to training with Tony, rather than focus training on repetitive drills. Tony's competitiveness improved significantly as a result, and he had a more enthusiastic approach to practice.

Abstract sequential and abstract random thinking (Gregorc, 1982) athletes think in concepts and ideas. They experiment and use analytical skills to test theories in relation to practice and competition, and they learn best in a non-authoritarian environment. They respond well to being included in leadership groups and to being given specific leadership roles. They are also creative and, if given the opportunity, bring significant positive changes to traditional competition preparation programs and traditional competition strategies.

INSTRUCTIONAL MODES

It is comforting for coaches to know that there are many ways to facilitate athlete development. In all situations, coaches must begin and maintain the development process by giving instructions to athletes. Methods for delivering instructions include oral instructions, written instructions, diagrams and demonstrations. The range of approaches to delivering these instructions includes problem solving, drilling, feedback and reinforcement.

ORAL INSTRUCTIONS

Oral instruction is the most common form of coach communication. It is used to give direction and impart knowledge. To provide quality oral instructions, coaches must mentally prepare each instruction, limit the information to two or three key points, be succinct and use voice and body language to ensure that the instructions are interesting and have high impact.

Once athletes become familiar with the detail of their coach's instructions, the coach can replace slabs of oral information with cues; for example, 'OK, team, let's warm up'. The 'warm-up' cue results in athletes performing a series of unprompted activities. Coaches can improve athlete self-management by including keywords or cues in their communications.

WRITTEN INSTRUCTIONS

Succinct and easy-to-follow written instructions are most useful when athletes have routines to follow and coaches want to avoid continually having to tell them what to do. This allows coaches to focus on other important duties. Some examples of written instructions in sport are a swimmer's training session written on a whiteboard beside the pool; exercise cards on the walls in weight-training facilities; written schedules for training camps; and team travel arrangements that include travel, meal and accommodation arrangements.

DIAGRAMS

Diagrams can be very helpful in facilitating learning for athletes. Quality diagrams have limited information, are easy to understand and are orientated and scaled to mirror the conditions on the playing surface, as if the athlete were looking down from directly above the playing surface. They are also accompanied by a brief explanation (oral or written) and use easy-to-recognise universal symbols and spatial conventions.

Diagrams are particularly useful to coaches of team sports. Most team sport athletes understand team strategies and their roles in them when the coach can accurately represent strategies in a diagram. Diagrams tend to be particularly helpful for males because of their acute spatial awareness.

Team coaches can also reduce the need for extensive follow-up strategy meetings with their athletes by providing each athlete with a playbook. A playbook contains diagrams of the game strategies, or plays, used in specific game situations. Athletes can refer to their playbooks at any time and can take time to memorise key plays away from valuable team practice.

Whiteboards are excellent for creating diagrams right at the moment. Good coaches quickly enhance athletes' understanding of their roles or of the team strategy by drawing informative diagrams on whiteboards during game breaks.

DEMONSTRATIONS

Demonstrations are a very effective coaching method for visual learners. The demonstration must accurately display the required action, and athletes should be given the opportunity to practise the action as soon as possible after the demonstration. Inviting an athlete with model technique that results in quality performance outcomes to give a live demonstration can result in significant and immediate improvement in the technique and approach of other, less capable athletes.

PROBLEM SOLVING

Requiring players to participate in solving problems they are having with their own performance or the team's performance entrusts them with ownership of aspects of their programs. Some athletes appreciate being responsible for their development, whereas others would rather be guided entirely by the coach. Problem situations are often managed effectively when the athlete is involved in the process of developing a solution.

Players in all sports can participate in finding solutions to both simple and complex problems that confront coaches. An example of a simple problem is determining the order in which track athletes are to run a 4×100-metre relay. Factors to consider include each runner's ability to run bends versus the straight, preference for leading versus chasing, speed and endurance capability and baton-changing ability. The coach can arrange a meeting with the runners and ask them to choose the running order based on their knowledge of each other's ability and of the opposition relay teams.

An example of a complex problem is players' lack of confidence in each other and themselves. The coach can invite team members to identify, in private individual meetings with the coach, personal areas of concern with their performance as well as concerns they have about the performance of other members of the team. The coach can then collate the views of the players. In addition to inviting all players to develop plans to confront their own lack of confidence, the coach can empower a leadership team to find a solution to team confidence issues.

Once any problem worthy of attention has been recognised by the athletes, it is essential that they work with the coach to develop an action plan. The plan should include a target outcome, the training activities to be undertaken, a time frame for completing the task and who is responsible for implementing the program. Simple problems often do not require a sophisticated plan; however, complex problems can place extensive demands on the planning process. Many elements of a competition, including the following categories, can pose problems for coaches and athletes. Examples of each category of problem are provided.

- **Environmental factors.** Unusual weather conditions, varying playing surfaces, poor preparation areas, extensive travel demands
- **Mental issues.** Poor motivation, lack of concentration, lack of confidence, misdirected aggression, excessively high or low anxiety levels
- **Competition strategies.** A lack of strategies to avoid exposing weaknesses, poor ability to cope with fatigue, the loss of a quality player in the team, a lack of variety in defensive and offensive plays
- **Technique difficulties.** A lack of skill routines to suit critical situations, a lack of automation of basic skills, a high skill error rate caused by poor technique, vulnerable performance areas caused by poor technique, which limit skill options
- **Opposition analysis.** High-quality opponents; aggressive opponents; inflated opposition reputations; physical differences in accuracy, consistency and endurance

DRILLING

Coaching would be relatively easy if athletes needed to receive instructions only once before being able to carry them out to perfection. The number of times an instruction must be reiterated and the number of times a training exercise must be repeated to guarantee that all athletes meet the required expectations vary depending on the type of instruction and the capability of the athletes.

Drilling is an essential part of athlete development and performance maintenance programs. Coaches should be aware that by constantly changing instructions and practice routines to avoid staleness, they may delay the necessary automation and fine-tuning of responses required in most advanced competitions. The dichotomy of drilling and variety

in coaching is one of the intriguing aspects of the coaching process. Quality coaches achieve the high levels of drilling required to develop athletes by incorporating a range of motivation techniques in association with the instruction or activity. They can change up the drill by modifying time and space demands, having groups compete against other groups doing the same drill, or adding defensive pressure. Drills are also more motivating when coaches stress their importance in helping athletes overcome particular opposition strategies or choose team leaders for each drill group.

FEEDBACK AND REINFORCEMENT

Feedback and reinforcement are not about instructing athletes about how or what to perform. Feedback informs athletes about how closely their actions approximate a coach's instructions, and reinforcement is designed to increase the frequency of correct action. Nevertheless, coaches would do well to link instructions to the delivery of feedback and reinforcement.

Occy, when coaching his beginner surfers, was commenting to his young grommets about their ability to get to their feet on the board at the time of catching a wave. He said to Kylie, 'Your technique was perfect, quick movement, feet spread, arms out and balanced [feedback]; you can have 15 minutes of free surfing [reinforcement]'.

Occy also noticed that Joel had a very solid and overweight build, which was causing him to have difficulty getting to his feet in one movement. Occy said to Joel: 'I liked the way you positioned yourself on the board [reinforcement] with good balance, powerful paddle and in front of the wave [feedback]. Many of my surfers need to get up onto the board in two stages [reassurance and instruction]. Joel, what I want you to do is first try getting up with one knee on the back of the board and the foot of the other leg near the middle of the board; then try to stand up as quickly as possible [instruction]'. Occy noticed that Joel became more relaxed and less tense and was able to get to his feet using the two-stage approach.

FOCUS ON SPORT

During practice and games, a coach should direct observations and feedback at the specific focus of the activity. This approach to coaching is encapsulated in the SPORT acronym, which represents the following coaching sequence:

- **Show.** Demonstrate the activity, emphasise no more than three key points and check for understanding.
- **Practise.** Allow players to immediately practise following the demonstration and revisit the key points. Repeat the demonstration if needed.

- **Observe.** Observe for 15 to 20 seconds at a minimum. Orally remind players about key points and provide further instruction if necessary.
- **Reinforce.** Praise good effort, acknowledge achievement, be enthusiastic and value the efforts of all players.
- **Time.** Place the newly learned activity into a practice session. Encourage making the activity a habit, and ensure that the key points are adhered to throughout the practice.

PRACTICAL WISDOM

Practical wisdom is often described as 'having eyes in the back of your head' and 'being ahead of the game'. It typically develops with experience as a coach. The ability to predict and anticipate athlete behaviour provides the coach with an opportunity to prepare the athlete for new situations. It also improves the coach's ability to manage groups of athletes and to make responsive tactical decisions during competitions.

Coaches can develop practical wisdom by raising their sensitivity to cause-and-effect events in the sporting context. Being alert and mindful of the need to make a mental note of what works and what does not work in the sporting context increases the coach's store of useful information and response strategies. This applies to making observations in all sport contexts as well as in the sport to which the coach is specifically aligned.

PLANNING AND ORGANISATIONAL CAPACITY

Planning and organisation are used not only to define the direction and structure of a program, but also to enable athletes to focus entirely on the task of performing. Good planning and

organisation limits confusion, reduces athlete frustration and ensures that athletes are working together to achieve their goals.

A coach with planning and organisation skills incorporates an in-depth analysis and understanding of contexts in which the athletes will perform, and includes up-front strategic goals and aims into each section of the program. Such a coach is flexible, can revert to a back-up plan if needed and attends to detail, but also delegates tasks to empower others and be free to focus on the overall performance agenda.

SITUATIONAL ANALYSIS

The ability to analyse situations usually requires extensive experience with coaching sporting teams or individual athletes. Changes in the environment and opponent strategies, varying opponents, athlete injury, motivation concerns, changes to schedules and unusual travel arrangements require that coaches as well as athletes be able to analyse situations and respond accordingly.

Angela was aware that her state track and field team had significant free time between heats and finals for their individual events at the national titles. Some athletes were scheduled to complete their competitions midway through the ten-day championships. She assessed the schedules of each athlete and decided to require all members of the team to use their free time to either support their teammates or attend organised recovery sessions. On the few occasions when all athletes had free time, Angela arranged for the team to visit local tourist attractions.

Angela ensured that all of the extra commitments would not unduly fatigue the athletes by consulting with the team fitness adviser and physiotherapist. She also placed different demands on athletes according to the workload associated with their individual competition schedules. Not only did the athletes remain focused throughout the championships, but also the free time activities enhanced team spirit and facilitated healthy relationships, particularly between the younger and older athletes.

Effective coaches identify what they know and what they do not know about a situation. Those who don't know how to respond to a situation should consult assistants or specialists who can provide educated advice.

A coach may notice that the athletes appear to be lacking energy and motivation. However, without a thorough understanding of the impact of training and competition workloads, the dynamics of the group or the effects of a demanding travel schedule, the coach will have difficulty identifying the reason for the problem. In such situations coaches can ask the more mature athletes what they think may be causing the problem, or they can seek the advice of experts in sport physiology and sport psychology.

STRATEGIC PLANNING

At the end of a competitive season, a quality coach begins developing a strategic plan for the next season and beyond. The plan should include a mission statement: an overarching aim that guides the program for the next one to five years.

A strategic plan should be divided into relevant sections, such as conditioning, recruitment, skill development, team building and performance strategies. Each section should contain a set of specific goals with associated action plans including the identification of who is responsible for achieving each goal

and a time frame for achieving it. Although it is important to consider all key elements of athlete development when designing a strategic plan, the most important consideration is that each goal be achievable within the designated time frame.

FLEXIBILITY

In all sports unforeseen circumstances arise that make it difficult to adhere to a strategic plan or make an informed situational analysis. For example, a key player may suffer a match-ending injury, a major sponsor may withdraw funding at the last minute and compromise the integrity of a preparation program, or security at a venue may not be as promised and deemed to be inadequate. When confronted with unusual circumstances, coaches should do the following:

- Remain calm and objective.
- Consult with others to identify the best approach.
- Consider a range of options.
- Act decisively if the situation occurs during a competition.
- Have an open mind about what is possible.

Sport environments often generate high levels of intrigue because of the possibility that anything could happen. How coaches manage the unpredictable is often indicative of the quality of their coaching.

ATTENTION TO DETAIL

Coaches can readily increase their effectiveness by attending to the detail associated with performance. The following examples show the benefits that attention to detail can provide for coaches and athletes:

- A rowing coach understands the importance of correctly rigging the boat to suit the body structure of each rower. Devoting time to each specific element of rigging can result in a few extra centimetres produced with each stroke of the oar.
- A team coach who masterfully manages the details of the pregame routine provides

the players with the assurance that they are ready to compete.

- Coaches of ball sports who teach the positioning of passes to the advantage of teammates, and then construct rigorous drills that automate succinct offensive passes at all levels of intensity and combinations of time and space, significantly increase ball retention.
- A racquet sport coach who takes time to observe upcoming opponents and develops a detailed analysis of their strengths and weaknesses can structure practice sessions to construct appropriate game plans for the athletes.

How much coaches and athletes can attend to detail is limited by the time they have to devote to their involvement in sport. However, by attending to organisation and administration detail, such as delegating duties, developing self-managed athletes and including smart technology to communicate all aspects of the program, a coach can, in fact, create more time to focus on performance detail.

Performance details are best managed during training. When performing in competitions, athletes need to limit their focus to a few critical elements that generate appropriate automated responses. A golfer may use a slight forward press of the hands to initiate the backswing, which triggers the formation of each component of the backswing—legs, hips, shoulders, wrists, backswing arc and timing. A coach who takes the time to teach the finer detail of sport performance and then conditions the athlete to automate detailed responses as part of a skill or game play routine will significantly improve the performance of that athlete in competition.

DELEGATION

Not all coaches have the luxury of qualified assistant coaches to whom they can delegate tasks. Following are guidelines for delegating coaching duties:

- Delegate specific areas of development to specialists, such as fitness coaches, skill coaches, defensive and offensive coaches and tactical coaches.
- Assign tasks to individual athletes or groups of athletes. Such tasks may include reflecting on a performance, assessing upcoming playing conditions, providing support and advice to a teammate who is out of form and compiling personal performance statistics using video analysis.
- Delegate authority to a leadership group. This authority can be designated to any area of the program and can include social activities as well as performance activities.

Delegation must be preceded by a clear explanation of the powers and jurisdiction of the person in the delegated role and of the coach's expectation of the commitment of the athlete(s) to that delegated person. Coaches must empower by providing some autonomy to those to whom they assign tasks. If they continue to be involved at too detailed a level, they do not reap any benefits from delegating, and the recruited supportive person may become frustrated.

In each of the three seasons of coaching his rugby union team, David started with a number of volunteer assistants who offered their time to the team. However, it did not take long before David was left to coach the team on his own. The initial enthusiasm of the assistants quickly diminished as they became aware that David was a control freak. He would allocate roles to the assistants, and then not only interfere while they were trying to coach, but also contradict them.

On a visit to the rugby academy, established to develop the nation's best youth players, David was astounded by the lack of presence of the head coach, Grant. Groups of players rotated through individual skill sessions, scrum and backs sessions, rehabilitation sessions, individual conditioning programs and game analysis meetings with different people in charge of each area, and players seamlessly fulfilled their daily and weekly commitments. Grant devoted most of his time to consulting with assistant coaches, coordinating schedules, analysing potential recruits and generating game plans.

David sought Grant's advice. Grant admitted that he was fortunate to have considerable finances to establish a coaching team. However, he said that the important aspects of delegation are recruiting the help of trustworthy people, giving the assistant coaches ownership of their roles and letting the assistants and the athletes know that they are highly regarded as coaches. David appreciated the advice and couldn't wait to contact potential assistant coaches for the next season of rugby.

Coaches can also delegate the role of mentoring to 'well-performed' or recently retired athletes. Mentoring is one of the most effective strategies for enhancing sport performance. Coaches who can no longer perform activities at the required level should consider delegating mentoring to others. When assigning a mentor to an athlete, usually an experienced performer with a developing athlete, the coach needs to ensure that the mentor is a respected person, consistently reinforces the coach's approach and is able to provide a model to which the athlete can aspire.

The mentor can work one on one with the athlete and provide immediate modelling of appropriate sport performance, explain ways to acquire higher performance levels and give immediate feedback about the athlete's progress. The mentor can take on the role of a training partner or a more sophisticated role as a team leader who acts as a coach when required.

By delegating administration tasks, coaching duties and organisation communications, a coach can more effectively monitor the athletes. Informed analysis of athlete responses is possible if the coach is not immersed in an activity, worried about the effectiveness of the organisation of a drill or thinking about what comes next. Also, the deployment of assistant coaches and an administration assistant provides the coach with time to think about worthwhile initiatives to enhance the overall program or stimulate the progress of individual athletes.

SUMMARY

- Coaches should consider a leadership style that complements their personality as well as the sporting context in which they coach.
- The authoritarian, democratic and submissive coaching styles are typical approaches to leadership in sport.
- When choosing a leadership style, coaches should consider the age, gender and learning and thinking styles of the athletes.
- A strong command of effective instructional skills combined with high-quality planning and organisation skills helps coaches of every leadership style achieve their goals.

REFERENCES AND RESOURCES

Gardner, H. (1993). *Multiple intelligence: The theory in practice.* New York: Basic Books.

Gregorc, A. (1982). *An adult's guide to style,* Columbia, CT: Gregorc Associates Inc.

CHAPTER 3

Qualities of Respected Coaches

——— Ken Davis

Coach Top Gunn strides into the dressing room one hour prior to game time, and the players immediately gather around. They are glued to his every word. He knows their strengths and weaknesses very well, and in preparation for this game, he has clearly defined each player's role in the team. One by one he checks on their readiness and calmly reiterates the key aspects of their role for the day. He says, 'I expect you to work hard to achieve the objective'.

In preparation for the game, Coach Gunn has scouted the opposition, noting their strengths and weaknesses. When the opposition is better on paper, he works out a way to trouble them and outlines this plan to his players. In doing this, he not only attacks the opponent's weaknesses but also recognises and uses his own team's strong points.

Coach Gunn is relaxed, composed, pleasant but firm. He notices an edginess in his team as the start of the big game nears. Adjusting his routine, he takes the players into a small room and asks them all to lie down and relax and imagine themselves performing in a cool but purposeful manner. He knows that they can perform under pressure because they have trained that way.

The players take to the court, and Coach Gunn takes up his position on the bench, exuding confidence in his players. He rotates players according to the standard of the opposition: if they are not strong, he gives more game time

to his lesser lights. He calls some set plays, and when individual players are subbed off, he takes time to speak to them about how their performance is going in relation to their outlined role and prepares them for their next stint on the court. He cares for the players and never berates or demeans them. The players respond to his requests and enjoy the challenges he has set. They know that if they try their hardest and play smart, their coach will be happy.

This vignette is an actual account of a coach at work. One could be excused for thinking that Coach Top Gunn is an elite professional coach, given the number of outstanding coaching qualities he displays. However, he is, in fact, a volunteer coach who rearranges his work schedule so that he can coach a primary school basketball team. Skills and respect, you see, are not exclusive to professional coaches.

Respect, as acclaimed hockey coach Ric Charlesworth says, must be earned and can be achieved at any level of sport. Coach Gunn is a respected coach, and his players all respond to his guidance because his knowledge and methods do much to enhance the performance of team members in an enjoyable yet purposeful environment. Coach Gunn is one of many coaches who fulfil their roles commendably. They employ coaching practices and demonstrate qualities that earn the respect of players, peers and parents.

To elaborate further on successful approaches and attributes and show how they have been applied, this chapter focuses on five coaches who are widely regarded as being or having been among the very best in their sports. All of them have enjoyed long coaching careers and are highly respected by the athletes in their charge. Many more qualities than those outlined in this chapter can help coaches to gain respect. The qualities discussed here are those that form a core of good coaching behaviour. Some less orthodox and idiosyncratic practices are cited as well to encourage creativity and fitting one's approach to one's personality.

The coaches featured are Sir Alex Ferguson, coach of the Manchester United football team; John Buchanan, former coach of the Australian cricket team; John Wooden, former coach of the most successful U.S. college basketball team, the UCLA Bruins; Ric Charlesworth, coach of the Australian men's hockey team; and Joyce Brown, former coach of the Australian women's netball team. All five are held in high regard for their depth of knowledge and their sustained success at the highest level, but even more so for their consistent demonstration of what a coach should strive to be.

SIR ALEX FERGUSON

Ferguson started his coaching career at East Stirlingshire in July 1974, a lowly club in the Scottish Second Division, and is currently coaching Manchester United in the English Premier League (EPL). He has coached Manchester United since 1986 and has been awarded Manager of the Year the most times in football history. In 2008 he became the third British manager to win the European Cup on more than one occasion. Following are some of the key qualities to be gleaned from his biography *Managing My Life* (1999):

- **Rely on repetition.** Ferguson is a firm believer in the value of repetition and regarded having a variety of drills to keep players interested as a 'dangerous evasion of priorities' (p. 137). He contends that athletes need to concentrate on refining technique to the point that difficult skills become a matter of habit. So, practice of the basics formed a large part of his training program. He wrote, 'I believed strongly that being able to pass the ball well was crucial, and I don't think there was a training session that did not incorporate passing' (p. 151).

- **Learn from mistakes.** 'Although I was making mistakes, I was not repeating them', Ferguson wrote (p.143). Such an approach, although sounding simple, is not always easy because coaches form their philosophies and methods over a considerable time, and many may be etched in stone. Coaches who continue to examine their performance, acknowledging and correcting any mistakes, ensure that they are constantly evolving.

- **Practise quick decision making.** Ferguson wrote: 'When I reached decisions quickly I was drawing a positive response, especially from players. I tested myself all the time. When a player was talking to me, I was making rapid analyses and assessments in my head, so that I could give quick clear answers' (p. 143). The notion of practising quick decision making is commendable. Players appreciate clear directions and quick solutions to their problems rather than leaders who mull over issues for an inordinate amount of time.

- **Provide positive reinforcement.** From Ferguson: 'All they needed was direction and somebody to say "well done" from time to time. Those are the best two words in football. There is no need to elaborate. "Well done" says it all' (p. 143). Often, in elite sport in particular, there is a school of thought that says that players know when they've done well and don't need reminding. That may be appropriate for robots, but humans appreciate praise for their efforts. Reinforcing both effort and outcomes can help to keep players on the track towards their goals.

- **Encourage visualisation.** 'I was trying to add imagination to my coaching, emphasising the need for players to have a picture in their minds, to visualise how they could have a creative impact on the shifting pattern of a game' Ferguson wrote

AP Photo/Jon Super

Successful coaches, such as Sir Alex Ferguson, know the importance of praising their players.

(p.151). Visualisation is a powerful tool for embedding correct techniques into the mind of athletes.

- **Improve the culture.** When Ferguson took over a club, as he did at both East Stirling-shire and Manchester United, he was quick to work on the drinking culture, which he considered the curse of British football: '[Excessive drinking] can take a damag-ing hold on a club and any manager who turns a blind eye, shouldn't be in the job. . . . Boozing should have no place in the lifestyle of a professional sportsman. Any player who thinks otherwise doesn't last long with me' (p. 152).

- **Foster fair play.** Ferguson had his own issues with self-control and admitted he wasn't an ideal role model in this respect, having been sent off the field when man-aging his team. However, he always put his faith in his skills and 'never in dirty or rough tactics' (p. 155).

- **Prepare for continued success.** Ferguson wanted to lay a foundation for every club he worked for to be successful over a long period. He did not want to allow the club's playing staff to age without giving suf-ficient attention to ensuring that younger replacements of the right quality were ready to stake claims for regular places in the first team. Hence, he believed that list management was crucial to the long-term success of a club. He also believed that scouting and recruiting structures aimed at bringing in talented young players were important for continued success.

- **Be persistent.** When we look at Ferguson in his current role, we see a man in charge of a team that is at the top of the English Premier League. However, that wasn't always the case. When he took over the role at Manchester United in 1986, the team had gone 19 years without a title. It took the club five years to win a title, and in that time Ferguson experienced many tests of his durability: 'Those times brought me far more lows than highs as I struggled to cope with a forbidding list of problems . . . where we finished in the league table in my first five seasons will show why I sometimes felt I was taking one step forwards and two backwards' (p. 243). By sticking to his beliefs and persisting, he was able to eventually turn the club into the powerhouse it is today.

- **Make connections.** Ferguson believes it is important to know and communicate with all people in the organisation. Knowing each person's name and interests and taking time out to talk to them can build and cement strong relationships that can assist in developing loyalty and commitment from all concerned in the club.

The previous list contains just some of the qualities exhibited by Alex Ferguson. With the exception of the piece on changing a drinking culture, all would be relevant for coaching at any level in any sport. One could contest the need for variation in training, but repetition is vital in mastering the basics. Perhaps a more balanced view may be the preferred option here: By all means coaches should have athletes practise the basics repetitively, but try to vary training drills to minimise the possibility of player burnout and perhaps ensure more enthusiastic practices.

JOHN BUCHANAN

John Buchanan will always be renowned for delivering Queensland its first Sheffield Shield title in the 1994-1995 domestic season, his first season with the Bulls. In his five years coaching the Queensland Bulls, the team won the Sheffield Shield and the domestic one-day competition twice. Buchanan took over as the coach of the Australian cricket team and was at the helm during an unprecedented period of success from 1999 to 2007. He led the team to a world record of 16 straight Test match wins and an unbeaten record of 24 One-Day International victories in two successful world cups.

The fact that Buchanan achieved this success at a time when coaches at the elite level were not totally embraced by the cricket fraternity, and that he had not played cricket at Test level, speaks volumes about his performance. Buchanan's background in education ensured that he would be an organised and thinking coach. Some of the qualities gleaned from reading his book *If Better Is Possible* (2007) are outlined here:

- **Have a vision.** Buchanan believes in developing a vision that is shared by the majority of his team, and especially by the leaders. He always strove to be better. The vision, he contends, has to be inspiring to the team, challenging and exciting in the sense that it has never been done before. The vision also has to be monitored and kept to the forefront of the athletes' minds at all times. Buchanan encouraged coaches to 'Challenge individuals and teams with possibilities and take them outside their comfort zones into the realms of uncertainty' (p. 1).

- **Initiate change.** When appointed to a new position, most coaches look to make change in some areas. Buchanan identified the systems and processes of planning, training, communication, behaviour, rewards, team hierarchy and support staff as critical aspects in his quest for change management. When working with the Queensland Sheffield Shield team, which had experienced limited success, he committed to an injection of new life. This plan involved the following: 'Different training regimes and routine; greater responsibilities for some off-field decisions about dress, travel, accommodation and social events; more detailed and precise preparation through meetings and accompanying visual and data analysis; and the selection of the right staff to deliver these messages practically' (p. 65).

In trying to create a legacy, Buchanan identified the younger players as key elements to support and maintain this change. In so doing, he encouraged no structured hierarchy within the team so that no matter how experienced they were, all players were given respect.

- **Know the whole person.** Buchanan strove to get to know his players as much as they wanted to let him into their lives. He wrote: 'When I am most satisfied with what I am doing as a coach, I am putting in time with those around me. I feel I am "in touch" with my players and staff. As a consequence I am in position to best help them should it be required' (p. 16). Knowing what motivates or disturbs a player, understanding players' backgrounds and their impact on their behaviour and discovering their interests are just some of the ways coaches can better engage with their athletes.

- **Create an environment in which the coach becomes increasingly redundant.** Increasing their own redundancy is a bold move by any coach, but Buchanan believes in the importance of continually developing players who are their own best coaches. Ultimately, when players can analyse their own game, adapt to changing competi-

tive circumstances and recognise ways to correct technical and mental weaknesses, then the coach has essentially completed his teaching role. He then becomes more of a support person and a resource for the players to call on when needed.

- **Decide and then move on.** According to Buchanan, life is about choices. Once you make a choice, it can't be undone. He encouraged coaches not to regret the bad choices they make but to learn from them.

- **Plan but be flexible and inclusive.** Buchanan is an organised, systematic planner who makes lists of everything that needs to be done. He concedes that such regimentation is not for all; however, everyone follows some form of plan. He is particularly mindful of being flexible with his plans and inclusive of all players in the planning stage: 'My experience shows that the best way to achieve a plan is to be flexible. Everybody needs to be included or at least have had the opportunity to have their say' (p. 81).

AP Photo/Rick Rycroft

Communicating and being in touch with players and staff helps coaches, such as John Buchanan, be of the most use to their team.

- **Scout the opposition.** The ability to dissect the opposition's players based on hard data was an important part of Buchanan's approach. He was one of the pioneers of computer analysis in cricket. He tried to establish predictability or patterning of the opposition, asking questions such as: What is the opposition more likely to do in certain game situations? and, What strategies do they use? He also found it useful to identify the best matches for his bowlers against opposition players. His scouting process also helped him discover new techniques being used by opposition players and provided insights into how to combat the conditions experienced in other countries.

- **Seek new horizons.** As the title of Buchanan's book suggests, he was always looking to be better. Some of Buchanan's innovations included using skills from baseball to improve fielding, creating multidimensional players who could use both sides of their bodies or could adequately bowl both pace and spin, using technology to enhance game analysis and practice performance and devising more efficient ways to practise skills.

- **Encourage adaptability.** Buchanan was strong on the notion that strengths can often be weaknesses. Although he encouraged players to understand and use their strengths as often as possible, he believes that a formula for success requires a built-in range of fallback options and strategies.

- **Communicate.** An ability to be in the moment and give full attention to the person not just the coach's agenda helped Buchanan become an optimal communicator. Like Ferguson, he preferred to recognise people for the good they do rather than the negative. He tried never to assume how people felt and recommended finding out by talking with them.

- **Manage the star players.** Buchanan believes that star athletes, by virtue of their talent, are often overlooked, so he always tried to keep lines of communication open to them. One of those star players, Justin Langer (former opening batter and current batting coach for Australia), in a personal communication with the chapter author, summarised Buchanan's influence as a coach in the following way: 'John Buchanan was a visionary who dared to be different and challenged everyone in his team to strive for constant improvement. He was courageous in his convictions and always challenged us to take the road less travelled in our pursuit of excellence. He had a strong work ethic and showed great passion for the game. His broad outlook on individual and team development helped develop people as well as cricket players, and I know I benefited from having him as coach of the Australian team through an extraordinarily successful period'.

JOHN WOODEN

Between 1964 to 1975, legendary UCLA basketball coach John Wooden coached teams that won 10 NCAA national championships, and seven of those championships were back to back. During this time, this six-time coach of the year's teams won 88 consecutive games. A summary of the many qualities that Wooden possessed were gleaned from his book *Wooden: A Lifetime of Observations and Reflections On and Off the Court* co-written with Steve Jamison (1997). According to Bill Walton (college and NBA basketball hall of famer who wrote the foreword to Wooden's book), Wooden taught his players teamwork, personal excellence, discipline, focus, organisation and leadership.

- **Emphasise attention to detail, intensity and repetition in each practice.** Bill Walton described the intensity of Wooden's practices as 'non-stop action and absolutely electric . . . crisp and incredibly demanding' (p. viii). To Walton, games actually seemed like they happened at a slower pace, such was the intensity of their practice. Often athletes can settle into 'cruise' mode at training, but not so under Wooden's guidance.

- **Plan thoroughly; then adapt as needed.** Denny Crum, former assistant coach to Wooden, said Wooden was first of all a teacher and 'was a master at organizing what needed to be done down to the last detail and then teaching it the same way' (p. xi). Wooden claimed he would 'spend almost as much time planning a practice as conducting it' (p.133). Similar to Buchanan, Wooden also was adaptable. He believed it was important to focus on preparing for any eventuality rather than a particular style of play from a particular team. Bob Costas (NBC sports commentator) also said Wooden was 'able to adapt to changing circumstances without bending to every trend, and without compromising what was at his core' (p. xiv).

- **Set an example.** Wooden lived his life according to the principles he espoused as a coach. According to Bill Walton, he gained respect by his personal example: 'He worked harder, longer, smarter, and was more dedicated, loyal, concerned, caring, detailed, meticulous, and enthusiastic than anyone I have ever worked with' (p. viii).

- **Listen to others.** Many coaches who reach the top in their field can become satisfied with the strategies that have worked for them in their journey to success. Not so with John Wooden. Assistant Coach Denny Crum explained: 'His willingness to listen to the ideas of others and his lack of ego allowed him to change and keep up with the ever-changing game' (p. xi). Wooden claimed that 'leaders should be interested in finding the best way rather than their own way' (p. 145).

- **Remain cool in a crisis.** Legendary LA Lakers star Kareem Abdul-Jabbar said

John Wooden's methodical preparation led the Bruins to many wins, including the night of their 88th straight victory.

he learned to appreciate Wooden's coolness under pressure. 'Coach taught us self-discipline and was always his own best example. He discouraged expressing emotion on the court, stressing that it would eventually leave us vulnerable to opponents' (p. xiii). Clearly, in the coaching cauldron, emotions can run high and can often erupt to produce behaviours that are far from cool. Calmness under pressure helps a coach make rational decisions.

- **Focus on the process.** In a world in which fans and media are obsessed with the outcome of a contest, Wooden believed that the most important question to ask players after competition was whether they tried to do all they could to influence the contest. If they did, then the players are winners, regardless of the result. By focusing on the process, coaches are continually working to improve the performance of their athletes regardless of the outcome.

- **Be prepared.** Wooden did not believe in rousing speeches pregame to motivate his players to try to rise to the occasion. He said, 'Let others try to rise suddenly to a higher level . . . we would have already attained it in our preparation' (p. 124). He believed that the time to prepare is not after you've been given an opportunity, but rather long before that opportunity arises. 'Once the opportunity arises it's too late to prepare' (p. 130). Traditionally, coaches have perhaps placed too much emphasis on the period immediately before a contest to ready players for competition. Wooden was perhaps a pioneer for a higher level of preparation that is now more prevalent in contemporary sport.

- **Have a sound, thoughtful philosophy.** Clearly, Wooden was a deep thinker on sport and life. He formed a philosophy that had many enduring principles that directed his approach to coaching. It is likely that all respected coaches develop a philosophy that provides the backbone of their success. Wooden conceptualised this philosophy in his Pyramid for Success, the

cornerstones of which are industriousness, cooperation, friendship, loyalty and enthusiasm. From there the journey to competitive greatness requires the building blocks of self-control, alertness, initiative, condition, skill and team spirit (Wooden and Jamison 1997). With the preceding in place, only then, according to Wooden, can the athlete perform consistently with poise and confidence. He also developed a checklist of factors that he could consult from time to time to see whether he was still on track for success.

RICHARD CHARLESWORTH

Ric Charlesworth has become a highly decorated coach after a stellar career as both a hockey and cricket player. In field hockey he represented Australia at four Olympic Games, winning a silver medal in Montreal in 1976, and then the world cup in London in 1986. He then coached the national women's team, the Hockeyroos, to Olympic gold in 1996 and 2000 and world cup victories in 1994 and 1998. He is now coaching the national men's team, the Kookaburras, which won the world cup in 2010. As a cricketer, Charlesworth represented his state Western Australia for several years as an industrious and competitive opening batter.

Charlesworth exhibited many of the qualities mentioned previously as he embarked on a coaching career. Like the other coaches, he was adamant that training needed to be designed to be 'physically, mentally, and tactically more complex and difficult than the game' (Charlesworth, 2001, p. 74). He believed in a flexible approach to the game plan; sometimes, just to make sure his coaching group was flexible, he would deliberately change playing structure during a match, claiming it developed confidence in his players that they could handle whatever came their way.

Although at first perceived as somewhat of a know-all, Charlesworth learned to appreciate the value of listening to his players, as the following reflection indicates: 'Anyone who thinks they know me will tell you that I always think I am right! I am an opinionated know-all, stubborn, and argumentative. I think they are only partially right for those who know me best know that while I will contest strenuously ideas and views I disagree with, I am also always listening. I think I am a user of good ideas, and I am absolutely convinced that the more people in the group contributing, the more likely we are to get the best way of doing things' (p. 79). Hence, the ability to discuss issues as they arise and to act on the good ideas presented is an important characteristic of respected coaches.

Fundamental to Charlesworth's coaching was a positive approach. He believed that 'there is no place for abusing players in any way. The message can be made without ever having to denigrate or humiliate players . . . . Every player, even the greatest champion, responds to positive encouragement and feedback' (p. 82). As well as the ability to listen and to be flexible, in his book *The Coach: Managing for Success* (2001), Charlesworth identified the following key strategies for good coaching:

- **Acquire knowledge.** Of course, knowledge is important in all domains, but all of the aforementioned coaches in this chapter have had a never-ending thirst for knowledge. Charlesworth realised that acquiring such knowledge was not all that difficult: 'You can do anything and know anything if you can read' (p. 75). Armed with this knowledge, Charlesworth contended that the coach should stand for and require quality.

- **Show diligence and a willingness to learn.** As an example of this quality, Charlesworth established a Lateral Inputs Committee whose role was to find out and relay information from techniques or approaches used in other sports.

- **Uphold standards.** Although most respected coaches believe in treating each person as an individual, every coaching environment contains a core of non-negotiables that should be modelled by the coach and strictly followed by the players. Charlesworth stated, 'coaches must uphold standards and require them of the athletes' (p. 81).

- **Display honesty.** According to Charlesworth, honesty is perhaps the most critical commodity a coach must have. He wrote, 'The coach worth their salt will develop in the team an appreciation of objectivity and truth that transcends ego and frustration. Then they will have a team that is fixed on what is happening and not on what others may think is happening . . . .' (p. 82). Of course, such honesty needs to be blended with tact because giving excessive honest criticism to players can deflate their confidence.

- **Stay on the attack.** Another interesting quality emerged in Charlesworth's approach to coaching. His match day approach was always attacking; he stressed that it is most unwise to try to defend a lead. 'What happens to teams is that they become very determined about defending in such circumstances but forget about attack. They lose form and structure and suffer diminished endeavour when they get the ball, and so it keeps coming back at them and pressure mounts' (p. 87).

In a personal communication with the author, Triple Olympic gold medallist and former captain of the Australian women's field hockey team, Rechelle Hawkes, had this to say about Charlesworth's qualities as a coach: 'He was one of the most professional and inspirational coaches of all time. His work ethic and attention to detail are second to none. He has the ability to inspire, motivate and extract the most from his players. His major strength is his ability to take a good team and turn them into an all conquering, powerful, dominant force . . . . There was always an air of invincibility surrounding teams when he was at the helm'.

Not only did Charlesworth expect his players to continually work to improve their games, but he too was on a never-ending journey to develop his coaching expertise. He continually sought feedback from both his assistants and his players. Such an approach went a long way in ensuring his long-term survival as a coach.

JOYCE BROWN

Joyce Brown, former coach of the world championship–winning Australian Netball Team, has had a long history of involvement in sport. Brown captained the Australian team that won the first world championship in 1963; then coached Australia to world titles in 1975, 1983 and 1991. In one period from 1963 to 1991, as a player and coach, her teams were undefeated at 46 world tournament matches.

Brown is a deep thinker about sport and coaching. She shares a number of qualities with the four previously mentioned coaches. She believed in simulating match pressure at training, scouted the opposition thoroughly, appreciated the need to develop her listening skills and was constantly learning about coaching from those within and outside netball. The book *No Limits: Joyce Brown* by Edie Smithers and Chris Appleby (1996) highlights some qualities and strategies, not yet mentioned in this chapter, that Brown possessed as a coach. These strategies help explain the high status Joyce Brown enjoyed in the sport of netball.

- **Stress the importance of recovery.** In recent times this notion has become widely accepted, but Brown realised this at a time when hard work was often followed by more hard work. Brown said that 'it's one thing to work your players hard, it's another to do it without proper recuperation time' (p. 76). 'If coaches don't see "work" written on their program, they don't think they're doing their job. . . . I think that reading players and understanding the value of rest is just as important as getting them extremely fit and mentally ready to play' (p. 140).

- **Scout the opposition by watching live games.** Like many contemporary coaches, Brown accumulated a stack of videos on both her own team and the opposition. However, she believed that 'being at a game was 10 times more useful than watching a video. [With video] you are at the mercy of the cameraman and what they follow is not all that coaches see in match play. Sometimes in hard games you find

players have their favourite moves which they go back to under the stress of play' (p. 78).

- **Create team bonding opportunities.** A strong commitment to team can be enhanced when athletes enjoy each other's company off the field, as Brown explained: 'Friendships off the court pay dividends on it. If the network of friendship and bonding is extremely close, then the teamwork is going to be spot on' (p. 81).

- **Have a clear mind.** Although most of the focus precompetition is directed at enhancing the performance state of the competing athletes, coaches also need to ensure that they themselves are in a relaxed, positive and focused state of mind. Brown used to take herself off and walk through a park to clear her brain and try to get her heart rate down. She said, 'I hate to be rushed and fussed before a big game because you have to be very sure that your mind is clear for your players to tap into and for you to tap into them' (p. 81).

- **Build confidence.** A reality of dealing with humans in elite sport is that even the great players go through periods in which they lose confidence and therefore form. According to one of her players, Keeley Devery, when Brown took over as coach, the team was a bit flat and low in confidence, but 'she made us feel very positive and proud of our achievements and that made a difference' (p. 84). Brown identified that women, in contrast to men, tend to be crushed very easily if they express self-esteem in their words and actions. Therefore 'they have to be thoughtful about how they behave but have a strong resolve about their worth' (p. 97). Brown wanted her players to recognise how good they were as people and netballers.

- **Use mental skills consultants.** At a time when training mental skills was still viewed with some suspicion in the sporting arena, Brown embraced the involvement of sport psychologists Colin Davey and Anthony Stewart in her program. She not only saw value in having the players consult these experts on mental skills, but also appreciated their input into improving her own mental skills. In Stewart's case she said, 'he's watched me at training and given me feedback on what I've done and who I've been hard on and why I was hard on them. You are never what you think you are' (p. 92). This ability to self-reflect and accept suggestions for improvement is not easy for coaches who typically have been leaders for a long time and are often set in their ways.

- **Show compassion.** Historically, coaching has been dominated by males, and the typical image portrayed in the media has been of a hard-nosed, tough minded, ruthless and, dare I say it, heartless person in charge. Thankfully, women have been given more opportunities to coach in recent times, and their more empathetic and compassionate approach has not only affected their coaching but also changed the approach of many male coaches. Brown believed that caring about players' feelings, understanding the impact of stress in their lives and supporting them when they are down does not mean that a coach can't demand a strong competitive instinct within the team. Sport psychologist Anthony Stewart described Brown's compassion as an 'enormous strength' and suggested that it is 'one not often shown, in my experience, by elite male coaches' (p. 93). Obviously, a variety of personalities exist in coaches of both genders, but the point is well taken.

- **Make considered decisions.** Although most coaches would support Alex Ferguson's assertion about the need to be able to make quick decisions during competition, Brown learned that when dealing with players, she needed to be careful about making snap decisions about them: 'If there is one thing that the help of a sport psychologist had taught me, it's never to make snap decisions on people, to realise that people are all different' (p. 104). Clearly, the need to balance a core set of non-negotiables, while recognising

the need for different approaches and expectations for various players, remains a constant challenge for all coaches.

- **Keep learning.** It is apparent that all the coaches in this chapter have had an insatiable appetite to keep learning, and this has contributed to their continued growth as coaches and their long-term success. According to one of Brown's star players, Vicki Wilson, 'Brown realised she didn't always know the answers, there's always one more thing on the learning curve that means opening up to others, taking suggestions, heeding advice and copping criticism' (p. 138). This quality is extremely important but difficult to embrace when you already have experienced success as a coach.

The smart coach, though, is always trying to be ahead of the pack, and this involves constantly evaluating and modifying current practices. Jill McIntosh, who played under Joyce Brown and later coached the Australian netball team to two world championships and two Commonwealth Games gold medals, confirmed Brown's commitment to learning, while developing the skill and self-belief of players. She made the following comments about Brown to the chapter author: 'After each term as National coach, Joyce grew as a person and coach, learning from experiences along the way. She was single-minded but very consultative with her players. She knew the capabilities of each player and believed in us. Although thoroughly prepared pregame, it was not so much about the opposition as encouraging us to play our game. She was a stickler for skill and believed our game was good enough to win and we did'.

COACHING QUALITIES AND INDIVIDUAL SPORTS

Although different coaching methods may be apparent in individual sports, all of the qualities of the five team sport coaches described in this chapter are equally relevant to coaching individual sports. Coaching is an emerging art and science that will continue to grow. We can learn from other sports and will no doubt continue to learn from research into sport. However, the sporting arena will always provide opportunities for coaches to experiment and discover new techniques and strategies. This is what makes coaching such an exciting profession.

As mentioned in the introduction, this chapter could never have included all the qualities that have ever been demonstrated by coaches throughout the history of sport. It is hoped, however, that those presented in this chapter, from the five elite coaches to Top Gunn, will encourage all coaches to continue to grow.

Fundamentally, coaches prepare athletes to meet the ever-changing challenges of competition with consistent focus and application to their task. In giving acclaim to his coach, Noel Donaldson, triple Olympic and multiple world champion Australian rower James Tomkins said in a personal communication to the author: 'There is nothing better than sitting on the starting line knowing that you are as prepared as you can possibly be, and ready to trust that preparation'.

All the coaches mentioned in this chapter have managed their athletes for extended periods of time. In a climate in which coaches are often replaced when they are not initially successful, Tomkins alerts us to the benefits of developing a long-term relationship with a coach:

'I was extremely fortunate to have Noel Donaldson as my rowing coach at Carey Grammar School and at the international level of our sport. Noel was passionate about rowing, heavily committed to his crews, and each individual within them, and was always looking for new and better ways to improve their performance. The consistency of our relationship meant that he knew my strengths and limitations and was always able to keep me motivated and improving'.

Everyone associated with hiring coaches should be aware of the value of coaches building relationships with athletes. They need to show patience in the journey to success, rather than replacing coaches at the first sign of decrements in performance. Otherwise, we are continually losing the benefits of the relationship that has been built and the knowledge of how to handle and motivate the athlete. Coaching clearly is a complex task. It is almost impossible to do a perfect job. Hopefully, by consistently demonstrating the range of qualities outlined in this chapter, coaches will not only retain their jobs but also continue to have success in their quest for perfection.

SUMMARY

- A review of the biographies of five esteemed coaches in different sports and some observations of a volunteer coach reveal a number of qualities of respected coaches.

- The qualities of successful coaches are not the exclusive domain of professional coaches. However, a volunteer coach is more time poor and may not be able to embrace all aspects of successful coaching.

- Several attributes and approaches are common among the most respected coaches, including having a vision of the best way forward, a willingness to learn new methods and adapt existing ones, an intimate knowledge of their own sports and others, a commitment to understand the whole athlete and the opposition and the ability to develop a positive and inclusive culture.

- By adopting a calm but firm persona, respected coaches seek to challenge athletes to continue to improve by providing activities that specifically prepare them for various roles in competition.

REFERENCES AND RESOURCES

Buchanan, J. (2007). *If better is possible.* Prahran, VIC: Hardie Grant Books

Charlesworth, R.I. (2001). *The coach: Managing for success.* Sydney: Pan Macmillan.

Ferguson, A.B. (1999). *Managing my life: My autobiography.* London: Hodder & Staughton.

Smithers, E., & Appleby, C. (1996). *No limits: Joyce Brown.* Lilydale, VIC: Varenna.

Wooden, J., & Jamison, S. (1997). *Wooden: A lifetime of observations and reflections on and off the court.* New York: Contemporary Books.

PART II

MANAGING THE PROGRAM

CHAPTER 4

Planning and Evaluating the Program

—— Sue Hooper

Planning and evaluating the program, the foundation of the coach's role, help coaches use their technical knowledge and skills more efficiently and effectively to improve their athletes' and teams' performances. These skills increase the satisfaction for coaches and everyone else in the program.

Coaches constantly plan and evaluate the elements of their programs that affect all aspects of an athlete's or team's experience. Plans vary in scope and duration, from annual plans to seasonal plans, periodised plans and plans for single training sessions. Planning and evaluating becomes more detailed as the athlete and team advance through the developmental stages. The process moves from a largely session-by-session approach for a novice athlete to an intricate career-orientated and detailed approach for an elite athlete.

At the most fundamental level, program planning and evaluation involve three steps performed by the coach:

1. Identify the program's goals.
2. Develop a course of action.
3. Review the outcome.

But that explanation is too simplistic to describe what actually transpires. In fact, the process is a cyclical one involving continual monitoring, feedback, decision making and action components, as depicted in figure 4.1.

This process is often referred to as the 'plan–do–review' of coaching. The general sequence is as follows: planning, executing the plan, evaluating the plan and then, to bring the process full circle, using information gained in the evaluation to improve the plan. The best way for coaches to learn and improve their planning and evaluation skills is to study a component of the program, evaluate its present performance, institute a plan to enhance it, monitor and gain feedback on its impact and use that data to modify the plan to function at optimal efficiency and effectiveness. The remainder of this chapter discusses the components of planning and evaluating in more detail.

KEY CONSIDERATIONS IN PROGRAM PLANNING

In its simplest form, planning requires the coach to answer the following questions:

- Who? Athletes and others interested in the program
- Why? Goals to be achieved
- What? Tasks to be completed
- When? Time, frequency and duration
- Where? Facilities, use of space and equipment
- How? Structure, sequencing, integration and style of tasks

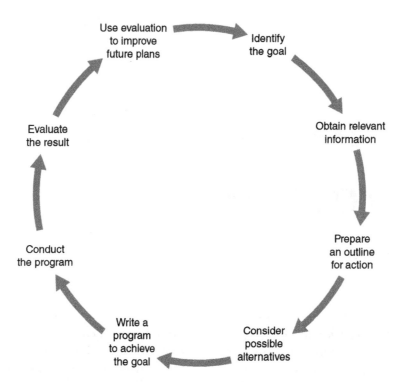

Figure 4.1 The planning and evaluation cycle.

The order of their consideration and the complexity of each question may differ according to the coach's role and the performance level of the athlete(s).

ATHLETES AND OTHERS

Coaches plan primarily for their athletes, but they must also consider the roles and tasks of other interested parties—in particular, the people who have an existing or future interest in the program. They may include the athletes' parents, family and friends, assistant coaches and trainers, strength and conditioning coaches and sports science and sports medicine practitioners.

Planning the tasks of other people and involving them in the planning process encourages them to commit to making the coach's plan work. Doing so also allows coaches to draw on their collective expertise when developing the program and to consider and manage the needs of those involved. In reality, the opportunity for these people to provide input into planning is often limited, but at a minimum, coaches should actively seek to involve them in program evaluation.

Athletes have other commitments in addition to sport. Education, work and family commitments commonly affect when athletes can train and the total time available for training. The challenge for the coach is to consider these factors when planning the program and to understand that, at times, athletes' other commitments may take priority over sport.

GOALS

Regardless of the sport or the athlete's level, goals are the foundation for the program plan because they provide direction for planning and function as key performance indicators for evaluation. Goals set a framework for achieving a long-term outcome (career and season goals) and shorter-term goals (phase, cycle or session goals). Coaches set themselves up for success when they set goals that are SMART: specific, measurable, attainable, relevant and time bound. (See chapter 13 for additional criteria and information.)

Long- and short-term goals help identify the program's purpose and set a time line for achievement. The time line may run for a season or a year for non-elite athletes, or for a two- or four-year competition cycle related to major events such as world championships or Olympic or Paralympic Games for elite athletes.

Long-term goals are set first and have an outcome focus. They are substantial, tangible objectives usually related to performance. They should be limited to fewer than four and should outline what the training program aims to achieve, such as reaching qualifying times to compete in three events at state championships or making the finals in one event in the state championships.

Short-term goals have a process focus and should relate directly to a means for achieving each long-term goal. They are set at session, cycle and phase levels. For example, a phase

Michael Weber/image broker/age fotostock

Athletes need long-term and short-term goals based around cycles for major competitions. For an elite gymnast, such as Lauren Mitchell, this might be a 4-year cycle targeting the Olympics.

goal might be to increase training to six sessions per week, the related cycle goal might be to improve vertical jump performance by over a centimetre and the session goal might be to include recovery exercises in every session.

In setting SMART goals, coaches must achieve a balance between having attainable goals and having ones that stretch the athlete and provide something worthwhile to work towards. The coach must consider any potential for confrontation or resistance to the goals. One good method is the CCOT analysis used in business; it stands for capabilities, challenges, opportunities and threats. In team sports, a CCOT analysis could be conducted for both the team and the individual athletes. It asks questions about each category:

- Capabilities: What are the athlete's strengths? How will these be kept as strengths?
- Challenges: What are the athlete's weaknesses? How can these be improved?
- Opportunities: What opportunities are there for this athlete? How can they provide an advantage?
- Threats: Are there any threats to goal achievement? How can they be minimised?

LOGISTICS

In addition to planning the content (tasks) of the training program, coaches must also plan for and allocate the resources needed to initiate the program. These resources might include the use of facilities and equipment, human resources such as assistant coaches and trainers and other pertinent logistics of the sport. This addresses the what, when, where and how of planning.

The content of the program (what) is considered later in this chapter and in other chapters. In considering when, where and how, the coach should give thought to these elements:

- Use of facilities, space, time and equipment
- Tasks for other people involved with the program
- Availability and allocation of adequate funds

In planning a session, coaches should do the following:

- Maximise participation and enjoyment.
- Include all athletes (e.g., those with special needs and medical conditions).
- Set performance learning goals (e.g., movement skills, values and attitudes).
- Ensure safe experiences and focus on standards of behaviour.
- Share some responsibilities with others (e.g., athletes lead warm-ups, parents keep records).
- Evaluate after each session to improve the planning for later sessions.

During the planning process, coaches should consider how they are going to evaluate the training program. This provides a structure for assessment and reflection and leads to more complete evaluations. Identifying key performance outcomes for sessions, cycles and phases and their method of evaluation helps coaches check their progress towards the long-term program goals.

LONG-TERM AND ANNUAL PLANS

Coaches consider two plans when preparing for their coaching roles each year: a long-term plan and an annual plan. Together these two plans provide the training and competition schedules to meet athletes' health, welfare and performance needs.

LONG-TERM PLAN

The long-term plan has a career-orientated focus that identifies sequential stages for optimal training, competition and recovery to ensure the athlete's best physical, mental and emotional long-term development. This plan may span 20 years with the goal of lifelong participation in sport and physical activity. The plan changes as the athlete moves through the stages of development in the sport. Table 4.1 shows an example of the considerations required by the coach in long-term planning.

In some sports, such as gymnastics, diving and swimming, specialisation occurs early; this reduces the length of the stages. Coaches should be careful to always keep a long-term development perspective even in early specialisation sports. They need to consider the individual athlete's readiness to move through the stages because missing or rushing through stages may have negative ramifications such as less well-developed skills and burnout.

To adjust each individual athlete's long-term plan, the coach should consider the following:

- Developmental stage including abilities and capacities
- Social and cultural background and language skills
- Motivations and expectations
- Special needs such as disabilities or medical conditions
- Other life activities (to manage the risk of negative outcomes such as overload)

ANNUAL PLAN

The annual plan is usually set around the individual athlete's stage of development, the sport program calendar and other commitments such as school, work and holidays. Periodisation allows the annual plan to be divided into manageable sections targeted at optimal performances at the required time. Periodisation involves structuring training, competition and recovery periods and integrating sports science, strength and conditioning and sport-specific technical and tactical activities in a sequence of phases. These phases may place different emphases on the volume, frequency and intensity of training to build athletes' capacity, help them peak for optimal performance and help them avoid excessive fatigue and injury.

The annual plan should be flexible enough to meet the changing needs of the athlete and the changing sport environment. It also needs to recognise that continuous work without variations in volume, intensity and methods ultimately leads to plateaus in performance, boredom and lack of motivation to train.

The phases of the annual plan are usually set by breaks in competition or the varying importance of competitions. These phases may be broken into smaller planning units such

Table 4.1 Stage and Age-Based Long-Term Plan for Athlete Development

Stage	Age (years)	Focus	Ratio of play to deliberate practice
Beginning	0–6	Learn fundamental movements	Minimal deliberate practice
Learning fundamentals	6–9	Build overall motor skills	4:1
Beginning training	9–12	Learn all fundamental sports skills	3:1
Training to participate	12–15	Consolidate sport-specific skills and try competing	1:1
Training to compete	15 +	Optimise sport, event or position skills Develop competition skills and strategies	1:4
Competing to win	18 +	Maximise event, position or performance skills	1:4
Active life	any age	Maintain lifelong physical activity and involvement in coaching, officiating or administration	Any

as macrocycles, mesocycles and microcycles. A macrocycle often covers the calendar year, although it may be four years for an Olympic athlete. Macrocycles may have one or several peak cycles, depending on the number of minor and major competitions in that cycle. Team sports often have a single peak or two peaks, but a macrocycle involving three or more peaks is common in international athletics.

Each peak cycle is broken down into training phases, most commonly identified as preparation, competition and transition. These phases are further broken down into subphases differentiated by their aims and priorities (discussed later in this chapter), and these are broken down further to mesocycles (usually three to six weeks) and then microcycles (one week). Microcycles have multiple training units such as technical training or speed training, and a single training session may include more than one unit. For example, stretching is often included with strength and speed work. Generally, three to six microcycles make up one mesocycle, and six mesocycles make up one peak cycle.

After identifying the individual athlete's development needs, competition calendar and other commitments, the coach can tackle the details of the plan in the three phases (preparation, competition and transition). These phases are considered differently for different sports. For the sake of simplicity, three general types

of sport are considered here: endurance, speed and team.

Preparation Phase The prime objective of the preparation (also called preseason) phase for any athlete is to develop a sound fitness base for the more intense and specialised training. This phase includes the general preparation subphase (one or two mesocycles) and the specific preparation subphase (one mesocycle). The first mesocycle typically involves a high volume of low- to moderate-intensity training that is progressively and gradually reversed. For example, volume may be reduced and intensity of training increased over the remainder of this phase.

Training methods in this phase vary with the type of athlete. Table 4.2 shows activities appropriate for endurance, speed and team athletes and considers psychological, nutritional, strength, power, technical and tactical applications.

Competition Phase The aim of the competition (in-season) phase is to develop an athlete's specific fitness and readiness for competition to maximal levels. Training is at a high intensity with a gradually reducing volume as the competition date draws near. Usually one mesocycle, the precompetition subphase, is the most demanding period of training in the cycle. To bring athletes' specific fitness and skills to

Table 4.2 Preparation Phase Activities Specified by Athlete Type

Type of athlete	Preparation phase	
	General subphase	**Specific subphase**
Endurance	Low-intensity aerobic training (more)	Low-intensity aerobic training (less)
	Anaerobic threshold training (less)	Anaerobic threshold training (more)
	Group goals and group performance	Awareness of individual differences
	Self-monitoring skills	Perceptual skills and decision making
	Technical training	
	Fartlek training	
	Endurance weight training	
	General flexibility	
	Recovery training	
	General sports nutrition	
Speed	Alactic anaerobic training (75% of max)	Alactic anaerobic training (>80% of max)
	Lactic anaerobic training (75% of max)	Lactic anaerobic training (80-90% of max)
	Anatomical adaptation	Maximal strength
	Group goals and group performance	Awareness of individual differences
	Self-monitoring skills	Perceptual skills and decision making
	Technical training	
	Low-intensity aerobic training for recovery	
	General flexibility	
	Recovery training	
	General sports nutrition	
Team	Low-intensity aerobic training (more)	Low-intensity aerobic training (less)
	Maximal aerobic training (less)	Maximal aerobic training (more)
	Alactic anaerobic training (75% of max) (less)	Alactic anaerobic training (80-90% of max) (more)
	Anatomical adaptation	Maximal strength
	Simple individual skills	Complex individual skills and team skills training
	Group goals and group performance	Awareness of individual differences
	Self-monitoring skills	Perceptual skills and decision making
	Technical training	
	Fartlek training	
	General flexibility	
	Recovery training	
	General sports nutrition	

their peaks for the competition subphase, this mesocycle includes high-intensity training (at or very near race or game intensity) with moderate volume. Recovery training is a key component; peaking and tapering processes should be planned carefully in the competition subphase (see chapter 9 for additional information).

The competition subphase may last several months, and fitness should be at a peak when entering this subphase. Fitness is then maintained with high-intensity training and relatively low volume. Several mesocycles may be needed, and these may need to be flexible to cater to fatigue, injury and illness. Sample activities are listed in table 4.3.

Tapering is the final phase of training before a major competition and is essential to an athlete's performance. The taper involves reducing the training load, usually the volume, and aims to alleviate the accumulated physiological and psychological fatigue and improve the training adaptations to achieve optimal performance (peaking).

For endurance and speed athletes, the final microcycle before competition focuses on tapering. Planning tapers for individual athletes requires consideration of their needs for rest and psychological preparation for competition. Tapers may be very short, such as days or a week for competitions of low importance, and may be several weeks long for important competitions.

Team athletes who compete weekly require a different approach: their recovery and lower-intensity training sessions are scheduled early in the week to allow them to recover from the previous game. The main training session of moderate to high intensity and volume is performed midweek, and a brief quality workout is scheduled for one or two days before the next game. Microcycles of this nature are designed to allow a mini-peak for each game throughout the competition phase. Some other examples of periodised fitness training programs are described in chapter 9.

Transition Phase The main objectives of the transition (off-season) phase are to maintain a reasonable level of endurance fitness and to prevent too much detraining. This is also a time for the athlete to rest and allow injuries to heal. The transition allows coaches and athletes to benefit psychologically from a break after the competition phase, and it is a good time for review, evaluation and planning. This can also be a time to focus on the specific weaknesses of individual athletes because they can spend time correcting these weaknesses without interference from other types of training. Table 4.4 provides sample activities for this phase.

Considerations for Annual Plans Coaches must consider a number of additional factors when developing their annual plans. These factors include training intensity and volume, individualisation for each athlete, periodisation and contingencies.

Training intensity and training volume are fundamental to the annual plan. Generally, when volume is high, intensity is low, and vice versa. The physiological adaptations may differ between high-intensity/low-volume training and low-intensity/high-volume training. Training volume can be increased by increasing either the duration or frequency of training units or both. The intensity of training is varied by adjusting the training load placed on the athlete, and this may be assessed using, for example, heart rate, rating of perceived exertion or blood lactate level. Balancing the intensity and volume of training for each athlete through the annual plan is a key part of the science and art of coaching.

Ideally, coaches plan for both their teams and their individual athletes. Planning only for the team and not for individual athletes reduces coaching effectiveness. An ideal way to individualise the plan is to involve the athletes and others in the planning. This will ensure that their personal interests, expectations and commitments are included and that they take some ownership of their development.

Coaches of team sports must match individuals to positions based on their character, talent, skills, physical attributes and other attributes, and then plan their training accordingly. Factors to consider include the individual response to stress and rate of, and limits to, improvement. Table 4.5 provides a more complete list of factors to consider. The coach should plan

Table 4.3 Competition Phase Activities Specified by Athlete Type

Type of athlete	Competitive phase	
	Precompetition subphase	**Competition subphase**
Endurance	Low-intensity aerobic training	Low-intensity aerobic training (recovery)
	Recovery training	Recovery training plus tapering
	Team-building exercises	Team activities and recreation
	Pressure, exertion and coping strategies	
	Mental preparation and recovery	
	Anaerobic threshold training	
	Maximal aerobic training	
	Endurance weight training (maintain)	
	Maintenance of general flexibility	
	Competition-specific nutrition planning	
Speed	Conversion to power, muscular endurance or both	Maintenance
	Recovery training	Recovery training plus tapering for peak performance
	Team-building exercises	Team activities and recreation
	Pressure, exertion and coping strategies	
	Mental preparation and recovery	
	Competition-specific nutrition planning	
	Maximal alactic anaerobic training	
	Maximal lactic anaerobic training	
	Low-intensity aerobic training (for recovery)	
	Maintenance of general flexibility	
Team	Maximal alactic anaerobic training	Maximal aerobic anaerobic training
	Conversion to power, muscular endurance or both	Maintenance
	Recovery training	Recovery training plus tapering
	Team-building exercises	Team activities and recreation
	Pressure, exertion and coping strategies	
	Mental preparation and recovery	
	Low-intensity aerobic training (for recovery)	
	Maximal aerobic training	
	Game-specific individual skills and synchronisation of team skill training	
	Maintenance of general flexibility	
	Competition-specific nutrition planning	

Table 4.4 Transition Phase Activities Specified by Athlete Type

Type of athlete	Transition phase
Endurance	Low-intensity aerobic training (cross-training) Maintenance of basic nutrition Maintenance of mental skills
Speed	Low-intensity aerobic training (cross-training) Alactic anaerobic training (60-80% of max) Lactic anaerobic training (60-80% of max) Compensation and endurance weight training Strength weight training Maintenance of basic nutrition Maintenance of mental skills
Team	Low-intensity aerobic training (cross-training) Compensation and endurance weight training Strength weight training Maintenance of basic nutrition Maintenance of mental skills

Table 4.5 Factors a Coach Should Consider in Creating an Individualised Annual Plan

Factors	Examples
Abilities	Dexterity, stamina, strength, speed, skills
Attitude	Open, closed, neutral to new experiences
Body type	Stocky, tall, short, lean, muscular, round
Capacities	Low, moderate, high limits
Cultural background	Ethnicity, race, religion, socio-economic status
Emotional make-up	Bored, excited, fearful, joyful
Language skills	Low, moderate, high
Learning style	Visual, verbal, kinaesthetic
Maturation	Immature, intermediate, mature
Motivation and expectations	Low, moderate, high drive for success
Other life activities	School, employment, volunteer roles
Personal background	Parent or guardian support
Social expertise	Works best one-on-one, in small groups, in large groups
Movement experiences	Recreational, instructional, competitive
Special needs	Disability, injury, medical condition

for skill development, improvement in game awareness and the integration of the athlete with other athletes in the team. Individualising athlete development helps optimise the innate capacity of athletes and thus their contributions to the team.

All of the planning units come together in a periodised plan of macrocycles, mesocycles and microcycles. Figure 4.2 shows an annual training plan for a junior elite basketball team and illustrates the tools that coaches can use to focus on both their short- and long-term goals.

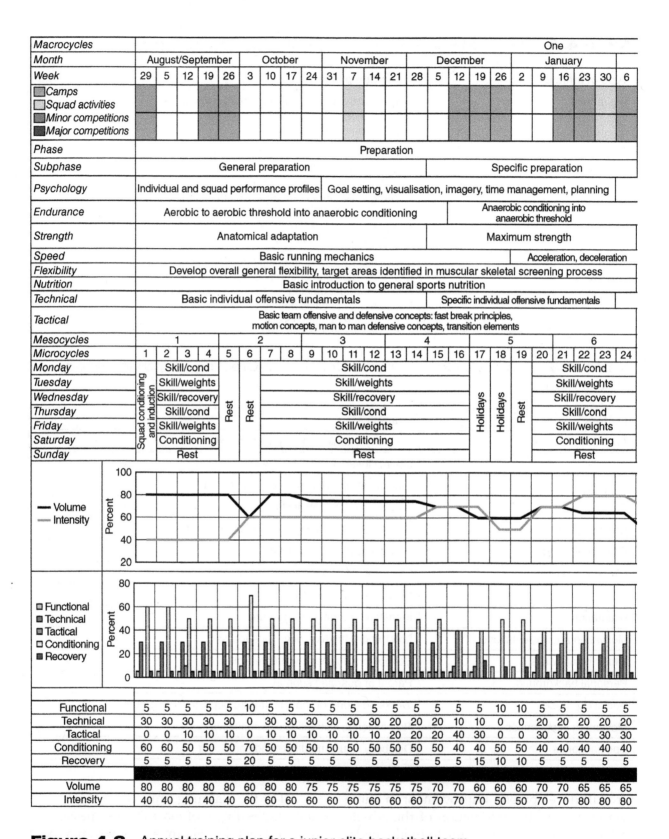

Figure 4.2 Annual training plan for a junior elite basketball team.

Annual periodisation plan

	February			March					April			May					June				July			Two August			
	13	20	27	5	12	30	19	26	2	9	16	23	30	7	14	21	28	4	11	18	25	2	9	16	23	30	6	13

Competition																			Transition								

| Precompetition | | Competition | | | | Transition | Precompetition | | | | Competition | | | | | | Transition | | | | | | | | | | |

Effective communication, mental recovery, mental preparation, maintenance of previous skills | Dealing with adversity, maintenance of previous skills | Active rest, regenerate, de-stress

Game type conditioning, repeat sprint work, specific multidirectional | Specific multidirectional, game type conditioning | Aerobic, aerobic threshold

Conversion to power | Cease all | Specific strength work | Max strength, power | Maintain | Cease all | Compensation

straight line speed, turning | Agility, turning, cutting | Reaction, contact | Cross training

Maintain general flexibility, continue to target areas identified in muscular skeletal screening process | Maintain general flexibility

Competition specific nutrition planning | Maintenance of basic nutrition

Individual offensive and defensive fundamentals | Individual offensive and defensive fundamentals in a game situation | Cross training

Advanced team offensive and defensive systems, decision making | Synchronise offensive and defensive concepts, problem solving situational plays

7				8					9			10					11					12		13			
25	26	27	28	29	30	31	32	33	34	35	36	37	38	39	40	41	42	43	44	45	46	47	48	49	50	51	52

Week 26–32: Skill/recovery, Squad/weights, Rest, Squad/weights, Rest, Competition, Rest/travel
Week 25: Rest
Week 33: Major competition
Week 34: Rest
Week 35: Rest
Week 36–40: Recovery, Squad/weights, Competition, Rest, Squad/weights, Squad/weights, Game/travel
Week 41: Rest
Week 42–45: Recovery, Squad/weights, Competition, Rest, Squad/weights, Squad/weights, Game/travel
Week 45: Travel, light practice
Week 46: Major competition
Week 47: Rest
Week 48: Rest
Week 49–52: Squad conditioning

10	5	5	5	5	5	5	5	5	10	10	5	5	5	5	5	10	5	5	5	5	5	10	10	10	10	10	10
0	20	20	20	20	20	20	20	10	20	20	10	10	10	10	10	0	10	10	10	10	0	0	0	40	40	40	40
0	50	50	50	50	50	50	50	60	0	0	70	70	70	70	70	0	70	70	70	70	80	0	0	0	0	0	0
40	20	20	20	20	20	20	20	20	20	20	10	10	10	10	10	20	10	10	10	10	10	0	0	30	30	30	40
10	5	5	5	5	5	5	5	5	20	20	5	5	5	5	5	20	5	5	5	5	5	20	20	20	20	20	20
50	50	45	45	45	45	45	40	40	50	50	50	50	50	45	45	40	45	45	45	30	30	40	40	50	50	50	55
70	80	80	90	90	90	90	95	95	70	70	80	80	70	80	80	60	70	90	90	95	95	50	50	60	60	60	60

Coaches who incorporate contingency planning within the planning process reduce their risk of being caught unprepared for the challenges that invariably occur. Contingency plans provide strategies for dealing with unexpected change. The ability to anticipate problems and to include some flexibility in the plan to take advantage of unexpected opportunities is a skill that coaches develop over time.

Contingency plans are useful when they include alternative activities, facilities, equipment or competition schedules. For example, a coach may need to change a session plan based on an athlete's attitude or physical condition on a given day. Contingency plans can be especially important in team sports, in which player availability can change suddenly.

EVALUATING THE PROGRAM

Evaluation involves reviewing the outcome of the program and the planning process. It begins at the session level and progresses to the long-term plan. Relevant questions include: Did we achieve the session goal? And, Are we on track to achieve the cycle goal?

In everyday practice, coaches use informal evaluation methods such as reflection on what they observed during the program. This is best documented in a planning and evaluation diary and can be supported by a regular formal evaluation that includes requests for feedback from athletes and others who influence the program. It is much better for the coach to provide a systematic opportunity for athletes and others to provide timely feedback than to learn at the end of the season about dissatisfaction with some aspect of the program from the beginning of the season, which negatively affected goal achievement. Providing opportunities for both formal feedback (e.g., meetings) and informal feedback (e.g., a feedback box for comments) from athletes and others ensures that they remain involved in planning and evaluating the program and increases the likelihood of their continued commitment to assisting the coach.

It is good practice for coaches to dedicate time after each session to evaluation. This is important because the original assumptions and expectations often change after planning. For example, athletes come and go, information that affects the program becomes available and competition schedules change. Having some flexibility in plans is important to cater for these alterations, which may also affect the goals.

The evaluation considers the results of the session (outcomes) and how these were achieved (processes). After sessions, coaches should ask themselves the following questions:

- Were the session's goals achieved?
- Are the athletes on track for achieving the goals of the cycle or phase?
- How did the athletes perform during the session?
- What was done well?
- What could have been done better?
- What strategies could improve the session?

Following are questions coaches should also ask themselves regarding the processes that were used:

- Was the session plan adhered to?
- Was the use of space and equipment efficient?
- Was the communication effective?
- What improvements could be made?

This structure for evaluation should be continued for each cycle and phase. Keeping records of changes that were made and why gives the coach a record to use for future planning and improves the coach's planning and evaluating skills.

COMPLETING THE CYCLE

The final step to complete the planning and evaluation cycle is to integrate the evaluation outcomes back into the program plan. This maintains important links among the goals, the annual plan and the long-term plan. By comparing the evaluation outcomes at each level, from session to long-term plans, coaches retain a sense of the time line for the achievement of short- and long-term goals.

WAIS WOMEN'S GYMNASTICS PROGRAM

The women's gymnastics program at the Western Australian Institute of Sport (WAIS) has had great success since it was introduced in 1984. The program was built around a strong spirit of cooperation and benefited from careful planning and continual evaluation. The program developed early and close connections with club programs in Perth to provide gymnasts with access to experienced coaches along the entire pathway from grassroots to high-performance squads. The program culture promotes gymnasts belonging to the program rather than any particular coach, and the overall philosophy is to develop solid foundations early with a delayed emphasis on winning. This program culture pervades all planning considerations.

In 1988 Liz Chetkovich became the first full-time WAIS gymnastics coach, converting to program manager in 1997. She was able to use the skills she learned as a coach in planning and evaluating programs to set long-term goals to build her coaching team. In a personal communication with the author, she said, 'Coaches need to have a clear picture in mind about what they wish to achieve and then, as opportunities arise, take a step by step approach in their planning, implementation and evaluation of strategies to reach their goals'.

Chetkovich's strategic recruitment of overseas coaches to join her, including the Russian national women's coach Andrei Rodionenko and later Russian Nikolai Lapchine, was important in her planning. The engagement of these coaches aided the development of homegrown coaches Joanne Richards and Martine George, both of whom have contributed significantly to the success of the program in recent years. The WAIS coaching team now comprises 10 full- and part-time coaches.

Because of the rigorous demands of the sport and the age of the participants, injury is a constant concern and requires continual monitoring and controlling of training load and strategies for injury prevention and management. One of Lapchine's recognised skills is regulating the training load especially during competition preparation. His planning is regulated daily, based on an evaluation of the gymnast's physical, technical and mental states; what was accomplished in previous sessions; and the point in the competitive season.

During the early 1990s, the program produced outstanding gymnasts such as Michelle Telfer and Jenny Smith, followed later by Commonwealth champion and world championship medallist Allana Slater, and more recently by world champion Lauren Mitchell. It is worth noting that these and other gymnasts from the program have also successfully pursued tertiary education that their coaches had to take into consideration in their program planning. These are great examples of how coaches can prioritise the commitments of their athletes to help them achieve success in sport and life.

Part of completing the cycle should also be a recheck of the CCOT analysis, especially those elements of the analysis relating to any changes in the athlete's internal and external environments. For example, a previous challenge for an athlete may have developed into a capability, and new opportunities and threats may have developed externally. A change in any of these areas affects the balance of components in the training program and therefore the pathway to achieving goals. The coach must consider these in planning for program delivery in the future.

SUMMARY

- Planning and evaluating are essential skills for every coach.
- The cyclical nature of planning and evaluation means that good coaches are continually planning, executing the plan, evaluating the plan and using information from the evaluation to improve the plan. Thus, they are always improving these important coaching skills.
- Seeking input from athletes and others who influence the program throughout the process is important for ensuring their ongoing commitment to the plan.
- Effective planning and evaluating requires coaches to adopt an individualised approach for each athlete that includes goal setting, logistics, contingency plans and periodisation. Coaches must also evaluate both processes and outcomes.

REFERENCES AND RESOURCES

Bompa, T.O., & Haff, G.G. (2009). *Periodization: Theory and methodology of training.* Champaign, IL: Human Kinetics.

Cross, N., & Lyle, J. (Eds.). (1999). *The coaching process. Principles and practice for sport.* Oxford: Butterworth-Heinemann.

Leonard, R. (2005). *The administrative side to coaching: A handbook for applying business principles to coaching athletics.* Morgantown, WV: Fitness Information Technology.

Mujika, I. (2009). *Tapering and peaking for optimal performance.* Champaign, IL: Human Kinetics.

CHAPTER 5

Creating a Positive Team Culture

—— Sandy Gordon

A sign above the entrance to the University of California at Berkeley swimming pool reads: *The aim of this establishment is to create an environment where champions are inevitable.* All sport organisations aspire to stage an environment where champions are inevitable. However, a very small percentage succeed in actually doing so.

In the business world there is ample evidence that values-driven organisational cultures are more successful as measured by profitability, growth and long-term survival. Such cultures also minimise unethical conduct and both attract and retain star performers. There is little evidence-based support for similar findings in sport, yet the development of effective organisational and team environments has long been regarded as the link between culture and performance. In addition, although the ability to foster effective cultures is widely considered the hallmark of effective sport leadership, in practice, many administrators and coaches are intimidated and frustrated by the significant challenges involved in such an undertaking.

This chapter describes processes that coaches working in school, community or high-performance contexts can use to establish effective organisational cultures. Examples of the implementation of these steps and processes are presented in addition to recruitment philosophies and ideas on strengths-based strategic planning.

Leaders from a variety of sports and all levels of sport participation will benefit from the discussion of contemporary and cutting-edge cultural change processes in this chapter. They should also gain confidence in implementing the strategies and ideas discussed here.

TERMINOLOGY FOR TEAM CULTURE

Before we examine the process, a review of some related terminology is in order. Although the following terms may be familiar, their meaning and usage are often either misused or misunderstood.

Sport culture refers to the values and assumptions that are shared within a sport team or organisation. Shared assumptions are often unconscious, taken-for-granted perceptions or beliefs that have worked so well in the past that they are considered the correct way to think and act towards problems and opportunities. All organisational cultures have at least three functions:

- A form of social control
- The social glue that binds people together
- A way to help members make sense of their workplace

The culture should not be so strong that it drives out dissenting values, which may form emerging values for the future. Sport organisations should have adaptive cultures so that all staff and other parties involved with the program, including athletes, support ongoing change in the organisation and their own roles.

Sport teams or organisations can also have *subcultures* as well as the dominant culture. Subcultures may be created by officials and administrative staff, as well as athletes and coaches, and maintain the overall organisation's standards of performance and ethical behaviour. Subcultures are also often the source of emerging and more contemporary values that replace ageing core values.

A *vision* describes what a team or organisation is striving to achieve; a *vision statement* declares the future the organisation wishes to create. A *mission* describes the core business of an organisation; a *mission statement* identifies the organisation's primary activity. An organisation's vision represents a deeper (higher) level of motivation than its mission. While the mission describes the means, the vision describes the end.

Values refer to individual, stable and evaluative beliefs that guide or dictate our preferences for behaviours or courses of action in a variety of situations. *Values-based behaviours* exemplify each value and should be overt and observable, assessable, trainable, hireable and rewardable. *Artefacts* are the observable symbols and signs of an organisation's values and culture. Broad categories of artefacts include organisational stories and legends, rituals, traditions and ceremonies, language and physical structures and symbols.

Values that have been 'behaviourised' ultimately drive an organisation's operations and dictate behaviour. This is because values directly influence ethical behaviour and interpersonal relations, or how people treat each other. They also affect how people perceive situations and circumstances, such as success versus failure and problems versus opportunities. Values also determine an organisation's priorities and ultimate goals.

A *values-based cultural change* is particularly appropriate when an organisation is being outperformed in its category by other organisations, personnel turnover is high, or its financial situation is declining, or it simply wants to go from 'moderate to good' or 'good to great'. When an organisation transforms to a values-based culture, three important changes occur:

1. First, the organisation moves from being success driven to being values driven.
2. Then, the organisation leaders begin to measure success in terms of its emotional, mental and spiritual health.
3. Finally, the role of leaders and managers moves from being predominantly controlling to being predominantly empowering.

The key to creating and sustaining a values-based culture that works is values enactment, which means living the values every day and bringing values-based words and phrases to life by spelling out actions, behaviours and standards. Leaders, in particular, play a critical role in establishing effective cultures by projecting their individually held values and personally 'walking the talk'. Long-term behaviour within any organisation is best predicted by aligning behaviour to what people in the organisation collectively value.

COACH'S ROLE IN ESTABLISHING VALUES AND A VISION

Contemporary leaders of sport organisations, clubs and teams are expected to create stability by engaging in *management behaviour*, including solving problems, organising staff and planning and designing budgets. However, they are also expected to engage in *leadership behaviour*, which produces change and adaptable performance cultures.

Leadership behaviour typically requires setting a clear vision and direction or purpose for the club and aligning, motivating and inspiring people towards achieving that vision. This is called *transformational* leadership, and it is important to note that although management is not leadership, and vice versa, contemporary leaders need to engage in both types of behaviour. Leaders also need to understand

GEELONG CATS FOOTBALL CLUB

The Geelong Cats Football Club participates in the national 17-team professional Australian Football League (AFL) competition. In 2005, after experiencing some lean years, the club decided to invite all people involved in player development and welfare to an interactive planning workshop. The participants in the discussions included the directors, administration staff, coaching and support staff, players, sponsors and representatives from the sport's governing body.

The specific purposes of the workshop were to clarify the objectives of the club in terms of its long-term development and agree on its core values and performance indicators. The process that was subsequently undertaken involved engaging everyone involved in player relocation and entry, induction, development and transition programs. This included host families, parents and friends, coaches, support staff, community and corporate personnel and the player development manager. The club was keen to develop not only good players but also good people who trusted and showed respect and support for each other in an environment of open communication.

Following a 'leading teams' course, a leadership group was established that included both older and younger players whose task was to ensure that all the members of the playing squad lived the core values that had been established. An inclusive process involving important people both within and outside the organisation has been conducted each year since 2005 to review the performance indicators, strategies and values of the club. Brian Cook, chief executive officer of the club, described to the editor of this book, Frank Pyke, the values the organisation created: 'We hold our values deep to our heart and the soul of our club and believe they create the uniqueness in our lives'.

In the time since the organisation made its changes, the Geelong team has tasted great success on the national stage, winning premierships in 2007 and 2009 and finishing runner-up and third in 2008 and 2010, respectively. It has also grown in financial strength and popularity as a result of having the right people involved and the right culture in place. They have fulfilled their initial intention of turning a good club into a great club.

This case study is based on a detailed version prepared for Sport Knowledge Australia by Dr. Caroline Ringuet from the Griffith University Business School in 2008. Based on Ringuet 2008

the trends, influences and perspectives of staff members from the various generations (builders, boomers and generations X and Y) and adapt their management styles accordingly.

In addition to creating a vision, leaders also carry the responsibility of defining the club's mission statement, results, performance goals and attitudes and behaviours. However, as illustrated in the vision model for a professional cricket organisation depicted in figure 5.1, underpinning everything are core values that guide and shape the way the organisation fulfils its purpose as well as creates its distinctive way of playing the game.

Implementing a values-based cultural change process involves the six steps described

in the following sections. Some real-life examples are provided to illustrate how sport organisations have applied each step and navigated their way to the final step: creating a shared vision.

STEP 1: CREATING A VALUES BLUEPRINT

Culture comes alive when teams or organisations that are engaged in the same business (sport) compare themselves to one another. To create a values blueprint for the first time, leaders may simply ask, How do others go about their business? How do others (organisations, clubs, coaches, players, fans) regard us? and,

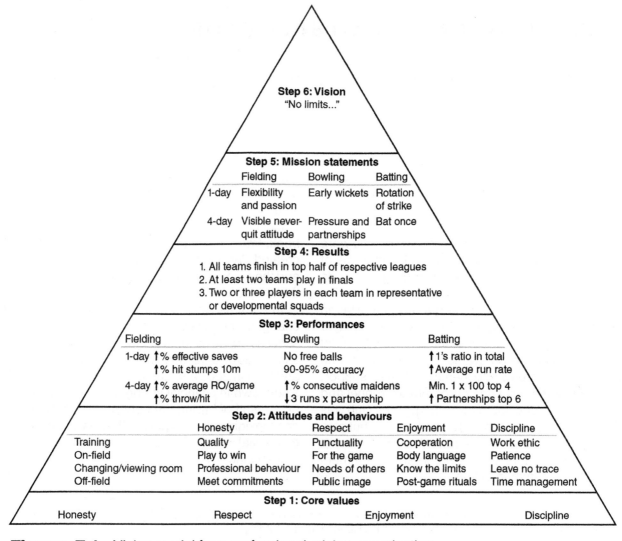

Figure 5.1 Vision model for a professional cricket organisation.

How do we want to be regarded? Quite often, participants engaged in this exercise experience considerable discomfort either because they quickly realise that they have no core values, or if they do, that their behaviours are not aligned with those values—they are not 'walking the talk'.

An easy-to-manage exercise that taps into players' and coaches' personal values for the first time is illustrated in figure 5.2. Each individual in the organisation responds to the question, What should be the core values by which our organisation, club or team operates? Once participants have individually identified three to five values from the list, they gather in pairs and negotiate their combined values down to three to five. Pairs then take on another pair and do the same, which double the number of participants (2:2, 4:4, 8:8, etc.) until the whole group arrives at five to seven core values, or preferably fewer. This exercise can take one or two hours (even a whole day), but however long it takes, it is always time well spent.

To revisit values that were previously created in an organisation, the leader could start conversations in focus groups with these questions: Which values do you believe are currently in place? Do those values actually drive our behaviours? Are they understood by everyone? Are senior leaders actually living the current

Figure 5.2 Identifying Core Values

What should be the core values by which our organisation, club or team operates? Look over the list of values below. Circle any values that jump out because of their importance to you. Then number your top three to five values in order of importance. Feel free to add values if needed.

Ethics	Peace	Originality	Service
Efficiency	Loyalty	Candour	Profitability
Initiative	Clarity	Prosperity	Freedom
Environmentalism	Security	Respect	Friendship
Power	Accountability	Fairness	Influence
Control	Love	Order	Justice
Courage	Persistence	Spirituality	Quality
Competition	Sincerity	Adventure	Hard work
Excitement	Fun	Cooperation	Responsiveness
Creativity	Relationship	Humour	Fulfilment
Happiness	Wisdom	Discipline	Purposefulness
Honour	Flexibility	Collaboration	Strength
Innovation	Perspective	Resources	Self-control
Obedience	Commitment	Dependability	Cleverness
Financial growth	Recognition	Trust	Success
Community support	Learning	Excellence	Enjoyment
Integrity	Honesty	Teamwork	Support

values or only giving them lip service? Whether creating values for the first time or revisiting existing values, leaders need to keep two key general questions in mind: What do we want our organisation to do? and, What do we want to stand for? Leaders also need to understand that culture develops in any organisation regardless of whether it is defined, that the best set of values are stated simply, and that no more than seven values should be identified because people will not remember more than this.

Some organisations have developed acronyms from the list of core values to help participants remember them. For example, as described in Pyke and Davis (2010), the Geelong Cricket Club in Victoria identified six core values: self-discipline, teamwork, excellence, preparation, unwavering courage and passion, which collectively formed the acronym STEP UP. Similarly, the Victoria State women's team's core values acronym was SPIRIT, which represented self-discipline, preparation, integrity, resilience, initiative and team. Finally, leaders need to avoid choosing values that are strongly associated with any religious or cultural mindset; one way to do this is to ask representatives of each major cultural or religious group in the organisation to vet suggestions and questions.

STEP 2: MATCHING BEHAVIOURS AND ATTITUDES TO EXPRESSED VALUES

The next step is to align both behaviours and attitudes to the expressed core values, which involves individuals' aligning their personal goals with the organisation's goals. For example, in figure 5.1 if the cricket organisation's core values include honesty, members of the organisation need to know what that actually means in terms of individual behaviour at training, on the field, off the field and in the changing room or viewing room. What behaviours will be observable? What attitudes will people share? This step is called 'behaviourising the value' or simply 'walking the talk' and is critical in identifying desirable and productive behaviours and attitudes. Table 5.1 illustrates examples of behaviourising various types of core values.

In addition to behavioural values, which are arguably the most important for both creating and changing culture, relationship and strategic values are common (see table 5.1). Relationship values, considered essential for developing trust, refer to both the quality and means by which leaders and coaches communicate with others. They also refer to how players interact with each other. Strategic values refer to the amount of time spent on sport-specific elements that coaches often consider core to the 'way we

should play'. For example, in volleyball, core elements might include serving, blocking and hitting fundamentals as well as fitness. Some coaches convert strategic values to a metric to monitor player development as well as for recruitment purposes.

In addition to determining core values and attitudes and behaviours, one other outcome from step 2 is the identification or creation of artefacts, such as songs or poems that symbolise or crystallise the essence of organisational membership. Imagery, words and melodies of songs can evoke powerful emotions and serve as reminders of desired values and attitudes. National anthems usually achieve this effect and bond players to each other, their team and their national values.

Other examples include the New Zealand All Blacks 'Haka' and songs of John Williamson that have become identified with Australia's rugby union and cricket teams: 'A Number on My Back' and 'Waltzing Matilda' for rugby union and 'Sir Don', 'The Baggy Green' and 'True Blue' for cricket. One common value or message in these songs is to be fair dinkum, authentic and real. Other artefacts include the décor and appearance of rooms and various other cultural drivers, such as how the organisation celebrates its traditions and anniversaries and how it bestows recognition for achievements.

Table 5.1 Behavioural Examples of Relationship, Strategic and Behavioural Core Values

Core values	On-court (on-field) behaviours	At-training behaviours	Off-court (off-field) behaviours
Relationship: *communication*	Encourage all teammates all the time.	Buddy-up and provide full support during each training session.	Look after teammates particularly when they are struggling.
Strategic: *commitment*	Focus on achieving game plans (team and individual).	Complete all prescribed exercises to the best of one's ability.	Rest, rehydrate and refuel healthily at all times.
Behavioural: *hard work*	Strive to improve at least one aspect of performance in every game.	Give everything to every session, and if feeling capable, ask to do more.	In discretionary time stretch or exercise in ways that add overall personal benefit and value.

STEP 3: ESTABLISHING PERFORMANCE AND PROCESS GOALS

In the vision model (refer to figure 5.1), performance and process goals refer to what the opposition will come to expect from the cricket team's style and approach to playing the game, including how they bowl, bat and field in both limited-overs cricket and longer forms of the game. Table 5.2 lists examples of performance and respective process goals set by a first-class cricket team specifically for one-day (50-overs) cricket.

In creating both performance and process goals, consistency (or repeatable good performance) rather than peak or optimal performance is advised because the latter may be both unrealistic and unnecessarily elitist. Performance appraisal systems should also be considered here. Recently, both amateur and professional coaches and players have come to expect both formal and informal feedback on a regular basis. Player unions in some sports and nations encourage their organisations to move towards formal appraisal processes on a more regular basis. For example, increasingly, performance-based contracts for players are replacing tenure-based contracts in some professional sports.

STEP 4: DETERMINING THE RESULTS

Results refer to comparisons made usually with other teams in the same division or league. Examples or results for any sport organisation might be to finish in the top three (for promotion) or the top two for a final. But results may also mean comparisons with the organisation's previous performances in firsts, seconds, colts and under-age group competitions. Results could also refer to the number of junior and senior players selected to state and national representative teams or to age-group development squads.

An appropriate results goal could also be to play to win every game, which unfortunately often reads: to win every game. Clearly, the latter is not the best measure of any organisation's results over a season because winning or outcomes are uncontrollable. Playing to win, on the other hand, is controllable and can easily be translated into performance and process goals for both teams and individuals.

STEP 5: STATING THE MISSION

Mission statements can be written for units within an organisation and a team (e.g., in cricket for batsmen, bowlers and specific fielders), as well as for units playing in various

Table 5.2 Sample Performance and Process Goals for One-Day Cricket

One-day cricket	Performance goals *Targets or measures*	Process goals *Methods or strategy*
Bowling	Maintain four runs per over 25% maidens per innings First ball dot ball every over	Execute game plan Bowl in partnerships Start of over focus
Batting	Wickets in hand first 15 overs 1 × 80 run partnership Minimum two dot balls per over	Assess conditions first 15 overs Set partner targets and roles Turn strike over
Fielding	One run-out per game Hit stumps 50% ratio +1 over rate at close	Anticipate and hunt in packs Perform balanced and decisive throws Hustle between overs

competitions such as limited-overs or four-day cricket fixtures (refer to figure 5.1). For teams, each statement should be a realistic and current assessment of what is possible with the players available and, as such, should add value to the overall vision. However, leaders should encourage all organisational units, including coaches, rehabilitation personnel (physiotherapists, trainers), selectors, curators and marketing and media liaison managers, to have mission statements.

STEP 6: SHARING THE VISION

Finally, the organisation's vision may be a brief and simple slogan or statement. However, it must explain, represent or symbolise the shared purpose within the organisation, which needs to be communicated regularly.

RECRUITMENT PHILOSOPHY AND SOCIALISATION

Organisational culture is strengthened by attracting and hiring people who already embrace important cultural values. This process, along with weeding out people who don't fit the culture, is explained by the attraction-selection-attrition (ASA) theory (Schneider, 1987). This theory states that organisations have a natural tendency to attract, select and retain people with values and personality characteristics that are consistent with the organisation's character, resulting in a homogenous organisation with a strong culture.

In sporting organisations, players, coaches and administrative staff often naturally avoid employment in organisations whose values seem incompatible with their own. Similarly, they often actively look for evidence of culture, such as artefacts, even when the culture is not advertised. At the same time, organisations also screen prospective employees for their cultural fit and acknowledge that people with a poor fit often leave voluntarily.

Organisational socialisation is the process by which individuals learn the values, expected behaviours and social knowledge necessary to assume their roles in the organisation. It is a process of both learning about the work context and adjusting to new work roles, team norms and behaviours. Effective organisations recognise the value of socialisation agents in the socialisation process. These are people, such as former players and mentors, whose role is to provide information and social support during the socialisation process.

STRENGTHS-BASED STRATEGIC PLANNING

All organisations recognise the need for strategic planning, which is an important aspect of transformational leadership. The best way to create a strategic vision is to invite conversations among everyone in the organisation—players, coaches, managers, administrative personnel, parents, fan club representatives and relevant parties from both the public (government) and private (commercial) sectors. Such conversations are crucial because these people are responsible for carrying out the activities of the strategic plan.

Harrison Owen (2008), the originator of Open Space Technology (OST), recognises that all organisations are 'self-organised' and that people, not individual leaders or systems, author and control cultures. OST is a small- or large-group process in which participants are invited to gather and create the agenda for discussions on whatever is important to them around a particular topic or theme. OST is a powerful facilitation tool for leaders who truly seek the opinions of every person that has a stake in the organisation's future. See the article 'Building the Optimal Cricket Operation' (Gordon, 2011) for an example of how OST was used with a national cricket team.

Another effective technique that involves organisation-wide participation is SOAR, which stands for strengths, opportunities, aspirations and results (Stavros & Hinrichs, 2009). This strategic planning framework also focuses on including the voices of all the people involved with a program. SOAR integrates a transformational process, known as appreciative inquiry, or AI (Cooperrider, Whitney, & Stavros, 2008), that builds on the existing strengths of an organisation, or what can be called the organisation's positive core. To deliver innovation, respond to daily challenges and create a vision for the future, leaders must include the perspectives and ideas of people at all levels who influence the program, and these perspectives and ideas must be considered on an ongoing basis. SOAR creates strategic conversations grounded in values using questions similar to those in figure 5.3.

An example of a strengths-based strategic planning event using AI conducted for the Western Australian Cricket Association's

Figure 5.3 Representative Questions Used in SOAR Strategic Planning Conversations

Strengths: *What can we build on?*
- What are we most proud of as an organisation? How does that reflect our greatest strength?
- What makes us unique? What can we be best at in our world?
- What is our proudest achievement in the last year or two?
- How do we use our strengths to get results?
- How do our strengths fit with the realities of our core business?
- What do we do or provide that is world class for our current and potential stakeholders?

Opportunities: *What are the various people involved with our organisation asking for?*
- How do we make sense of opportunities provided by the external forces and trends in our business?
- What are the top three opportunities on which we should focus our efforts?
- How can we best meet the needs of people involved with our organisation, including employees, shareholders and community?
- How can we distinctively differentiate ourselves from existing or potential competitors?
- How can we reframe challenges to be seen as exciting opportunities?
- What new skills do we need to move forwards?

Aspirations: *What do we care deeply about?*
- When we explore our values and aspirations, what are we deeply passionate about?
- Reflecting on our strengths and opportunities conversations, who are we, who should we become and where should we go in the future?
- What is our most compelling aspiration?
- What strategic initiatives (e.g., projects, programs and processes) would support our aspirations?

Results: *How will we know we are succeeding?*
- Considering our strengths, opportunities and aspirations, what meaningful measures would indicate that we are on track to achieve our goals?
- What are three to five indicators that would create a scorecard that addresses our vision and mission statements?
- What resources are needed to implement vital projects?
- What are the best rewards to support those who achieve our goals?

Cricket Operations unit follows (and is described fully in Gordon, 2011). Briefly, in 2008 Graeme Wood, the CEO of the Western Australian Cricket Association (WACA), requested a two-day session on Building the Optimal Cricket Operation with his current cricket operations staff. The staff included the CEO, the high-performance manager, the game development manager, the human resources officer, the team manager and head coach, the cricket officer manager and an executive board member.

Participants of this session first had to understand the four phases of the AI 4-D cycle.

- **Discovery**—To explore what gives life to the organisation when it is at its best
- **Dream**—Based on what is discovered, to envision what the organisation might look like in the future
- **Design**—To co-construct organisational arrangements to support the shared dream or vision
- **Destiny**—To determine ways and means of sustaining commitment to the future

In the discovery phase and prior to day 1, participants were asked to select and interview three to five people whose opinions on their areas of responsibility in the current cricket operation they respected. Interviewees included current and non-current WACA staff and others involved in the organisation. Sample interview questions are provided in table 5.3. On day 1 participants shared their interviewee stories about when they had experienced or observed the WACA (or other) cricket operation at its most alive and most effective.

During the dream phase, participants reflected on all the interviewee data collected by the whole group and agreed on which aspects of this history and these memories of peak performances and past experiences represented the WACA's calling. The group also created provocative propositions specifically for cricket operations that reflected the overall WACA strategic plan.

On day 2, in the design phase, participants created a WACA social architecture (how people will work together in the future) that both reflected the provocative propositions

Table 5.3 Appreciative Inquiry (AI) Interview Questions

Stage in AI 4-D cycle	Questions and instructions for interviewees
Discovery	What is or has been going positively? Think of a peak experience or high point in your own work or experience here (or at another organisation). Interviewers should note all accomplishments and prideful recollections before proceeding to the next question.
Dream	What do we need to do at this organisation to create more of these positive experiences? How could we use these positive experiences to create a vision of a desired future state? Interviewers should encourage provocative ideas and encourage the interviewees to focus on future possibilities, not current processes.
Design	What action plans will create and sustain the future we want, in terms of leadership, infrastructure, policies and systems? What new or different arrangements would support the proposed changes? Interviewers should get some ideas, but should not push for specifics—aim for suggestions for improvement, not perfection.
Destiny	How do we deliver these plans of action? What innovative teams do we need to create, and who will champion each team? What specific goals should each team endeavour to achieve? Interviewers should link this to the previous question and still search for new ideas as well as more of what already works.

Adapted, by permission, from S. Gordon, 2011, "Building the optimal cricket operation," *Appreciative Inquiry Practitioner* 13(2): 60-64.

created in the dream phase and represented compelling new ways of carrying out cricket operations. The destiny phase focused on action planning and goal setting regarding the delivery of new systems of working together and achieving group outcomes.

CEO Wood seemed impressed both with AI and its immediate and sustained impact and provided the following feedback: 'The appreciative inquiry approach . . . was extremely successful in allowing the key players to open up and be encouraged to volunteer their views on how the group could work more effectively together to achieve the agreed vision. The session was instrumental in effecting change and managing the change process in an effective manner over the following three-year period' (Gordon, 2011, p. 64). Appreciative inquiry (AI), which was clearly effective in this example, is an inclusive and democratic approach that engages everyone in the change process. Most of all, however, by obtaining buy-in from people at every level of any program, AI injects energy into the change process, which every sport organisation needs to sustain any change initiatives.

SUMMARY

- Sport leaders can create effective organisational cultures using a six-step approach, starting with establishing core values and, more important, values enactment, and then setting performance and process goals that are aligned with desired results and outcomes, setting mission statements that provide the 'means to the end,' and sharing the vision.
- When sport leaders clearly engage everyone involved in conversations around the direction and values of their organisations and teams, and consistently connect their own actions to these values, cultural change is not only possible but highly likely.
- The role of leaders is essential, particularly in ensuring that values are maintained and constantly made real to all of the people involved in the organisation.
- Strengths-based strategic planning processes provide contemporary leaders with easy-to-implement techniques for conducting important organisation-wide conversations about transformational change.

REFERENCES AND RESOURCES

Cooperrider, D.L., Whitney, D., & Stavros, J.M. (2008). *Appreciative inquiry handbook: For leaders of change* (2nd ed.). Brunswick, OH: Crown Custom.

Duda, J.L., & Balaguer, I. (2007). Coach-created motivational climate. In S. Jowette & D. Lavallee (Eds.), *Social psychology in sport* (pp. 117-130). Lower Mitcham, SA: Human Kinetics.

Gordon, S. (2008). Enhancing the team work of the Sri Lankan cricket team: A case study of applying Appreciative Inquiry. *InPsych, 30* (1), 12-13.

Gordon, S. (2011). Building the optimal cricket operation. *Appreciative Inquiry Practitioner, 13,* (2), 60-64.

Owen, H. (2008). *Wave rider: Leadership for high performance in a self-organizing world.* San Francisco: Berrett-Koehler.

Pyke, F., & Davis, K. (2010). *Cutting edge cricket.* Lower Mitcham, SA: Human Kinetics.

Ringuet, C. (2008). *The Geelong Football Club & key stakeholder management: A case study of player welfare management.* Griffith University, Brisbane: Sport Knowledge Australia.

Schneider, B. (1987). The people make the place. *Personnel Psychology, 40* (3), 437-453.

Schroeder, P.J. (2010). Changing team culture: The perspectives of ten successful head coaches. *Journal of Sport Behaviour, 32* (4), 63-88.

Stavros, J.M., & Hinrichs, G. (2009). *SOAR: Building strengths-based strategy.* Bend, OR: Thin Book.

CHAPTER 6

Relating to Others

—— Paul Kiteley

In theory, coaching environments are supportive settings in which working relationships grow and prosper and all those involved are focused on improving individual and team performance. However, the reality can be significantly different, with support for the coach varying from extremely positive to very poor.

In professional sport the loss of support can result in the termination of employment of a coach even though the team's or athletes' on-field results are very successful. A positive win–loss record does not guarantee ongoing tenure when any or all of the management team, board members and key sponsors are unhappy. The same applies at the junior level. Once the support of the parents disappears, the effectiveness of the coach to work with athletes is reduced significantly, and a parting of the ways inevitably follows.

Coaches who are admired and respected by the athletes they guide and assist are often highly esteemed by other members of the organisation. The people skills that are vital to teach, develop and enhance the capabilities of athletes are also crucial for coaches to have in building relationships with others.

The coach development pathway is often similar to that of the athlete. It begins as a volunteer at junior level and progresses to possible employment as a full- or part-time professional coach. Along the journey, coaches need to appreciate and strengthen the relationships they develop. This chapter highlights strategies and principles that will assist coaches in involving others and ensuring effective communication throughout the program.

WORKING WITH PARENTS

In coaching probably no single behavior is more important than communication (Spink, 1986, p. 6). A critical period in establishing and building relationships occurs when new athletes and their parents first come to meet the coach. In team sports, this usually occurs in the preseason phase. One key ingredient is to 'develop open lines of communication making it a priority to talk to parents outlining your approach and discussing any of their concerns' (McClean, 2008, p. 13). The induction phase is often the key window of opportunity to build a collaborative and positive relationship with parents. In team sports, individual meetings as well as a group presentation are recommended.

Coaches need to 'understand that parents cannot be truly objective in evaluating their son or daughter's ability and performance' (Schilling, 2007, p. 48). The challenge for coaches is to win the trust of the parents so that they speak positively about them and facilitate the best possible athlete–coach relationship. A common cause of concern and disquiet from parents involves decisions about their child's role within a team as well as the amount of on-field (or on-court) time allocated to the child.

In sports such as football, hockey and netball, the issue of time allocation is frequently linked to players in the midfield and forward, or offensive, roles. In bat and ball sports such as cricket, softball and baseball, most contested by parents are the top order batting positions, bowling and pitching duties and wicket keeping and catching roles. These are the roles and positions that are often dominated by the most talented and skilful athletes. A coach with individual athlete development as a priority will endeavour to ensure that all athletes have the opportunity to undertake a range of positions and roles.

Coaches in junior sport often start the year by focusing on individual development rather than team results. However, maintaining this approach for the entire season is often a challenge. The philosophical premise of seeking improvement for every team member is easier to implement in round 1, when the team results receive less scrutiny and the focus is not on positions on the competition ladder. The true test comes as the team strives to qualify for finals and especially once the finals campaign begins. The best strategy for coaches to follow once they have developed a coaching philosophy and have explained it and received support from players, parents and club officials is to stick with it for the entire season

The temptation to cut back on player rotations and keep the better-skilled athletes on the field longer is understandable especially when the 'crunch' comes in close games. After an under-14 Australian football grand final, I once observed parents consoling their distraught son who was denied the opportunity to take the field. In a very close game, his team had won the match, but the coach had not used him at any stage, keeping him on the interchange bench for the entire game.

I learned later that this was the first time the entire season that the coach had not allowed everyone to participate. The competition rules allowed for an extended bench of six players to encourage maximal participation, but coaches were not obligated to use all of the players named in the team. The player involved in this incident was much smaller than his teammates, but regardless of his size, physical strength and playing ability, the coach had no excuse for not giving all members of the team a chance to participate. A number of this player's teammates and their parents were also likely to be anxious and disappointed with this outcome.

Conversely, I once saw an experienced junior cricket coach implement and maintain a pre-determined maximal participation bowling rotation from the first game to the final match. The strategy involved all members of his team, including the wicket keeper, equally sharing the bowling duties. They were defeated in the grand final in a close game, but the players' spirit and enthusiasm remained very positive throughout the match. Every player was striving very hard to win, and the coach had no intention of making any alteration to the game plan during the finals. Implementing these inclusive strategies can reduce the normally high dropout rate from junior sport, bucking the trend of only the more skilled or dominant athletes continuing to senior participation.

ESTABLISHING COMMUNICATION AND SETTING EXPECTATIONS

Whether starting a new job or attending their first training night at a new club, most coaches experience feelings of uncertainty and unease, and understandably so. Coaches can temper these feelings by making sure they have a well-organised and comprehensive induction process. Their first aim should to ensure that every athlete feels welcome and comfortable. Next, they should begin the education process by explaining their key coaching philosophies and outlining their expectations of the athletes and their families. Every new season should begin with a comprehensive information meeting for athletes and their parents. The aim is to create a confident and optimistic impression for all athletes and their families.

As the former head coach of the Geelong Falcons in the under-18 Australian Football League (AFL) competition, Aaron Greaves had a transparent and unambiguous philosophy that was focused on maximising individual player development. In interviews with the author while he was still serving in his role as head coach, Greaves said: 'Our role is to facilitate the best possible environment to enhance the opportunities for our players to be selected in the AFL draft. We work proactively to provide as much information and feedback as we can to all our players and their families'.

Greaves' parent education program at the Geelong Falcons was very comprehensive and began with a detailed informational induction evening that all listed players and their parents were expected to attend. The presentation was led by Greaves and the regional football manager, Michael Turner. They aimed to build trust and rapport with the athletes and their families. In an up front and honest manner, they would deal with the issues that they knew could sometimes be concerning to the athletes and especially their parents.

The challenge for many coaches is articulating and explaining their key coaching strategies and philosophies in such a way that their audience can comprehend and ultimately develop a shared understanding. Where possible, coaches should consider using real-life scenarios when providing information and strive to clarify any potential misunderstandings by encouraging questions, discussions and feedback.

Greaves believes that using examples of previously drafted players was very beneficial. During his presentation he was aware that parents' knew that many drafted athletes were dominant players and leaders in their local junior teams. He explained: 'The athletes and their families have a strong interest in the performances of any recently drafted players from our region. They all desperately want to be able to play at the highest level and will usually listen attentively to any advice that may enhance their prospects'.

At the 2011 induction presentation, Greaves and Turner outlined the example of 2010 Geelong Falcons player Luke Dahlhaus. Luke was playing well for the team in a half forward and midfield role in the first part of the season. Michael Turner, along with 2010 coach Paul Hood who has regular feedback sessions with the AFL recruiters, agreed that Luke would play a series of games on the half-back flank so

Aaron Greaves used proactive communication with players and all others involved with a club to ensure on-field success.

Photo courtesy of AFL Media.

they could observe his defensive skills and his adaptability to a new role. At 18 years of age, he was selected by the Western Bulldogs Football Club in the 2011 AFL preseason rookie list draft. He has since made a very promising start to his career, playing well in a number of games in the seniors in 2011. Greaves and Turner used this example to help everyone understand that being played in various positions is not a negative outcome and actually enhances the chances of being drafted.

Using personal experience or the knowledge of colleagues to anticipate and proactively deal with contentious issues before they occur is a very worthwhile strategy for coaches. For example, parents can become very anxious about selection decisions, game or court time, team leadership roles and balancing educational pressures and commitments. The induction phase of the season, including the group information forum and individual follow-up meetings, is the ideal time to develop realistic expectations about these athlete issues. The extra effort of proactive communication is well spent; it can help coaches avoid having to respond to frustrated and irritated parents who believe their son or daughter has been treated unfairly.

Aaron Greaves recognised that a common concern of parents relates to team selection and players missing opportunities to participate. Greaves and his coaching staff appreciated that skilled and talented players are in very high demand (e.g., on school teams and state representative teams).They were also acutely aware of the research that has highlighted the injury risks from overuse and fatigue that these young athletes face. Greaves said: 'Parents need to understand that missing a game or two during the season will not be detrimental to players' chances of AFL draft selection. AFL recruiters have a very strong vested interest in wanting the drafted players to be fit and injury free. They do not need to see them play every week to make a clear judgement'.

Greaves also explained to parents and athletes that the athletes' training and playing loads are being closely monitored and reviewed. He explained that they tell 'players and parents that players should expect to be rested at certain stages of the season and this will usually occur when their workload increases (school football, increased game or training time, etc.). They need to appreciate that this is a proactive measure and has nothing to do with form'.

Coaches enhance the relationship and rapport with parents when they look for opportunities for ongoing dialogue and seek their feedback. For example, talking to parents before and after training is appreciated and contributes significantly to their developing a positive, supportive connection with the coach.

Greaves and his assistant coaches welcomed feedback and promoted an environment of open communication. Detailed player information and analysis was provided every week to all players. These reports gave feedback on strengths as well as areas needing improvement. These reports were often an excellent trigger for discussions between athletes and their parents. Greaves believes that the sharing of information and feedback was a key component in a constructive working relationship with the parents. He and his team strived to create an atmosphere in which ideas, differences and disagreements could be aired openly and in a non-threatening environment.

PROVIDING A POSITIVE ENVIRONMENT

All coaches need to understand that they are role models for those around them. The behaviour, body language, attitudes and maturity they display are always important, but especially in the junior sport environment. The goal should always be to ensure that all athletes feel safe and are able to enjoy their participation. Inappropriate behaviour by parents or any other people involved in the club must be dealt with immediately and consistently.

Behaviours parents may display that can have a negative impact include 'over emphasising winning, holding unrealistic expectations and criticising their child' (Raeburn, 2006, p. 34). These behaviours can create situations that will not only impact on that particular individual but potentially other members of the team. During my time in junior sport, I recall a close friend and teammate receiving a loud and aggressive verbal assault from his father at halftime. Sitting next to him at the time, I found that I was more upset than he was. Apparently, the behaviour was typical of the father, and my teammate received these assaults regularly.

Coaches should ensure that the clubs and associations with which they are involved develop and enforce parental guidelines that facilitate a safe environment for athletes. The coach should always be vigilant and act quickly to stop inappropriate behaviour at any time, including during training sessions, competitions or any other sanctioned club activities. As Australian basketball icon Andrew Gaze has said, 'Sport should be a fun and healthy environment, not one that is compromised due to the inappropriate behaviour of coaches, parents and spectators. If sport is not a positive experience then it is highly unlikely juniors will maintain their participation and fulfil their potential' (Strathmore Unicorns Basketball Club, 2009).

Everyone associated with the team should be given a copy of the club or association code of conduct. An ongoing education campaign outlining the philosophies regarding the behavior of parents and other spectators should become part of the fabric of the club. This code of conduct should also address the behaviour of coaches and support staff as well as players. Following are key principles coaches should promote to parents and other spectators to create a positive sporting environment:

- Spectators should respect officials and their decisions, and they should not publicly criticise officials.
- Spectators should respect players and spectators from both teams.
- Spectators should read and abide by the club's code of conduct.
- Spectators should be supportive, whether their team is winning or losing.
- Spectators should discourage negative behaviour during club matches or other events.
- Spectators should alert a club official if someone is behaving inappropriately.

- Parents should be good sports themselves and set a good example for their children.
- Parents should encourage their children and support their efforts.

WORKING WITH EDUCATIONAL INSTITUTIONS

Working with aspiring athletes who are pursuing their sport with dedication and commitment creates situations that require proactive communication with their educational institutions. Teachers at schools, universities and TAFE vocational schools are not always knowledgeable about the additional challenges talented athletes need to overcome. The staff may develop negative attitudes towards student-athletes because they are unaware of and do not fully appreciate their individual circumstances.

Coaches should be aware of the educational status of all of their athletes and try to proactively assist them in developing a positive relationship with the teachers or administrators supporting their education. Following is a summary of the main issues that arise with talented athletes and how they may affect their educational goals:

- **Training and competition commitments.** Athletes often face a significant challenge in combining their educational programs with their sporting commitments especially if they are secondary school students. Training programs for elite junior athletes usually involve commitments of at least 15 hours and often up to 30 hours per week. These training sessions are typically undertaken either before or after the school day. On weekends there is usually extensive involvement with competition obligations.
- **Physical and psychological demands.** Mastery of the intense physical and technical elements of elite sport requires many hours of specific strength and conditioning training along with the practice required to master complicated skills and tactics.

Sports such as gymnastics and diving require great precision to execute routines, requiring heightened perceptual and fine motor skills. The coaches expect total focus during their intensive training sessions to minimise injury risks. A very common and understandable consequence is that athletes arrive at school in a fatigued state both mentally and physically. Teachers can underestimate the extra demands these student-athletes are dealing with and can become frustrated when they appear listless and have concentration lapses in class.

- **Travel requirements.** Athletes who are following a high-performance sporting pathway almost always need to undertake regular interstate and possibly overseas travel. This can result in extended absences from school and consequently an interruption in face-to-face contact with teachers. Every effort should be made to inform the school management in advance of any forthcoming travel or competition demands that student-athletes will be required to undertake. A number of schools have implemented flexible and alternate options to support young athletes competing at elite levels. This has happened because the schools have been given appropriate lead times so they can make allowances for elite athletes' circumstances, while minimising the disruption to other students and the teaching staff.

- **Health and injury issues.** As a consequence of the heavy demands of training and competition, student-athletes often have to deal with injuries. Medical appointments with specialists that enable student-athletes to return to full training as soon as possible can be difficult to come by, which may result in their being absent from regular school time. School communities sometimes underestimate the time, dedication and commitment student-athletes are investing to excel in their sport.

Ultimately, coaches are not directly responsible for the educational outcomes of their athletes. However, a supportive and well-informed coach can help athletes and their families implement processes and strategies to positively influence these outcomes. Following are some helpful initiatives:

- Coaches can undertake individual meetings with all of their athletes to gain an understanding of their educational aspirations and explore any possible conflicts with their upcoming sporting commitments (e.g., a world junior championships selection that clashes with a Year 12 exam period). If any clashes are identified, the coach can encourage both athlete and parents to contact the school immediately to begin discussions about alternative arrangements.

- Coaches can encourage the athlete to undertake personal development sessions to enhance their time management skills and processes. Many talented athletes have successfully combined their sporting careers with extremely high-level academic and career aspirations. This is almost always achieved by athletes who can effectively manage their busy schedules.

- Supporting parents to provide some background information to the teaching staff so they may gain a greater insight into athletes' training and competition demands is a helpful role for coaches.

- Athletes need support during the key times of exams and finalising important assignments. Coaches can help by adjusting training loads at critical times and allowing student-athletes to maximise their potential to achieve their educational goals

- Coaches can encourage the family to build a relationship with and seek regular advice from the school careers adviser especially on subject selection, course applications and university entrance. A coach might suggest that the family investigate the option of doing the year 12 over a two-year period if the athlete is going to miss a significant portion of the academic year because of overseas and interstate travel commitments.

- A senior educational staff member who understands the issues faced by talented athletes can be very helpful for an athlete who needs an individualised way to meet his or her educational needs. A coach can help the athlete identify such a person (e.g., the year level coordinator, head of sport or assistant principal) and foster a positive relationship between them.

Coaches need to do more than just make positive statements about the importance of education. They need to actively engage with parents and provide a consistent and very clear commitment to support the athlete's educational goals. Geelong Falcons coach, Aaron Greaves, understands the importance of his athletes to be committed to achieve the best results they can in their year 12 studies. He expects his athletes to feel confident that they can discuss with him the need to miss training if they need extra time to prepare for important exams and assignments.

Those who coach athletes who are part of the national sports institute or academy network can benefit from the very comprehensive service available to them as part of the National Athlete Career and Education program (NACE). (See the Australian Sports Commission's website for more information.) This is an extremely valuable individualised service that helps athletes resolve many of the issues and challenges they face as they strive for excellence both on and off the sporting field.

Integrating education or a career and a personal life with a sporting career is never an easy task. The challenge is to find a way to help athletes achieve sport and life goals by balancing and proactively managing the substantial time demands. The role of all coaches should be to help their athletes get the most out of their sporting career while continuing to achieve excellence in their studies and careers outside sport.

The importance of addressing the sport and life balance is becoming well recognised and appreciated. This has resulted in most professional sporting teams and clubs facilitating the appointment of player welfare managers, reducing the need for coach involvement in

this area. The player welfare manager has the key responsibility of supporting and assisting the athlete in meeting educational goals and ambitions. Nevertheless, professional coaches should always maintain an active interest in the outside interests and ambitions of all of the athletes they coach.

WORKING WITH SUPPORT STAFF

Leadership styles vary considerably. Some leaders are very hands-on and choose to be heavily involved at all times; others are comfortable delegating many key tasks to their assistant coaches and support staff. Others operate with a combination of both strategies, depending on the circumstances. Whatever approach they choose, coaches should always remember that the standards they set and the way they conduct themselves will set the benchmarks for all members of their team.

Head coaches should strive to provide all members of the team with a clear understanding of their roles and guide them towards having a shared commitment to a common goal, or getting everyone on the same page. A leader must be able to convey a vision in terms that inspires others to commit to it. Head coaches must communicate openly and passionately to gain the confidence of those with whom they are involved. Positive leaders also need to have the tenacity to work towards their vision with resilience and confidence as they deal with challenges and setbacks that inevitably arise.

Successful leaders welcome both positive and negative feedback from their colleagues. Regardless of coaching level, 'One thing is for certain: if you want to get better at what you do you should use some system to get feedback from key stakeholders and develop strategies to enhance your strengths and strengthen your weaknesses' (Davis, 2004, p. 6).

Following are some identified traits of positive leaders. Coaches who seek to improve their capacities in these areas enhance their chances of developing united and cohesive support teams.

- **Flexibility** is being able to listen and respond to new ideas, even if they do not match your usual way of thinking. Good leaders are able to defer judgement while listening to others' ideas, as well as embrace new methods and strategies. A flexible and open-minded approach builds mutual respect and trust between leaders and their support team, and creates an atmosphere in which new ideas may emerge. Highly regarded Australian Rules coach David Parkin was well known for most of his career for implementing an authoritative and unyielding coaching style. Though his approach was successful in the early 1980s, leading to premierships with the Carlton Football Club, in 1995 Parkin embraced and implemented a new strategy, which involved passing on significant responsibilities for some of the key components of the athlete preparation to his player leadership group. This approach was vindicated by a very successful team performance in winning the 1995 AFL premiership.

- **Commitment** is setting a standard for investing the needed time to a task and inspiring others to follow this approach. It is much easier to expect athletes as well as the other coaches and support team members to strive for excellence when the head coach demonstrates a very high level of commitment. Olympic Gold medal–winning rowing coach Chris O'Brien sets a standard of meticulous preparation and dedication that inspires all members of his support staff to want to reach. O'Brien also undertakes a comprehensive athlete feedback process aimed at challenging everyone involved with the athletes to strive to enhance and improve their contributions to ensure that the team achieves the agreed-on performance benchmarks.

- **Innovation** is the ability to think creatively and seek solutions that may seem radical at first but ultimately can prove to be very successful. New ideas should always be encouraged, and the team environment should be a setting in which all people involved believe they can contribute at any time without fear of criticism or ridicule. Occasionally, the left-field solutions produce the most significant improvements in individual athlete performances or team achievements.

An excellent example of an innovative high-performance sport development program is that of the Australia aerial skiing team. Geoff Lipshut, CEO of the Australian Olympic Winter Institute, developed and implemented a unique talent transfer program that facilitated the transition of elite gymnasts to the aerial skiing team. It was recognised that the power, strength and acrobatic skills developed by gymnastics training can yield success in aerial skiing. The track record of this initiative is outstanding and includes Olympic Gold medalists Alisa Camplin and Lydia Lassila as well as multiple world champion Jacqui Cooper.

- **Impartiality** means dealing with everyone in an unbiased and consistent manner. Coaches should always strive to ensure that all of their athletes feel they are being treated as equals. The temptation to be more lenient with the highly talented athletes can be compelling, especially in the lead-up to important games. The ongoing consequences of special treatment for one individual can have significant repercussions for team morale. Athletes who believe they have they have been treated unjustly lose respect for the team leader, and trust can be extremely difficult and often impossible to rebuild.

- **'Team first' attitude** means proactively giving credit where it is due. Head coaches should always acknowledge and highlight the efforts of assistant coaches and the support team in all team and athlete achievements and successes. They should always go out of their way to acknowledge the efforts of everyone involved. On the other hand, head coaches must shoulder the blame and accept responsibility for any failings or mistakes that athletes and members of the support team make. A team leader should never publicly humiliate or demean anyone for a failing. Head coaches, as the leader of the group, accept that any mistake is ultimately their responsibility.

- **Self-confidence and assertiveness** enable coaches to deliver honest messages when needed to get desired results. In some situations, clear and decisive action is required

SUCCESSFUL SUPPORT STAFF–COACH RELATIONSHIPS

Ernie Merrick was the inaugural head coach of the Melbourne Victory Football Club from 2005 to 2011. His excellent coaching record includes two A-League Premiership victories in 2006/2007 and 2008/2009. Prior to his appointment at Melbourne Victory, he was the football program head coach at the Victorian Institute of Sport from 1992 to 2005. Merrick delivered a comprehensive development program that produced a number of athletes who graduated to successful professional football careers.

One of Merrick's particular strengths was the ability to build excellent camaraderie and a sense of purpose in his support team. This continued when he was appointed the inaugural coach of the Melbourne Victory Football Club, and not surprisingly, a number of his VIS support team joined him as staff members at Victory. Merrick understands the importance of creating an environment in which everyone on his support team feels valued and appreciated. About these relationships, he said: 'The responsibility for staff cohesion and cooperation rests with the coach. The coach must adopt a management style that allows all staff members to feel that they are important members of the group. Success is dependent on their expertise. The major influence on the group, staff, and players will be the culture of the club. This has to be developed over time and have a solid foundation based on honesty, integrity, loyalty, and respect'.

Establishing agreed-upon goals and objectives for everyone involved at a club or team is widely accepted as one of the most important strategies for a head coach to implement. Merrick advocated for a process in which all involved believe their input and ideas are valued and considered. He said: 'Setting goals, establishing a vision, and stating the club mission is a consultative process. All staff and the playing squad must take ownership of the stated goals and therefore be accountable and responsible. The long-term plan and vision should be clear and concise. The short-term goals of the club must be measurable'.

Developing an environment that builds the confidence of the support staff requires a proactive approach. Everyone should feel that their views are appreciated and carefully considered. Merrick said: 'Healthy discussion and debate needs to take place to determine various staff roles and appropriate intervention on player programs. Input should be valued and rewarded. The assessment of performance and the evaluation of staff roles should be regular and ongoing'.

In media interviews after significant team victories, Merrick would often praise and acknowledge his support team. He also sometimes named people who had played significant roles and provided quick summaries of their contributions and how they were instrumental in the team's success. About providing praise to his support staff, he said: 'The responsibility for both success and failure needs to be shared. Good performance should, on occasion, be publicly acknowledged in the media'.

The planning process should always be undertaken with great care and attention. Coaches should understand and appreciate that a comprehensive plan helps to coordinate everyone's efforts. It facilitates the delegation of key tasks so that all team members are clear about their roles and responsibilities. Of this, Merrick said: 'Good planning optimises team performance. Therefore, it is always worthwhile spending time on scheduling, setting standards and delegating responsibility. It has often been said that success lies in the details'.

and everyone needs to understand what is expected and that they are accountable. A common mistake is acting in an authoritarian rather than assertive way. Coaches can avoid this by seeking regular and honest feedback from athletes, support staff and parents (if involved with junior sport) and responding appropriately if there is a negative perception. This may include enrolling in personal development programs aimed at enhancing communication skills. When difficult decisions are needed, coaches should try to deliver the information with clarity and self-assurance. They should be firm and resolute and always strive to make well-informed, clear decisions.

- **A sense of humor** is another positive trait exhibited by effective team leaders. It is a very useful tool to relieve tension and boredom, as well as to defuse hostility. An amusing anecdote or funny story delivered at the appropriate time can help the group move on quickly in a much better frame of mind. Elite sport is often a very tense and highly emotional environment; coaches who can retain their sense of humour will provide a calming influence for their athletes at critical times.

Traits of positive leaders adapted from Hakala 2008.

BUILDING RAPPORT

Showing appreciation involves encouraging and motivating people through praise, recognition and acknowledgement of their achievements and the challenges they face. Building rapport is about connecting with others at a personal level. This means understanding who they are, their interests and some of the things that are important to them.

Coaches should take the time to consider how well they know their assistant coaches, team managers and support staff. Building rapport requires that they take the time to be on familiar terms with everyone they work with, which enables them to build positive and productive working relationships. A good start is to know something about the families, hobbies and interests of co-workers outside of sport or club involvement. Finally, some everyday personal details are also very helpful to know, such as birthdays and favourite coffee orders. When purchasing a take-away coffee on the way to a training session or selection meeting, a coach will be much more popular if he or she brings key support staff one as well!

LISTENING

Improving listening skills also enhance coaches' working relationships with support personnel. The way to become a better listener is to practice active listening; this involves not only making a conscious effort to hear the words but also paying attention to the feelings and attitudes behind the words. The type of listening coaches need is 'deep emphatic listening' and it 'involves listening carefully to voice tone, emotional content, being able to reflect back and tuning in to what the person is saying' (Greene & Grant 2003, p. 115). To do this, coaches must concentrate on what the other person is saying and avoid being distracted by whatever else may be going on or by thinking about contradictory arguments to make when the person stops speaking. They must not allow themselves to get bored and lose their focus on what the other person is saying.

Support staff struggle to trust and have confidence in coaches with poor listening skills. To instil confidence and build trust, coaches need to convince others that they are listening attentively. They should always try to respond in a way that persuades the other person to continue the dialogue, so they can gather all of the information. Body language is very important, as is eye contact. The following active listening tips can help coaches improve their skills:

- Show that you are genuinely interested by nodding occasionally, smiling and encouraging the speaker to continue with positive verbal comments such as 'yes' or 'I agree'.

- Provide feedback. Use paraphrasing by saying things like 'In other words . . .' or 'What I am hearing is . . .'.

- Ask questions when you need clarification and to let the other person know you understand the message.

- Avoid the temptation to interrupt.
- Maintain eye contact.
- Display open and relaxed body language (avoid fidgeting).
- Never take calls or check your phone for text messages while someone is speaking to you.

DEALING WITH CONFLICT

Sporting environments are emotional settings. People are usually involved with sport because they are very passionate and sometimes fanatical. In this environment, conflicts are unavoidable, and coaches need skills and strategies for resolving them. When conflict is handled poorly, relationships suffer and may always be compromised. As with any human interaction, the potential for conflict increases when people believe they have been taken for granted.

Coaches should understand that conflict is not always a negative thing; when handled in a mature manner, it can often result in positive outcomes. Conflict can 'clear the air by getting issues into the open. It can also help to reveal true feelings which can be a positive driver for change. Finally, disagreements and differences being openly discussed can also rejuvenate team spirit and energy levels which have been impeded by unresolved issues and concerns' (Fox, 2002, pp.65-66). The following list* outlines strategies and helpful tips for managing conflict with support teams or others involved in the program:

- Be professional: Speak clearly and stay composed in heated situations. This demonstrates confidence in managing the situation. Avoid confrontational argument or debate.
- Remain calm: Don't over-react. Stay relaxed and adopt a low-key posture/body language. Use objective, neutral language.
- Address the problem—not the emotions: Try to put aside the emotions of all parties. Emotions inevitably inflame the situation. By dealing with the facts and the available evidence, you are more likely to be seen as making a fair and appropriate decision.

- Be fair: Avoid team or individual bias at all costs. Demonstrating integrity is vital to maintain trust within the group.
- Be confident and open: Don't be defensive or try to justify actions. Clarify decisions when appropriate, based on the facts and the evidence presented.
- Be firm: Deal with unacceptable behaviour firmly and quickly. Set boundaries in a polite, professional and assertive manner.
- Remember that 90% of conflict occurs not because of what was said, but the tone in which it was said.

*Reprinted, by permission, from Australian Sports Commission http://www.ausport.gov.au/participating/officials/tools/communication/Conflict

WORKING WITH SPONSORS

Sponsorship has become an important consideration for all sporting organisations. In the junior sport scene, sponsors often provide vital support through the provision of in-kind goods and services as well as monetary resources. In professional sport, sponsorship is typically a critical component to maintain the financial viability of the club or sporting organisation.

A proactive coach who promotes sponsors in public forums and during media opportunities plays a significant role in contributing to a flourishing partnership. On the other hand, a coach who shows little or no interest publicly acknowledging or building rapport with club sponsors can be very detrimental to the relationship. Head coaches should never underestimate the important influence, both positive and potentially negative, they have on the club–sponsor relationship.

Once the club or sporting organisation has entered into a commercial sponsorship agreement with a company, certain rights and benefits are outlined. Before contractual arrangements are finalised, head coaches should seek information about clarification of any ways they or the players will be directly involved with sponsors.

After reviewing the information, coaches should immediately communicate any areas in which they have concerns or reservations. Consider a situation in which a club's major sponsor has requested admission to the team change rooms prior to and after all matches as one of their benefits. After consideration, the coach decides to allow sponsors to interact with him and the players at the conclusion of the games. However, the coach feels strongly that during the pre-game preparation period, admittance to the change rooms and warm-up areas should be restricted to the coaches, players and support staff.

In this scenario, the coach needs to immediately clarify and explain his view to club management emphasising the possible impact of any distractions on the team performance. He should also emphasise to all the involved that the protocols will remain in place if the team qualifies for finals. The excitement of team success can create tension when people want to interact with the team and personally wish the players luck just prior to the game on Grand Final day. In these team access and competition day scenarios, coaches need to ensure that club officials, sponsors and supporters are given clear and consistent information so misunderstandings do not occur.

Most businesses like to feel involved and kept informed about what's happening with their sponsorship arrangements and the club's activities. Inviting sponsors down to meet with the coaches and players in the pre-season and making them feel appreciated helps to build the foundation for a positive relationship. The aim should then be to provide regular opportunities to meet with them during the season to reinforce the important role they play in assisting the team and the club. The following are helpful hints for the coach in keeping the sponsors happy:

- Work with club management to ensure that sponsorship agreements are in synch with your coaching philosophies and expectations.
- Acknowledge and thank the sponsors in all of your public speeches and at presentation events; always recognise the important contribution they are making.
- If you and the players are required to wear clothing with the sponsor's logos, show leadership by always wearing the correct attire and being neat and well presented.
- If the sponsor also provides branded product, then show loyalty by promoting and using the product at all times. (For example, if you have a sports drink sponsor, make sure you always use its product. A published photo of you sipping the opposition product will not be well received.)
- Remember that even during your free time away from the club, your conduct and actions will have consequences for the image of the club and consequently the relationship with sponsors, so practice exemplary personal behaviour.

WORKING WITH SPORTS ADMINISTRATORS AND BOARDS

In many sporting organisations, the boards of management are made up of volunteers who have a long history of involvement of the sport. Their experience will, for the most part, be an asset to operations and the conduct of the club or association. However, coach–board relationships can be an area in which conflicts and tensions can develop. One of the key areas in which these differences can occur relates to differing expectations about the levels of time, commitment and responsibility that are reasonable and fair for all staff and volunteers.

Professional coaches have the added pressure of potentially losing their jobs if they lose the support of management. An obvious cause of tension and conflict is team or athlete results. Individual sport coaches are also subject to close scrutiny by management if they are perceived as not helping their athletes achieve expected results.

Coaches need to provide as much information as possible to the board of management to help them understand their athlete devel-

Photo courtesy of Australian Paralympic Committee.

Brad Dubberley knows that management must be apprised of and understand his strategy for getting results on the court.

opment plans. Consider a golf coach who is appointed to support the state team to compete at the national championships in six months. She identifies a technical swing fault in one of the most talented athletes that she believes needs to be rectified to maximise the athlete's long-term skill development and potential.

The coach and the athlete believe that this swing change needs to be implemented immediately, but they both recognise that this will definitely have a short-term negative impact on the athlete's performance. The coach believes that the athlete will be achieving optimal competition performances in time for the national championships; however, her scores and results in tournaments and events for the next three months will likely be much worse than expected.

In this scenario, the coach should explain the situation to everyone involved with the team. Doing so will help them understand the strategies in place and hopefully minimise

the chances of any misunderstanding or tension while the athlete is undergoing the swing changes.

Following are other tips for working with administrators and board members:

- Communicate your plans clearly because more information is always better than not enough.

- Build a positive relationship with all of the key people and develop an understanding of their perspectives on major issues.

- Be aware that political infighting often occurs within sporting organisations. When it happens, strive to be seen as an impartial and dedicated person who has the best interests of the organisation at heart.

- When conflict or disagreements occurs, be tactful and diplomatic. Try to find solutions in a timely manner.

PROACTIVE APPROACHES TO RELATIONSHIPS

The Australian Wheelchair Rugby team won silver at the 2008 Beijing Paralympics and the 2010 world championships. Their arch rival is Team USA, the reigning Paralympic and world champions before the 2012 London Paralympics. Brad Dubberley, the National coach for the Australian team, explained his goal for the team as 'the absolute goal is to ensure we have the best possible opportunity to win a gold medal in London'. The team achieved their goal and won the gold at the 2012 London Paralympics.

Dubberley is very aware that he needs to communicate proactively with the senior management of the Australian Paralympic Committee (APC) and keep them fully informed regarding his plans for the team at every tournament and event. In this regard, he said: 'Players [need to] have the opportunity to play in different positions, and the team needs to trial new offensive and defensive tactics under match conditions. Of course we want to win every match we are involved with, but sometimes the results in some of the lead-up events are less critical than ensuring we are ready for any challenge'. He communicates this same message clearly to the APC so everyone understands that what might be perceived as setbacks are in fact steps towards preparing for a peak at the Paralympic Games.

Dubberley also strongly advocates for recognising the importance of the roles played by his support staff. He believes that recognising them in a public forum can be very beneficial. In the lead-up to the 2010 world championship competition, Dubberley invited all of the athletes and support staff to the official uniform presentation function, a longstanding tradition in team sports in which athletes are awarded their individual singlets with their names and numbers displayed.

Dubberley secretly arranged for additional official Australian singlets to be made specifically for all of his support team. Before the athletes were presented with their singlets, the team manager, assistant coach, team mechanic and other members of the support team were individually called to the stage to receive their Australian team singlet with their names emblazoned on the back. Dubberley said: 'The support staff were all very grateful to receive their own official team singlets; I believe it helped everyone involved to feel they were all a vital part of the team. They were worn with great pride'. This reinforced to everyone the key role the support staff play in the achievement of the team results.

SUMMARY

- A supportive and encouraging work situation creates the best opportunity for coaches to achieve their personal goals and maximise the performances of their athletes.
- Coaches who are admired and respected by the athletes they guide and assist often are highly esteemed by others involved with the team or club. The people skills vital in teaching and developing the skills of athletes are also crucial in building relationships with others on the team.
- In junior sport, proactive communication with parents is recommended to educate them about key coaching philosophies and strategies.
- Coaches should also be aware of the education status of all of their athletes and try to help them develop positive relationships with the people who are supporting their studies.
- Coaches who enhance their listening skills and their capacity to deal with any conflicts increase their chances of developing united and cohesive support teams.

- Coaches should show appreciation for their support team through praise, recognition and acknowledgment of their achievements.
- A cooperative and positive link with boards of management and sport officials as well as the club sponsors requires a proactive and persistent approach.

The author of this chapter thanks Aaron Greaves, Ernie Merrick and Brad Dubberley for giving interviews and sharing their insights. The author also thanks Bernadette Sierakowski for her assistance in the preparation of this chapter.

REFERENCES AND RESOURCES

Barker, C.,& Coy, R. (2003). The 7 heavenly virtues of leadership Sydney, NSW: Australian Institute of Management; McGraw Hill.

Davis, P. (2004). Coaching performance: What sort of job are you doing? *Sports Coach, 27*(1), 6-8.

Fox, A. (2002).*Managing conflict.* London: Spiro Press.

Gilbert, W.,& Hamel, T. (2011). Enhancing coach-parent relationships in youth sports: Increasing harmony and minimizing hassle. *International Journal of Sports Science & Coaching, 6*(1), 37 - 41

Greene, J., & Grant, A. (2003).*Solution focused coaching.* Harlow, Great Britain: Pearson Education.

Hakala, D. (2008). The top 10 leadership qualities. www.hrworld.com.

Hellstedt, J. (1987). The coach/parent/athlete relationship. *Sport Psychologist, 1*(2), 151-159.

ITF Commercial Department. (2009). Fundamentals of sport sponsorship. *Coaching & Sport Science Review, 48,* 8-10.

McLean, K. (2008). Dealing with parents: Promoting dialogue, *Sports Coach, 30*(1), 12-13.

Reaburn, P. (2006). Theory to practice: Parental influences on kids sporting success. *Sports Coach 29*(2), 34.

Schilling, E. (2007). A game plan for mom and dad. *Coach & Athletic Director, 77*(5).

Spink, K. (1986). *Coaching for sporting excellence: Enhancing the natural potential of children in sport.* London: Macmillan.

Strathmore Unicorns Basketball Club. (2009). *Encourage the kids, support the game campaign.* www.strathmoreunicorns.org.au

CHAPTER 7

Managing Risk

——— Paul Jonson

If one of your athletes undertakes a warm-up exercise that you can see might cause injury, you would not hesitate to step in and advise the athlete how to perform the exercise correctly. Easy enough. But what would you do to defuse racial tensions in a team that you were about to begin coaching? Or what if you were tipped off that one of your athletes might be partaking in doping practices? Or how would you respond to media allegations or questions about one of your athletes being involved in off-field behaviour that has serious legal implications?

Issues such as these will arise, and accidents *will* happen. Try as they may, coaches cannot shield their athletes from all harm—not if they want to offer their athletes the necessary challenges and opportunities for maximal development. Playing it too safe equates to playing not at all. Every day in every practice and at every competition, risks are inherent to a lesser or greater degree in every sport.

This chapter identifies the most prevalent risks to which coaches must be alert and provides recommendations for how to deal with those risks. It also discusses how coaches can ensure the safety and well-being of others as well as themselves. Risk management is a necessary part of good coaching practice. It is achieved by becoming aware of and planning for contingencies in relation to the whole coaching enterprise, and then acting in accordance with that plan when such contingencies occur.

RISK MANAGEMENT

Each type of risk has its own set of dimensions, so there is no such thing as 'one size fits all' when it comes to risk management. Risk management costs time and often money but not necessarily large sums of either. Decisions need to be made based on the best information available at the time, and therefore it is an ongoing process. Further, risk management accomplishes many goals, including optimum performance; productive relationships among athletes, coaches, administrators and parents; and organisational efficiency. At the end of the day, risk management is part of creating an environment in which the coach and athlete can flourish along with the organisation and everyone who supports it.

Definitions of risk abound, but the one that appears in the Australia and New Zealand Standards for Risk Management (AS/NZS ISO 31000, 2009; an important resource) is succinct: 'the effect of uncertainty on objectives' (2.1, p.1). Risk management involves the use of a coordinated set of activities to control the many risks that can affect an organisation or person seeking to achieve objectives, and it requires the use of risk management principles and a risk management framework and process. The important point to note from these definitions is that risk management is about helping people and organisations achieve objectives through preventive practices. In other words, it is about taking positive steps to reduce the likelihood of issues arising that will hinder on-field success.

Risk management is both a legal and ethical imperative of coaching. Many laws pertaining to sport coaching *must* be observed. These are discussed in the following sections. The time coaches take to learn how to address these matters properly is time well spent when considering the toll of a lawsuit. However, there is also the issue of what coaches *should* do. Even in the absence of legal imperatives, coaches are generally expected to follow certain moral rules. These may be found in codes of conduct discussed later or in the culture of the sport. Hence, although moral rules of behaviour are not always compulsory, they are expected and so a coach needs a set of ethical values to guide decision making. Again, risk management relates to both what not to do as much as what to do.

According to the Australian and New Zealand Standard, a *risk management process* systematically applies management policies, procedures and practices to a set of activities to establish the risk context; communicate and consult with everyone involved; and identify, analyse, evaluate, treat, monitor and review risk (AS/NZS ISO 31000, 2009: 2.8, p.3). This is a very helpful definition because it sets out the basic steps required to achieve effective risk management practice.

In essence, risk management requires the coach, together with the organisation, to do the following: Identify all risks by becoming familiar with issues, analyse and evaluate how to treat the risks in a reasonable fashion, and then implement the treatment when necessary. In practical risk management terms, this means acquiring as much knowledge of the risks as possible and then deciding what can be done to minimise their occurrence. It is important to monitor and maintain the risk elements and processes and to conduct regular and systematic reviews of all of them.

The next step, the treatment of risk, need only be *reasonable* according to the standards of the sport. What is reasonable will change according to the situation, the level of experience of

the coach and the characteristics (age, gender, disability, etc.) of the athletes. It should also be noted that any standards are guidelines only and must be adapted to non-standard situations. It is here that a risk management plan, knowledge and experience come to the fore to help coaches with decision making.

PRIMARY RISKS IN COACHING

Beyond the general principles and processes of risk management are the laws coaches must observe to manage risk. These laws relate to risk situations that coaches may encounter at some point in their careers as they deal with athletes and the associations that either employ them or organise the sport and the events in which their athletes participate.

NEGLIGENCE

Increasingly, greater responsibility is being imposed on coaches to prevent or minimise the risk of injuries to athletes, in both training and competition. Coaches usually have the most direct control over athletes, and as such, they have the primary duty to minimise their risk of injury. Coaches may be liable for the negligent supervision of an athlete (*Foscolos v. Footscray Youth Club*, 2002); use of inappropriate tactics that result in injury to either their own player or an opposing player (*Bugden v. Rogers*, 1993); failing to give the right advice or take the right precautions (*Vowles v. Evans*, 2002); or forcing or 'encouraging' an athlete to participate while injured or unwell or to consume drugs that cause illness or are banned under the anti-doping rules, to assist participation. Coaches must, at all times, instruct athletes about the correct or most acceptable methods of safely performing the tasks of a specific activity and inform them of the risks involved in participating in the activity, when such risk is not obvious.

In informing athletes of possible risks, however, the coach is often faced with a conflict of interest. When coaching in a club environment, coaches owe a duty to both the athlete and the club. However, the interests of the club to have the athlete participating whenever possible and the interests of the athlete may be in conflict when the athlete is injured or unwell. Coaches should always act in the best interests of the athlete.

Duty and Standard of Care The law of negligence states, in essence, that coaches have a duty to exercise reasonable care to prevent foreseeable risk of harm to all athletes in their care and control. In terms of managing risk, this means that the coach must do or not do what a reasonable coach of similar standing would or would not do in the same circumstances.

Coaches should note that Australian law underwent a significant change in 2002 that is helpful to coaches. Coaches are not liable for injuries arising from risks that would have been obvious to a reasonable athlete in the situation. Whether the athlete knew about the obvious risk is no longer relevant. If a reasonable athlete in that situation would have realised that the situation involved a risk, the coach is not guilty of negligence.

This law also applies to inherent risks in sport activity. Inherent risks are those that cannot be removed or avoided by the exercise of reasonable care. Injury or illness suffered as a result of such risks carries no liability. Therefore, coaches need do nothing to minimise the danger. Indeed, in some cases it would be difficult or impossible for coaches to minimise the danger. In other words, the only way to avoid the inherent risks of a sport is to avoid the sport altogether. Having said that, a coach may still choose to advise athletes of risks so they can take precautions where possible. Furthermore, it does not matter that the activity is dangerous (one that involves a significant risk of harm). If the risk is obvious, even if the activity is dangerous, the coach will not be liable for any injuries arising from that risk.

However, when the relevant risk of injury would not have been obvious to a reasonable athlete in that situation, the coach will be liable for negligence if injury results. Coaches in such cases should manage the risk by giving athletes appropriate warnings and instructions.

An important distinction must also be made between volunteer and paid coaches. Volunteer coaches who are unpaid or recover reasonable expenses will not be liable for any negligence

David Woodley/Actionplus/Icon SMI

All sports, even those with less physical contact than Australian rules football, have inherent risks. Although coaches cannot prevent all risks or injuries, they should advise athletes of non-obvious risks and encourage them to take precautions when possible.

committed while doing sport-related work, which includes coaching. Coaches who are paid, however, may be found liable for negligence if they breach the standard of care expected of them in that situation.

So how careful does the professional coach have to be? Basically, if a professional coach acted in a manner that is widely accepted in Australia by peer professional opinion as competent professional practice, then the coach will be regarded as not having acted negligently.

The law of negligence is no different when coaching children than when coaching adults: Coaches must exercise the degree of care that a reasonable coach would exercise in that situation. However, the standard of care required when coaching children, who are generally less capable than adults of taking care of themselves and realising risks and dangers, is different from that required when coaching adults. The standard of care when coaching disabled athletes is different again. One important risk management step especially relevant to children is to match athletes according to their skill, experience and size. Coaches of children should refer to *The Safety Guidelines for Children and Young People in Sport and Recreation* and the national Smartplay program, which detail safety (risk management) practices for children.

Essential Duties All coaches in all coaching situations are required to perform certain essential duties to provide for the welfare of their athletes. It is incumbent on coaches to do the following:

- **Ensure that athletes are capable of undertaking the sport activity.** Athletes must have the level of knowledge, skill and fitness required to undertake the sport activity expected of them. Coaches can ensure this by being knowledgeable about their athletes and providing the relevant coaching and training as well as appropriate medical checks. This requires coaches to keep up-to-date with information relevant to what they are doing and to be sure activities do not go beyond athletes' levels of competence.

- **Provide safe equipment.** The coach should ensure that athletes are using the correct equipment and that it is in good order, particularly if that equipment was supplied by the coach. The coach should undertake regular checks or advise athletes to either check equipment themselves or to take it to an expert.

- **Provide a safe environment.** Coaches should ensure that athletes are participating in an environment, on grounds and in facilities that do not pose any unusual or 'non-obvious' dangers. Coaches can accomplish this by undertaking or arranging for regular assessment.

- **Provide proper supervision.** Coaches must ensure that athletes are properly supervised, especially children and other less able athletes. They can do this by either personally being present or having systems to ensure that someone who is suitable for the task is in attendance.

Returning to risk management principles, the key is foreseeability: planning *and* acting to minimise or avoid risk as is reasonable in the situation. 'Reasonable' suggests that acting in this way should not involve significant expense, difficulty or inconvenience.

Should an injury or illness occur, coaches must take prompt and proper action to treat the problem, which may involve either acting to the best of their ability or organising assistance as necessary to ensure the well-being of the athlete. In this regard, coaches who assist injured athletes will not be liable for negligence if they cause further injury while trying in good faith to help. This is known as the Good Samaritan provision.

Good risk management practice in relation to injury and illness involves keeping good records (including diary notes) of strategies and actions taken to ensure athlete safety. Injuries happen, athletes do become ill, and when coaches can show the court that they have at all times taken reasonable steps (that is, that they have done or not done what would be expected of a reasonable coach in the situation that led to the injury or illness), then neither they nor their employers will be liable for negligence. More important, they will know they have done what was expected of them to minimise the risk of injury and illness to the athlete.

DISCRIMINATION

'Human rights are about recognising every person's inherent right to be treated with respect and self-worth, which includes a person's right to live free from discrimination' (Thorpe et al., 2009, p. 426). One would hope and expect that in this day and age, coaches no longer knowingly discriminate on the basis of gender, sexual orientation, religion, race, disability or the like, except where necessary. (Specific lawful exceptions are described later in this section.) Thus, the important risk management strategy here for coaches is to be aware of the laws that relate to discrimination:

when they are discriminating and should not be, and when they can and should discriminate. The objective is to create a safe, respectful and harassment-free sport environment.

To be very clear, it is illegal for a coach to be discriminated against by an employer or selector or for a coach to discriminate against an athlete in providing coaching services, including making selections on the grounds of the athlete's age, disability, race, gender, sexual orientation, trans-sexuality, colour, ethnicity, nationality, pregnancy, breast-feeding, marital status, religious beliefs, political conviction or irrelevant criminal or medical record. Exemptions to these rules are addressed later; suffice it to say that discrimination is allowed when it is fair and reasonable, as defined under the law.

The definition of discrimination is treating someone less favourably than others based on one of the aforementioned characteristics. Discrimination can be either direct or indirect, and coaches should ensure that neither occurs if they wish to avoid prosecution in addition to public contempt. Direct discrimination is overt behaviour that effectively states discriminatory practice. Indirect discrimination is surreptitious behaviour that results in discriminatory outcomes. An example of direct discrimination is to say that anyone who is of the Jewish faith cannot participate in the training session run by coaches. An example of indirect discrimination is to have all coaching classes and selection trials on Friday nights, which is when practising Jews are not allowed to participate in sporting activities.

Exemptions exist for certain forms of discrimination. For example, a coach may exclude one gender from participating in the sport if strength, stamina or physique is relevant and if the athlete is over 12 years of age. Note, however, that an employer cannot discriminate against a coach on these grounds. In some situations a coach may be permitted to practise reverse discrimination. For example, if the competition is for disabled athletes or competitors of a particular gender, the coach may select only athletes with the relevant disability or of that gender.

Another exemption is that a coach can discriminate if not doing so would result in unjustifiable hardship to the coach or his employer (the sport association). In determining whether the observance of non-discriminatory practices would result in unjustifiable hardship, all relevant circumstances must be taken into account including financial implications. The Disability Discrimination Act also states that discrimination on the ground of infectious diseases is permissible if reasonably necessary to protect public health.

It should be noted that a coach who in any way encourages or assists another person to commit acts of discrimination may be liable as an accessory. This principle of liability as an accessory also applies to instructions to an athlete to commit a criminal act such as 'taking out' a player on the opposing team with an illegal manoeuvre. Such action may also result in the coach's employer being liable under the principle of vicarious liability. It should also be noted that vilification (publicly or openly offensive, insulting, humiliating or intimidating comments or gestures based on race, colour or national or ethnic origin) is itself a form of discrimination.

The risk management strategy regarding discrimination is very simple. Coaches should not in any way, shape or form become involved in or tolerate discrimination unless it is necessary for the nature of the competition; will be dangerous for persons 12 or older; or will result in unjustifiable hardship or a risk to public health and safety.

HARASSMENT, SEXUAL MISCONDUCT AND CHILD ABUSE

Harassment, sexual misconduct and child abuse include both illegal and inappropriate behaviour. Under no circumstances should a coach justify or tolerate such behaviour. Harassment is any kind of unwelcome advance be it sexual, abusive or otherwise 'which a reasonable person, having regard to all the circumstances, would have anticipated that the person harassed would be offended, humiliated or intimidated' (Sex Discrimination Act 1984 [Cth], s 28A). Harassment includes not only physical actions but also either verbal or written statements or gestures and can be a single incident or a series of incidents.

It must be remembered from a risk management perspective that sexual harassment is always about the experience of the victim. Therefore, coaches must think how athletes might react to their actions. If a coach thinks the athlete *might* be offended, humiliated or intimidated, or if the athlete reports such a feeling, then the coach should stop the act immediately, no matter how innocent the act or unintended the athlete's response might be.

In addition to familiarising themselves with legal prohibitions, coaches should read, understand and carefully apply the Member Protection Policies developed by the Australian Sports Commission as well as those developed by individual sports. They should also consult the IOC's Consensus Statement, 'Sexual Harassment and Abuse in Sport'.

Codes of conduct are also important instruments in educating and directing coach and athlete behaviour. (See the Codes of Conduct section later in this chapter.) Developing, monitoring and evaluating the implementation and impact of policies and procedures to prevent harassment; developing educational and training programs; promoting and exhibiting equitable, respectful and ethical behaviour; and fostering strong partnerships with parents or caregivers to prevent harassment are all recommended risk management strategies to help coaches create a harassment-free environment.

The coaching of children, as outlined earlier, requires special steps to ensure their safety. There are also special laws that relate to working with children, whether the job is voluntary or paid. In essence, laws require coaches working with athletes under 18 years of age to undergo police checks to ensure they have no convictions for serious child-related offences. They also prohibit people with such convictions from working with athletes under the age of 18. The imposition is therefore on both the coach and the employer.

There is no national law regarding working with children, and so the law is different in every state and territory. Coaches in New South Wales and South Australia must undergo this screening each time they begin coaching children with a new association. Queensland, Victoria, Western Australia and the Northern Territory have a certification system that, while also mandatory, is transferable to each workplace.

Only under Queensland law is a risk management strategy required regarding children. The strategy must include a commitment to the safety, well-being and protection of children; a code of conduct; reporting procedures; recruitment, training and management procedures; breach management procedures; and compliance procedures. This applies to coaches as both employees and employers.

From a practical point of view, the best risk management strategy is to never coach a child one-on-one unless it is in public view. It is strongly recommended that those coaching children individually always have at least an assistant coach or a parent present. Any coach who has any concerns about a child's behaviour or that of any other person in such matters is under a duty to report them immediately to either the employer or the police as appropriate.

MEDIA RELATIONS

An important risk management warning that coaches should heed is to be very careful about what they say about their sport and others in their sport, both publicly and privately and especially to the media. Two sides to this issue need to be examined: what the coach should and should not say in and to the media, and what the media can and cannot say to the public.

Although we do have freedom of speech in Australia, it is not unlimited. Two exceptions are of particular importance to coaches: defaming someone else and doing serious damage to an employer's reputation.

DEFAMATION

In relation to defamation, although coaches can make critical comments of others (and others can make critical comments of them), coaches and their critics must not do so in a way that untruthfully or unfairly damages the reputation of the other. A defamatory remark is one that may injure the professional reputation of

TALKING TROUBLE

In September 2008, the Melbourne Storm star player and captain, Cam Smith, was suspended from playing for two weeks by the National Rugby League's judiciary panel for an illegal tackle. The effect of this was that Smith was unable to play in the grand final.

Two days after the suspensions were made, Smith's coach, Craig Bellamy, and the Storm's CEO, Brian Waldron, alleged at a press conference that the judiciary decision was unreasonable based on the lack of action against players from other teams who had committed similar tackles, and that the decision was predetermined based on the betting odds surrounding the likelihood of Smith's suspension.

The members of the judiciary panel were offended by the implied allegation that they had acted without full fairness and equity in reaching their decision and believed their integrity had been attacked. The panel members commenced legal proceedings against the coach and CEO for defamation and were awarded $105,000 plus costs in October 2010, two years after the incident. The NRL had already, in 2008, fined the Storm $50,000 over the comments.

a person by causing others to ridicule, hate, avoid or lower their estimation of that person. Importantly, any form of communication to any sized audience beyond the defamed person is enough to permit a lawsuit. Note also that anyone repeating a defamatory statement made by someone else is also liable for defamation.

There are two defences against a charge of defamation. Truth is a complete defence, but in New South Wales, Queensland, Australian Capital Territory and Tasmania, only if the statement was made for the public benefit or is a matter of public interest. Private activity is a matter of public interest only if it has some relevance to that person's capacity to perform public activities. The second defence is that the offending remarks were fair comment on a matter of public interest.

The moral of this story from a risk management perspective is that coaches should make sure they have the correct facts and are very genuine and honest in their opinions. But even then, malicious remarks are still likely to be regarded as defamatory.

DISREPUTE

Most employment contracts or codes of conduct contain a clause in which the coach agrees not to bring the sport into disrepute. It may be worded something like this: *The coach agrees not to engage in conduct that brings or is likely to* *bring the coach, the coach's athlete, the sport or the association into disrepute.*

What amounts to disrepute will be decided by the facts of each case, but in general it is determined by what the court (or the sport association) believes ordinary members of the public or the relevant sporting fraternity would think of the reputation of the coach, the athlete, the sport, or the association after the remark or act came to the public's attention. As with defamation, if the remark or act caused others to ridicule, hate, avoid or lower their estimation of the person, sport or association, it would be deemed to have been disreputable. This may result in termination of the contract. Typically, however, it results in a sanction by the sport association itself, such as a fine, suspension or reprimand.

What rights do coaches have with the media? To be blunt, other than the right to sue for defamation as outlined earlier, they don't have any, other than breach of privacy, which doesn't do much other than prevent the release of private and personal details. Coaches cannot prevent anyone from publishing their photo (unless they improperly try to associate the coach with an event, service or product) or anything they say or do (unless the information is gathered illegally such as recording a conversation without the coach's knowledge, but even in this case there are exceptions).

Again, the warning here is quite simple: There is no such thing as 'off the record' with the media. Coaches should always be sure of their facts and be careful about what they say in public, particularly if it is a critical comment. Nothing a coach says should ever be malicious.

DEALING WITH ETHICAL ISSUES

Most coaches know what to do and what not to do in most risk situations—especially when the law is involved as outlined earlier. But issues are not always clear-cut. Often, coaches face situations that require them to make judgement calls that are outside of the realm of the law. Consider, for example, a coach who is advised that the drug testing authority is coming to test her athlete and the athlete has to suddenly be elsewhere . . . again. What if the coach suspects that the athlete uses drugs? What if this athlete is a key member of the team, which has a very good chance of winning? How should the coach respond to this scenario? The risks here to reputation, finances, success and fair play are not insignificant and need to be managed. One helpful strategy is using ethical guidelines.

CODES OF ETHICS

Ethics is the branch of philosophy that examines morality—the problems and processes for making judgements. For coaches, ethics is about the decision-making process behind the actions they take that have moral repercussions. It helps to define fair and proper behaviour (as distinct from legal behaviour). Ethics requires that coaches determine which rules they will follow when faced with a choice and which rules will take precedence if there is a conflict.

It is not appropriate to suggest to coaches what ethics should be; others have done that, as we shall see. However, a process exists to help coaches arrive at their rules of behaviour. In other words, choosing an ethical code in advance is a good risk management strategy.

Ethical codes should be formulated in the 'cool light of day'—that is, not when coaches are under pressure to make a decision, but when they can think things through, objectively and theoretically. Such codes should be created when there are no competing interests, without emotions and solely on the basis of what is right and wrong. No one at the time should be in a position to be affected by the code; the coach should only be concerned with formulating the code itself. Further, rules must be unaffected by what people might think of or even do to the coach. This is not about popularity. Finally, the coach needs to establish a priority of rules in case of a conflict.

CODES OF CONDUCT

Most sports today have their own sets of ethical principles in the form of codes of conduct. The Australian Sports Commission has established a very effective generic code as well. These are valuable documents for several reasons: They define acceptable behaviour; they promote exemplary standards of behaviour; they establish a framework for decision making; and they are a mark of identity. They spell out what coaches stand for as coaches and as human beings. Above all, they are fundamental to sustainable coaching practice because most athletes want to be associated with sport associations and coaches who have an ethical approach.

MINIMISING RISK

A subset of risk management is *risk minimisation*, which basically involves passing on or avoiding risk. The following sections discuss the three key strategies for minimising risk.

INCORPORATION

One way of reducing financial risk is to create a corporate entity to own the coaching business. This is achieved quite simply and relatively inexpensively through an accountant or solicitor. Although some formalities are involved, these are greatly outweighed by the reduction in the risk of financial hardship should the company be sued for a coach's mistake. The effect is that coaches are not personally liable nor are their personal assets available to cover any debts or damages if they are successfully sued.

MONEY IS NOT EVERYTHING

At the 2008 Beijing Olympic Games, one of Australia's best gold medal prospects, Jessica Schipper, was beaten by a Chinese swimmer. The defeat was particularly galling because the Chinese swimmer had purchased Schipper's training program from Schipper's coach, Ken Wood. The program Wood sold included detailed information on stroke technique, weight training, diet and methods of preparation for elite swimmers.

Wood admitted he had sold the program for a significant sum of money without saying just how much. But he was quite unrepentant about his action. Wood claimed that because of the low pay received by swim coaches, even the top ones, he had little choice. He noted that he runs his own business, and he acknowledged that he takes in international swimmers (whom he charged a lot more than locals), although he works for Australian Swimming.

Asked if he had cost Schipper a gold medal, Wood said: 'I don't know. I can't answer that. But I wanted Jess to win. I feel bittersweet, I do'. Woods said he did not provide any coaching or assistance of any kind after the Australian Olympic trials and believed that he had not betrayed Schipper. He said that he felt he had to make a living and that he did not actually coach the Chinese swimmer at any point in time.

Adapted from P. Badel, 2008. Available: http://www.foxsports.com.au/schippers-coach-sold-swim-plans/story-e6freyp0-1111117214136.

INSURANCE

Whether or not the business is incorporated, a very prudent risk minimisation step is to take out relevant insurances. These are best discussed with an insurance broker who can advise on the type and amount of insurance cover needed. When taking out insurance, coaches must be totally honest about their previous histories and the activities involved in their coaching. Failure to provide a full previous history can lead to a loss of insurance cover, and not listing all coaching activities may result in not being covered at all. Coaches also should advise their insurers (which can be done via a broker) of any changes in their coaching activities, especially those that involve riskier behaviour.

The two most common and fundamental types of insurance for coaches are public liability and professional indemnity. Public liability covers legal liability for bodily injury or property damage suffered by members of the public, including athletes, as a result of negligence. Professional indemnity covers liability for breach of duty of care and includes cover for wrong advice that leads to loss. The other insurance that coaches *must* take out if they (or their company) employ anyone is workers' compensation. This is compulsory under Australian law. It may also be wise for coaches to take out personal accident insurance in case of personal injury to themselves. The main message here is that coaches should talk to their insurance brokers and report everything that has *any* relevance to their insurance coverage.

EXCLUSION CLAUSES

The use of exclusion clauses (which include waivers, releases, disclaimers and limited liability clauses) is both a potentially effective risk minimisation strategy and ethically contentious. These clauses, which may be included in a contract with the athlete or appear in signs, in essence say that if the coach does something that causes injury or loss to the athlete, the athlete cannot obtain compensation for that injury or loss.

Under the Civil Liability Acts, coaches do not owe a duty of care to their athletes if the risk was the subject of a risk warning, which may include a sign or clause in a contract. The risk warning must be given before the athlete begins any training or competition, can be given in writing or verbally and warns of the general nature of the particular risk. Note that risk warnings need only be given once and not before every session, provided the nature of the risk has not significantly changed. However, the coach cannot escape liability if the harm to the athlete resulted from the coach's violation of a law relating to personal safety or if the athlete was forced to participate by the coach. If the athlete is a child or otherwise lacks mental capacity, the coach must give the risk warning to the parent or person in control of the athlete.

However, a word of warning: Although the courts will uphold exclusion clauses, they need to be sufficiently clear. Hence, a further risk management strategy is to seek legal assistance in drafting the wording of the clause or sign.

The ethical issue involved here is whether coaches should seek to avoid liability if they contributed in some causal way to an athlete's injury. If the insurance contract includes a requirement to do so, then the coach is left with little choice, but if not, or if there is uncertainty as to the extent of the exclusion or liability limitation, then the coach must ask, Do I want to escape responsibility for injuries that I have caused by my behaviour to my athletes—those who have put their trust in me?

If the proper risk management practices and strategies are in place, the likelihood of injury is significantly reduced and the need to rely on exclusion clauses is reduced. Prevention is best achieved through good risk management planning and behaviour.

SUMMARY

- Risk management is about coaches' caring for the safety of both themselves and their athletes. It can relate to physical safety, financial well-being and the right to participate.

- Risk management may present ethical dilemmas as well as challenges to self-control. But at all times, it means thinking ahead about the consequences of one's actions. That thinking is best done with knowledge.

- Knowledge of the laws of negligence, child protection, discrimination, harassment, rights to privacy and reputation, contractual obligations and codes of conduct all assist in risk management planning and decision making.

- Strategies such as incorporation, insurance and the use of exclusion clauses can be very effective barriers to personal liability. However, they all need to be understood and acted on with one aim: providing an environment in which the athlete and coach can excel.

- The best approach to risk management is to think, plan, implement and coach!

REFERENCES AND RESOURCES

Australian Sports Commission. Coaching Code of Ethics. www.ausport.gov.au.

Buckley, E. (1998). *Sports law: Name and image.* Potts Point, NSW: The National Publishing Group.

Bugden v. Rogers (unreported, BC9302234, SCNSWCA 40069/91; CA40073/91, 1993 Australian Torts Reporter). Frankena, W. (1973). *Ethics* (2nd ed.). NJ: Prentice Hall.

Foscolos v. Footscray Youth Club [2002] VSC 148.

Gibson, A. *Australian Sports Law Reporter.* Sydney: CCH.

Healey, D., & Leonte, D. (2005). *Insurance and risk management in sport.* Kensington, NSW: Faculty of Law, University of New South Wales.

Smartplay. www.smartplay.com.au

Sports Medicine Australia. *Safety guidelines for children and young people in sport and recreation.* www.smartplay.com.au

Thorpe, D., Buti, A., Davies, C., Fridman, S., & Jonson, P. (2009). *Sports law.* Melbourne: Oxford University Press.

Vowles v. Evans [2003] 1 WLR 1607.

PART III

DEVELOPING THE ATHLETE

CHAPTER 8

Evaluating the Athlete

—— David Pyne

Every sport contains elements of fitness, skill and motivation. Evaluating these elements through a well-organised testing program can provide the coach and athlete with important information. The results of testing can assist the coach in improving daily training programs and eventually competition performance.

The testing program should be integrated with other elements of the annual plan. The major and minor competitions are programmed first, then the main training blocks, followed by details of the testing and support programs. In the planning stage the coach needs to determine the purpose of testing and how the results will be used in planning, prescribing and reviewing training programs. The head coach works with assistant coaches, managers, sports science and sports medicine staff and other officials to determine the selection and timing of testing throughout a training and competitive season.

A wide range of applications and benefits can be obtained from a testing or evaluation program. Some programs provide benefits to both coach and athlete immediately, whereas others, such as talent identification and research projects, may take months or years to pay dividends. The choice of test and how the results are implemented depends on the individual circumstances of the coach, athlete and sporting program. A small battery of tests targeting the most important aspects of training and competitive performance is suggested. A common mistake is to try to measure too many things at once, which is time consuming and possibly distracting for the coach and athlete. The main purposes of athlete testing follow:

- **Identifying and developing talent.** Testing younger athletes identifies those with the physical, technical and behavioural characteristics needed to be successful senior athletes. Initially, many talent identification (TID) programs focused narrowly on simple anthropometric and fitness characteristics, but more recent approaches incorporate lifestyle and behavioural assessments.

- **Assessing characteristics of individual athletes.** The traditional testing of athletes is used to identify their current status. Testing can be undertaken in a clinic, laboratory or office setting; in the regular training environment; or during an actual game, tournament or competition. One-off testing is useful, but serial monitoring of an athlete over time, such as a training season, yields more valuable information on the progress of that athlete.

- **Assessing groups of athletes, teams or programs.** In team sports players are often tested as a group or subgroup (e.g., forwards and backs in rugby; guards, forwards and centres in basketball; rookies, seniors and veteran players in Australian football).

- **Analysing game and training.** The increasing availability of digital technology has expanded the opportunities for game and training analysis. Athletes can be monitored remotely (or afterwards using postgame processing) with simple notational analysis or more sophisticated video-based time-and-motion analyses.

Key performance indicators such as points scored, penalties conceded, shots made and missed, rebounds and assists made, turnovers made and tackles made and missed are routinely quantified in national and international games.

- **Evaluating training and lifestyle interventions.** Testing athletes to determine the effectiveness of training (general fitness training, skills and drills, team plays and tactics) and general lifestyle (dietary, time management, sleep management, hygiene, psychological skills training, athlete career and educational programs) interventions forms a major part of many testing programs. Such testing can be conducted routinely in regular training or in larger, more controlled research studies.

- **Managing injury.** Injury is a reality of many sports, and musculoskeletal testing of athletes is a critical element of diagnosis at the time of injury, management during the immediate recovery period and guidance of the rate of return to full training and competition.

- **Evaluating sporting equipment and technology.** Testing is also useful for evaluating the utility or benefits of new sporting equipment and technology ranging from clothing, uniforms, bats, clubs and balls to the rapidly emerging digital technology such as smart phone apps, sport-specific software applications, instrumented strength testing apparatus, global positioning systems (GPS), heart rate telemetry and digital video analysis.

PHYSICAL DEVELOPMENT AND MATURATION

The evaluation of younger athletes is heavily influenced by their individual rates of physical development and maturation. The period of the adolescent growth spurt (typically 12 to 15 years for females and 14 to 17 years for males) is characterised by wide variations in the rate of development of physical, psychological and skill attributes. The peak height velocity of 8 to 10 centimetres (3 to 4 in.) per year is typically attained around the age of 12 years for girls and 14 years for boys (see figure 8.1). Aerobic training can be increased after peak height velocity is reached. Strength and power training is accelerated a little later in boys, typically around 15 or 16 years of age.

The awkward adolescent phase in which motor skills decline transiently during periods of rapid growth is well known to most coaches

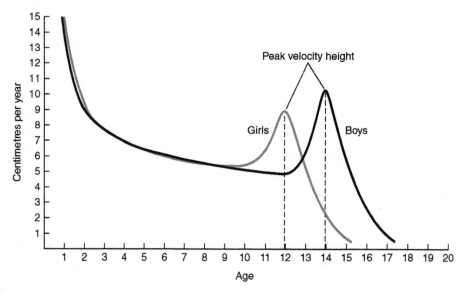

Figure 8.1 Peak velocity height curve for girls and boys showing the increase in stretch stature (height) expressed in units of centimetres per year.

From http://www.brianmac.co.uk/ltad.htm

of adolescent athletes (Beunen & Malina, 1988). For these reasons, testing programs are generally introduced when athletes reach about 15 or 16 years of age.

From early childhood to maturation, people go through several stages of development: prepuberty, puberty, postpuberty and maturation. Each stage has a corresponding phase of athletic training. Various models of long-term athlete development have been developed to assist the coach in preparing junior and adolescent athletes. The two most well-known of these models are the theory of periodisation of training as described by Tudor Bompa (Bompa & Haff, 2009) and the long-term athlete development (LTAD) model by Istvan Balyi (Stafford & Balyi, 2010).

The LTAD model has two versions, each comprising sequential stages to assist the coach in planning the development of younger athletes. The early specialisation version of the LTAD is for athletes starting at a younger age in skill-oriented sports such as gymnastics. The four stages of this version are training to train, training to compete, training to win and retirement and retainment. The late specialisation version is primarily for athletes in team or strength or power sports. The five stages of this version are FUNdamental (ages 5 to 9), learning to training (ages 8 to 12), training to train (ages 11 to 16), training to compete (ages 15 to 18) and training to win (older than 17). Training loads increase gradually as younger athletes progress through to senior ranks.

An important question for the coach is when to start basic testing or evaluation of a junior athlete or team. Athletes should be introduced to the concept of testing around the age of 13 or 14 with very basic tests of performance, fitness and skills. The focus at this point should be on education and providing a foundation of knowledge and experience for more advanced testing undertaken in later years. Athletes should also be taught the basics of stretching, recovery practices, nutrition and hydration, mental preparation and tapering and peaking for competition.

More organised testing is introduced at age 15 or 16 as the athlete matures and more time is allotted to training and competition. The key

areas of fitness and conditioning, psychological preparation and technical development can all be supported by a testing and evaluation program. By age 17 or 18, the athlete's physical, technical, mental, personal and lifestyle capacities have evolved, and the focus of training shifts from development to maximisation of performance.

DEVELOPING A TESTING PROGRAM

A testing or evaluation program typically comprises three main steps:

1. Determining the most important attributes or characteristics needed for successful competitive performance
2. Testing and evaluating attributes or characteristics in the clinic or laboratory as well as the training or competitive environments
3. Prescribing individualised training, lifestyle or intervention programs that match the athlete's attributes with the characteristics or attributes required for a particular event or sport

The initial step of determining the most important attributes is often undertaken by sports scientists using observational analysis of games and training and measurements of physiological, psychological and technical attributes. Some of this work is completed in discrete research projects involving collaborations among team staff, sports scientists, university partners and private enterprise. In professional sports with substantial resources, such as the Australian Football League (AFL), most teams undertake continual monitoring of the characteristics needed for success. The tactics and strategies in sports evolve quickly, so the best-prepared teams continually monitor trends in player preparation, recovery, game and training analysis and conditioning and skill drills.

The second step of evaluating or testing players is the visible part of the process and involves the coaches and players at various stages of the season. Although some research projects can proceed quietly in the background, the formal testing of athletes must be well organised and concise and result in minimal interruptions to the regular training program.

Prescribing individualised training is the final step in the process. In individual or solo sports such as athletics, swimming, triathlon and cycling and the racquet sports such as tennis, badminton and squash, programs need to be tailored to the requirements of each player. However, even in these sports, athletes often train together in groups under the direction of a single coach. The challenge for the coach is to find the balance between general group training and the small modifications needed for individuals. This task is particularly challenging in junior sports in which a larger number of athletes make it difficult to prescribe individualised training. In team sports, the training program can be individualised to subgroups of players according to their particular needs.

Coaches need to consider the following elements when prescribing individualised training programs to improve fitness and performance:

- Current level of fitness
- Desired level of fitness
- Short-term and long-term training history or background
- Current or recent injuries, illnesses or bouts of fatigue
- Effectiveness of various training activities
- Time available
- Venue, facilities and equipment availability
- Coach availability

EVALUATING ATTRIBUTES AND PERFORMANCE

The coaching group determines which areas of an athlete's program need to be assessed and how this will be undertaken. No coach will have all the necessary time, skills, expertise or experience to perform the tests alone. Sports science and sports medicine specialists who are experts in the field can be enlisted. Assistant coaches, managers, parents and the athletes themselves can also provide support during testing sessions. Laboratories are the most controlled environments, but the question of how well these results transfer to the field should be addressed (Rampinini et al., 2007).

Testing can take the form of assessing several attributes in isolation or involve assessing the

AIS SWIMMING PROGRAM

The Australian Institute of Sport (AIS) swimming program has a 30-year history of preparing and managing elite swimmers participating in national and international competitions. A key element of the program is the regular assessment of swimmers in training and competition. The swimmers undergo regular video and biomechanical filming in the pool to improve their skills and swimming techniques. Physical therapy support includes weekly massage, minor or major treatment and injury management and occasionally clinic-based assessments of functional movements. Strength and power attributes are assessed in the gymnasium to ensure that dry land training programs are effective and complement the pool-based training.

Physiological testing involves a series of established pool-based tests of speed, speed-endurance and endurance and regular (observational) monitoring of selected training sets and sessions in consultation with the coach. Results are typically returned in real time to the coach and swimmer via telemetry or digital video or verbally. Psychological attributes are assessed occasionally via questionnaires, interviews or one-on-one consultation with the sport psychologist. Full support team meetings are organised at key points in the annual plan (preseason, midseason, precompetition and postcompetition) to plan and evaluate programs and performances and to review each swimmer's progress on an individual basis.

performance itself. In individual time-based sports such as running, swimming, cycling, rowing and triathlon, measuring performance is relatively straightforward. The sidebar, AIS Swimming Program, details a comprehensive testing program in swimming from the Australian Sport Institute.

In team sports measuring performance directly is more difficult. The usual approach is to measure factors *contributing* to performance rather than the performance itself. For example, a team sport coach might test various aspects of fitness and conditioning, skills, recovery and load indicators and psychological measures.

Some athletes perform well in training or testing, but have difficulty reproducing that level of performance in competition. For this reason, it is worthwhile to see how athletes respond under pressure in training by using time trials and performance tests (for individual sports) and simulated games or team practices (for team sports).

AGE, GENDER AND DISABILITY CONSIDERATIONS

Most sporting organisations have developed specific coaching programs for junior, senior and masters athletes to cater for all ages of participants. The opportunities for athletes in these groups have increased substantially in recreational and competitive sport settings. Junior programs are typically conducted by local clubs and schools and involve volunteer coaches or physical education teachers. Generally, the focus of club and school programs is participation, fun and learning the skills and culture of various events and sports. Basic testing of athletes is introduced for older juniors as they approach senior ranks. Physical capacities and therefore test results vary considerably during the adolescent years (Mujika et al., 2009). At the recreational level, enjoyment, health, physical activity and fitness are the primary aims of sport participation, and there

Testing athletes for team sports, such as netball, usually relies on testing factors that contribute to performance. As a result, evaluating players in pressure situations is essential.

Daniel Swee/Actionplus/Icon SMI

is little need for a formal testing or evaluation program.

Masters- or veterans-level programs have evolved in many sports, but similar to junior and recreational programs, these have little need for comprehensive testing programs. The participation of middle-aged and elderly people in physical activity, exercise and competitive sports has increased substantially in the past few decades. Masters athletes can maintain high levels of training and competitive performance despite the normal ageing process. Inevitably, physical performance tends to decline. A decline in maximal oxygen consumption by around 10 per cent per decade is the primary mechanism causing age-related reductions in physical performance (Tanaka & Seals, 2008). A gradual decline in musculoskeletal and strength and power attributes also contributes to a reduction in sporting performance.

Male and female issues have been around as long as organised sport. Although similar testing programs can be employed for both male and female athletes, different reference ranges are needed for selected anthropometric and physical fitness tests. Males are typically taller, heavier and stronger than females, although of course there is wide individual variation within and between genders. A gender difference is particularly evident in strength and power testing (Walsh et al., 2007).

Psychological and psychosocial testing may also be needed on a gender-specific basis. Given gender differences, it is usual practice to test males and females in separate groups. Mixed-group testing can be problematic for some athletes of either gender, particularly females, some of whom may feel intimidated performing in front of their male counterparts. In a conversation with the author, Shannon Rollason, the head swimming coach at the Australian Institute of Sport, remarked that 'Coaching junior and senior female athletes is very rewarding providing you treat each and every girl with fairness, respect and consistency'.

Some exercising females experience symptoms associated with the female athlete triad syndrome relating to energy availability, menstrual function and bone mineral density (Thein-Nissenbaum & Carr, 2011). Clinically, these conditions can manifest as disordered eating behaviours, menstrual irregularity and stress fractures. At-risk school- and university-age athletes should be assessed for triad components at the commencement of and during higher-level training programs. Athletes, parents, coaches and trainers should be educated and informed about the female athlete triad syndrome.

In the presence of triad symptoms, further evaluation and treatment by a multidisciplinary team is strongly recommended. Fluctuations in the menstrual cycle can influence exercise and sporting performance and need to be considered in both the training and testing of female athletes. Some studies indicate substantial variation in physiological responses and the athletic performance of female athletes at specific phases of the menstrual cycle (Rechichi, Dawson, & Goodman, 2009). Variations in measures of aerobic performance, anaerobic capacity, anaerobic power and muscular strength in female athletes therefore warrant careful interpretation. Because the effects of oral contraceptives on hormonal profiles and athletic performance differ among athletes, this issue should be managed on a case-by-case basis.

Disability issues represent a special challenge for coaches. In general, the key elements of a testing or evaluation program for athletes with a disability are broadly similar to those of able-bodied athletes. However, the nature of the specific disability must be considered for each athlete. Some disabilities affect posture and movement, whereas others influence skills and techniques. For physical testing, specialised or modified equipment, venues and facilities are often required for disabled athletes. Sports science personnel with specific knowledge of disabilities should be consulted, and all parties should be briefed by the coach, athlete or parent or guardian when testing or evaluation programs are being developed.

Serial testing of physiological function and performance capacities can provide a quantitative assessment of improvement or decline in the condition of the athlete. A multidisciplinary approach involving kinetic (force), kinematic

Ady Kerry/PA Archive/PA Photos

Female athletes who train and compete at high levels need to be educated about the female athlete triad syndrome to ensure health and continued athletic success.

(motion) and electromyographic (muscle activity) testing is needed to identify underlying conditions responsible for abnormal gait and elevated energy costs.

TALENT IDENTIFICATION AND TALENT TRANSFER

Many sports devote significant resources to developing talent identification and talent transfer programs to increase the number of athletes with potential for success at a senior level. Talent identification programs typically involve the prediction of performance over a variable period of time by measuring physical, psychological, physiological and technical abilities.

A first step in this process is the assessment of elite athlete qualities to develop a model of success in particular events or sports. A number of longitudinal studies have been conducted to verify whether the proposed models have been successful in identifying talented athletes. More recently, experiential studies of talent identification and development involving case studies, interviews and personal histories have complemented the more traditional experimental approaches. These experiential studies provide a rich source of information and are often more accessible, personable and meaningful for coaches and athletes.

A recent study of cricket fast bowlers illustrates the experiential approach. Eleven international fast bowlers who cumulatively had taken more than 2,400 Test wickets in over 600 international Test matches were interviewed using an in-depth, open-ended and semistructured approach (Phillips et al., 2010). Qualitative data were analysed to identify key components in the development of fast bowling expertise.

Contrary to expectation that bowlers had followed a similar pathway of learning and development from junior to senior ranks, there was a wide range of development pathways. Coaches need a broad view on talent development, and there is no single pathway to success even in a given sport.

The interaction of physical, psychological, environmental and social factors is critical in producing elite-level performance. Extensive mental preparation, focus and commitment, clear goal setting, support from family or friends and opportunities to participate in high-level training programs are needed as athletes move through the talent development pathway. The sidebar about the Australian Football League details the league's highly regarded talent identification program.

The final sidebar details the talent transfer program for women's skeleton, an event on the Winter Olympic program. Although most talent transfer programs to date have focused on sports with lower participation numbers such as skeleton, rowing or sprint cycling, there are few apparent limitations on the choice of donor and recipient sports. Assessment of anthropometric and physiological characteristics has been the most common approach, but increasingly, the aptitude for the training and culture of the recipient sport is being addressed. Sports with common elements, such as somersaulting or acrobatics in gymnastics and aerial skiing or high-intensity paddling in surf ski and sprint canoeing, are obvious candidates for talent transfer.

IMPLEMENTING A TESTING PROGRAM

A testing or evaluation program needs to be well organised and managed to provide useful information. A good place to start is to examine the successful testing programs of other coaches in the sport. Coaches at the junior and senior levels who are willing to share their ideas and approaches to testing could be

---

AUSTRALIAN FOOTBALL LEAGUE NATIONAL DRAFT PROGRAM

The Australian Football League (AFL) has for 20 years conducted an annual draft program in which the best 18-year-old players in the country are chosen by each of the league teams in a centrally coordinated process. The national draft program culminates in the annual AFL Draft Combine, in which the top 120 players attend for medical and psychomotor screening, musculoskeletal assessment, psychometric testing of adolescent coping skills and resilience and anthropometric and fitness testing. The evaluation of players also includes video analyses of game performances; match reports from coaches, observers and managers in the recruiting network; and a face-to-face interview with coaches and team officials.

In the fitness testing program, players' test scores are presented as a percentile rank (from 0 to 100) to assist the clubs in comparing players. Position-specific reference ranges have been developed and benchmark scores (top 10 scores of all time) have been used widely to inform players and club officials. Given the large volume of test data and the various formats (digital video, numeric test results and written text), a sophisticated data management system has been implemented to generate individual player profiles and group summaries.

Talent transfer programs are designed to identify athletes in a variety of sports who might have the attributes necessary for success in a particular sport. Talent transfer has traditionally been a focus for lower-profile sports that often struggle to attract participants in a crowded sport calendar dominated by high-profile mainstream sports. However, even more popular sports, such as AFL, cast a wide net for potential champions from rival sports like basketball and international sources.

WOMEN'S SKELETON

The article 'Talent Identification and Deliberate Programming in Skeleton: Ice Novice to Winter Olympian in 14 Months' is a useful case study describing a successful talent transfer program (Bullock et al., 2009). The primary aim of the study was to transfer the talent of, rapidly develop and qualify an Australian female athlete in the skeleton event for the Winter Olympic Games.

Quantifying the volume of skeleton-specific training and competition undertaken through the program was a key aspect of the program. Initially, 26 female athletes (primarily from summer sprint-based sports) were recruited through a talent identification program based on their best 30-metre running sprint times.

Attendance at a selection camp revealed the 10 most suitable athletes, who then undertook an intensive skeleton training program. Four of these women were selected to compete on the world cup circuit for Australia. The athlete chosen to represent Australia at the Torino Winter Olympic Games had completed 300 start simulations and 220 training and competition runs over a period of 14 months.

The success of this case study highlights the importance of a well-targeted identification and development plan that integrates the physical, technical and tactical elements of a sport. An overlooked aspect is the importance of offering a pathway or opportunities for those athletes who don't make the final cut.

From http://www.ncbi.nlm.nih.gov/pubmed/19191166.

contacted. Local or state sporting associations and national organisations are other useful sources of information.

Upon completion of testing, the first step the coach needs to take is to decide which data or test results offer the most value and how they can be communicated to the athlete. Data can take the form of text in written reports; numeric values in a spreadsheet or database; and increasingly, digital video of testing, training and game activities. The following details should be included in the fitness testing report for a team sport:

- Player name, age, address and contact details
- Date, location and time of testing
- Sport or team details
- Name of coach
- Current test scores
- Previous test scores
- Magnitude of change from previous testing (improvement or decline)
- Group, team or squad averages
- Reference ranges where available
- Comments
- Test protocol details
- Scientist contact details

The visual presentation of results is important; most coaches and athletes prefer figures or charts rather than large tables of numeric data. One useful method for comparing an individual player's results with the team average is a Z-score chart. A Z-score indicates how many standard deviations a player's result is above or below the mean score for the team. Figure 8.2 shows a junior rugby league player who has excellent endurance and speed but is slightly below average in lean body mass.

The second step in managing the testing program is to determine who will have access to the data and test results. If the data are sensitive, such as medical, physiotherapy or psychology reports or contain important tactical and strategic information, password protection is critical to prevent unauthorised access. The organisation of the online data structure (naming the files and creating a hierarchical system of folders) is a key consideration. The best way to transfer and synchronise data

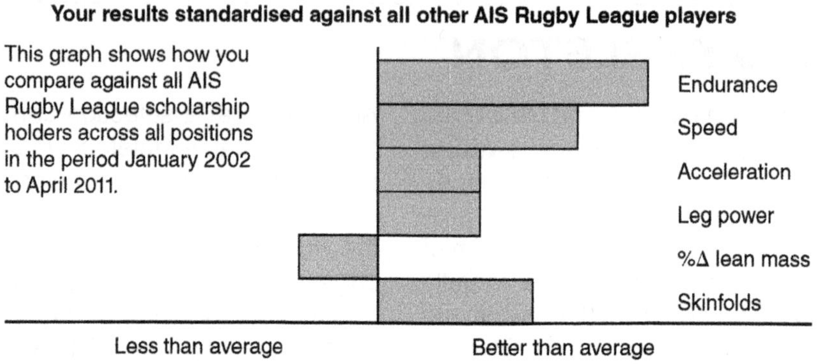

Your results standardised against all other AIS Rugby League players

This graph shows how you compare against all AIS Rugby League scholarship holders across all positions in the period January 2002 to April 2011.

Endurance
Speed
Acceleration
Leg power
%Δ lean mass
Skinfolds

Less than average   Better than average

Figure 8.2 A Z-score chart.

Reproduced by courtesy of the Australian Sports Commission.

between computers or systems should also be considered. At senior levels, coaches typically delegate the management of testing data to an administrator or to IT or support staff personnel. At junior levels, coaches or team managers or both generally have to manage the results themselves. Parents are a good source of support, and adults should keep in mind that these days young athletes often have a better grasp of computing and IT skills than their coaches, team managers and parents.

Other technical issues include choosing an appropriate file format(s) and software for the various types of digital data. Data should be stored on a server or in a data storage device or system. A backup system is probably the most important consideration in the management of testing data because hard drives on desktop and laptop computers can fail. Team and sporting organisations should have automated backup systems. An off-site backup is recommended if large amounts of valuable data have been captured, collated and stored. The hardware, software and time required for data management can be expensive and should be included in the team's or organisation's annual budget. The transfer or handover of key information is essential during the turnover of coaching or management staff.

SUMMARY

- Evaluations can yield important information about both junior and senior athletes.
- Athletes' physical capabilities, skills and techniques and levels of emotional development are key factors.
- Important attributes can be assessed in isolation or in actual or simulated sporting competition.
- Testing measures should relate to the specific requirements of the sport or event and the demands of competition.
- Age, gender and disabilities should be accounted for when appropriate.
- Talent identification, development and transfer programs are increasing in number and sophistication.
- A well-organised and well-managed evaluation program will yield useful short- and long-term benefits for the athletes, coach and sport.

REFERENCES AND RESOURCES

Beunen, G., & Malina, R.M. (1988). Growth and physical performance relative to the timing of the adolescent spurt. *Exercise and Sport Sciences Reviews, 16,* 503-540.

Bompa, T.O., & Haff, G.G. (2009). *Periodization: Theory and methodology of training.* Champaign, IL: Human Kinetics.

Bullock, N., Gulbin, J.P., Martin, D.T., Ross, A., Holland, T., & Marino, F. (2009). Talent identification and deliberate programming in skeleton: Ice novice to Winter Olympian in 14 months. *Journal of Sports Sciences, 27,* 397-404.

Mujika, I., Spencer, M., Santisteban, J., Goiriena, J.J., & Bishop, D. (2009). Age-related differences in repeated-sprint ability in highly trained youth football players. *Journal of Sports Sciences, 27,* 1581-1590.

Phillips, E., Davids, K., Renshaw, I., & Portus, M. (2010). The development of fast bowling experts in Australian cricket. *Talent Development & Excellence, 2,* 137-148.

Rampinini, E., Bishop, D., Marcora, S., Ferrari Bravo, D., Sassi, R., & Impellizzeri, F. (2007). Validity of simple field tests as indicators of match-related physical performance in top-level professional soccer players. *International Journal of Sports Medicine, 28,* 228-235.

Rechichi, C., Dawson, B., & Goodman, C. (2009). Athletic performance and the oral contraceptive. *International Journal of Sports Physiology and Performance, 4,* 151-162.

Stafford, I., & Balyi, I. (2010). Coaching for long-term athlete development. www.1st4sport.com/p-1122-1st4sport-com-coaching-for-long-term-athlete-development.aspx.

Tanaka, H., & Seals, D.R. (2008). Endurance exercise performance in Masters athletes: Age-associated changes and underlying physiological mechanisms. *Journal of Physiology, 586,* 55-63.

Thein-Nissenbaum, J.M., & Carr, K.E. (2011). Female athlete triad syndrome in the high school athlete. *Physical Therapy in Sport, 12,* 108-116.

Walsh, M.S., Bohm, H., Butterfield, M.M., & Santhosam, J.W. (2007). Gender bias in the effects of arms and countermovement on jumping performance. *Journal of Strength and Conditioning Research, 21,* 362-366.

CHAPTER 9

Designing a Training Program

—— Brian Dawson

The planning (or periodisation) of a training program involves adopting a sensible, logical and ordered approach to developing athletes and teams for competition, to maximise training gains and performance improvement. Although planning ahead might seem like a chore, not doing so results in an ad hoc and disorganised approach to training, which will guarantee suboptimal results. The importance of a planned and structured approach to training is reflected in two well-known coaching adages: *Failing to plan is planning to fail* and *Plan ahead for success; no plan is needed for failure.*

In designing a training program, coaches should first know and understand the technical, tactical, psychological, and fitness demands of the sport. Next, they must assess the strengths and weaknesses of their athletes so they can prescribe a training program that meets the requirements of the sport and their athletes' individual needs. An important consideration here is to develop (as much as possible) individualised training programs, rather than rely solely on group methods, which will invariably produce lesser outcomes.

PRINCIPLES OF TRAINING

A number of fitness training principles have evolved over many years, based both on scientific research and coaching experience. These include the principles of overload, recovery, specificity, reversibility and individuality, which provide the framework on which to plan a training program. For positive adaptation to fitness training to occur, sensible and suitable nutrition and sleep patterns must be in place, as outlined in figure 9.1. Coaches should always remember that although a training session provides the stimulus for athlete improvement, the adaptations that improve their athletic capacity occur between sessions, principally when sleeping and recovering.

OVERLOAD

Simply stated, to improve their present fitness level, or 'athletic shape', athletes must carefully and sensibly overload their current capacity in training. Exceeding the current fitness capacity introduces fatigue and strain to the body, which gradually adapts to cope with these increased demands. Therefore, applying overload to athletes is fundamental to improving their fitness.

The difficulty for coaches is in determining the degree of overload appropriate for each of their athletes. If the training stimulus applied is too weak, the body has no need to adapt and performance does not improve. Conversely, if the training stimulus is too strong, the body becomes chronically fatigued and unable to adapt, and performance worsens (see figure 9.2). In this situation, in the short term (one to two weeks) an athlete is said to be overreaching (failing to tolerate the training load), which can be corrected by appropriate rest and

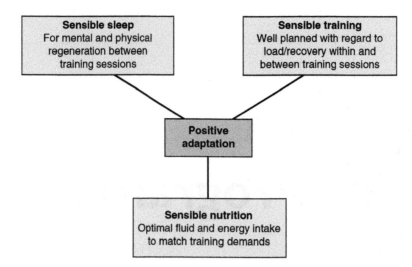

Figure 9.1 The conditions necessary for positive adaptation to training.

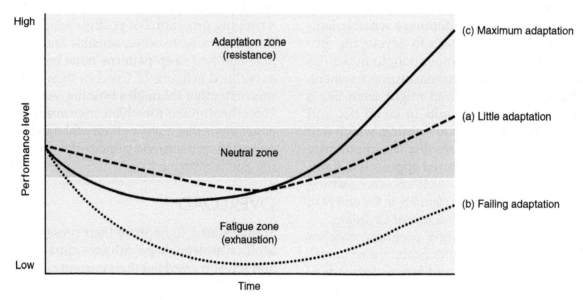

Figure 9.2 The performance of athletes under three different training loads.

Reprinted, by permission, from F. Pyke, 2001, *Better coaching: Advanced coach's manual*, 2nd ed. (Champaign, IL: Human Kinetics), 102.

recovery over a few weeks. However, if the training stimulus is too strong over a longer term (several weeks), the athlete may develop full-blown overtraining syndrome, which is seriously debilitating and may require months to years to recover from, and can often be career threatening.

Overload is a function of the volume (intensity and duration) and frequency of training sessions (as well as competition efforts). How the body adapts depends on how the sessions are planned and managed, as well as the starting fitness level of the athlete. In this regard, the following points are important:

- Stepwise increases (approximately 10 per cent at a time) in load should be applied gradually, usually across a training week, rather than within a training session.

- Training loads should be cyclic, with harder sessions or weeks alternated with lighter ones.

- Coaches must always carefully consider the fatigue level of each athlete. Other stressors, such as emotional disturbances, travel, missed sleep, poor diet and high altitude or hot climates can also contribute to fatigue.

RECOVERY

To gain optimal benefit from the training load applied, athletes must be given sufficient recovery time between training sessions; otherwise, fatigue gradually accumulates and the body does not adapt to the training stimulus, resulting in suboptimal performance. Therefore, the coach must plan recovery time and training sessions into the overall training program and ensure that athletes understand their importance. Because the training principles of overload and recovery are the two most important, and because they are complementary, they should be considered in tandem when planning a training program. The coaching adage *Work hard and recover well = best performance* appropriately sums up the interaction between these principles.

Another commonly used adage is *The harder I train, the luckier I get.* Although this is true to a point, unless hard, fatiguing training is cycled with low-intensity and recovery training sessions, the hard work will be in vain. This is because the body will not have the opportunity to recover and adapt, which is crucial to

UNDERLOADED WAIS UNDER-19 FOOTBALL PLAYER

Early in the competitive season, a midfield player for the Western Australia Institute of Sport (WAIS) was identified by his coach as lacking sufficient specific repeat effort fitness to perform at his best. With input from the WAIS sports science staff, the coach decided to increase the training load in a careful and prescribed manner over an eight-week period to improve the player's fitness. The increased training load equated to one extra 45- to 60-minute training session per week that consisted of high-intensity repeated interval efforts and short sprints interspersed with short, active recovery. Cold water immersion (10 °C, or 50 °F, for five minutes) was used after each session.

Examples of the training sets completed were as follows: four 90-second hard (80 to 90 per cent maximal effort) runs with 45 seconds of recovery between them and repeated two or three times, and eight 30-metre maximal sprints with 25 seconds of recovery between them and repeated two or three times.

The table that follows presents the changes that were noted from the start to the finish of the eight weeks. As noted, a reduction in body fat (skinfolds) and an increase in repeat effort fitness (yo-yo level 2 and repeat sprint test) occurred, and both coach and player agreed that match fitness and performance had improved markedly.

Measurements and tests	Start	Finish	Amount of change
Body mass (kg)	61.50	59.90	(Δ −1.6 Δkg)
Sum of seven skinfolds (mm)	113.2	97.8	(Δ −15.4 mm, −13.6%)
Yo-yo level 2*	16:2	17:3	(Δ +1:1, +7%)
Total time(s) for repeat sprint test (6 × 20 m on 20 sec)	21.41	20.85	(Δ −0.56 s, −2.6%)
Vertical jump (cm)	50	50	No change

*The yo-yo level 2 test involves repeated 20-metre shuttle efforts at gradually increasing speed until exhaustion, with a 10-second rest between shuttles.

improving performance. The following guidelines are useful when designing a program:

- Hard training sessions should be followed by lighter ones.
- Heavy weeks or phases of training should be followed by lighter ones.
- After every moderate-to-hard training session and competition, athletes should practise some form of postexercise recovery.
- Generally, recovery from running training takes longer than recovery from cycling or swimming training.

Recovery procedures such as cold and contrast water immersion have received much scientific attention in recent years, and most professional sporting clubs (e.g., the AFL and NRL) and sport institutes have dedicated facilities (e.g., cold baths, saunas, swimming pools) for these purposes. Cold water immersion is perhaps the most popular postexercise recovery procedure presently used by athletes to reduce inflammation and muscle spasm. Table 9.1 details several recovery methods available to athletes; one or more of these should be used regularly. However, which is best for promoting fast recovery after training is not yet known, and may well vary among individuals.

In addition to these methods, diet is extremely important in the recovery process. Adequate intake of protein, carbohydrate and fluid after training and competition is critical for tissue repair, muscle glycogen replenishment and fluid balance restoration. Having sufficient and good-quality sleep is also essential for full recovery. Sleep is the most powerful recovery procedure available to athletes, both for tissue repair and adaptation and mental regeneration and stabilisation. Coaches should encourage athletes to develop good sleeping habits. Table 9.2 provides an example of these recovery procedures as used during the competitive season for an AFL player.

A final example of the importance of the principle of recovery (and that the adage *More is better* does not apply) is illustrated by the improved performances of athletes following a tapering (or peaking) phase in training just prior to major competitions. In a taper, the volume of training is reduced (by about a third to a half of normal), but the intensity is maintained. Research evidence, plus the experience of many coaches and athletes, shows that this process enhances performance. When athletes have the opportunity to 'unload' from hard training, they gain both physical benefits (improved speed and power and aerobic efficiency) and psychological benefits (more positive mood states, less tension, more vigour) as fatigue levels in their bodies diminish.

SPECIFICITY

Strong scientific evidence underscores the fact that training should engage the specific muscles and actions involved in the sport most of the

Table 9.1 Common Postexercise Recovery Procedures

Recovery procedure	Likely effects
Active (10-30 min of low-intensity exercise)	Remove lactic acid, increase blood flow to muscles
Cold water immersion (10-15 °C for 5-15 min)	Reduce peripheral blood flow, inflammation, muscle spasm, pain
Compression garments (especially for travel and sleep)	Increase venous return and lymph drainage
Contrast water immersion (35-38 °C and 10-15 °C alternated for 1-2 min, repeated three to five times)	Reduce swelling and inflammation by alternating dilation and constriction of blood vessels
Massage (30 min—self or masseur)	Remove waste products, increase lymph drainage and muscle relaxation
Stretching (15-30 min on large-muscle groups)	May reduce muscle soreness, increase joint range of motion
Warm water immersion (35-40 °C for 5-15 min)	Increase body temperature and peripheral blood flow

Table 9.2 Daily Schedule for an AFL Player

This schedule assumes a seven-day break between games. The ratings of well-being are based on a 7-point scale, in which 1 is very, very good and 7 is very, very bad.

Day	Recovery or other activities	Rating of well-being
Saturday	• Away game (interstate travel: four-hour flight to get home) • Immediately postgame: carbohydrate/protein and fluid intake during coach debrief, then weighed to assess loss of body mass; small snack eaten while stretching, then cold water immersion (10 °C for 12 min) • Spaghetti meal at airport prior to flight for carbohydrate replacement • Compression garments used on plane, plus walk every hour • Upon return, sleep is a priority	6
Sunday	• After nine hours of sleep, 20 min walk/jog, then 30 min stretch followed by 1 min pool walking and 3 min cold water immersion (10 °C), repeated four times • Weight checked again • Afternoon nap encouraged	6
Monday	• AM training: light weights and mobility circuit • PM training: 15 min low-intensity skills • Contrast baths posttraining (38 °C and 10 °C alternating for 2 min each, repeated three times)	5
Tuesday	• Day off (complete same recovery as Sunday to accelerate recovery) • 20 min walk/jog, then 30 min stretch followed by 1 min pool walking and 3 min cold water immersion (10 °C), repeated four times	4
Wednesday	• 60 min high-intensity main training session followed by stretching and 12 min cold water immersion (10 °C)	3
Thursday	• 20 min light-intensity skills session, then active cool-down for 10 min • Increased carbohydrate intake	3
Friday	• 15 min moderate- to high-intensity session (match preparation) • High-carbohydrate diet • Increased fluid intake	2
Saturday	• Match	

time. This may suggest that the best form of training is performing the sport. However, although there is some logic to this, to prepare well for competition, athletes need to practise selected parts of a race (start and finish) or game situation (forward and defensive set-ups and ball movement) intensively in training. This allows for more (and many) high-quality repetitions than would normally occur in a race or game and is important for optimal training overload and performance improvement.

In considering the application of specificity, coaches should understand that for optimal development of the necessary performance capacities, the primary sporting movements and energy systems must be trained regularly. Put simply, swimmers must swim, cyclists must cycle and runners must run, so that the specific muscles are overloaded and provided with a training stimulus.

However, in some situations, what appears to be non-specific training may still be beneficial, particularly for providing variety in training, for recovery purposes, for fitness maintenance when injured and as foundation work for developing or maintaining base endurance. So-called cross-training (e.g., a runner performs swim or cycle training, which use quite different muscle groups to running) may still provide a training stimulus for central (heart-

Zuma Press/Icon SMI

Training for athletes, such as swimmer Stephanie Rice, must be specific to the sport to ensure development of performance capacities.

lung-blood) endurance adaptations, because heart rate and stroke volume remain elevated for long periods. However, the specific (calf) muscle fibres important for optimal running performance are not trained by these methods; muscle-specific adaptations require specific training. This is why the majority of the training program must consist of activities that are directly related to competition.

REVERSIBILITY

Essentially, the training principle of reversibility simply says, *Use it or lose it*. During enforced breaks due to injury or illness, the training adaptations developed within the body (both physical and mental) are gradually lost and must be redeveloped when the athlete recovers. Scientific studies have shown that over a two- to three-week period, endurance capacity declines by approximately 25 per cent (after bed rest) and 10 to 15 per cent (after injury-forced inactivity). Coaches and athletes must understand and respect the fact that training at the

same intensity and volume as before a lay-off is not possible, and attempting to do so may lead to unnecessary injury or soreness. Generally, it will also take at least the amount of time as the lay-off, but usually longer, to return to the previous level of endurance fitness after recommencing training.

Muscle strength and power have been found to decline more slowly (over several weeks) than endurance when training is interrupted. However, if a limb is immobilised because of injury, the principle of reversibility comes strongly into play, as demonstrated by the rapid loss in size and strength of the injured part. Injured athletes, following medical clearance, should be encouraged to maintain their endurance or strength and power by exercising other body parts or using other modes of training. For example, an Australian rules footballer with an ankle injury can work hard on swimming or cycling to maintain central (heart-lung-blood) endurance fitness, as well as upper-body strength and power, while unable to run or bear weight during recovery.

During the transition between seasons, fitness capacities may decline as athletes take a rest from normal training routines. During this period they should remain active, perhaps with some cross-training, to both recover from the specific demands of the season that just ended and prepare for the next preseason training phase. Athletes who are inactive during the off-season and gain weight often spend the preseason trying to regain their former fitness levels, rather than extending their capacities further; this limits their potential improvement. Athletes who return to training overweight and unfit also risk being overloaded and suffering injury as they try to keep pace with their peers during preseason training.

INDIVIDUALITY

Because athletes have their own strengths and weaknesses and their own individual anatomical, physiological and psychological make-ups, obviously they need individually tailored training programs for optimal development. However, because training athletes in groups is easier, the important training principle of individuality is often overlooked. Coaches must take the time to plan individual programs for their athletes to produce the best results.

Following are examples of why training programs need to be individualised:

- Some athletes respond better to hard training than others do, and therefore require less recovery time. Coaches must carefully consider how athletes handle training loads and how much recovery they need between sessions.
- Athletes with a low fitness base have greater potential for improvement than others, and younger athletes have greater potential for improvement than older athletes do.
- Some athletes are more affected than others by exposure to altitude, air pollution, or hot and humid climates (unacclimatised athletes especially), lessening their ability to cope with group-designed training programs.

- Family, social and work stressors affect an athlete's ability to tolerate a training load, which should be modified to compensate for these demands when necessary.
- Nutritional preferences can affect the ability to train. For example, vegetarians are more susceptible to iron deficiency, which can easily affect their endurance capacity. Heavy alcohol drinkers can develop a vitamin B1 deficiency, which will affect their energy production.
- Chronic and past injury can limit parts of a training program, because it may be unwise to risk further injury by attempting the full program. For example, rowers with previous lower back injuries may need to avoid weight programs involving heavy barbell squats.

PLANNING A TRAINING PROGRAM

The planning (or periodisation) of a training program involves dividing the training year (or season) into phases. In each phase one or more of the physical (or tactical and mental) requirements of the sport are emphasised, depending on the dates of major competitions. For sports such as swimming, cycling and track and field, working backwards from the date of the most important competition (e.g., national championships or Olympic Games) may be wise when planning the training program. In contrast, in team sports such as Australian football and rugby, which involve a five- to six-month competitive season, it may be more appropriate to frame the training program around the start of the season and then plan the in-season program accordingly.

The three main training phases in any annual plan are the preparation (preseason), competition (in-season) and transition (off-season) phases. Each of these has subphases, which have different training emphases as competition dates get closer. The phases and subphases of training are then further split into macrocycles (sometimes also called mesocycles), which are blocks of training generally extending over four to five weeks, and microcycles, which are typically one week long. As such, four or five microcycles make up one macrocycle.

The microcycle is the hub of the training program, because it involves all of the training sessions for the week. Generally, because the rate and degree of improvement and athletes' tolerance to training cannot always be accurately predicted, only one or two microcycles might be planned in advance. Coaches must be both flexible and sensible in applying the training program. By contrast, the macrocycles should always be planned in advance so there is a clear direction and purpose to the training block. Table 9.3 presents the typical training year, divided into its various phases, subphases and cycles.

PREPARATION PHASE (PRESEASON)

The prime objective in the preparation phase is to develop a sound fitness (endurance) and skill base on which the higher-intensity and specific sport training necessary for competition can be built. Most coaches and athletes agree that a good preseason training phase is key to a successful season. Having a good base should allow athletes to adapt more quickly and easily to higher-intensity training and to perform more consistently during the competition phase.

Three (or more) macrocycles are often involved in the preparation phase. One or two are allocated to the general preparation subphase, which usually involves a high volume of low- to moderate-intensity training. However, this will be progressively and gradually reversed in the following specific preparation subphase, in which one or two macrocycles emphasise higher-intensity and competition-specific training. Table 9.4 presents a typical macrocycle for an endurance runner during the preparation phase.

In table 9.4, the athlete has just begun to prepare for the next competitive season, so the goal of the macrocycle is to develop suitable base endurance (both cardiorespiratory and muscular). The training sessions are spaced over each microcycle (week) so there is only one training session per day; as well, the athlete runs on consecutive days only once (Friday and Saturday), which is followed by a recovery day. After the first two microcycles, more intensive running training (fartlek and anaerobic threshold) is gradually introduced to provide overload, in preparation for future (more intense) macrocycles.

Table 9.3 Sample Training Year

	Yearly plan																						
Phases of training	**Preparation (preseason)**													**Competition (in-season)**										
Subphases	General preparation									Specific preparation				Precompetitive (practice matches and events)					Competitive (weekly or regular competition)					
Macrocycles (months)	1					2				3				4					5					
Microcycles (weeks)	1	2	3	4	5	6	7	8	9	10	11	12	13	14	15	16	17	18	19	20	21	22		

To ensure a peak at the optimal time, the training phases in sports such as cycling need to be scheduled working back from the date of the most important competition.

																			Transition (off-season)									
																			Transition										
6					7					8				9				10				11				12				
23	24	25	26	27	28	29	30	31	32	33	34	35	36	37	38	39	40	41	42	43	44	45	46	47	48	49	50	51	52

Table 9.4 Typical Macrocycle in the Preparation Phase for a Club-Level 10K Runner

Type of training	Days											
	M	T	W	Th	F	Sa	S	M	T	W	Th	
Low-intensity aerobic training (long and slow)	X		X		X	X		X		X		
Fartlek training (mixed speed)												
Anaerobic threshold training (more intense)												
Endurance weight training (high reps, light loads)		X		X					X		X	
Recovery days (beach swim)							X					
Objectives	Develop base endurance: cardiorespiratory and muscle Minimise muscle soreness in first week						Develop base endurance: cardiorespiratory and muscle 10% increase in weekly km					
	Microcycle 1						Microcycle 2					

ASSESSING FUNCTIONAL FITNESS TO PLAY

The centre position in netball requires good aerobic capacity, good repeat effort ability and strong passing and receiving skills. A player who succeeds at this position will also have good decision-making skills. The following questions and sample answers provide an example of how a coach might assess a netball centre player to determine her functional fitness to play. These types of questions may be important in assessing whether the player is fit and capable to play in the aerobically demanding position of centre for the first round of the competitive season.

- Does she score as expected in endurance tests (e.g., 12 or more on 20-metre shuttle test)? *Yes, score has improved from level 10 shuttle 8 (two months ago) to level 12 shuttle 6.*

- Does she score as expected in repeat sprint fitness tests (e.g., improvement in her 6 × 20-metre total time)? *Yes, score has improved from 24.6 seconds (two months ago) to 23.4 seconds.*

- Are her skinfold and weight values acceptable (e.g., decreased since preseason training began)? *Yes, a sum of seven skinfolds and weight have reduced from 105 millimetres (4.1 in.) and 66 kilograms (146 lb) (two months ago) to 88 millimetres (3.5 in.) and 62.5 kilograms (138 lb).*

- Has the preseason training period been injury-free? *Yes, apart from one week of reduced training as a result of minor illness.*

- Are her passing and receiving skills and decision making at a high level? *Yes, but more improvement could be made.*

- Can she make position and recover quickly? *Yes, in practice matches this has been a strength.*

If the answers to any of these questions were no, the coach would want to consider other options for the game: perhaps a different player or plan to rotate players through the centre position.

	F	Sa	S	M	T	W	Th	F	Sa	S	M	T	W	Th	F	Sa	S
	X	X		X				X			X				X		
					X			X					X				
																X	
					X		X					X		X			
			X							X							X
				Develop base endurance: cardiorespiratory and muscle Introduce fartlek training for pace change 10% increase in weekly km Increase reps by five for weight training							Develop base endurance: cardiorespiratory and muscle Introduce anaerobic threshold training for higher quality						
				Microcycle 3							Microcycle 4						

COMPETITION PHASE (IN-SEASON)

In the competition phase, the objective is to develop not only the specific fitness of the athlete, but also the technical, tactical and mental requirements for optimal performance. Training is generally of high intensity and quality in this phase and involves periods of tapering prior to competition, which may be either for a few of the most important events in individual sports, or weekly for team games.

The precompetitive subphase of training normally comprises one macrocycle and has the goal of achieving peak athletic shape for competition. Practice events or games occur during this subphase, which must be factored into the overall training plan. The competitive subphase usually lasts for several months and many macrocycles and may involve semiregular competitions or weekly contests.

Because of the rigours of competition, training in the competition phase is designed to maintain (rather than improve) fitness; other performance elements such as skill, psychol-ogy and strategy may receive more emphasis. Because of the regular competitive efforts required, recovery and good sleep and nutritional practices are also very important in this phase. The coach must be flexible and adaptable in planning each weekly microcycle, taking into account the recent competition results. Table 9.5 presents an example of a typical microcycle for an Australian footballer during the competition (in-season) phase.

The objective of the microcycle in table 9.5 is to promote good recovery from the previous game and to prepare well for the next one. The microcycle presented here is a moderate-intensity week, being the third in a four-week block of training leading up to a bye in the middle of the season. Squad training is spread across three days (Tuesday, Thursday and Friday) with a full recovery day (Wednesday) separating the two most intense sessions. There is a heavy emphasis on recovery procedures (cold and contrast water immersion, stretching, massage and compression garments) throughout the week. There is also a 'mini taper' at the end of the week, prior to the Saturday game.

Table 9.5 In-Season Microcycle for an Elite Midfield Australian Football Player

Day	Time	Activity	Training/focus
Sunday	AM	Walk/jog 15 min on grass	
		Swim 500 m (easy) Cold water immersion at 10 °C for 10 min	Cross-training and recovery
	PM	Afternoon nap	
Monday	AM	Gym: 40 min Weights: 2 or 3 sets of 6 to 10 repetitions of 6 to 8 exercises	Resistance and muscular strength and power
		Cold water immersion (10 °C) for 10 min	Recovery
	PM	Strategy meeting: 50 min Team meeting (whole squad): 30 min Review of previous game and early focus on next opponent. Line meeting (midfield players): 20 min. Review of midfield impact in previous game and early focus on next opponent.	Strategy and skill and tactics
Tuesday	AM	Team meeting (whole squad): 20 min	Strategy: confirm things to practise during training
		Squad training: 45-60 min Skills and game play and conditioning involving three or four drills with footballs and tackle pressure in one or two drills	Interval training with ball; repeat efforts and skills
		Contrast water immersion (38 °C and 10 °C for 2 min each, repeated three times)	Recovery
	PM	Squad training: 80 min Specific skills, 30 min: general kicking, kicking for goal, marking	Individual and team skill practice
		Flexibility, 30 min: 8 to 10 stretches held for 30 to 40 s and repeated twice for each major muscle group	Static stretching and joint range of motion
		Massage, 20 min: focus on legs	Massage and recovery
Wednesday		No training; may choose optional activities (boxing, cycling and swimming)	Cross-training or recovery
Thursday	AM	Team meeting (whole squad): 20 min	Strategy: focus on opponent's style of play
		Squad training: 45-60 min Skills and game play and conditioning involving two or three drills with footballs and shadow pressure. Focus on clean, skilled ball movement.	Interval training with ball; repeat efforts and skills
		Cold water immersion (10 °C for 5 min)	Recovery
	PM	Gym: 40 min Weights: 2 or 3 sets of 6 to 10 repetitions of 6 to 8 exercises	Resistance and muscular strength and power
		High-carbohydrate snack and fluid	Glycogen loading
		Fly east for game (wear compression garments)	
Friday	PM	High-carbohydrate diet	Glycogen loading
		Squad training: 30 min 2 or 3 drills with emphasis on touch and skills and no pressure	Interval training with ball and game readiness
		Strategy meeting: 50 min Team meeting (whole squad), 30 min: focus on opposition and own game style Line meeting (midfield players), 20 min: focus on match-ups	Strategy and tactics
		Massage, 20 min: focus on legs	Massage and recovery
Saturday	AM	Walk/jog 15 min	Loosen up and wake up
		High-carbohydrate diet	Glycogen loading
	PM	Game: 4 hours (including warm-up and recovery) Total distance ~13.6 km; number of high-intensity efforts (≤15 km/h) ~295; number of high-intensity sprints (≥20 km/h) ~77	Competition—repeated, very hard efforts and skills
		High-carbohydrate/protein snack and fluid	Recovery
		Stretching for 15 min	Recovery
		Cold water immersion (10 °C for 10 min)	Recovery
		Fly west to home (wear compression garments)	

TRANSITION PHASE (OFF-SEASON)

The main objective of the transition phase is to maintain a reasonable level of fitness while enjoying a break from the physical and mental rigours of training and competing. It is also a time to treat niggling injuries without the need to continue to train and play. The transition phase may last one to three months, and macrocycles involving cross-training for exercise variety, as 'active rest', should be encouraged during this phase. Specific weaknesses in an athlete's profile, such as lack of skill on the non-preferred side, joint flexibility or upper-body strength can also receive intensive attention without interference from other modes of training.

Although the transition phase is extremely important in allowing athletes to become refreshed and re-energised prior to commencing training for the next season, it is vital that they return to training in reasonable athletic shape; otherwise, much of the next preseason training phase will be wasted in merely returning to their previous fitness levels. For ongoing performance improvement, stepwise increments in athletic shape must occur from one year to the next.

TRAINING PROGRAM ELEMENTS

This chapter has covered all the key principles of training and explained how a program should be implemented in phases through the year. The danger of such a presentation is that coaches may perceive periodisation as something to be implemented in a very mechanistic manner, with little room for judgement or modification.

Indeed, any successful program places a priority on athletes' needs, abilities and interests. Moreover, athletes should take PRIDE in engaging in and completing the program. Therefore, when constructing a sport training program, coaches should remember to account for the following:

- *P* is for *planning*. To ensure progress and the achievement of desired development, training sessions need forethought. Each training block should build on the next.

- *R* is for *responsibility*. Where possible, athletes should be involved in decisions about the training program and competition preparation. Giving them input into the decision-making process will increase their sense of ownership and commitment to the program.

- *I* is for *injury*, which is likely to occur at some point. Coaches must exercise due care and minimise injury risk wherever possible, and also not rush injured athletes back into training before they are cleared by qualified medical personnel.

- *D* is for *development*. A training program can arm athletes with many life-enhancing skills such as the ability to set goals; manage time; handle adversity; and persevere through fatigue, muscle soreness and training plateaus. The long-term development of athletes is what matters most.

- *E* is for *education*. As a result of the program, athletes should be knowledgeable about the requirements of the sport. This knowledge should include information about nutrition and fluids, injury prevention and treatment, mental preparation and recovery procedures.

SUMMARY

- The planning (or periodisation) of training programs is fundamental to achieving optimal performance improvement.
- The training principles of overload, recovery, specificity, reversibility and individuality provide the framework for planning a training program.
- Overload should be applied gradually with small (~10 per cent) increases applied across a full training week.
- Training should be cyclic with harder sessions and weeks alternating with lighter ones.
- Recovery procedures must be incorporated into the training program, and athletes should be instructed about their importance.
- Coaches should always consider the fatigue levels of athletes, watching for signs of failing adaptation to training (overtraining).
- Training programs should be individually planned.

REFERENCES AND RESOURCES

Martens, R. (2004). *Successful coaching* (3rd ed.). Champaign, IL: Human Kinetics.

Pyke, F.S. (Ed.). (2001). *Better coaching* (2nd ed.). Canberra, ACT: Australian Sports Commission. Reaburn, P., & Jenkins, D. (Eds.). (1996). *Training for speed and endurance.* Brisbane, QLD: Allen and Unwin.

Rushall, B., & Pyke, F.S. (1990). *Training for sports and fitness.* Melbourne, VIC: MacMillan.

Whipp, P. (Ed.). (2010). *Physical Education Studies 3A-3B.* Perth, WA: UWA Publishing.

CHAPTER 10

Implementing Training Methods

——— Peter Reaburn

Once a training program has been designed for an athlete, a key determinant of its success will be how it is implemented. Clear and effective explanations and instructions, complete and easy-to-follow schedules, useful forms or other recording tools to track adherence and improvement, and careful monitoring of technique are just some of the key elements in making the training program a success.

This chapter provides a quick look at the many training methods used in a training program to develop athletes. It presents both scientifically based guidelines and specific details on developing endurance, speed, strength, power and flexibility. Examples are presented from a wide range of sports to help coaches understand the universal and activity-specific approaches that work best.

ENDURANCE TRAINING

Endurance is the ability to last. Running a marathon, racing 40 kilometres (25 miles) on a bike, competing in a six-minute rowing race and swimming 1,500 metres all require the capacity to finish the event. Team players such as basketball, netball, hockey and football players also need endurance, not only to last the game, but also to recover from sprints during the game, from game to game at a daylong event or on successive days at a major competition.

Five factors determine endurance abilities: genetics (75 per cent of endurance or aerobic capacity is genetic), gender (females generally have a 10 per cent lower aerobic capacity than males), body composition (the need for low body fat), age (aerobic capacity drops 0.5 per cent per year in athletes over 35 years) and training (aerobic capacity can increase about 25 per cent depending on the level of aerobic fitness at the start of a program).

Sports science has conclusively shown that training for endurance means developing a number of specific physiological characteristics, each of which is trainable. Through the correct training techniques, athletes can adapt their bodies to maximise each of the following factors:

- **Maximal oxygen uptake ($\dot{V}O_2$max), or aerobic capacity.** $\dot{V}O_2$max is the maximal amount of oxygen that can be transported to and consumed by an athlete's working tissues. Historically, it was thought (and still is by many coaches!) that $\dot{V}O_2$max was the most critical factor in endurance. Although it is important, a far better predictor of endurance performance is what percentage of that $\dot{V}O_2$max can be maintained for the duration of an event—in other words, the anaerobic threshold. Training at, near and above anaerobic threshold raises $\dot{V}O_2$max.

- **Anaerobic threshold.** This is the percentage of the athlete's $\dot{V}O_2$max that can be used at race pace—the 'hurt but hold' intensity. Top marathoners and road cyclists can maintain 80 to 85 per cent of their $\dot{V}O_2$max, whereas less elite athletes can sustain only 70 to 75 per cent of their $\dot{V}O_2$max for the same distance. Training at or near anaerobic threshold raises both $\dot{V}O_2$max and anaerobic threshold.

- **Fatigue resistance.** This is the ability of an endurance athlete to maintain pace during endurance exercise. A major adaptation to long-duration, low-intensity endurance training is fatigue resistance.

- **Economy of motion.** This is the oxygen cost required to maintain a specific speed. Elite endurance athletes use better technique and up to 15 per cent less oxygen to maintain the same pace as recreational athletes. Technique training is critical in improving economy. Long, slow distance training, drills and goal-pace training all improve economy. For example, if a 10K runner wants to complete the distance in 40 minutes, then a set of 400- or 800-metre runs at a four-minute per kilometre pace should be part of the training program.

- **Fuel usage.** At higher race speeds, athletes rely more on carbohydrate than on fat as a fuel for energy production. However, well-trained endurance athletes can make greater use of fats as a fuel during racing than less-trained athletes, thereby conserving valuable liver and muscle carbohydrate (glycogen) stores. Long, slow distance training increases the ability of the body to burn fat and thus conserve glycogen stores.

ENDURANCE PERFORMANCE TRAINING

One of the most common and scientifically correct ways to train endurance is to use heart rate monitoring. This is because science has shown a direct relationship between heart rate and exercise intensity. To use the heart rate training zones outlined here, coaches must know the athlete's maximal heart rate (MHR). Historically, the following formula was used to estimate MHR:

$$MHR = 220 - age\ 10\ beats/min$$

Recently, a new formula has been developed and validated for use by healthy adults:

$$MHR = 208 - (0.7 \times age)\ beats/min$$

However, research and experience tells us that the MHR of individuals varies greatly. Thus, coaches who do not know the exact MHR of their athletes either under- or overestimate the training intensities they need. MHR can vary within a person depending on the following factors:

- **Muscle mass used.** In general, the larger the muscle mass, the higher the MHR, meaning that a triathlete's MHRs for swimming, biking and running may be different, or a swimmer may have a higher MHR for butterfly than for freestyle.

- **Body position.** In general, the more an athlete's heart works against gravity, the higher the MHR, meaning a triathlete may have a lower MHR when swimming than when running.

- **Water pressure.** Deep-water running generally lowers MHR compared to the same action on land.

- **Drug use.** Drugs can affect an athlete's MHR. For example, a type of blood pressure drug called beta-blockers reduces the ability of the heart to beat quickly. This may be a factor in older athletes.

Although a sport-specific MHR test in a laboratory at a university, academy or institute of sport is the recommended method for endurance athletes, the following field tests can be used to determine MHR:

- **Step test.** After warming up well, the athlete does 10 continuous one-minute increases in intensity starting easy and gradually building until the last effort is all-out. Examples include runners doing ten 400-metre runs; swimmers doing ten 100-metre swims; cyclists starting in low gears and increasing gearing every minute on a wind trainer; and rowers or kayakers increasing ergometer stroke ratings, wattage or time per 500 metres or gradual increases in rating and pressure within the boat.

- **Two 4-minute efforts.** After warming up, an athlete does an all-out four-minute effort (e.g., 1-kilometre run; 300- to 400-metre swim; timed effort on a bike, wind trainer or ergometer), has a two-minute recovery and then goes again.

Athletes doing MHR tests should wear heart rate monitors and follow the test with a cool-down.

ENDURANCE TRAINING ZONES

Sports science has shown that as athletes exercise harder, their heart rates increase in direct proportion to the speed or power at which they achieved MHR. MHR, velocity at $\dot{V}O_2$max ($v\dot{V}O_2$max) or power output at $\dot{V}O_2$max can be measured using a heart rate monitor, GPS or power meter, respectively. Once coaches know this, they can use table 10.1 to establish training zones.

For the endurance athlete, the vast majority of training should be in zones 2 through 4 with spikes of zones 5 through 7 depending on the training phase. When using heart rate zones and a heart rate monitor, coaches should remember that heart rates are higher when athletes exercise in hot or humid conditions. Research suggests that heart rates can increase by 1.4 per cent for each degree above 21 °C (70 °F). For example, at a constant pace, a heart rate of 140 at 21 °C (70 °F) becomes 160 at 31 °C (88 °F).

Zone 1 is the recovery zone and can be achieved using the sport the athlete is training for or some other method such as water running. The intensity is low and the duration is short. This type of 'training' is useful after racing or hard training sessions such as those at zones 5, 6 or 7 or when the athlete feels that it's time to lighten the load.

Zone 2 is the minimal intensity required to achieve an endurance training response. The beginner endurance athlete might start out at 65 per cent of MHR, but as fitness improves or the years accumulate, the intensity required to gain adaptations will increase to 70 to 75 per cent of MHR. This is commonly called LSD (long, slow distance), or conversation pace, training.

Zone 3, together with zone 2, forms the basis of endurance training and should be performed for a minimum of 30 minutes depending on the event being trained for. Obviously, an ironman or long-distance triathlete would need to spend many more hours of zone 2 training than an Olympic distance triathlete. Zone 3 training is done at 75 to 80 per cent of MHR for long periods. Examples are 10- to 30-kilometre (6.2- to 18.6-mile) runs, 40- to 120-kilometre (25- to 75-mile) bicycle rides, 5- to 15-kilometre (3.1- to 9.3-mile) rows or 1,500- to 3,000-metre swims, or longer sets of intervals around this intensity.

Zone 4 training is performed just below anaerobic threshold (80 to 85 per cent of MHR). Because the intensity is lifted, the duration is reduced. Examples are 5- to 20-kilometre (3.1- to 12.4-mile) runs, 30- to 80-kilometre (18.6- to 50-mile) bicycle rides, 5- to 10-kilometre (3.1- to 6.2-mile) rows or more intense intervals. Importantly, the intensity is just below the 'hurt but

Table 10.1 Endurance Training Intensities

Zone	Name	% MHR	%v$\dot{V}O_2$max	% Max Power	RPE (1-10)
1	Recovery	< 65%	< 65%	< 65%	2 (Very light)
2	Aerobic	65-75%	65-75%	65-75%	3 (Fairly light)
3	Extensive endurance	75-80%	75-80%	75-80%	3 (Somewhat hard)
4	Intensive endurance	80-85%	80-85%	80-85%	4 (Moderately hard)
5	Anaerobic threshold	85-92%	85-90%	85-90%	5 (Hard)
6	Maximal aerobic	> 92%	> 90%	> 90%	7 (Extremely hard)
7	Speed	Not applicable	> 100%	> 100%	Not applicable

MHR = maximal heart rate; v$\dot{V}O_2$max = velocity at $\dot{V}O_2$max; RPE = rating of perceived exertion hold' anaerobic threshold intensity and is thus often described as 'strong but comfortable'.

It is difficult to understand how training at large volumes below planned race pace can prepare athletes for racing (zones 5 and 6), unless the athletes are marathoners or long-distance triathletes. Athletes must therefore undertake some training at anaerobic threshold, or zone 5. This type of training exposes the body to sustained exercise corresponding to the endurance athlete's highest current steady state pace—the 'hurt but hold' pace. The intensity of training is elevated to 85 to 92 per cent of MHR and can be done through continuous work of at least 15 minutes but no longer than 90 minutes, such as in 5- to 20-kilometre (3.1- to 12.4-mile) runs, 20- to 60-kilometre (12.4- to 37.2-mile) bicycle rides or 4,000- to 5,000-metre swims. After 90 minutes (or less), the working muscles can run out of carbohydrate.

Another form of zone 5 training is interval training with short recoveries that are half or less of the work time, such as 15 to 20 100-metre swims, 15 to 20 1-kilometre (0.6-mile) bicycle rides and 8 to 10 400-metre runs. It is critical with anaerobic threshold intervals that the quality of the last interval be as good as the quality of the first, and the recovery between intervals must remain relatively short compared to the interval duration. This type of training should be performed at the most twice per week, should be preceded by a good warm-up and followed by a longer cool-down and generally be preceded and followed by an easier day or training session (zone 1 or 2).

Anaerobic threshold is the most important quality for an endurance athlete—even more important than $\dot{V}O_2$max. The higher the anaerobic threshold relative to $\dot{V}O_2$max, the better the athlete will race. Research has shown that both interval training and medium-long continuous sessions elevate both anaerobic threshold and $\dot{V}O_2$max. Anaerobic threshold intervals should have the heart rate elevating 5 to 10 beats above the anaerobic threshold heart rate (approx 85 to 92 per cent of MHR) during the interval and recovering to 10 to 20 beats below during recovery. Figure 10.1 shows an example of how the heart rate increases and decreases during work and recovery when performing anaerobic threshold interval training.

The principle of specificity (see chapter 9) says that athletes should train the way they race. That generally means continuous workouts for endurance athletes. Continuous anaerobic threshold workouts should be 15 to 20 minutes plus in length, and the intensity should be held at that 'hurt but hold' pace. Theoretically, there is not enough carbohydrate in the muscles and liver to go longer than 90 minutes at this pace, unless the athlete is well trained or uses sports drinks or gels to keep up the energy supply.

Zone 6, or maximal aerobic ($\dot{V}O_2$max) training, employs intervals with speeds that are greater than planned race pace but with long recoveries. The overall training volume during such a session is reduced, but the intensity is lifted. Examples are three- to eight-minute repeats (300- to 400-metre swims, 3- to

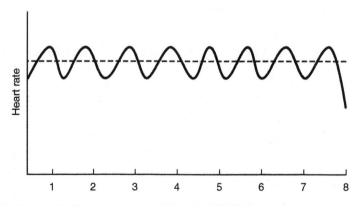

Figure 10.1 Heart rate during anaerobic threshold interval training.

5-kilometre [1.9- to 3.1-mile] reps on the bike, 1-kilometre [0.6-mile] reps on the running track) with two- to five-minute active recoveries (easy swim, spin or jog).

In zone 6, intensity is 90 to 100 per cent of MHR for each interval, but recovery intensity is down to 60 to 70 per cent of MHR. Athletes should be well warmed up and build into the first 10 to 20 seconds of each interval. Repetitions depend on individual tolerances, but 4 to 10 reps would be suggested depending on the athlete's training age (years of training), fitness level and predisposition to injury. At the most, two sessions of zone 6 per week should be used with easy recovery work in between.

Zone 7, or speed work (e.g., 3- to 20-second all-out efforts with long recoveries), is done in short bursts once or twice a week depending on the training phase. Two or more days of recovery at lower-intensity zones are needed for recovery because muscle damage is likely, especially in larger athletes and runners.

ENDURANCE DEVELOPMENT FOR TEAM SPORTS

Most team sports require the development of speed, strength and power and endurance. However, often the development of one of these components can inhibit the development of another. Therefore, the coach needs to periodise athletes' training so that each capacity can be optimally developed.

Research has shown that doing strength and endurance training together can reduce the development in strength with no effects

Imaginechina via AP Images

Athletes in highly aerobic team sports, such as soccer, must train strategically to develop the required endurance.

on endurance performance. Limited research has examined combined sprint and endurance training, but suggests that a combination of both sprint and endurance training leads to not only good gains in speed, but also gains in aerobic performance. From a practical point of view, these results suggest that training in highly aerobic team sports, such as hockey, soccer, Australian rules and depending on player position rugby league, rugby union and netball, should place a strong emphasis on endurance development through a combination of sprint and endurance training.

Based on the preceding results, plus knowledge of physiology and training theory, a team coach wanting to maximise athletes' speed, endurance and strength might consider the following guidelines:

- Sprint training should be completed at the start of a training session when the athletes are fresh.

- Strength training should be completed in the evening following at least 48 hours' rest since the previous session for the particular muscle groups used.

- Endurance training should be periodised so that the time between endurance sessions and strength or speed sessions are long enough to allow appropriate recovery.

Table 10.2 provides a sample preseason weekly training schedule for a team sport player completing speed, strength and endurance training concurrently. Table 10.3 provides a sample in-season weekly training schedule for a team sport player completing speed, strength and endurance training concurrently.

SPEED TRAINING

Speed and power are critical for success in racing sports (swimming, cycling and running); all field and court sports; acrobatic, racquet, combative and bat and ball sports; and power sports such as track and field. Speed is the distance covered divided by the time it takes to cover that distance. In sports such as swimming and running, the speed occurs in a straight line. However, speed for a touch, netball or water polo player may also mean changing direction while moving.

The following types of speed need to be defined and trained differently. Table 10.4 suggests which of the types of speed are important for which sports.

- **Maximal speed** is the highest speed an athlete can reach. This normally occurs three to five seconds after a start from a stationary position.

Table 10.2 Preseason Training Schedule for Concurrent Speed, Strength and Endurance Training

	Monday	Tuesday	Wednesday	Thursday	Friday	Saturday	Sunday
AM	Endurance	Rest	Endurance	Rest	Endurance	Rest	Rest
PM	Strength	Flexibility, speed and skill	Strength	Flexibility, speed and skill	Strength	Endurance or flexibility and speed	Rest

Table 10.3 In-Season Training Schedule for Concurrent Speed, Strength and Endurance Training

	Monday	Tuesday	Wednesday	Thursday	Friday	Saturday	Sunday
AM	Rest	Rest	Endurance	Rest	Rest	Rest	Rest
PM	Speed, skill and endurance	Flexibility and strength	Rest	Flexibility and strength	Speed and skill	Game	Rest

- **Acceleration speed** in sports such as touch, netball, basketball, football and tennis is crucial. These are sports in which short sprints are done and maximal speed may not be reached. The ability to get into space, get off the mark or take a gap is more important than maximal speed in these sports.

- **Speed endurance** is the ability to sustain maximal speed or near-maximal speed and to withstand the effects of fatigue. Events longer than five seconds (e.g., 100- to 400-metre runs, 50- to 100-metre swims) and team sports (e.g., touch, netball, basketball, water polo) and individual sports (e.g., tennis, squash, badminton), in which the time between sprints isn't long enough to recover, require high levels of speed endurance.

- **Change-of-direction speed** is crucial in most team and racquet sports. The ability to evade or chase an opponent in team sports and change direction quickly in racquet sports requires agility as well as acceleration speed.

DEVELOPING SPEED

It is beyond the scope of this chapter to give a specific formula for developing speed in every athlete of every age and gender for every sport. However, the following guidelines can help develop speed in any athlete of any age or ability:

- **Be fresh.** All speed training should be performed when the body is fully recovered from a previous event or training session. Tired, sore or overtrained athletes cannot improve their speed.

- **Master correct technique.** Correct sprinting technique is developed through many repetitions to reinforce skill development. Initially, this should be done at slower speeds, but then the speed should be gradually increased while maintaining correct form. Sport-specific drills are an excellent means of developing correct sprint technique. (See the References and Resources section at the end of the chapter.)

- **Warm up with intensity.** A warm-up should include low-intensity work that develops a light sweat, followed by static (holding) then dynamic (swinging, bouncing) stretching of the specific joints and muscles used in the sport or event. This should be followed by specific drills and then gradually increasing intensity to the speed required in training.

- **Recover between efforts.** All sets and repetitions of a speed training session must be followed by adequate recovery so the next effort is high quality. The shorter the effort is, the shorter the rest should be. As a general rule, a 1:4 to 1:6 work-to-recovery ratio is recommended.

- **Vary the training.** Speed training sessions should vary among light, medium and heavy days.

Table 10.4 Relative Importance of Speed Types for Common Sports

Sports	Maximal speed	Acceleration speed	Speed endurance	Change-of-direction speed
Tennis, squash, badminton	1	3	2	3
Basketball, netball, touch	1	3	3	3
Soccer, rugby union, rugby league, Australian rules	3	3	3	3
Swimming, cycling, running	3	2	3	NA

1 = minor importance; 2 = some importance; 3 = major importance; NA = not applicable

- **Monitor training volume.** Coaches should track the total distance covered during each maximal speed training session to ensure a gradual progression in distance or number of repeats.

- **Develop speed endurance with longer intervals or shorter rests.** Doing longer intervals (e.g., 150- to 400-metre runs, 50- to 100-metre swims or 30- to 60-second bike efforts) or decreasing the rest between shorter intervals (10- to 20-metre runs, 12.5- to 25-metre swims or 5- to 10-second bike efforts) develops speed endurance. The aim should be sport specificity. Obviously, a touch football player needs to do short sprints up and back with short recoveries, but after, say, six 10-metre efforts, a long rest of two to three minutes might be taken so the quality of the next set of six 10-metre efforts is high.

- **Develop strength and power.** The sprint athlete needs to focus on developing muscle mass, strength and power in the gym or using resistance and exercises that are sport specific (see the section Strength and Power Training).

- **Include flexibility training.** Decreased flexibility results in decreased speed due to the stride or stroke length decreasing.

With these principles in mind, let us now examine a six-step progressive model for developing speed in competitive athletes.

1. **Basic training.** Developing a training base early in a season, during the transition phase between seasons or in the off-season gives an athlete a foundation on which to develop speed and power without getting injured. Stretching, strengthening, skill drills and the development of some endurance should be keys.

2. **Functional strength and power.** Developing muscle mass, strength and power in the gym under the guidance of a strength and conditioning specialist should be a priority. The Strength and Power Training section later in this chapter outlines the guidelines for developing these attributes.

3. **Plyometric training.** This step focuses on hopping, jumping, bounding, hitting and kicking exercises that must be explosive and sport specific. Donald Chu's *Jumping into Plyometrics* (1998) and *Explosive Power and Strength* (1996), and *Training for Speed, Agility, and Quickness* by Lee E. Brown and Vance A. Ferrigno (2005) are excellent resources for sport-specific exercises with great diagrams and descriptions of exercises and drills. Plyometric training should be undertaken only by athletes with a high training age or a well-developed base of strength and power training in the gym.

4. **Sport loading.** This step focuses on sport- or event-specific speed and loading the athlete with relatively light resistance that develops speed and power without changing sprinting form. Speeds should be 85 to 100 per cent of maximum. The ways to increase resistance include weighted vests, harnesses, parachutes, uphill sprinting, stairs, sand, weighted sleds and drag suits for running athletes; leg ties, buckets or tethers for swimmers; large gears, slow cadences, headwinds and hills for cyclists; and tyre tubes for rowers.

5. **Sprinting form and speed endurance.** This phase develops sprinting technique and the ability to maintain speed by using longer sprint repeats.

6. **Overspeed training.** This phase involves applying 5 to 10 per cent extra speed through the use of overspeed training techniques such as downhill sprints, harnesses, elastic bands, fins in swimming or low gears in cycling. The aim is to train the nervous system to increase stride rate in runners, stroke rate in swimmers and rowers and cadence in cyclists.

SPEED TRAINING METHODS

Numerous training methods can develop speed, acceleration, speed endurance and agility speed in team and racquet sports. Table 10.5 presents general principles for developing maximal speed, acceleration, speed endurance and agility speed. Brown and Ferrigno (2005)

Table 10.5 Program Variables for Developing Maximal Speed, Acceleration, Speed Endurance and Agility Speed

Variable	Maximal speed	Acceleration speed	Speed endurance		Agility speed
Intensity (%)	95-105	100	95-100		100
Interval length (seconds)	2-5	2-5	2-5	10-60	2-5
Rest between intervals	Complete (2-3 min)	Complete (2-3 min)	30-90 s	3-8 min	Complete (2-3 min)
Number of intervals	6-12	6-12	3-10		6-12
Start method	Flying	Stationary or slow walk	Not applicable		Various but sport specific
Frequency (times per week)	2	2 or 3	2 or 3		2 or 3
Base qualities	Aerobic and power	Strength and aerobic	Speed and aerobic		Speed and aerobic

offer some excellent drills for each of these methods and, in particular, agility drills that can be used or adapted to any sport.

Sprint-Assisted Training (Overspeed Training) Various types of sprint-assisted training all aim to increase leg or arm frequency and thus speed. For sprint runners this might include downhill running (<3 per cent grade), being towed by a partner attached to an elastic or inelastic cord, treadmill sprinting or high-speed stationary cycling. Cyclists may use drafting behind a motorbike or high-cadence work. Swimmers may use elastic tubing or flippers or have the coach or a training device pull a hip harness or tethers.

Speed should only be increased by approximately 5 per cent because more than that increases the risk of injury or of developing poor technique. Distances should be short, warm-ups and stretching and cool-downs should be longer and the number of intervals should be reduced. Overspeed training is recommended for athletes with a higher training age and good technique, core strength, balance and specific strength. The guidelines for this type of training are as follows:

- Athletes should warm up with walk-jog-stride-sprint cycles, then specific static and dynamic stretches, followed by a repeat of

the walk-jog-stride-sprint cycle. (Cyclists should replace *walk* with *cycle*.)

- Athletes should focus on correct technique and strong communication with the coach.
- Towing should be done on a grassy surface.
- Overspeed training should occur at the start of the training session, when the athlete is fresh.

The *Sports Speed* book by Dintiman, Ward and Tellez (1998) is an excellent resource for overspeed training programs for runners.

Acceleration Sprints Acceleration sprints gradually increase from a rolling start, through jogging, to striding out and eventually sprinting at maximal pace. This type of training is useful for emphasising maintaining sprint technique as speed increases.

Sprint-Resisted Training (Sport Loading Training) Sprint-resisted training, such as uphill running, stair running, sand or sand dune running, water running, weighted vest running, tethered swimming or towing a parachute or sled, increase strength and speed endurance. As with sprint-assisted training, these training methods are for experienced athletes with good form, balance and strength. Again, *Sports Speed* (Dintiman, Ward, & Tellez, 1998) is an excellent resource for sprint-resisted training programs for runners.

The following methods and guidelines are suggested for sprint-resisted training:

- Weighted vests increase leg power dramatically. Athletes should complete three to eight sprints of up to 120 metres with complete recoveries.

- Harnesses are an excellent means of increasing leg power. A partner of similar body weight and power holds back the runner in the harness, who tries to run at about 90 per cent effort. Athletes should use progressively increasing repetitions of 3 to 10 short efforts (10 to 60 metres) with complete recoveries.

- Parachutes are available in various sizes. Athletes should run at about 90 per cent effort for short distances (10 to 60 metres) and then have complete recoveries.

- Uphill sprinting develops starting speed and acceleration speed with steep grades of about 8 per cent, or start speed and speed endurance with grades of 1 to 3 per cent.

- Stair climbs develop leg power but must be done safely (treads should be non-slip) and well spread out to allow correct technique. Ideally, the inclines should be between 3 and 8 per cent.

- Sand running places high loads on runners' knees, ankles and hips. It should be used sparingly to develop leg strength and power.

- Weighted sleds and pulling tyres develop power and strength. To maintain correct form, athletes should choose weights that allow them to maintain correct form over 5 to 40 metres.

Hollow Sprints Hollow sprints are accelerations and brief sprints interrupted by periods of recovery in the form of jogging or walking. For example, athletes might accelerate for 30 metres, jog for 30 metres, accelerate for 30 metres and walk for 150 metres. This form of sprint training is appropriate for team players because it offers a variation in speed and tempo within each sequence.

Repetition Sprints Repetition sprints involve running distances at a constant speed (75 to 100 per cent of maximal speed) with recovery periods of sufficient length to allow the athlete to maintain form. They develop speed endurance and allow a sprinter to 'finish on' in a sprint race or team players to recover quickly for the next effort rather than dying in the last of five sprints. The following guidelines are recommended for developing speed endurance:

- Athletes should sprint up to 30 seconds at 90 to 95 per cent of maximal speed or at maximal speed for 10 to 20 seconds.

- Rest periods should be one to five minutes longer so athletes can recover for the next maximal effort of 10 to 30 seconds.

- Team players should use distances specific to their playing positions.

- Coaches should gradually increase the distances or shorten the recovery time to progressively overload athletes.

Resistance or Weight Training Resistance or weight training involves the strengthening and then power development of the muscles used in the sport or event. In sprint running, the gluteals, hamstrings, quadriceps, calf, abdominals, lower back and hip flexor muscles are critical. In sprint freestyle swimming, the latissimus dorsi, triceps and pectorals are important. As a guide, table 10.6 summarises the training phases and specific exercises that a sprint runner might undertake leading up to a major event. A strength and conditioning specialist should be consulted to develop a specific program in consultation with the coach.

Plyometrics Plyometrics involves the athlete moving small resistances (such as body weight) with speed. Examples are hopping, jumping and bounding for the lower body and swinging, quick-action push-offs, catching and throwing weighted objects (medicine balls, shot puts, sandbags), arm swings and pulley throws for the upper body. Table 10.7 describes the four types of movements used in plyometrics and provides exercises for each.

Dintiman, Ward and Tellez (1998) and Brown and Ferrigno (2005) offer excellent diagrams and descriptions of over 50 plyometric exercises. (See the References and Resources section at the end of the chapter.) Exercises

Table 10.6 Exercises for Various Training Phases for a Sprint Runner

Training phase	Specificity	Objective(s)	Exercises
General preparation	Low	Injury prevention, hypertrophy	Squat, deadlift, hip extension, hip flexion, bench press, trunk stabilisation
Specific preparation	Medium	Strength development	Half-quarter squat, lunge, power clean, push press
Precompetition	High	Power development	Sled sprint, inclined sprint, speed bounding, vest sprinting, hopping, depth jumps
Competition	Very high	Specific power	Sled sprint, inclined sprint, speed bounding, vest sprinting
Transition	Low	Recovery, rehabilitation	

Table 10.7 Types of Plyometrics and Sample Exercises

Type	Description	Exercises
Jumps	One- or two-legged	Jumps in place: tuck, pike, split squat, squat, jump squat, skipping Standing jumps: long, triple, lateral
Hops	One-legged	<10 repeats or >10 repeats depending on the specificity of the event or sport Speed hop, lateral hop
Bounds	Going for distance starting on 1 leg and landing on the other	>10 repeats or <10 repeats depending on the specificity of the event or sport Going for distance (e.g., 30-100 m)
Shock	Depth jumps, jumps for height	Depth jumps off a box

that simulate specific movements of the sport or event should be chosen. Although many athletes may be strong, it is the speed of plyometrics movements that develops the power critical for sport.

Plyometrics are recommended as long as the athlete has developed both general strength and core stability. Plyometrics programs should be initially overseen by a strength and conditioning specialist who monitors the progression of the program. The main myth about such training is that injury rates are high. However, the research data suggests that injury results not from performing explosive actions, but from performing the exercises with incorrect technique or not adhering to the following guidelines:

- The exercises should correspond to the form, muscle actions, direction and range of motion of the sport.

- Athletes should explode at the beginning of the action and let inertia move their limbs through the range of motion.

- Athlete should use their bodies for resistance. Too much extra weight (vests, ankle weights) may increase strength without increasing power, and it also increases the risk of injury. Weights less than 5 per cent of body weight (e.g., <5 kg, or 11 lb) are enough extra resistance.

- Athletes should have as little wall, implement or ground contact time as possible. The faster a muscle is forced to lengthen, the more powerful the resulting muscle contraction will be.

- When landing or pushing, athletes should handle the forces with as little joint bending as possible. This reduces contact time, making the resultant muscle contraction more powerful.

- Athletes should focus on both speed and form.

Apart from these guidelines, the following safety precautions are suggested with plyometrics:

- Athletes should limit plyometrics to two sessions a week at least 48 hours apart and not immediately after or the day after heavy strength training, unless lower-body strength training is combined with upper-body plyometrics training.
- Beginners should not exceed 100 jumps per session.
- Complete recovery is required between sets (e.g., two to four minutes) to maintain the quality of each set at a high level.
- Athletes should begin with low intensity (e.g., skipping, wall pushes) and progress to two-foot jumps in place, to standing jumps (e.g., standing long or triple jumps or jumps over cones), to multiple jumps and hops (e.g., double-leg hops, single-leg hops, cone hops, repeat triple jumps), to double-leg depth jumps or box jumps, to single-leg depth jumps or box jumps, to bounding for distance.
- Athletes need to have a strength base.
- A strength specialist can help initially with form and program design.
- Athletes should warm up with walk-jog-stride-sprint cycles, then specific static stretches followed by dynamic stretches.
- Footwear should have ankle and arch support and a non-slip sole.
- The surface should be shock absorbing such as grassy areas, artificial turf or mats. Plyometrics should never be done on asphalt, cement or hard gym floors.
- Boxes should have non-slip tops.
- With depth jumping (e.g., jumping off one box and onto another), the heights should be less than 0.75 metre (30 in.), or for heavy people (>100 kg, or 220 lb), less than 0.5 metre (20 in.).

STRENGTH AND POWER TRAINING

This section outlines the basic principles of developing a program for athletes' sport, event and individual needs. However, it is beyond the scope of the chapter to give specific details for every athlete in every sport or event. Numerous performance benefits arise as a result of an effective strength training program in both male and female athletes from all sports. The sport performance benefits include increased muscle mass for strength and power development, stronger connective tissue (ligaments, tendons, cartilage) to increase joint stability and help prevent injury, increased daily energy expenditure and loss of body fat and improved self-confidence and self-esteem.

Strength is the maximal force that can be generated by a muscle group with one maximal effort. Strength can be further divided into three areas:

- **Absolute strength** refers to the maximal force or weight that can be lifted once. It is generally measured as an RM (repetition maximum). For example, an athlete's 1RM for the squat exercise may be 100 kilograms (220 lb).
- **Relative strength** refers to the 1RM relative to body weight. Thus, if two athletes have a 1RM squat of 100 kilograms (220 lb) but one athlete weighs 100 kilograms (220 lb) and the other weights 75 kilograms (165 lb), the 75-kilogram athlete has much greater relative strength and theoretically should perform better. Sports such as weightlifting and field athletics require both absolute and relative strength.
- **Strength endurance** is the ability to sustain a high level of muscular force for a relatively long period under conditions of fatigue. Sports such as rowing, in which athletes must sustain 50 per cent of 1RM for six minutes, demand strength endurance.

Power is the rate of applying force or strength. A powerful movement is one that involves

DETERMINING IRM

The maximal amount of weight that can be lifted in one lift, not two, is called a 1RM (repetition maximum). Similarly, 10RM stands for the maximal weight that can be lifted 10 times, but not 11. Strength specialists may use 3RM or 12RM or a percentage of 1RM (e.g., 50 per cent of 1RM). When strength specialists develop weight training programs, they should use RMs to determine what load to lift.

Following are the steps to safely determine 1RM:

1. The coach or strength specialist selects the exercise for 1RM testing.

2. The athlete warms up with 10 repetitions of a light weight and then rests for a minute.

3. The athlete performs five repetitions with a medium weight and then rests for two minutes.

4. Taking two to three minutes between lifts, the athlete makes three to eight attempts to gradually increase the weight to determine the heaviest weight that can be lifted only once (1RM) for that exercise.

---

speed. Thus, most sports demand power. The power-to-weight ratio is of major importance in sport. That is, if two athletes have the same power output but one is 25 kilograms (55 lb) lighter than the other, the lighter athlete has a far greater power-to-weight ratio. Most sports also demand *power endurance,* or the ability to sustain powerful contractions over a period of time.

STRENGTH TRAINING METHODS

Like coaching, strength and power training is part science and part art. It is recommended that strength and power programs be developed under the supervision of a trained strength and conditioning specialist working in close consultation with the coach. The Australian Strength and Conditioning Association (ASCA) website homepage has a 'Find a Coach' link to help coaches find strength and conditioning specialists in their areas.

Following are some of the ways to develop the types of strength and power discussed previously:

- **Hypertrophy training.** Hypertrophy training is crucial for athletes wanting to increase muscle size, such as young footballers wanting to 'bulk-up' or masters athletes over 50 years of age whose muscle mass has started to decrease significantly. Medium weights are used, and the repetitions are relatively high.

- **Maximal strength.** Maximal strength training occurs after hypertrophy training and develops strength in the larger muscles. The weights are heavy, and the number of repetitions is low.

- **Isometric training.** Isometric training involves pushing against an immovable object with the muscle contracting but not moving. Rock climbers and racquet sport players who need to develop isometric strength in the forearms for gripping benefit from isometric training. Given that most sports demand that muscles move, this type of strength training has limited application in sport except when coming back from injury or in some specific sports and positions (e.g., a rugby front-row forward's neck strength for scrumming).

- **Eccentric training.** Eccentric training involves the muscle lengthening while it exerts force. Examples might be squats in which the quadriceps at the front of the thighs lengthens while the body is being lowered. This type of training is a must in sports involving running or sprinting. Because this type of muscle contraction leads to the most muscle damage and soreness, it must be gradually introduced into a training program.

- **Power training.** Power training should be done after developing strength because the greater the strength, the greater the power that can be developed. Power training involves rapid movements of lighter weights and just a few repetitions. Power training is essential for sprinters in all sports. However, it should be done after hypertrophy or maximal strength training and with correct technique, because it can lead to injuries if poor form is used.

- **Power endurance training.** Power endurance training is what most sport is all about—contracting muscles quickly to generate powerful contractions to get speed. As in power training, correct form is essential. Because this type of training develops endurance, fairly light weights are used but repetitions are high.

- **Plyometrics.** Plyometric training is excellent for developing power. It involves rapid movements such as hopping, jumping, bounding and leaping. (Refer to the Plyometrics section in the section, Speed Training.)

- **Core stability training.** The body's core is the trunk—the abdominals and lower back. If that area is not strong and stable during sport, the legs are not driving off a stable base and the upper body will move off line if the hips wobble. Lack of strength in this area is one of the most common causes of lower back pain. Two excellent books are available to assist coaches with this type of training: Jason Brumitt's *Core Assessment and Training* (2010) and *Strength Ball Training* by Loren Goldenberg and Peter Twist (2007).

Developing Muscle Strength   Strength is the foundation of power, power endurance and muscle endurance. It is highly dependent on the size of the muscle as well as the nerve stimulation the muscle receives, both of which are trainable. Strength initially increases quickly as a result of nervous system changes. After four to eight weeks, an increase in muscle size takes place and increases strength further. Table 10.8 summarises the key factors to consider when developing strength.

Developing Muscle Hypertrophy   Hypertrophy, or muscle enlargement, weight training is important for developing muscle mass in youth players and competitive masters athletes. Athletes with a higher proportion of fast-twitch fibres, such as sprinters, appear to hypertrophy more than predominantly slow-twitch-fibred endurance athletes. Muscle damage, seen more with eccentric (muscle-lengthening) exercises than concentric (muscle-shortening) exercises, stimulate muscle hypertrophy. This suggests that the tempo (speed) of the eccentric action in any exercise should be longer than the muscle shortening phase. It can take up to eight weeks of strength training to see an increase in muscle size. Table 10.9 summarises the key factors to consider when planning a muscle hypertrophy weight training program.

Developing Muscle Power   Muscle power is the key to sport performance. Power means doing actions quickly so that a muscle's rate of force development is increased. Given that the greater the strength is, the more power can be developed, strength must be developed first with heavier loads. Loads should then be lightened and the speed of contraction increased progressively. However, once athletes have developed strength and then have started developing power (speed-strength), they must continue to maintain strength by doing one or two sessions per week of strength training. Table 10.10 summarises the key factors to be considered when developing muscle power.

Developing Muscle Endurance   Most sports demand some level of muscle endurance. Although strength training itself can improve muscle endurance, research has shown that specificity of training produces the greatest increase in muscle endurance. Improving muscle endurance requires a high number of repetitions or short recovery times between sets or both. Table 10.11 summarises the key factors to be considered when developing muscle endurance.

Table 10.8 Principles of Strength Development

Factor	Novice	Advanced
Muscle action	Concentric: muscle shortening Eccentric: muscle lengthening	
Loads	60-70% of 1RM	80-100% of 1RM
Repetitions	8-12	1-6
Progression	Reassess 1RM every 2-4 weeks Increase load 2-10%	Reassess 1RM every 2-3 weeks or drop reps and increase intensity 2-10%
Sets	1-3	2-3
Exercise selection	Single- and multi-joint exercises	Multi-joint exercises
Free weights or machines	Free weights and machines	Free weights
Speed of movement	Slow to moderate with good technique	Slow to moderate to fast depending on sport or event and with good technique
Rest between sets	2-3 min for multi-joint exercises (e.g., bench press) 1-2 min for single-joint exercises (e.g., leg curl)	
Frequency	2-3 times/week with 48 hr between sessions	4-6 times/week depending on sport, event or training phase
Range of motion	Complete or to individual tolerance	

Table 10.9 Principles of Muscle Hypertrophy Development

Factor	Novice	Advanced
Muscle action	Concentric: muscle shortening Eccentric: muscle lengthening	
Loads	70-85% of 1RM	70-100% of1RM
Repetitions	8-12	1-12 with majority 6-12
Progression	Reassess 1RM every 2-4 weeks Increase load 2-10%	Reassess 1RM every 2-3 weeks or drop reps and increase intensity 2-10%
Sets	1-3	3-6
Exercise selection	Single- and multi-joint exercises	Multi-joint exercises
Free weights or machines	Free weights and machines	Free weights
Speed of movement	Slow to moderate with good technique	Slow to moderate depending on sport or event and with good technique
Rest between sets	1-2 minutes	2-3 minutes for 1-6RM 1-2 minutes for 7-12RM
Frequency	2-3 times/week with 48 hr between sessions	4-6 times/week depending on sport, event or training phase
Range of motion	Complete or to individual tolerance	

Table 10.10 Principles of Muscle Power Development

Factor	Novice	Advanced
Muscle action	Sport specific	
Loads	30-60% of 1RM	
Repetitions	3-6	1-6
Progression	Reassess 1RM every 2-4 weeks Increase load 2-10%	Reassess 1RM every 2-3 weeks or drop reps and increase intensity 2-10%
Sets	1-3	3-6
Exercise selection	Multi-joint exercises	
Free weights or machines	Free weights and machines	Free weights
Speed of movement	Fast with good technique	
Rest between sets	2-3 min for multi-joint exercises	
Frequency	2-3 times/week with 48 hr between sessions	4-6 times/week depending on sport, event or training phase
Range of motion	Complete or to individual tolerance	

Table 10.11 Principles of Muscle Endurance Development

Factor	Novice	Advanced
Muscle action	Sport specific	
Loads	50-70% of 1RM	30-80% of 1RM
Repetitions	10-15	10-25
Progression	Reassess 1RM every 2-4 weeks Increase load 2-10%	Reassess 1RM every 2-3 weeks or drop reps and increase intensity 2-10%
Sets	1-3	3-6
Exercise selection	Multi-joint exercises	
Free weights or machines	Free weights and machines	Free weights
Speed of movement	Moderate with good technique	Fast with good technique for low reps Moderate for high reps
Rest between sets	1-2 min for high-rep sets	< 1 min for 10- to 15-rep sets
Frequency	2-3 times/week with 48 hr between sessions	4-6 times/week depending on sport, event or training phase
Range of motion	Complete or to individual tolerance	

Developing Power Endurance Following the development of strength and power using the preceding methods under the supervision of a strength and conditioning specialist, some sports and events demand the development of power endurance. Following are some ways to develop or maintain these qualities:

- **Body weight exercises** such as push-ups, sit-ups and squats can be done with minimal equipment, but the choices of exercises are limited and the resistance cannot be controlled easily.

- **Weight training** to develop power endurance should follow the guidelines in table 10.12.

- **Circuit training.** Circuit training involves using either body weight or weight training devices and performing one exercise immediately followed by another exercise (or running activity) using a different body part. Circuits can be based on time (e.g., 30 seconds at each work station) or number of repetitions (e.g., 20 squats). The exercises chosen should be sport specific and aimed at performance improvement or injury prevention. This type of training is very useful with many athletes and limited equipment.

- **Resisted sports movements.** Resisted sports movements include uphill running, stair or sand dune running, weighted vest running, tethered swimming, towing a parachute or sled, placing a tube on the front of a rowboat, cycling into a headwind or up hills, or doing low-cadence, high-resistance work on a wind trainer. These training methods are for experienced athletes with good form, balance and strength.

STRENGTH TRAINING AIDS

Numerous general and sport-specific strength training and power training aids are on the market.

- **Stretch cords** are commonly used by swimmers. They are cheap and available at swim shops and pools. Tubing can be found at surgical supply chemists or dive shops. With both stretch cords and tubing,

Table 10.12 Principles of Power Endurance Development

Variable	Value
Sets	2-3
Repetitions	20-40
Load (RM)	20-40
Tempo	0.5-0-0.5
Rest between sets (min)	1-2
Frequency (times/week)	2-3

the greater the thickness, the greater the resistance. They are light and portable and can be used to replicate exact sport or event movements on land. Page and Ellenbecker (2011) is an excellent resource for training tips using stretch cords.

- **Free weights or dumbbells** are relatively inexpensive, are available from fitness suppliers or sport stores and can be used in many ways to develop and maintain strength.

- **Swiss balls (Mediballs, Fitballs)** are widely used for developing core strength. For athletes with lower back pain or the need to develop strength in the abdomen and lower back, this type of training is essential. See the resources listed at the end of this chapter for help in this area or visit a sport physiotherapist or Pilates specialist for advice on core-strengthening programs.

- **Sport-specific aids.** Following are some of many sport-specific aids:

  o *Tethers* are fixed to a point while the swimmer works against the water to hold a position. They are excellent for strength and power development, but very stressful if used too often for too long.

  o *Drag suits* have pockets to catch water and make the swimmer work harder, thus developing strength and power endurance.

  o *Paddles* vary in size and shape and are used to develop strength in swimmers.

Small paddles should be used initially at slow speeds and short distances. Distance, speed and paddle size can be increased over time.

- *Resistance aids* for swimmers include shoes and buckets to tow. Runners can pull weighted sleds or small parachutes, and rowers can attach small tubes to their boats.

- **Medicine balls** are highly effective in developing strength and power endurance. They are also great for developing core body strength and action-specific strength and power such as that required by throwers. (See the resources at the end of this chapter for more on medicine ball exercises.)

- **Kettlebells** are cast iron weights resembling cannonballs with handles. They are used to perform ballistic exercises that combine cardiovascular, strength and flexibility training. Sizes may range from 1.8 to 79 kilograms (4 to 174 lb). Similar to medicine balls, they can be used to develop core strength as well as sport-specific strength and power. (See the end of the chapter for more on kettlebell exercises.) As with all resistance training exercises, coaches should ensure that athletes use the correct techniques and loads and that the exercises adhere to the principle of sport, event or position specificity.

FLEXIBILITY TRAINING

Flexibility is the range of motion around a joint or multiple joints. It facilitates the ability to perform specific tasks such as reaching, striding, jumping, stretching and catching. For example, in freestyle swimmers a high degree of shoulder and hip rotation flexibility is required to get a high elbow recovery, a catch, a long stroke and body roll. Track sprint runners need a good stride length, so hip flexibility becomes crucial. *Stretching* is the process of lengthening connective tissue in and around joints (ligaments, tendons, joint capsules) or muscles and other tissues.

Flexibility training is essential for freestyle swimmers to achieve an optimum stroke.

Ric Tapia/Icon SMI

For athletes, the benefits of flexibility training include improved performance as a result of a greater range of motion (e.g., increased stride or stroke length), mental and physical relaxation, improved body awareness, reduced risk of joint sprain or muscle strains, reduced risk of back problems, improved postural alignment, the prevention and treatment of many sport-related injuries and reduced muscle soreness and tension. Research has shown a relationship between poor flexibility and subsequent injury in the Achilles tendon, plantar fascia (arch of the feet) and hamstring tendons.

The following principles should be adhered to for a safe and effective flexibility program:

- Athletes should warm up using calisthenics, cycling or jogging for five minutes to increase body temperature and increase blood flow to muscles and connective tissue (ligaments, tendons) that limit flexibility. In cold weather, the warm-up might be more intense and athletes might wear more clothes.

- Athletes should isolate the muscle groups to be stretched.

- Correct limb alignment and technique are crucial.

- Exhaling going into the stretch facilitates relaxation during the stretch.

- Athletes should breathe normally during the stretch but accentuate exhaling when going deeper into the stretch.

- The stretch should be held at the point of tension, not pain.

- The stretch should be held for 10 to 30 seconds.

- Athletes should come out of the stretch as carefully as they go into it.

- Two or three repetitions are recommended for a 10-second stretch or one repetition for a 30-second stretch. Given that a lack of flexibility is due to connective tissue tightness, research has shown that low-force, long-duration stretching is the most effective to get increased range of motion about a joint.

- Stretching should be done three to five days per week.

- Because most sports demand dynamic flexibility, athletes should incorporate a progressive velocity flexibility strategy. That is, they should stretch in the following order:
  1. Static
  2. Slow, short of end-of-range dynamic stretching (below 75 per cent of actual sport speed)
  3. Slow, full-range dynamic stretching (again, below 75 per cent of actual sport speed)
  4. Fast, short of end-of-range stretching
  5. Fast, full-range stretching

The American College of Sports Medicine (ACSM) recommends that static stretches be held for 10 to 30 seconds. In contrast, proprioceptive neuromuscular facilitation (PNF) techniques (discussed later) should include a six-second contraction of the muscle followed by a 10- to 30-second assisted stretch. The ACSM also recommends at least four repetitions per muscle group completed a minimum of two days per week.

The types of stretching that follow are useful in a flexibility program. For the best discussion available on the science and methods of stretching, see the excellent book *Sports Stretch* by Michael J. Alter (1998), which describes 311 stretches for 41 sports, or the booklet *The Stretching Handbook* by Brad Walker (2011), which has great photos of a wide range of stretches for all the muscle groups and joints.

- **Static stretching.** In static stretching, once the muscle(s) and joint are stretched to the point of tension, the stretch is held to allow the connective tissue around the muscle and joint to stretch. No external force is applied to the body.

- **Ballistic stretching.** Ballistic stretching is associated with bouncing or bobbing in a rhythmic motion. The momentum of the limbs or body forcibly increases the range of motion, but the risk of injury is higher as is the likelihood of muscle soreness after stretching.

- **Dynamic, or functional, flexibility.** A controlled, soft bounce or swinging motion is used to force the joint past its normal range of movement. The force of the bounce or swing is gradually increased but always controlled. This type of stretching is beneficial for athletes who use full range of motion while moving (e.g., gymnasts, divers). It does have a risk of injury and so should be used only by well-trained and conditioned athletes and only after a static stretch.

- **Contract–relax, or proprioceptive neuromuscular facilitation (PNF), stretching.** The PNF method consists of alternating an isometric muscle contraction and static stretching. The area to be stretched is positioned so that the muscle is under tension in a static stretch. Then the athlete contracts the stretched muscle group while using a partner, stretch cord or wall to apply resistance against the contraction to keep the joint from moving. The athlete holds the contraction for six seconds or more. The muscle is then relaxed and a controlled stretch applied for the standard 30 seconds. After a 30-second recovery, the process is repeated two or three times.

PNF has been shown to be more beneficial than static, ballistic or functional flexibility exercises. The advantages of PNF are increased range of movement, increased flexibility and muscle strength development for performance and injury rehabilitation. PNF stretching is most beneficial to athletes who need strength at the end of range of motion, such as rugby forwards, divers, sprinters and sport athletes.

Stretching prior to an event has long been a part of warming up in sport. There is no doubt that stretching anecdotally and theoretically reduces injury, although no scientific evidence supports this claim. Although recent research suggests that stretching immediately prior to strength and power events may actually reduce power output and force production and thus performance in power events, more recent research is showing that when static stretching before an event is followed by dynamic stretching, power performance is not inhibited and may even be enhanced.

SUMMARY

- Every training program should be based on scientifically based training principles and training methods backed by research.
- Training programs should include training methods that are specific to the sport, the demands of the sport or the sport event , and in team sports, the positional demands of the sport.
- Most sports demand a combination of strength, power, speed, endurance and flexibility training with different sports, positions and events requiring different emphases of these qualities.
- Smart coaches invest in the services of strength and conditioning specialists to help them develop their strength and conditioning programs.
- Smart coaches seek additional resources, including those suggested in this chapter, to develop their sport-, event- or position-specific training programs.

REFERENCES AND RESOURCES

Alter, M. (1998). *Sport stretch* (2nd ed.). Champaign, IL: Human Kinetics. Available from Human Kinetics Australia (www.humankinetics.com). Contains 311 stretches for 41 sports. The classic book for sport stretching.

Bompa, T., & Haff, G. (2009). *Periodization* (5th ed.). Champaign, IL: Human Kinetics. Available from Human Kinetics Australia (www.humankinetics.com/). A training theory bible for coaches wanting to develop strength, power, endurance, speed and agility and unlocking the secrets to putting the plan together.

Brown, L., & Ferrigno, V. (Eds.). (2005). *Training for speed, agility, and quickness* (2nd ed.). Champaign, IL: Human Kinetics. Available from Human Kinetics Australia (www.humankinetics.com/). Contains numerous drills and exercises for sprint runners and team players. A classic book.

Brummit, J. (2010). *Core assessment and training*. Champaign, IL: Human Kinetics. Available from Human Kinetics Australia (www.humankinetics.com/).

Chu, D. (1996). *Explosive Power & Strength*. Champaign, IL: Human Kinetics.

Chu, D. (1998). *Jumping into plyometrics* (2nd ed.). Champaign, IL: Human Kinetics. Available from Human Kinetics Australia (www.humankinetics.com/). Contains numerous sport-specific plyometric exercises. Another classic book.

Dintiman, G., Ward, R. & Tellez, T. (1998). *Sports speed*. Champaign, IL: Human Kinetics. Available from Human Kinetics Australia (www.humankinetics.com/). The classic book for sprint runners.

Gambetta, V. (2007). *Athletic development: The art & science of functional sports conditioning*. Champaign, IL: Human Kinetics. Available from Human Kinetics Australia (www.humankinetics.com/). A great all-round book of particular interest to the team coach.

Goldenberg, L., & Twist, P. (2007). *Strength ball training*. Champaign, IL: Human Kinetics. Available from Human Kinetics Australia (www.humankinetics.com/).

National Strength and Conditioning Association (Editor, Brown, L.) (2007). *Strength training*. Champaign, IL: Human Kinetics. Available from Human Kinetics Australia (www.humankinetics.com/).

Page, P., & Ellenbecker, T. (2011). *Strength band training* (2nd ed.). Champaign, IL: Human Kinetics. Available from Human Kinetics Australia (www.humankinetics.com/).

Sandler, D. (2005). *Sports power*. Champaign, IL: Human Kinetics. Available from Human Kinetics Australia (www.humankinetics.com/). A great all-round book of particular interest to the coach of speed and power athletes.

Walker, B. (2011). *The stretching handbook*. Gold Coast, QLD: Walkerbout Health and Leisure. Available from www.thestretchinghandbook.com. This book has diagrams and guidelines for all major stretches.

www.gssiweb.com is the homepage of the Gatorade Sports Science Institute. It has an excellent range of articles relating to sport performance and good health and an easy-to-use search engine.

www.nsca.com is the homepage of the world's leading organization in strength and conditioning, the National Strength and Conditioning Association.

www.exrx.net contains information on strength training. This is a great website that can help coaches develop their own programs using scientifically based principles. The website also has a wide range of plyometric exercises, including kettlebell exercises, with video clips linked to each.

www.oztrack.com is an excellent website run by professional Australian sprint coaches. It has plenty of links to other speed-related sites and heaps of training tips and resources.

www.thestretchinghandbook.com contains information on stretching and access to a free newsletter.

CHAPTER 11

Analysing Technique

—— Elizabeth Bradshaw

An understanding of sports biomechanics arms the coach with technical insight into why and how the body moves. Biomechanics encompasses both anatomical and mechanical principles, and its purpose is to enhance performance and prevent or minimise injury. Most coaches use biomechanical techniques in their everyday coaching without always being aware of it. Before providing an athlete with observations of technique, a coach must visually analyse that athlete's movement. To provide feedback, the coach must then distinguish relevant from irrelevant factors in that particular movement.

COACHING BIOMECHANICS

An in-depth understanding of biomechanics can enable a coach to do the following:

- Select techniques and equipment that are most appropriate for an individual athlete's body size, body structure, physical development and skill level.
- Estimate the physical load (impact) of training and competition and incorporate that information into athlete management and training programs to achieve optimal training adaptations without injury.
- Analyse athletes' movements and help them refine their techniques to move more effectively and efficiently.
- Communicate with sports science and sports medicine practitioners regarding athletes' techniques or the treatment of injuries.

- Guide the athlete on the advice and treatment received from sports science and sports medicine practitioners to achieve a positive outcome, such as improved technique, improved performance, improved technique and performance or recovery from injury and return to peak performance.

The real value of biomechanics is that it enables coaches to treat every athlete as an individual. Coaches who understand biomechanics do not need to rely on their own experiences from being coached when younger or on the simple observations of others. They do not seek to copy the technical style of current champions and do not leave their athletes to learn unguided.

Incorporating video or other simple technology (e.g., timing gates and contact timing mats) into coaching practice can be a useful method of evaluating athletes' technique; such evaluations help coaches provide feedback that can help athletes progress in their training. Video, for example, enhances coaches' ability to view fast movements so they can give better feedback to their athletes. Other advantages are that the athlete can see what the coaches see during video playback, and coaches can keep visual records of their athletes' movements over time to track their progress.

Coaches need to make sure, however, that the technology they are using adds value to the training session. Using technology requires careful planning, especially if the coach has not used it regularly before. Determining when, where and how to use technology is crucial and depends on the age, level and aspirations of the performer, as well as the coach's experience. An experienced coach can distinguish key factors in a movement and, in particular, separate relevant from irrelevant factors.

Another important consideration to remember when using video is to view the athlete from more than one perspective. Many coaches, both inexperienced and experienced, always observe their athletes from the side. This can lead to overlooking important technical factors (or flaws).

Wanting to correct a flaw in technique immediately is a natural response, but before doing so, the coach needs to first evaluate the cause of the flaw, determine whether the athlete is psychologically ready for the feedback and decide how best to provide that feedback based on the athlete's learning preference. The coach should consider whether that athlete is a visual, auditory, read/write or kinaesthetic learner (see www.vark-learn.com for more on learning styles). The cause of the problem may be purely technical, or it may be caused by inadequate strength or flexibility or anxiety.

A technical flaw identified in the later stages of a movement can also be caused by a technical flaw during movement preparation that may be less obvious. Travelling sideways during a basketball jump shot reduces the player's shooting accuracy and is usually only noticeable if the coach watches the player's take-off and landing position. The cause is typically a technical flaw during the preparation phase of the shot such as a sideways lean while jumping and releasing the shot. It may be necessary to consider or assess physical, psychological and tactical aspects of the athlete's movement before making a decision and providing feedback.

BIOMECHANICAL PRINCIPLES

Anatomy refers to the physical structure of the human body and provides definitions to describe the basic movements of the body and its segments. In biomechanics the physical relationship of internal and external structures are examined. That is because loads imposed on the body affect the internal structures of the body. The internal structures that are most relevant to sport and biomechanics make up the musculoskeletal system and include the following:

- **Bones.** Bones provide a framework that gives the human body its form and shape. They also provide protection for the vital organs such as the heart, and when articulating together, they can act as levers that enable us to move. A lever is like a rigid bar with one end that is fixed and the other end that can move freely.

- **Cartilage.** Cartilage is a fibrous connective tissue that is viscoelastic, which allows for virtually frictionless movement. The primary function of cartilage is to transmit forces across joints, distribute these forces to prevent stress on one particular region of the joint and provide a smooth surface for the relative gliding of a joint.

- **Ligaments.** Ligaments connect bone with bone, increase the mechanical stability of the joints, guide joint motion and prevent excessive joint motion. Ligaments are mechanically similar to tendons, but are less stiff and weaker than tendons. Ligaments can carry high compressive (axial) loads and have more resistance to shear (parallel) loads than tendons do.

- **Joints.** Joints are where two bones meet and are held together by ligaments. They are classified in terms of their structure and function. Most relevant to sport are cartilaginous and synovial joints. Cartilaginous joints have limited movement and provide stability. Their main function is to allow bending. Synovial joints permit large movement and typically are formed between two long bones. Their main function is to enable movement.

- **Muscle.** Muscle is the active element of the musculoskeletal system. Muscle is capable of actively contracting to produce tension (pulling force) within itself and on the structures to which it attaches. Its functions are to produce movement and to create tension for maintaining posture.

- **Tendons.** Tendons connect and transmit pulling (tensile) loads between muscle and bone and therefore are involved in producing joint motion and maintaining body posture. Tendons also enable the muscle belly to be at an optimal distance from the joint on which it acts, without requiring a fully extended length of muscle. Tendons have a high tensile (pulling) strength, but have minimal resistance to loads from other directions.

Specific terminology is helpful for movement analysis. Tables 11.1 and 11.2 provide direction and movement terms used in movement analysis.

Table 11.1 Direction Terms

Term	Definition	Example
Anterior	Towards the front of the body	The toes of the foot are anterior to the heel.
Posterior	Towards the back of the body	The shoulder blades (scapulas) are posterior to the ribs.
Medial	Towards the midline of the body	The big toe is medial to the smallest toe.
Lateral	Away from the midline of the body	The ears are lateral to the nose.
Proximal	The origin of the body part or limb	The shoulder is proximal to the elbow.
Distal	The opposite end of the body part or limb to the origin, which often articulates with another limb	The wrist is distal to the elbow.

Table 11.2 Movement Terms

Term	Definition	Example
Flexion	• Bending the body or body segment (about a joint) • Decreases the angle at a joint	• Bending the hips and knees when squatting down in preparation to jump • Bending the elbow to lift a drink bottle to your mouth
Extension	• Straightening of the body or body segment (about a joint) until it reaches a straight alignment • Increases the angle at a joint	• Extending the body about the hips to stand up after touching your toes • Straightening your knee to rotate the lower leg and foot through for a soccer kick
Hyperextension	• Straightening of the body or body segment (about a joint) beyond a straight alignment • Occurs when a segment extends past its usual anatomical position	• Arching of the back during a volleyball spike or badminton smash • Hyperextending the shoulder (part of a combined movement) during throwing
Abduction	• Movement of a body segment or part away from the human body's midline	• Moving the arm about the shoulder laterally away from the body

(continued)

Table 11.2 Movement Terms *(continued)*

Term	Definition	Example
Adduction	• Movement of a body segment or part towards the human body's midline	• Moving the arm about the shoulder toward the body
Rotation	• Movement of the body or a body part about an axis inwards or outwards	• Performing a whole body twist when springboard diving • Rotating the arm about the shoulder during a windmill softball pitch
Varus	• The inward inclination of the distal end point of a bone • Describes the position of the lower leg (tibia and fibula) in relation to knee alignment, where the distal end point is the ankle	• Being bowlegged
Valgus	• The outward inclination of the distal end point of a bone	• Being knock-kneed
Pronation	• Transverse plane movement in which the forearm rotates so that the palm of the hand is facing down • Radius bone rotates over the ulna bone	• Pronating the forearm and creating forward spin during cricket bowling
Supination	• Transverse plane movement in which the forearm rotates so that the palm of the hand is facing up • Radius and ulna bones parallel to each other	• Supinating the forearm to create backspin during cricket bowling
Inversion	• Rotation of a body part inwards • Used to describe motion of the heel (calcaneus) or the foot	• Rotation of the sole of the foot inwards during the later (propulsive) phase of running ground contact • Rotation of the sole of the heel inwards
Eversion	• Rotation of a body part outwards • Used to describe motion of the heel (calcaneus) or the foot	• Rotation of the sole of the foot outwards during the early (braking) phase of running ground contact • Rotation of the sole of the heel outwards
Dorsiflexion	• The ankle joint motion in which the toes move towards the shin	• Heel strike on the ground during race walking
Plantarflexion	• The extension of the ankle joint in which the toes move towards the ground	• Plantarflexing the ankle during the push-off (propulsive) phase in sprinting
Elevation	• Moving a body part in the upward direction	• Elevating the shoulder during a tennis serve to attain a higher reach
Depression	• Moving a body part in the downward direction	• Depressing the shoulders to maintain good posture during dressage riding

The human body's movement is described with reference to three anatomical axes that pass through the body's centre of mass. The axes can be thought of like splitting the body in half in a specific direction. Movement planes describe the movement action direction about a specific axis. Figure 11.1 shows the three movement planes and axes, and table 11.3 further describes the movement that occurs in these planes and about these axes.

An understanding of the mechanical properties of the musculoskeletal system is important for sport performance, understanding the causes of injury and attempting to prevent injury. For example, lower back injuries became increasingly prevalent in the 1980s in fast bowlers, especially teenage players whose immature backs are more susceptible to injury under heavy loading. Biomechanical testing led by Professor Bruce Elliott at the University of Western Australia linked the injuries to what is now referred to as a 'mixed action' in which the hips and the shoulders do not remain aligned throughout the delivery.

The forces associated with this counter-rotation between the hips and shoulders,

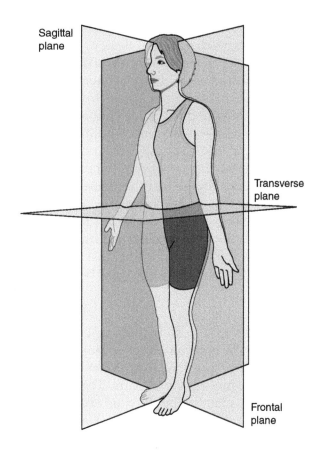

Figure 11.1 Movement planes and axes.

Table 11.3 Movement Planes and Axes

Term	Definition	Example
Sagittal plane (transverse axis)	• Movement of the human body (or body limb) in the forward or backward direction • Movement in one direction (linear), or rotational, which is in the rolling direction for this plane of movement	• Flexion and extension of the leg when running • Forward somersault in gymnastics
Frontal plane (sagittal axis)	• Movement of the human body (or body limb) sideways in the linear direction or as rotation, which is in the side spin direction for this plane of movement	• Swinging the leg outwards and inwards (abduction and adduction) • Cartwheel or side somersault in gymnastics
Transverse plane (longitudinal axis)	• Rotational movement of the human body (or body limb) in the twist direction	• Rotation inwards (palm facing down, or pronated) and outwards (palm facing up, or supinated) of the forearm • Twisting with a straight body during the airborne phase of an aerial ski jump

particularly if it exceeds 30°, include trunk movements, such as lateral flexion, that place greater strain on the intervertebral discs in the lower back and cause their degeneration. The implications of these findings was to encourage fast bowlers to modify their technique to adopt either a more side-on or front-on position during delivery, and to keep counter-rotation to a minimum. Overbowling, poor physical preparation and excessive fatigue are other causes of lower back injury that cricket coaches need to understand. The impact of the research is reflected in injury surveillance data collected during the past 20 years that show a reduction in back injuries, particularly among adolescent fast bowlers.

FORCE

Force refers to a push or pulling action that can cause the body (or object) to start moving, stop moving, speed up, slow down or change direction. Forces come in pairs. The action of one force is matched by an equal and opposite reaction force by the other object. For example, when you push downwards onto the ground, it creates a reaction force upwards. This force development pattern is used when preparing to jump vertically from the ground. The muscles of the legs generate internal forces that create an overall external force onto the ground.

When squatting downwards by bending the hips and knees, the muscles are lengthening and generating an *eccentric* internal force. When moving upwards by extending the hips and knees, the muscles are shortening and generating a *concentric* internal force. In both directions, the overall external human body force created acts downwards onto the ground, resulting in an upward reaction force from the ground. The ground reaction force during the downward leg action pushes upwards and enables the athlete to control the descending movement. During the upward leg action, the ground reaction force pushes upwards and is used by the athlete to accelerate the body into the air.

SUMMATION OF FORCE

Summation of force is when larger forces can be achieved by using as many force-producing body segments as possible. This is used for any sport skill that requires a maximal effort (e.g., soccer penalty kick). The force is developed sequentially, and therefore the combined force develops over time like a chain of dominoes. The largest segments, such as the trunk and hips, start the movement, and the smaller segments, such as the foot, end the movement.

Any pause in the force chain can cause some of the force developed to be lost. This can also be a mechanism for injury because the athlete has to restart the force chain later in the movement sequence, usually with smaller segments and muscles. For example, a pause at the end of the arm-cocking phase in the overarm throwing action of a softball outfielder results in the shoulder musculature having to compensate to reactivate the movement sequence. Over time that biomechanical pattern can result in an overuse injury of the shoulder.

BALANCE AND STABILITY

Balance and stability is when the athlete is able to resist a change (challenge, interference or both) to the body's motion. This can be either *static,* in which the athlete is holding a stationary stable position, or *dynamic,* in which the athlete is moving in a balanced manner. Increased body mass leads to greater stability. However, with the exception of sports such as sumo wrestling, increasing body mass is not usually the best method of increasing stability for most athletes.

Coaches should consider the size of athletes' base of support during movement and the position of their centre of gravity (also known as centre of mass) relative to their base of support in the vertical and horizontal directions. Athletes are more stable when they have a larger base of support, when their centre of gravity is horizontally positioned within their base of support, and when their centre of gravity is lower to the ground (see figure 11.2).

In racquet sports such as badminton, athletes can be high and unstable during offensive play court movement because they know where they need to be and when, and what shots they are executing. During defensive play court movement, however, they need to be low and stable because they do not necessarily know where they need to be and when, and what shot they

Figure 11.2 High stability results from *(a)* the centre of gravity being low to the ground and within a large base of support. Moderate stability is achieved when *(b)* the centre of gravity is within a small base of support. Low stability results from the centre of gravity being *(c)* outside and *(d)* high and outside a small base of support.

will be executing to counter their opponents' play. Stability during the athlete's movement therefore must take into account other performance requirements.

In court sports such as basketball and netball, a wide double-legged landing position is the most stable; players in this position can resist the efforts of opposing players trying to knock them over. This position is ideal for reducing the ground impact forces, but moving quickly into position for further play from this position is difficult. A staggered foot placement is an ideal compromise, but can restrict a player to a specific movement direction for further play because one foot is farther forward. The other option is a compromise between stability and speed for further play by having a slightly narrower double-legged landing position.

LAWS OF MOTION

Laws of motion are also known as Newton's laws of motion. There are four laws as follows:

1. A body remains in its current state of motion (velocity), unless acted on by an external force. This law describes the tendency of an object to keep its current state of motion (speed), and the difficulty in changing the state of motion of an object (resistance to change). Generally, this law applies only to sports such as women's artistic gymnastics in which athletes must hold a static position, and external forces such as friction are absent.

2. A force applied to a body causes acceleration of that body of a magnitude proportional to the force, in the direction of the force and inversely proportional to the body's mass. In simple terms, the direction of the force equals the direction of acceleration, and a larger force will result in faster acceleration. This law is more applicable to sports. For example, generating a larger horizontal force in the starting block action of sprinting results in a faster acceleration during the early phase of the race.

3. For every action, there is an equal and opposite reaction. This law describes force pairs: action and reaction force. During early ground contact when running, the foot and leg are forward of the body and the foot strikes the ground downwards. This creates a ground reaction force in the opposite direction, upwards and backwards against the runner's movement direction. The reaction force therefore acts to stabilise the foot and leg by decelerating its motion.

   During later ground contact, the foot and leg are behind the body and push downwards onto the ground. This creates a ground reaction force that acts upwards and forwards towards the runner's movement direction. This later reaction force therefore provides propulsion and accelerates the runner's motion into the following stride. Athletes can lessen the early deceleration phase of a sprint by wearing spikes to provide stability, and by striking the ground with a predominantly downward (vertical) action force. This is known as an active foot strike.

   The direction of the reaction force is also relevant to diving and gymnastics when trying to create angular rotation in the forward or backward direction. The application of the ground reaction force is opposite to the resulting direction of rotation. For a gymnast to generate forward rotation, the reaction force must pass upwards and behind (posterior to) the gymnast's centre of mass. For backward rotation, the reaction force must pass in front of (anterior to) the gymnast's centre of gravity.

4. All bodies are attracted to one another with a force proportional to the product of their masses and inversely proportional to the distance between them. In sports, the force that the particles of one body (e.g., a billiard ball) exert on the particles of another body is generally so small that its effect is imperceptible. The effect of gravity does not change until approximately 1.63 kilometres (1 mile) above sea level. Therefore, athletes competing at the 1968 Mexico Summer Olympics had a very slight performance advantage due to the 2.24-kilometre (1.4-mile) altitude and slightly lower gravity.

BODY MOTION

Body motion (or *kinematic concepts*) is a broad description of the body's motion. The following types of body motion are possible:

- Linear motion—All parts of the body show the same trajectory in a straight or curvilinear line. When a figure skater holds an arabesque position, all parts of the body follow the same movement path (line).

- Angular motion—Rotation about an axis. The axis can be internal (e.g., shoulder joint) or external (e.g., the high bar in men's gymnastics).

- General motion—A combination of linear and angular motion. This category of movement includes swimming the free-style stroke and sprinting when movement occurs in the forward (linear) direction, which is generated through the angular movement of the legs and arms.

- Whole body motion—A mixture of linear, angular and general motions of the segments. The best example of whole body motion is field events in athletics such as the discus and hammer throw.

MOMENTUM

Momentum is the quantity of motion that the human body (or object) possesses. Momentum is the product of a body's mass and its speed. Because an athlete's body mass is typically stable (fixed), developing faster speed results in greater momentum. Momentum can be in one direction (linear) or rotational (angular).

PROJECTILE MOTION

Projectile motion is when the human body (or an object) is projected into the air. A projectile is a body in free fall that is subject only to the forces of gravity and air resistance (including wind). For that reason, the human body's (or an object's) momentum is fixed (conserved) at the instant of take-off into the air. Therefore, the athlete's speed and direction of take-off are important for the resulting airborne movement. Landing errors in sports such as gymnastics and aerial skiing are usually the result of sub-optimal take-off mechanics (e.g., too much or insufficient take-off speed or incorrect take-off angle). Momentum can only be gained or lost in the air if the person comes into contact with another person (e.g., a collision while contesting for the ball in football or soccer) or an object (e.g., catching the horizontal bar after a release movement in gymnastics).

Projectile motion is affected by the (1) vertical release speed, (2) horizontal release speed, (3) height of release relative to landing position and (4) direction (angle) of release. Increasing the release (take-off) speed of projection increases the horizontal distance travelled (range) more substantially than either the release height or angle. When the release height is zero (ground level), the release angle that produces maximal horizontal displacement is 45°. As the release height increases (take-off position is higher than landing), the optimum release angle decreases below 45°. Alternatively, as release height decreases (landing position is higher than take-off), the optimum angle increases above 45°.

In sport there are many examples of projectile motion. Shot put, javelin, discus and long jump are examples of projectile motion in which maximal horizontal distance is the performance outcome. Maximal vertical displacement is the performance outcome for high jump and pole vault, whereas the accuracy and speed of the trajectory of objects is more important in golf, tennis, basketball and soccer.

CONSERVATION OF MOMENTUM

Conservation of momentum is when, in the absence of external forces, the total momentum of a given system (human body, object) remains constant. Athletes transfer momentum from one body axis to another to change their bodies' movements while in the air (e.g., change from a somersaulting motion to a twist) or to stabilise their bodies in the air by using counter-rotation of one half of the body with respect to the other (e.g., rotating the hips and legs in the opposite direction to the upper body during a volleyball spike; also known mechanically as a cat twist).

Athletes can also control their movement speed in the air by changing the position of their body parts relative to their centre of mass (also known as centre of gravity). By distributing their body parts wide and away from the centre of mass, they increase their moment of inertia (resistance to change in motion), which slows their rotational speed. If they pull their body parts in close to their centre of mass, they decrease their moment of inertia, which increases their rotational speed. This is often used by gymnasts to control their rotation. When gymnasts tuck their knees and arms in close to their bodies, they can rotate faster in somersaults because they have reduced their moment of inertia. They can slow their rotation by extending the legs and trunk into a more stretched position, which increases their

RECOGNISING EXPERT PERFORMANCE

Expert performance is often described with reference to sport legends such as Sir Donald Bradman (cricket), Nadia Comaneci (artistic gymnastics), Michael Jordan (basketball), Ian Thorpe (swimming) and Ronald Barassi (Australian rules football). This often then raises the question of what was superior or unique (or both) about the technique of these athletes.

Expert performance is typically described from a biomechanical perspective as an appearance of smoothness, coordination and grace; an efficient use of the athlete's physical abilities; a performance that is so efficient that it looks effortless; and a performance that is consistent even under pressure. It is for these reasons that attempting to simply replicate the technique of a sporting legend is unlikely to produce the next champion.

However, a common feature of sporting legends is that they do not leave any aspect of their performance to chance during their training and preparation for competition. Although this encompasses all training domains (e.g., psychological and physiological preparation), from a technical perspective, an expert per-former masters and maintains mastery of all of the fundamentals of the sport. For example, as a boy, Don Bradman hit a golf ball against a water tank using a cricket stump, which would have trained his eye–hand coordination.

Most sports contain one or many fundamental movements that need to be mastered such as running, jumping, kicking, throwing and catching either in isolation (e.g., distance running) or as a sequence (e.g., running and jumping in basketball). The constraints of these movements are physical (the athlete's anthropometry, strength, flexibility, training history), biomechanical (e.g., force generation) and environmental (rules, equipment). The importance of technical excellence has often been the domain of individual, judgement-based sports (e.g., diving, gymnastics), but is slowly emerging as an area of focus in team sports as well. In court sports such as netball, the opposing players are the judges. Technically excellent movement in netball can provide the advantage of being fast and hard to predict (e.g., deceptive plus interceptive, agile and adaptive, which results in better feeding of the ball up the court) as well as being less prone to injury.

moment of inertia. This is useful when they want to land after performing the somersault.

PRINCIPLES OF MOVEMENT ANALYSIS

There are two major categories of movement analysis principles: those that are universal and those that apply generally to most sports. These principles should be considered when analysing sport movement.

UNIVERSAL PRINCIPLES

Universal principles of movement analysis are aspects or elements that apply to all movements. They therefore can act as a guideline when assessing movement in sport. Universal principles enable the observation and assessment of generic features (e.g., arm-cocking action in throwing), as opposed to focusing only on known elements of specific sport technique (e.g., final arm-cocking position prior to the start of the arm acceleration phase).

Stretch-Shortening Cycle The stretch-shortening cycle describes a common muscle sequence in which the muscle is in an active state and stretches (eccentric contraction) prior to an immediate shortening (concentric contraction). The active stretch enables the muscle to produce more force than it could from an isolated isotonic (concentric) action.

For example, when running, the calf muscles are preactivated (active) prior to ground contact. The muscles are therefore ready to resist the impact with the ground, during which time they stretch eccentrically. The stretch phase is then followed by muscle shortening (concentric phase) during the propulsive phase (or thrust phase) of the running action.

A stretch-shortening cycle is also present in throwing when the pectoral (chest) muscles are actively stretched during the pre-cock arm action, followed by a shortening of the muscles during the arm acceleration phase.

In the softball windmill pitch, the pitcher performs a loaded start position during the preparatory movement, similar to a track start in athletics. The simple technical change of not pausing between the downward stretch movement and the upward knee drive into the pitch changes the technique to use a stretch-shortening cycle. The technical change results in a more forceful knee drive and resultant pitching motion, increasing the speed imparted to the ball.

Minimisation of Energy (Economy) and Reduction of Extraneous Movement As athletes become more skilled at a task, a reduction in extraneous or unnecessary movements that may have been present when they were first learning the skill occurs. This results in a more energy-efficient and economical movement pattern. This can be achieved from a better sequencing of the movement, from better control of individual joint patterns that maximise force generation and ideal application or both.

Even at the high-performance level, small technical corrections can further enhance the efficiency of an athlete's movement. For example, improved core stability can have a significant effect on running economy (see figure 11.3), especially if the athlete also has excessive upper-body rotation. Keeping the elbows closer to the body during the arm swing and driving with the elbows can also improve running efficiency by encouraging a more efficient and stable arm swing movement. An unstable and inefficient arm movement and core can also create instability in the lower extremities, which affects leg drive and the rear foot motion. This is because the human body is a linked-segment system.

AP Photo/Andres Leighton

In cricket, bowling takes advantage of the stretch-shortening cycle as the pectoral muscle is prestretched just before contraction.

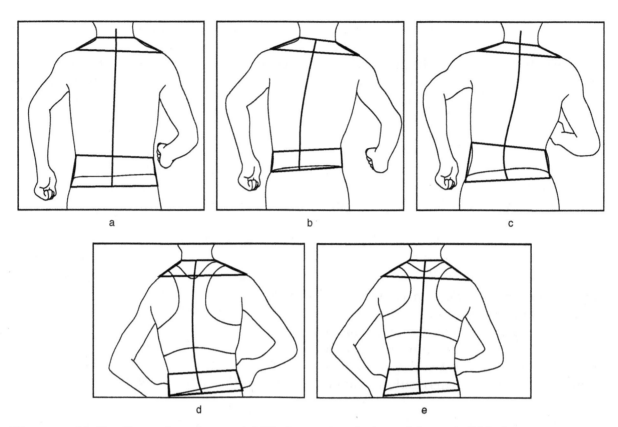

Figure 11.3 Examples of core stability in running that are *(a)* good, *(b)* below average, *(c)* poor, and *(d)* with excessive upper body rotation. *(e)* Improvement of poor core stability and reduced upper body rotation after two months of training intervention in a 17-year-old female distance runner.

SEMI-UNIVERSAL PRINCIPLES

Semi-universal principles are aspects or elements that apply to movement with few known exceptions. Like universal principles, they can suggest features to examine when assessing movement.

Sequential Muscle Sequencing The principle of sequential muscle sequencing is the same as the summation of force discussed earlier in this chapter. It is also known as a transfer of angular momentum, or the kinetic chain. It applies to sport activities that require maximal force or speed such as throwing and kicking.

Minimisation of Inertia The biomechanical principle of minimisation of inertia relates to increases in the acceleration of movement though the positioning of the distal (farthest end from the joint) end point of a body segment to minimise its inertia. For example, the flexion of the recovery leg during sprinting decreases the inertia of the leg, which increases its rota-

tional speed. This leads to a faster leg recovery phase. During the later drive phase of the leg, however, when the knee extends in preparation for ground contact, the inertia of the leg increases, which reduces its rotational speed. This slows the leg for the ground contact phase to enhance stability and force production.

Impulse Generation and Absorption Impulse is the product of force and time. This principle therefore applies to any sport that requires strength and speed. The generation of impulse produces a change in momentum (energy) of the body and can be achieved from a combination of a large force developed quickly and a smaller force developed over a long time.

An explosive and quick action is needed to generate impulse in most sport movements (e.g., a jump take-off). Therefore, the impulse is generated from a large force that has been developed quickly. During impulse absorption, the time of the action is long, which reduces the impact force (e.g., a jump landing). This tactic is also employed in catching tasks to absorb the momentum of the ball without injuring the hands.

Maximisation of the Acceleration Path Maximisation of the acceleration path relates to a change in mechanical energy and applies to sports that require strength, speed or both. This can be achieved from the generation of a large force or from increasing the distance over which the force is applied. For example, skilled soccer players lean their bodies away from the ball during a kick. This allows for a wider swing of the kicking leg, which increases its angular acceleration and the force imparted to the ball through the foot.

Balance and Stability Balance and stability can be either static (stationary) or dynamic (moving) and have been described earlier in this chapter. Increased stability in movement can enhance performance by increasing the efficiency, speed or economy of the movement. Improved stability also reduces the risk of injury during movement.

METHODS OF MOVEMENT ANALYSIS

A number of methods are used in analysing movement. The method selected depends on the knowledge and experience of the observer and the context in which the analysis is being performed. The three main methods of analysing the biomechanics of sport movements are movement phases, free body diagrams and deterministic models. Movement phases and free body diagrams are more frequently used by coaches and sports scientists, whereas

MOVEMENT ANALYSIS AND A SMOOTH SERVE

The 2011 US Open champion, Samantha Stosur, is widely regarded as having the best serve in the world in women's tennis. The universal and semi-universal movement analysis principles apply to Stosur's tennis serve. Her technique is coordinated and biomechanically sound, and this enables her to develop a high-powered and accurate serve with maximal spin. Tennis Australia mentor coach Rob Kilderry explained to the author of this chapter that Stosur has a smooth, rhythmic, relaxed and coordinated service action that adheres to sound biomechanical principles and enables her to generate maximal speed and spin.

Kilderry pointed out the following body positions and movement patterns in Stosur's service action. She commences the serve with a wide foot placement for good balance. As she steps her rear foot up under her right hip, she flexes her knees, placing the leg muscles on stretch to assist in the development of power. In the same action, Stosur rotates her hips and shoulders back, which stretches the chest muscles and loads them up with active energy. Her back foot comes up in unison with her left arm being raised to a perpendicular position with her head turned to the right and her racquet arm poised at a right angle at the elbow joint (often referred to as the trophy position), which helps to develop angular momentum.

The advantage of this technique is that it enables the release of energy from the stretched leg and chest muscles to accelerate the racquet head down the back and 'up and out' to the ball, while pronating the forearm and finishing with a wrist snap to maximise the speed of the serve. Stosur's body then follows through upwards and outwards into the court, with her legs making an arabesque movement as she lands on her left leg.

The speed of Stosur's serve is enhanced by excellent leg drive. Power in the shoulder joint of the racquet arm, created from the stretch-shortening cycle action and summation of forces, is conditional on the ball not dropping too far from the peak of the toss prior to impact.

Rob Kilderry believes that the challenge for tennis coaches in the future is to make better use of the body of knowledge, based on sound biomechanical principles, that is available for practical on-court teaching. This includes determining the cause of skill errors and the best methods for correcting them. In his opinion, 'Good teaching is the science of the future', which must commence when the player first picks up a tennis racquet.

deterministic models are used in more complex movement analysis and therefore more often in sports research.

MOVEMENT PHASES

A sport movement, especially for ballistic actions such as hitting, throwing and kicking, generally contain three main phases:

1. Preparation
2. Execution
3. Follow-through

The preparation phase contains all of the movements that prepare an athlete for the performance of the skill, such as the backswing during cricket batting and the run-up in long jumping. The execution phase is the performance of the actual movement that often includes a point of contact with an object (e.g., contact of the baseball bat and ball), the release of an object (e.g., discus) or a flight phase (e.g., long jump). Finally, the follow-through refers to all of the movements that occur after the execution phase (e.g., leg lift after kicking a football) that slow the body's momentum to prevent injury, to get ready for another movement or

both. These three main phases are often further broken into subphases or key elements.

Overarm throwing such as baseball pitching has three subphases for the preparation phase: the wind-up, the stride and arm cocking (see figure 11.4). Similarly, a standing shot in netball has three preparation subphases: stabilisation and preparation, aiming and loading. Other more complicated sport actions such as gymnastics vaulting can also be broken into movement phases, subphases and points of interest.

Gymnastics vaulting contains seven general phases: (1) the run-up; (2) the transition, which typically includes a hurdle step but may be also preceded by a round-off; (3) the board contact phase; (4) the preflight phase; (5) the table (horse) contact phase; (6) the postflight phase; and (7) the landing. The board contact phase can be broken into two subphases, the downward compression (loading and storage of energy in the springs) of the board and the upward reaction (recoil of the springs imparting energy back to the gymnast). A point of interest, for example, is the gymnast's take-off angle from the board and the table contact angle at the end of the preflight phase.

Figure 11.4 The subphases of the preparation phase of a baseball pitch: *(a)* wind-up, *(b)* stride and *(c)* arm cocking.

FREE BODY DIAGRAMS

A free body diagram is a visual diagram of the expected or predicted movement pattern; it is usually drawn as a simple stick figure. Coaches and researchers often use the technique to describe a subphase or point of interest in a movement pattern. Coaches may use free body diagrams to communicate to athletes or to illustrate to other coaches what they believe is good technique.

In research, a free body diagram defines the extent of the analysis and identifies the significant forces involved in the action using arrows, along with the directional coordinates relevant to that movement pattern (e.g., a two-dimensional or three-dimensional coordinate system). The free body diagram typically shows only the forces acting on the system and not those within the system (e.g., muscle forces).

DETERMINISTIC MODELS

A deterministic model is a concept map that describes the biomechanical factors determining a movement or action, starting with the primary performance factor(s) (e.g., jump dis-placement for long jump, race time in sprinting), followed by a breakdown into secondary factors (or derivatives) and so on. Hence, a deterministic model can have many levels. Figure 11.5 provides an example of a deterministic model. More examples of deterministic models can be found in *The Biomechanics of Sports Techniques* (Hay, 1993).

Regardless of the technique employed, movement analysis requires careful planning. These techniques may also suit qualitative or quantitative analyses of movement. Qualitative analysis assesses the technical quality of the movement (e.g., rhythm, posture), whereas quantitative techniques assess the movement using numbers (e.g., angles, distance, speed, force).

PROCESS OF MOVEMENT ANALYSIS

Movement analysis in sport contains six general steps:

1. **Question.** Identify a question, problem, idea or goal.

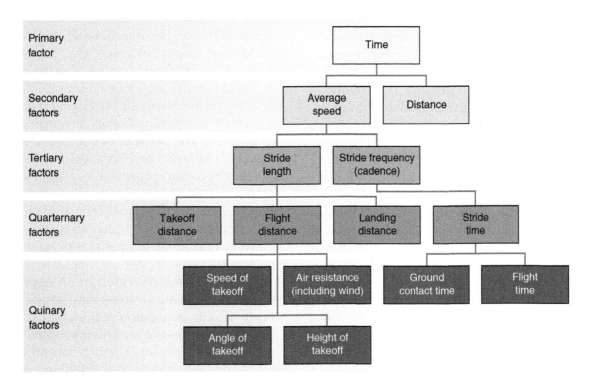

Figure 11.5 A deterministic model of running.

2. **Preparation.** Determine what and how to observe.

3. **Observation.** Observe the performance.

4. **Evaluation.** Detect faults and weaknesses.

5. **Intervention.** Provide feedback to the athlete and advise on how to improve a technique, correct a problem or both.

6. **Re-evaluation.** Evaluate the training intervention.

Movement analysis is used with athletes to identify a question, problem or idea. However, it may also be used to simply monitor changes in technique or predicted changes resulting from a training intervention, to monitor progress in rehabilitation from injury or to provide biomechanical data for research about that sporting skill.

During the preparation step, the purpose of the sporting skill should be identified. Movement analysis methods such as movement phases, free body diagrams and deterministic models are then used to identify the expected movement parameters and deviations, and determine what general biomechanical principles apply (e.g., stretch-shortening cycle muscle action). This also helps with planning how the movement will be observed and analysed.

When planning how to observe the movement, coaches should consider what information is required to answer the question. This will determine whether the movement is observed qualitatively using video or quantitatively using video with video analysis software or other methods (e.g., speed gun, timing gates, contact mats, force platforms, GPS tracking devices). This is also affected by the athlete's experience of receiving technical feedback. With athletes who have never received feedback on the biomechanics of their movements, it is important to start with simple, but often just as effective questions, evaluation and interventions.

Quantitative analyses are generally warranted for use with movements that occur too quickly and in which differences in position are too subtle to notice, especially when a high-speed camera is not accessible. Consideration should also be given to factors that affect sport performance such as environmental conditions, anxiety and fatigue. For a movement pattern to be valid, it should occur in a context closely related to normal performance such as training, a simulated competition or real-life competition.

Selecting how to observe the movement is also affected by how many times observations are needed to obtain a reliable assessment (usually at least three), whether any technical equipment will interfere with the regular environment, and if using video, the angles from which the observations must be made. Sometimes coaches need to familiarise athletes with the movement analysis protocol so they know what to expect and are comfortable. This is important if there are any equipment changes (e.g., a beat board instrumented with a contact mat in gymnastics) or objects or cables will be placed onto the athlete such as when using accelerometers (a method of measuring acceleration and estimating force) or electromyography (EMG, a method of measuring muscle activation patterns).

Following the performance observation comes the important step of evaluation. The evaluation depth and time depends on the original question, the athlete's expectations and experience, the relevance of the time of evaluation to performance (e.g., providing feedback two to three months after the observation is usually no longer relevant because athletes' performances have changed during that time), the minimal analysis required for an accurate and reliable evaluation and the observer's knowledge and experience. During this stage coaches must not lose sight of the purpose of the movement analysis, which is the original question, problem or idea. This can often occur during detailed quantitative analyses that involve large sets of numerical data.

Good feedback provided in an appropriate manner during training can significantly improve skill acquisition and enable a coach to modify or enhance an athlete's technique to improve performance. During normal training conditions, athletes are active in correcting errors; however, on some occasions they need further extrinsic feedback from coaches. Because coaches guide this training process, they can benefit from a strong understanding of biomechanics. Such an understanding helps them evaluate athletes' performances and choose training strategies that improve their athletes' performance while avoiding injury.

Specifically, coaches' feedback to athletes should be as simple as possible. Complex and detailed critiques of athletes' movement can be overwhelming. Athletes are best served by receiving a simple evaluation summary with a maximum of three key points (aided by feedback suited to their learning preferences such as video). Coaches should discuss with athletes how that information can be used in their training program (the intervention). These key points may lead to coaching cues to use during technical training.

The benefits of using movement analysis techniques in coaching practice can only be revealed if the athlete is re-evaluated after an appropriate intervention period (minimum of eight weeks). Re-evaluating the athlete may enable the coach and athlete to decide on a further technical area of focus that was not as important or apparent during the initial analysis. Finally, a coach who needs to seek help from a sports biomechanist or other expert because the cause of an athlete's movement problem is not apparent after simple investigations needs to have a clear understanding of what is needed, and the coach needs to lead the process. Because coaches know their athlete best, they should guide the process and associate any feedback with the athletes' training. Coaches should accompany athletes to any testing environment, and must not be afraid to ask many questions or debate the results.

TECHNOLOGY FOR MOVEMENT ANALYSIS

Technology for movement analysis is rapidly changing and improving, with standard consumer technology also now offering suitable tools for coaching. Technology applicable to movement analysis in sport can generally be categorised according to the biomechanical measures they provide, including the following:

- Temporal (timing) measures that describe movement
- Kinematic (position, angles, displacement, velocity) measures that describe movement
- Kinetic measures (force platforms, force transducers, pressure sensors, electromyography) that can explain the causes of movement, such as why one athlete can jump higher than another athlete can

It is impossible to discuss all of the technology available in sport, so this section outlines those most relevant to coaches and sports biomechanics practice. Temporal measurement systems include radar guns, laser distance measuring devices, timing gate systems, contact mats and video cameras. Contact mats have also been used by some sports practitioners to estimate ground reaction forces and jump power (i.e., kinetics); however, because these estimates are inaccurate, they should be avoided. Video cameras are a basic tool for temporal and kinematic analysis when combined with computer video analysis software. Other kinematic tools are electromagnetic tracking systems; global positioning systems; accelerometers; motion suits with built-in inertial sensors that can measure position, orientation and acceleration; and more advanced automated three-dimensional motion capture systems that are more often used in biomechanics testing centres and sports research laboratories.

Because video is popular technology in coaching, it is important to highlight some important points related to video camera selection and operation. When selecting a video camera, coaches should look for an adjustable shutter speed, a manual focus, and if working outdoors during sunset, a low light function. Adjusting the shutter speed is a key feature when collecting high-quality video in sport. Shutter speed is the length of time the shutter is open and the lens is exposed to light to capture the image. A standard shutter speed for everyday domestic filming is 1/25 s (1/25th of a second), whereas for faster movements in sport, a higher shutter should be used such as 1/250 to 1/500 s for athletics, and 1/1000 s for golf. This ensures a clear image when the video is played back frame by frame.

For fast movements such as a golf swing, standard video cameras do not capture key points of interest such as ball contact because of their limited capture speed. A high-speed camera is required to successfully capture ball contact in golf. Increasing the shutter speed or the capture speed will increase the lighting requirements. When videoing outdoors in bright sunshine, this is not a problem; however, in lower light conditions indoors, extra lighting may be required. Another important piece of equipment is a tripod to keep the camera stable and help capture a large view of the movement.

Force platforms are becoming a more accessible tool in sport as a result of new portable designs. Force platforms contain a force transducer in each corner, each of which acts much like a spring, compressing and expanding when loaded and unloaded. Force platforms can be used to measure loading patterns on the body during actual athletic movements such as long jump take-offs, or can be used to measure athletes' physical strength. A growing body of research shows that measures of peak forces are better estimates of sport performance than traditional measures of jump height or distance. For example, peak vertical take-off force during a counter-movement jump has been identified as a good indicator of floor tumbling ability in gymnastics. Hopping peak vertical take-off force and ground contact time and horizontal peak take-off force have been revealed as good indicators of sprinting ability.

Other kinetic measurement systems are pressure sensor shoe insoles, mats that measure the normal contact force applied per square centimetre and electromyography. Pressure measurements provide more detailed information on the loading patterns such as, for example, through the sole of the foot during running and in the saddle during dressage riding.

Electromyography enables the measurement of the muscle activation patterns and provides a rough estimate of how the muscle is producing force. Surface electrodes are used in sport because fine-wire (needle-like) electrodes are not appropriate for measuring movement. The limitation of surface electromyography is that it can only measure the more superficial muscles and not the deeper muscles such as the transverse abdominis. Electromyography can be used to identify potential causes of reinjury in athletes, especially when combined with other movement analysis techniques such as video.

Figure 11.6 shows the use of electromyography in running to identify imbalances in the muscle activation patterns of a footballer. The right ankle had been previously injured numerous times. When combined with video-based measures, this indicated that the athlete was predominantly plantarflexing his right ankle during ground contact, which effectively doubles the forces travelling through his ankle and Achilles tendon.

Related to electromyography is ultrasonography, which is more of a kinematic measuring technique of the movement of the muscle; it is also used for assessing tendons. Ultrasonography capturing frequency is now above 25 hertz, and therefore its applications in sport are slowly developing. Its limitation at present is the difficulty attaching and keeping the probe stable on the body's surface during movement; however, it is being used to assess tendon stiffness during vertical movements such as loaded squats.

SURFACES AND EQUIPMENT

Sport surfaces are usually complex structures composed of many layers of materials that all contribute to the overall behaviour of the surface and its interaction with the athlete. Sport surfaces include athletic track surfaces, natural and artificial turf, indoor and outdoor game surfaces (e.g., netball court) and gymnastics mats. Artificial turf for soccer fields attempts to mimic natural grass without the temperature and wearing degradations, and typically contains five layers: a rigid substratum of compact gravel or concrete, a deformable elastic layer, sand, rubber and then the artificial grass fibres.

Sports equipment also incorporates materials and includes clothing, protective equipment

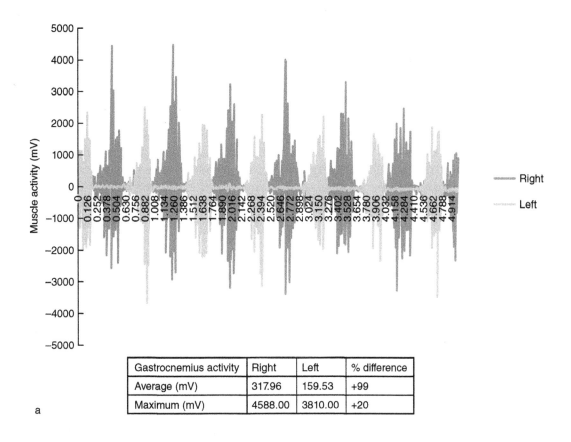

Gastrocnemius activity	Right	Left	% difference
Average (mV)	317.96	159.53	+99
Maximum (mV)	4588.00	3810.00	+20

a

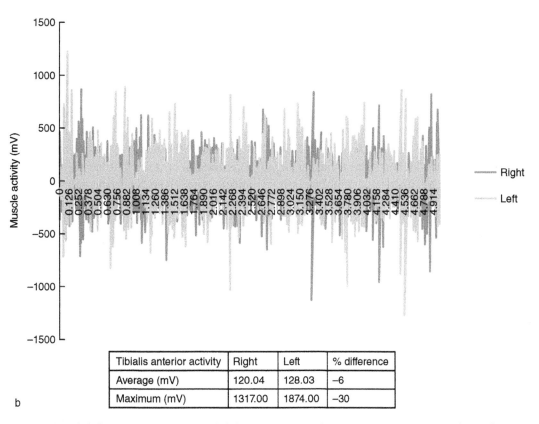

Tibialis anterior activity	Right	Left	% difference
Average (mV)	120.04	128.03	−6
Maximum (mV)	1317.00	1874.00	−30

b

Figure 11.6 *(a)* Gastrocnemius and *(b)* tibialis anterior activation patterns for a footballer.

and striking objects. Fencing incorporates all three of these. Fencing clothing includes a jacket, shoes, pants, socks and shoes. The protective equipment includes a mask, Kevlar material in an underarm protective jacket as well as in the main jacket, rigid plastic protectors that are gender specific (cups for males and breast plates for females) and a glove for the fencing hand. The striking object depends on the style of fencing and can be a foil, epee or sabre.

Because both surfaces and equipment can influence the athlete, any modifications (if within the rules of the sport) require careful evaluation that takes into account the athlete's anthropometry (physical dimensions) and any injury considerations. For example, a change in footwear or surface characteristics can alter the ground reaction forces (magnitude and direction). This leads to a change in the muscle activation patterns of the leg extensor muscles. The footwear–surface interaction in most sports can be a mechanism of injury if the biomechanics are suboptimal as a result of the frequency of contact.

Another example of the importance of equipment and surfaces is when fitting a bike to a rider. Making sure that the handlebars are not wider than the rider's shoulders is one simple step to ensuring good stability through the front wheel and steering ability. Another simple step is ensuring that the seat and its brackets are horizontally level when viewed from behind. Equipment misalignment such as a faulty or damaged bike seat can also be a mechanism of injury.

CHARACTERISTICS OF SPORT SURFACES

Biopositive and *bionegative* are terms used to describe the effect of a surface on the performer. A biopositive surface enhances athletes' movement, allowing them to perform movements that would not be possible on a standard surface. For example, the triple twist on the floor in gymnastics is only possible because of the elastic floor surface. A bionegative surface reduces the athlete's movement when compared to a standard surface. Sand is an example of a bionegative surface. Therefore, it is more difficult to play volleyball on a sand-based court than on traditional wooden flooring. Wearing shoes with spikes on a dry ground surface can lead to excessive penetration and increased energy cost because of the slowing of the foot movement that occurs when withdrawing the spikes. The shoe–surface interaction then has a bionegative effect on the athlete's movement.

Friction and *traction* describe the force created between a shoe or other object (e.g., bobsled, skis, snowboard, golf ball, tennis ball) and a surface. The force acts parallel to the contact area between the shoe and the surface. Friction often provides stability in a movement by stopping the object from sliding across the surface.

When an athlete is running, the friction force acts in the opposite direction to the rotating foot's motion, thereby stabilising the foot during ground contact. During the early to middle phase of ground contact, when the foot is creating braking forces, the friction force acts against the athlete's direction of travel. However, during the middle to late phase of ground contact, when the foot is creating propulsive forces, the friction force acts in the athlete's direction of travel, but against the backward pushing motion of the foot. The friction force generated depends on the object–surface interface coefficient of friction and the normal contact force between them.

The coefficient of friction is a dimensionless number (a quantity with no physical dimensions and therefore no units) that describes the object–surface interface during static and dynamic movement. It is specific to the two materials in contact with each other. For example, the coefficient of dynamic friction should be higher than 1.1 for running movements with or without changes of direction such as swerves, cutting and turning. To meet this requirement on an athletic surface, such as Mondo, athletes wear shoes with spikes. This creates a special form of friction force known as traction. Traction is the force created by the interlocking of two surfaces, which in athletics is the penetration of the shoes spikes into the Mondo surface. Friction that is too high or too low can have an association with injury. For example, friction is 10 to 40 per cent higher on artificial turf than on grass.

Friction can also be reduced by using lubrication (e.g., wax, oil) or increased by using a high-viscosity substance such as glue or honey. Ballet dancers often use a white powdery substance called rosin (made from the sap of fir trees) on pointe shoes to create a higher coefficient of static friction and a lower coefficient of dynamic friction. This enables the dancer to stick to the floor when on pointe for slower movements, but not during faster gliding, horizontal movements such as a glissade.

Resilience is a measure of the energy absorbed by the surface that is then returned to the striking object. For most surfaces in sports, this relates to the viscoelastic behaviour of the surface. The surface material for the ground, court or field also has an effect on its resilience. For example, a synthetic tennis court has a higher resilience than a grass tennis court. A lack of surface resilience can cause fatigue and therefore has a relationship to injury.

In cricket, ball bounce resilience relates to the description of the pitch surface as being fast or slow. When the surface is hard and dry, the ground reaction force from the impact of the ball on the pitch is higher so that the ball bounces more; a very fast pitch results from high resilience (R > 15.6 per cent). When the pitch is wet, moisture in the subsurface has a cushioning effect on the impact force of the ball. The ball bounces less and a very slow pitch results from low resilience (R < 7.8 per cent).

The compliance and hardness of a surface are not related to resilience. The compliance of a surface relates to its deformation when loaded; whereas the hardness of a surface relates to its resistance to penetration in its upper layer. Hard surfaces such as concrete have a low compliance, whereas softer surfaces have a high compliance. There is an optimum compliance and hardness for a surface in sport. Hard and low-compliant surfaces can increase the risk of injury as a result of larger impact forces. Soft and high-compliant surfaces can be fatiguing.

Force reduction describes the percentage of maximal impact force reduction experienced on the surface, compared with what would be experienced on concrete. Athletic tracks have a force reduction of 35 to 50 per cent; a fast track has a lower force reduction making it tolerable for international competition but not suitable for everyday training.

INJURY ASPECTS OF SPORT SURFACES

The likelihood of injury on a sport surface relates to the loading impact magnitude and rate, the resilience, its compliance and hardness, its consistency in these characteristics, the coefficient of friction between the surface and the shoe or object and how the athlete interacts with the surface. Impact loads, for example, are typically lower on surfaces that allow sliding such as tennis courts. Runners also adjust their foot strike patterns on hard surfaces by contacting the ground more through the forefoot than the heel.

A surface analysis completed on the Cirque du Soleil training stage provides a good example of the importance of a consistent sport surface. The compliance and hardness of the surface was revealed to be inconsistent, with minimal compliance on top of the supporting beams (<1 millimetre) and high compliance between the supporting beams (10 to 22 millimetres). This meant that the performers could not preactivate their leg muscles appropriately for their impact with the surface during their movements, resulting in a 25 per cent injury rate. To decrease the high-impact forces and vibrations on the performer, the company made the stage surface harder and more consistent.

Volleyball court surfaces may also play a role in the occurrence of injury, especially to the lower leg, because of the large number of vertical landing movements. The vertical impact force magnitude and rates are higher on traditional wooden flooring and tartan flooring surfaces than on artificial turf. Therefore, the obvious conclusion may be to change to an artificial turf surface for volleyball training. However, artificial turf has a lower resilience (energy return rate) and therefore is not ideal from a performance perspective. A surface combination with a higher resilience and compliance, such as a synthetic surface, may be required. This would necessitate careful testing because of the change of the surface–player interaction. The high lower leg injury rates in volleyball could also be caused by other factors such as the players' landing biomechanics as opposed to the court surface itself.

RUNNING SHOES

A good running shoe is designed to reduce repetitive ground impact forces, maintain stability of the rear-foot movement, provide adequate friction or traction for the athletic activity, allow for variations in foot-strike movement patterns, avoid exacerbation of any rear-foot movement or structural irregularities, be comfortable and dissipate heat. Shoes therefore contain specific structural features such as closed-cell polymeric foam (EVA) in the midsole and wedges of the heel. Coaches should look for key features in shoes for running, but need to keep in mind that athletic shoes can vary greatly in structural design for sport-specific purposes (e.g., sprinting, discus, high jumping, rugby, squash).

A shoe that is uncomfortable and exacerbates any rear-foot movement pattern abnormalities is not suitable for an athlete. Athlete characteristics coaches should also consider include the athlete's arch structure (high and flexible, flat and rigid, in between) and rear-foot motion, as illustrated in figure 11.7.

Normal rear-foot motion during ground contact involves a process of force dissipation and generation. It starts with a lateral-sided foot strike with the lower leg and foot aligned neutrally (lower leg and heel roughly vertical, foot aligned in the running direction). As the foot is loaded with the runner's body weight, the heel (calcaneus) rotates into an everted (valgus) position to stabilise the foot. During the later propulsive phase, the heel rotates into an inverted (varus) position, as the runner uses the generated ground reaction force to create momentum.

The first key feature of a running shoe is the shape of the sole, which is referred to as the last. A shoe with a straight rather than curved last reduces excessive rear-foot calcaneal eversion (commonly known as hyperpronation). A more rigid foot that does not adequately pronate requires a curved last.

The amount of lateral heel flare is a second key feature of a running shoe. Lateral heel flare increases the distance (moment arm) between the ground reaction force during the initial laterally sided foot strike and the subtalar (ankle) joint centre, which increases the rotational forces (torque). Lateral heel flare is therefore not suitable for hyperpronators but can be used to protect the Achilles tendon from large

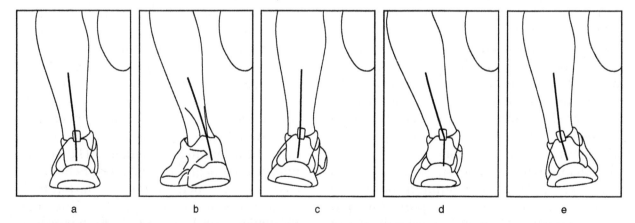

Figure 11.7 Types of rear foot motion: *(a)* normal, *(b)* forefoot abduction, *(c)* forefoot adduction, *(d)* excessive calcaneal eversion (valgus), and *(e)* calcaneal inversion (varus) at initial ground contact. The last two abnormalities are often reported as excessive pronation and excessive supination, respectively, but are not able to be accurately identified from two dimensional video or images.

forces when combined with a wedged insole for athletes prone to Achilles tendinopathy. The heel tab of the shoe also has a role in protecting the Achilles tendon; however, it should not be too high or too hard because these can cause inflammation of the tendon. Aside from these features, running shoes should be replaced regularly because they can lose a significant proportion of their shock-absorbing ability after only 800 kilometres (about 500 miles) of running, even though they can still appear as good as new.

SPORT-SPECIFIC SURFACES

There are numerous examples of sport-specific materials and surfaces. The 250 to 450 dimples on a golf ball reduce form drag (also known as pressure or shape drag) during flight, enabling it to travel farther. A pool's design determines whether it is classified as a fast or slow pool for competition. This is based on whether it contains features to reduce wave drag that develops when swimmers enter the water. The lane ropes float on the surface of the water and contain circular wheels that spin to diffuse wave drag developed by a swimmer in an individual lane. This reduces the wave drag that travels into another swimmer's lane. A gutterless pool design, which allows the water to spill over the edge, prevents the wave drag that results when water rebounds from the sides.

Smart materials that can harden when subjected to impact forces are now being used in protective zones (e.g., knee and elbow padding) in winter sports such as downhill and aerial skiing and also in ballet pointe shoes. Compression garments such as shorts, tights (leggings) and socks aim to improve circulation and reduce muscle vibration (oscillation) to aid performance and enhance recovery.

SUMMARY

- Coaches should consider the unique characteristics of each athlete when applying biomechanical principles (e.g., whether the athlete has the physical strength or flexibility to execute the target technique). Always viewing athletes from the side with the naked eye, or with a video camera, limits the coach's perspective. A better all-round perspective can be gained by viewing athletes from various directions.

- Athletes need to develop smooth and efficient movements to maximise performance and prevent injury. This often requires attention to the fundamentals (basics) of their movement patterns.

- Technology is very useful in monitoring the progress of athletes. Athletes should have the opportunity to have a practice session with new or unfamiliar technology before its use in training or competition evaluation, especially if the equipment is placed on the athlete's body (e.g. electromyography electrodes). This aims to ensure that the athlete is comfortable with the technology so that their normal movement patterns are captured.

- Simple video can provide a good visual resource for re-evaluating athletes' technical improvements against set goals and strategies. It removes the guesswork from evaluating whether the training intervention is working or requires modification.

- More advanced technology may be needed to properly answer some movement questions or problems, especially for fast movements. Electromyography, for example, can be used to examine activation patterns of superficial muscles which may provide insight on the cause of injury or re-injury.

REFERENCES AND RESOURCES

Bartlett, R. (1999). *Sports biomechanics: Reducing injury and improving performance*. London: E & FN Spon.

Carr, G. (2004). *Sports mechanics for coaches* (2nd ed.). Champaign, IL: Human Kinetics.

Cavanagh, P.R. (1990). *Biomechanics of distance running*. Champaign, IL: Human Kinetics.

Hamill, J., & Knutzen, K.M. (2008). *Biomechanical basis of human movement* (3rd ed.). Baltimore: Lippincott Williams & Wilkins.

Hall, S.J. (2010). *Basic biomechanics* (6th ed.). New York: McGraw-Hill.

Hay, J. (1993). *The biomechanics of sports techniques* (4th ed.). Englewood Cliffs, NJ: Prentice Hall.

McGinnis, P.M. (2005). *Biomechanics of sport and exercise* (2nd ed.). Champaign, IL: Human Kinetics.

Nigg, B.M., Cole, G.K., & Stefanyshyn, D.J. (2003). *Sport surfaces, biomechanics, injuries, performance, testing, installation*. Calgary: Topline Printing.

Potthast, W., Verhelst, R., Hughes, M., Stone, K., & De Clerq, D. (2010). Football-specific evaluation of player-surface interaction on different football turf systems. *Sports Technology, 3* (1), 5-12.

Severn, K.A., Fleming, P.R., & Dixon, N. (2010). Science of synthetic turf surfaces: Player-surface interactions. *Sports Technology, 3* (1), 13-25.

CHAPTER 12

Teaching Sport Skills

——— Damian Farrow

Improving athletes' acquisition of technical and tactical skills entails both the art and science of coaching. This chapter focuses on the sufficiently 'road-tested' scientific approaches that coaches can employ with confidence. At times this science directly challenges established coaching convention, and on other occasions, it is complementary.

The principles of advanced and fundamental skill acquisition do not differ; what does vary is the attention to detail a coach must invest in creating an effective skill learning environment. Athlete skill acquisition centres on the coach's effective manipulation of two key factors: (1) the design of the practice environment and (2) the provision of instruction and feedback. These two coaching tools can be used in a myriad of ways to create skill learning. This chapter presents the guiding principles that a coach should consider when determining when and how to manipulate these factors.

The chapter starts with a clear definition of skill learning followed by key skill practice guidelines that are accompanied by examples to show how they can be manipulated. These manipulations require an understanding of how practice conditions can be subtly modified to maximise athletes' skill learning. The final section features advanced instruction and feedback techniques that challenge coaches to rethink more traditional teaching methods and weigh the use of new technologies that can, when used inappropriately, undermine rather than promote learning.

SKILL LEARNING VERSUS SKILL PERFORMANCE

Following a skill development session or a series of sessions, many coaches feel uneasy because they are unsure whether the player has genuinely learned the new skill, implying a permanent change in skill level, or whether the player has simply made a transient improvement that will disappear before the next practice session. This is referred to as the *performance or learning* issue; understanding the difference between these closely related terms and, in turn, how they interact with various practice and feedback approaches is critical to creating genuine skill development.

Obviously, each time an athlete repeats a skill, he is *performing* the skill. If he is not influenced by factors such as fatigue, this performance is likely to be a good illustration of his level of skill learning. However, coaches need to understand some fundamental differences between performing and learning.

Skill *performance* is an athlete's observable skill execution at any particular moment in time. It is a transient state and can be highly variable, sensitive to conditions such as fatigue, motivation, environmental conditions and coach instructions (see Schmidt & Wrisberg, 2004). For example, a tennis player learning a new forehand swing pattern may hit a number of well-executed strokes in a row from a coach's hand feed, but as soon as she moves to a more open rally situation, her stroke performance becomes increasingly variable: The movement pattern disappears for a couple of strokes and then reappears and so on. These wild shifts in performance success are indicative of observable performance, which is strongly influenced in this case by the coach's ball-feeding ability.

Skill *learning* is regarded as a permanent improvement in skill performance as a result of practice, suggesting that some underlying mechanisms (e.g., muscle recruitment, nervous system control) have been developed in some way. Because these developing internal processes are difficult to observe, coaches need to assess learning by observing the athlete's performance. The trick is to make such assessment when transient influences such as coach instruction or fatigue have dissipated.

Two of the simplest and most effective methods to assess learning are retention (transfer) testing and dual-tasking. In retention testing, the skill is assessed following a period of no practice (e.g., after a day or a week). This reveals whether the skill change is permanent and not directly influenced by short-term but transient performance factors such as a previous practice session. Quite often, when focused practice is devoted to a particular skill, rapid progress is seen over a session as a result of the strong feedback and practice provided by the coach. At the end of such sessions, coaches often conclude that the players have picked up the skill really well or mastered the key component. Yet the reality is that they improved their performance of the skill; a retention test is required to more accurately assess skill learning.

A practical way to do retention testing in a coaching environment is to start a practice session with a test of what was practised in the previous session. An alternative method to test learning is to transfer the skill to a new context to see whether the skill change holds in this

Zuma Press/Icon SMI

When developing new skills, such as changing a golf swing, athletes and coaches must ensure the new skills carries over into the competitive environment.

transferred (or different) context. For example, the tennis player could now be asked to hit the new forehand in a rally situation rather than from a coach-fed ball.

Obviously, the ultimate test of transfer is whether the athlete can maintain a level of skill performance or technique when under competitive stress. Continuing with the tennis example, the coach should test whether the player can maintain her new forehand swing pattern in a match situation against an opponent hitting to her with a variety of depth, spins and ball heights. Coaches are understandably reluctant to send their players into competitive environments too early to assess whether the skill has been cemented as a permanent change.

A useful alternative to assessing learning in competition is to use a dual-task test. This test is based on a learning theory that as skill levels develop, performers are able to devote less conscious attention to the execution of the skill. In the case of dual-tasking, as the name suggests, the test requires the player to do two things at once. Our tennis player would be required to maintain her new forehand technique while rallying and performing a secondary task such as counting backwards in 3s from 100.

The logic of this test is that if the primary skill (the forehand, in this case) is cemented as a learned change, the player will have spare attentional capacity to complete the secondary task (backwards counting). If she cannot maintain her new forehand swing pattern while counting, the coach quickly knows that the skill is not yet permanent and that further practice is required. Any number of secondary tasks could be used (e.g., rhyming words, simple math sums); the aim is purely to load up the player's attentional capacity. An added advantage of dual-tasking is that players find this a fun activity.

EFFECTIVE SKILL PRACTICE

Skill practice has become a hot topic over the last decade in part as a result of society's fascination with how expertise is developed. A number of best-selling books written by journalists have been influential (see Coyle,

2010; Gladwell, 2008) in translating some of the theory into practice. The content of these books centres on the conditions (i.e., natural talent versus practice volume) required for expertise to be developed. Much of the impetus and scientific evidence reported has been drawn from Anders Ericsson's theory of deliberate practice (see Ericsson, Krampe, & Tesch-Römer, 1993; Ericsson & Starkes, 2003). Ericsson proposed that expertise can be explained by the accumulation of 'deliberate practice' or the time spent performing a task with a well-defined goal, set at a level of difficultly that will challenge current performance but can be mastered within hours of practice by concentrated effort, augmented with feedback and ample opportunities for repetition and corrections of errors (Ericsson, 2006).

This definition of practice is very specific, and any practice that does not meet this strict definition cannot be considered deliberate. Depending on what one has read, one could be convinced that deliberate practice is essential for the development of sport expertise. However, a number of unresolved issues should give coaches pause before blindly accepting all the assumptions of this approach.

For instance, there is great debate over whether competition should be considered part of the deliberate practice framework, in part because Ericsson's theory was first developed based on the practice habits of virtuoso violinists, not sport performers. Further, the typical experimental evidence collected has suggested that 10,000 deliberate practice hours are necessary to reach expert status in the sport or skill practised, yet Australian evidence demonstrates that team sport athletes seem to need far less (see Baker, Côté, & Abernethy, 2003). Although Ericsson's theory is persuasive and supported by experimental evidence, coaches need to consider the context in which theories are developed before they apply them to their programs.

Although there is not space here to detail the pros and cons of Ericsson's theory, a few key points should be made. No one disagrees that significant practice time and repetition are required to develop skill and that deliberate practice is part of this process. The notion that the 1st and 10,000th hours of practice should be equally challenging is appealing, yet there is still great debate on the specific nature of this practice (see Baker & Cobley, 2008, for more discussion). Additionally, some coaches have misinterpreted or misstated (neither the fault of Ericsson) this guideline and erroneously claim that athletes need 10,000 practice *repetitions* to become expert performers.

Irrespective of considerations of the previously noted misinterpretations, Erissson's theory only provides guidelines about the volume of practice required but doesn't really assist coaches with the microplanning of a practice session. So let's look at how the specific organisation and content of practice trials may actually generate various skill learning rates and subsequently alter the volume of practice required.

MAXIMISING PRACTICE VARIABILITY

How a coach organises and distributes practice repetitions within a session has a profound impact on how much learning occurs. Although a popular coaching adage is *Practice makes perfect*, skill acquisition practitioners have a different mantra: *Repetition without repetition*. In other words, it's not the repetition of an identical hockey hit that generates learning; rather, it's forcing a player to adapt his technique to achieve a consistent outcome goal. Put simply, a player who has to think (not necessarily consciously) about how to hit the ball to reach the intended target before every strike will generate greater skill learning than a player who only has to solve this problem the first time he strikes the ball in a drill, after which time every strike is the same, so minimal mental effort is required.

An important issue associated with adopting a practice approach that forces the player to engage in active problem solving rather than passive practice, is that it can often lead to highly variable skill execution and inconsistent performance outcomes within a given session. Many coaches perceive this inconsistency as negative and adapt the practice drills to remove the so-called error. However, this is the very

source of the advantage gained from variable practice. Learning is messy!

The challenge for coaches is to determine an acceptable range of messiness, or what is termed functional variability. That is, to achieve an acceptable learning rate, the player must be suitably challenged but able to achieve the task goal. The accepted range of variability may be narrower as the skill level of the performer increases. This can be called 'finding the challenge point' (Guadagnoli, 2007) and is discussed in the next section.

In short, well-organised practice (that is, with sufficient variability and challenge) can actually reduce the number of practice repetitions required for learning to occur. Practice variability can be created in many ways. Researchers have learned a lot about practice variability by comparing random practice and blocked practice and examining the role of mental effort in the results of both. It has been found that the greater the mental effort a learner uses, the better the resultant learning is.

Random practice involves alternating between two (or more) skills or variations on each practice attempt. For example, a swimmer may perform one start and then one turn and then repeat this process (start, turn and so on). Neither the start nor the turn is practised repeatedly by itself. Alternatively, blocked practice involves practising one skill continuously for a set of attempts before moving on to another skill. For example, the swimmer completes all start repetitions before performing any turning practice.

Research has found that blocked practice leads to better *performance* of the skills in the short term compared to random practice. This would seem logical because players can get into the groove on a given skill during a practice session. However, when the skills are examined over the longer term to determine whether the practice performance is permanent, random practice produces improved retention or *learning* of the skill. This is a good demonstration of the need to separate learning and performance effects to truly assess the value of a specific practice approach.

These paradoxical effects (i.e., blocked practice leads to superior practice performance

VARIABILITY AND REPETITION IN PRACTICE

Researchers have examined the issue of practice variability and repetition over a long history of skill acquisition research. The results have shown that even for relatively closed skills such as a basketball free throw, it is valuable to expose players to practice variability so they are required to problem solve and potentially adapt their technique to meet their task objective.

A classic study (Kozar et al., 1994) examining the basketball free-throw shooting accuracy of an NCAA Division 1 men's team in practice and in competition highlights the importance of making every repetition count. Players were found to shoot an average of seven or eight shots in a row each time they practised the skill. Contrast this to the game setting, in which either one or two shots in a row are the norm. Practice free-throw accuracy was 74.5 per cent, compared with game accuracy of 69 per cent. Of most interest was when the first two free throws in practice were analysed separately; the accuracy was 69.8 per cent, or the same as game performance. This highlights the importance of spacing repetitions so they all count equally. It also highlights the importance of practice specificity, or put simply, the amount of transfer from practice to the game depends on how closely practice conditions resemble the game.

These findings can be applied to set shot goal kicking in Australian football. Typically, this skill is done in blocks in which players kick 10 shots in a row from the same spot or various positions around the goal-face, often without a man on the mark. From a practice specificity perspective, better transfer could be expected if those 10 shots were taken in five blocks of two kicks or 10 blocks of one kick (if well planned and time permitted) throughout a training session and with a man on the mark.

but poorer learning than random practice) can be explained by the relative amount of mental effort generated by each approach. A random practice session results in higher levels of mental effort than a blocked practice session because of the need to continually switch between skills. Players are forced to more actively process the skill requirements each time they practise the skill, whereas in a blocked practice session learners can 'switch off' after repeating the same skill a few times in a row. Although random practice generates more learning than blocked practice does, the characteristics of an individual player and the purpose of a session both affect the choice of method in a practical setting (see Patterson & Lee, 2008).

FINDING THE CHALLENGE POINT

The skill level and experience of a learner determines whether random or blocked practice would be most helpful to learning. Specifically, beginners who have no experience or little skill in the tasks to be practised benefit more from blocked practice than random practice. It's argued that beginners need the opportunity to get an idea of the movement and establish a basic movement pattern before engaging in random practice. Blocked practice provides this opportunity because the learner can reinforce a desirable outcome or correct an error from the previous practice attempt without the interference of having to change to a different skill or perform a major variation of the same skill.

This seems logical if we consider the amount of mental effort a beginner applies to the learning of a new skill. Increasing that effort by introducing a high-interference practice schedule, such as random practice, would only cause an overload on a beginner's limited processing capacity. However, once learners have established the basic movement pattern, they should then be exposed to a greater amount of interference to increase the mental effort. Therefore, more skilled players benefit more from a random practice schedule than a blocked practice schedule. One qualification to this is that even skilled players may benefit from some blocked practice when they are learning a new technique. The blocked practice can be used initially when they are getting the feel of the new technique.

Coaches should also be mindful that the practice schedule itself can be manipulated between the extremes of pure random or pure blocked practice. Although the research has typically investigated changing skills after every trial (random practice) or completing large blocks of trials on one skill before changing (blocked practice), there are alternatives. Table 12.1 summarises some of these alternatives in hockey and shows how the amount of practice interference can be adjusted to suit the skill level of the player.

In his excellent book *Practice to Learn, Play to Win*, Mark Guadagnoli uses the analogy of Goldilocks and the Three Bears to explain the issue of finding the right challenge point. As the story goes, Goldilocks wanted porridge that wasn't too hot or cold, beds that weren't too hard or soft; rather, they needed to be just right! Similarly, practice needs to challenge the player so that it's not too easy requiring little investment or so hard that it's de-motivating (Guadagnoli, 2007).

DEVELOPING PERCEPTUAL–DECISION-MAKING SKILLS

The previous section illustrated the important connection between the brain and skill performance and learning. This connection is often underestimated when considered in relation to the tactical skills required in team sports, such as basketball and soccer, or for the execution of time-stressed skills common in interceptive sports, such as cricket, baseball and tennis. Although observable movement or action is an obvious component of skilled performance, coaches need to understand that any movement is reciprocally linked to perception and decision-making processes (referred to as perceptual–decision-making skills).

For example, before passing, a basketball player must first scan the court to identify a free teammate to pass the ball to. If all teammates are covered by opponents, the player must make another decision; for example, 'Should I keep dribbling the ball or take a shot?' This seemingly simple decision based on what the player sees in front of him is then further complicated by additional considerations such as the coach's team rules (e.g., wherever pos-

Table 12.1 Varying Interference Levels for a Hockey Player

Drill or activity name	Description	Level of interference
Block trials	Instead of switching from skill to skill after one practice repetition, players do a small block of each (e.g., five hits, then five dribbles).	Low to moderate
Variable practice	Instead of switching between two totally different skills, players practise variations of one skill (e.g., hit and then lift).	Moderate
Win shift–lose stay (around the world)	Goal-scoring practice: Players who score goals *win and shift* to a different hit location. Those who don't hit goals *lose and stay* and repeat the same shot on goal.	Player-generated difficulty based on current skill level
Skill circuits	Set up a number of different practice stations with each focusing on a different skill (e.g., goal hits, trapping skills, agility circuit, lifted hits). Practice for a defined amount of time at each station.	Moderate, depending on the amount of time and number of stations in the circuit
Practice-rest	The secret to making every repetition count is to be forced to forget the previous practice repetition. Having a chat about an unrelated issue between hits at goal may be all that's required.	Moderate

sible, look for 3-point shots) and the player's physical capacity. If the player is a poor outside shooter, despite the coach's team rule, his decision is going to be based primarily on his skill capacity; hence the player is likely to continue to dribble or pass the ball off. Although most coaches are more than aware of the reciprocal link between perceptual–decision-making skills and action, they often ignore it in a practice setting.

For many generations, kicking practice in Australian football has revolved around lane work drills in which players repetitively practise kicking skill in a closed situation with an absence of unpredictability. For example, players are kicking from the same distance and angle, using the same ball flight on each repetition. The movement patterns of all the players are known in advance as the players move in a stereotypical pattern (akin to a dance routine) without any opposition trying to disrupt the ball's movement. Such training could not look any more different to how the game is actually played, where every skill execution is typically completed under highly variable conditions with significant opposition pressure.

Coaches persist with these closed practice approaches because they associate them with performance success; they believe that the opportunity for high repetition gives players the chance to 'ingrain the skill'. Both coaches and players believe this based on how 'sharp' or successful players are during these drills.

This is a good example of a transient performance improvement rather than permanent learning. The drill with high repetitions of the same kick type removes much of the challenge for a player and in turn inflates current performance. Further, the absence of any perceptual–decision-making component in the drill also reduces the specificity of what is being practised. Consequently, such a drill provides a small learning legacy when transferred to the competition context. The only positive aspect of such a practice is that it does give players confidence, so it has its place if that is the coach's primary aim.

Effective practice of tactical skills requires perception and decision-making processes to be linked to the action. This is relatively easy to achieve by mimicking the common situations experienced by players in a game. The advanced coach, however, can create practice opportunities that scale and overload these common situations in a manner that maximises the practice time available, ensuring

GAME SENSE AND FUNDAMENTAL SKILL TRAINING

A recent debate emerging in many team sports is the relative contribution of what is termed game sense, or decision-making training, compared to skill-based training. Many practitioners have seemingly set these two practice approaches at opposite ends of a continuum, highlighting a common misperception about the application of game sense and fundamental skill training. The two practice approaches are not exclusive to one another. A skilled coach with an understanding of the key constraints of a sport would certainly be able to develop a game with appropriate challenge in which the focus is on a fundamental skill.

It should be noted that the game sense training approach starts with a focus on the player's learning how to play the game—or a focus on tactical awareness and decision making. However, it also explicitly highlights that when technique (fundamental skill) is the limiting factor to the game being played well, then technique should be the focus of the game. An appropriate fundamental skill game may involve practising a skill in pairs or a 6v6 keepings off game. In either case, because the perceptual–decision-making and action components are closely linked and not separated, transfer to competition is maximised.

that players get ample practice opportunities (see Farrow, Pyne, & Gabbett, 2008). Soccer is a wonderful example of a sport that has a practice culture of playing small-sided games (e.g., 5v5) to develop critical tactical elements that can transfer to the larger game.

How the coach helps players develop and understand the key tactical skills of their sport is another critical aspect of advanced coaching. Methods such as game sense coaching complemented by the use of indirect instructional approaches in which players take a more active role in the learning process through problem solving and guided-discovery practice are argued to be advantageous in the coaching of tactical issues (Davids, Button, & Bennett, 2008).

DEVELOPING INTERCEPTIVE SKILLS

Interceptive actions common in tasks such as cricket batting and playing tennis also emphasise the importance of practising the perceptual component in connection with the physical aspect of a skill. The time stress associated with skill execution in such tasks typically forces a performer to prepare a response to the opponent before the ball has left the bowler's hand (in cricket batting) or before the server has made contact with the ball (in the tennis return of serve).

Successful advanced preparation is termed *anticipation* and is a hallmark of skilled performers. In recent years, a large amount of research has investigated how such perceptual skills can be developed. The first critical aspect of developing skilled anticipation is for the coach to direct the performer's attention to the critical early information sources (cues) needed to predict an opponent's movement intention. For example, for the skill of cricket batting, a batter must understand what aspects of the bowler's mechanics provide the clues to where the ball is about to be bowled.

Sports scientists have demonstrated that for a swing bowler, the time between the bowler's front-foot impact on the bowling crease to ball release is when key cues such as the position of the bowling hand, wrist and arm must be presented (Müller, Abernethy, & Farrow, 2006). Knowing this information then allows the coach to develop perceptual training drills that help the batter link these advanced cues with the resultant delivery location.

TEMPORAL OCCLUSION

A variety of perceptual training drills have been examined experimentally, and they provide coaches with a number of practice options. Perhaps the most popular practice method has been temporal occlusion. In practical terms, temporal occlusion means blocking the vision of the outcome of a movement sometime before the appearance of ball flight. For example, video footage of a tennis server shot from the perspective of a receiver may be shown to a player, but the player's vision is occluded (the video clip is blackened out or paused) just at the moment of racquet and ball contact for the serve. This forces the returner watching the video to make a decision about serve location on the basis of precontact cues, such as the racquet head angle or ball toss position. Figure 12.1 shows an example of a temporal occlusion sequence for tennis serving. More information is helpful, but a receiver can extract key anticipatory information from the server before racquet–ball contact (end of row *c*). Such practice is advantageous to players.

The logic of such training is simple: When players are forced to learn which key kinematics of a server's action forecast the resultant serve location, they can then use this perceptual skill in the live situation to buy themselves the necessary time to prepare and execute their return. Recently, this video-based training activity has become even more realistic through the use of liquid crystal occlusion goggles that allow players to experience temporal occlusion as they return serve or bat in cricket against a live opponent. Figure 12.2 shows a pair of liquid crystal occlusion goggles being used to train the perceptual (anticipatory) skill of a tennis returner. With the push of a button, the coach can occlude the vision of the player.

Figure 12.1 A temporal occlusion sequence. When the vision is occluded at the peak of the ball toss (end of row *b*), the receiver must predict the serve's direction earlier in the movement.

Figure 12.2 Player wearing liquid crystal occlusion goggles when *(a)* open and *(b)* closed.

Because not all coaches have access to advanced technology as previously described, less technologically dependent strategies are available. For example, asking tennis receivers to close their eyes at racquet–ball contact, getting servers or bowlers to complete their service or bowling actions from a position closer to the receiver or batsman to increase the time stress experienced, or even using items such as a coloured dishwashing glove on the bowler's hand to draw the batman's attention to the location of critical advance information are all useful approaches for developing perceptual skill.

SIMULATION TRAINING APPROACHES

As technology has evolved, coaches have increasingly used interactive simulation training to develop the perceptual–decision-making skills of their players without the physical cost of playing the game. Players are usually presented with video footage or animations of a game situation and must make decisions by pressing a button, moving a joystick or simulating a movement response. Such technology is most evident in team sports such as gridiron, soccer and Australian football.

More commonly referred to as perceptual training in the research literature, these approaches are supported by an emerging

volume of evidence (Farrow & Raab, 2008). The key factors thought to be critical for a successful simulation experience can be summarised as follows:

- Coaches need to be clear about the critical information players should be attending to in a situation to drive their perceptual–decision-making responses.

- Forcing players to attend to the critical information by pausing or occluding the scenario at a critical point is useful for creating time stress on the player and in turn developing anticipatory skill. This is particularly the case for interceptive actions such as returning serve in tennis or cricket batting.

- After a period of perceptual training, players should recouple the perceptual skills with action by physically practising the skills they rehearsed in simulations.

- More interactive simulations (see figure 12.3) that require physical responses to the situations are more valuable than purely computer-based tasks (See figure 12.4).

A final point on the training of anticipatory skill, which has also become a hot topic for sports scientists, is the issue of disguise or deception. At the same time that performers are attempting to better understand and train to react to opponents' key cues, those opponents

Figure 12.3 An Australian footballer simulating skills.

Figure 12.4 An Australian footballer completing a touch screen–based decision-making task.

are working on methods to disguise these same cues so that they become more difficult to pick up, or even creating deceptions by having existing cues lead to different or unanticipated responses.

One of the most famous practice examples of disguise was the method adopted by Peter Fischer, an early coach of the legendary tennis player Pete Sampras. Coach Fischer would stand behind a young Sampras as he was in the act of serving and yell what type of serve he wanted. The effect was that Sampras could not predetermine the type of serve he wanted to hit. As a result, he developed a service action that allowed him to hit with great variety so he could respond successfully to the coach's requests. Consequently, Sampras was renowned in professional tennis for having one of the most difficult serves to anticipate.

EFFECTIVE INSTRUCTION AND FEEDBACK

The use of instruction and feedback is the other most powerful skill acquisition tool at the disposal of coaches. Attention to detail with the medium of instruction and feedback is generally poor and, as a result, often can be counterproductive to skill learning despite the coach's best intentions (Abernethy, Masters, & Zachry, 2008). Due to the general lack of quality in instruction and feedback, coaches may be tempted to use any of the myriad of technology-based feedback methods available today. Many of these tools can be useful, but coaches need to be judicious in their selection of technology tools.

New technologies for providing feedback appear in the coaching landscape almost weekly. For instance, many coaches would be able to point to firsthand experience in either using or having a sports scientist support their program with GPS units, heart rate monitors, accelerometers, skill analysis and feedback software, video applications, force plates and gaze-tracking technology.

In addition to capturing an aspect of skilled performance, these devices all provide *augmented feedback,* or objective information about a performance to the coach and athlete in some form of visual representation often in real time. For instance, 'Your knee flexion during that service action was recorded at 50°'. This is considered augmented feedback because it adds (augments) to the coach's and the performer's own perceptions of how much knee flexion was achieved. This section discusses a number of key factors that coaches need to consider about these technologies.

A critical starting point is to understand what feedback information is naturally available to a performer both during and at the completion of a movement (commonly referred to as intrinsic feedback) and how this is interpreted. For instance, a golfer can *see* the result of his swing by observing whether the ball was sliced, hooked or hit straight. Similarly, a springboard diver may *feel* that she did not tuck sufficiently as her rotational speed in the air was slowed and consequently struggled to complete the dive sequence.

In the preceding examples, the feedback information was visual (see the ball) or kinaesthetic (feel the tuck), but could also be based on any other sensory information such as audition (hearing the sound of racquet–ball contact), haptics (touch—the feel of a new grip) or any combination of these. A critical point is that, as performers' skill levels develop, their capacity to interpret this intrinsic feedback improves. In fact, a defining characteristic of elite performers is their capacity to self-monitor. This has important consequences for the learning value of many augmented feedback strategies, both in regards to the nature and type of feedback information provided and to the timing or delivery of this information.

A useful starting point for a coach is to decide what element of an athlete's performance requires feedback. Although this may seem logical, all manner of augmented feedback is provided to athletes simply because supporting technology can provide it. For instance, just because a force–velocity profile of a rowing stroke can be shown to an athlete at the completion of an effort does not mean that it should be.

Skilled divers and other athletes can interpret intrinsic feedback and use it to improve performance.

Stephen Pond/EMPICS Sport/PA Photos

A common abuse of technology is the seemingly overreliance on heart rate monitoring, lap times and stroke rates in athletics and swimming environments. Given that elite performers tend to develop highly refined self-monitoring skills, shouldn't a coach assist this process by first asking the athlete to estimate a lap time or stroke rate before feeding back this information? This simple strategy of placing the onus of performance evaluation first on the athlete has the twofold advantage of developing self-monitoring skills and simultaneously removing an athlete's dependency on augmented feedback.

Related to this discussion of augmented feedback is the nature of the information provided to the performer. A large amount of empirical work has been devoted to the question of whether instructions and feedback should lead to an internal or external focus of attention (see Wulf, 2007, for a review). Internally focused instructions direct athletes' attention to their movement mechanics, such as focusing a player's attention on how to drop the ball when kicking. In contrast, externally focused instructions direct athletes' attention to the effect of the movement on the environment, such as focusing a player's attention on the ball flight after the kick or the sound of the ball contacting the boot. Interestingly, many feedback technologies provide internally focused information.

Research has consistently demonstrated that focusing externally leads to better skill learning than focusing internally. In simple terms, it is argued that internally focused instructions may force an athlete to interfere with the movement coordination that would usually operate without the need for conscious attention, whereas externally focused instructions allow the athlete to self-organise movement coordination and in turn support more effective learning and performance (see also Davids et al., 2008).

A third content issue relates to the precision of the feedback provided. Along with advances in technology, the level of measurement precision available to a coach has continued to evolve. Yet the evidence for an athlete's capacity to interpret and use this information to make a change in performance is limited. For example, athletes from all sports are commonly subjected to high-speed motion analyses of their techniques with the aim of providing feedback about the efficiency of their movement kinematics or kinetics.

Common performance metrics may relate to critical angles at various phases of the movement and coordination or timing profiles. Although such detailed information is certainly useful to skill analysts and coaches, they need to carefully consider what information to feed back to the athlete. For instance, after completing a full three-dimensional motion analysis of a rugby union hooker's line-out throwing action, a coach concluded that he needed to extend his knee angle by 10°, because his set-up position was too crouched. Rather than telling the player that he needed to extend his legs by 10°, the coach told him to adopt a set-up position as if he were sitting on a bar stool. This image captured the essential information required to change the player's performance in a far more accessible manner than providing the feedback generated by the measurement system. The use of analogies to summarise critical performance information confers additional learning advantages over more traditional explicit coaching instructions or feedback (Masters, 2008).

SUMMARY

- Knowing the difference between learning and performance is critical for understanding how to manipulate the learning environment. Performance effects are transient and variable, whereas learning effects are permanent changes in a player's skill. Coaches should try using retention, transfer or dual-task tests to assess players' learning.

- Although practice volume is important, varying practice conditions and ensuring that perceptual–decision-making processes are linked to the action are critical for generating effective learning.

- The provision of feedback and instruction needs to be carefully considered by asking the following question: Are athletes developing the capacity to monitor their own performance? Coaches who answer no need to consider changing the way they provide feedback or instruction.

REFERENCES AND RESOURCES

Abernethy, B., Masters, R.S.W., & Zachry, T. (2008). Using biomechanical feedback to enhance skill learning and performance. In Y. Hong & R. Bartlett (Eds.), *Routledge handbook of biomechanics and human movement science* (pp. 581-593). New York: Routledge.

Baker, J., & Cobley, S. (2008). Does practice make perfect? The role of training in developing the expert athlete. In Farrow, D., Baker, J., & MacMahon, C. (Eds.), *Developing sport expertise: Researchers and coaches put theory into practice* (pp. 29-42). London: Routledge.

Baker, J., Côté, J., & Abernethy, B. (2003). Sport-specific practice and the development of expert decision-making in team ball sports. *Journal of Applied Sport Psychology, 15,* 12-25.

Coyle, D. (2010). *The talent code.* New York: Arrow Books.

Davids, K., Button, C., & Bennett, S. (2008). *The dynamics of skill acquisition.* Champaign, IL: Human Kinetics.

Ericsson, K.A. (2006). The influence of experience and deliberate practice on the development of superior expert performance. In Ericsson, K.A., Charness, N., Feltovich, P.J. & Hoffman, R.R. (Eds.), *The Cambridge handbook of expertise and expert performance* (pp.683-703). New York: Cambridge University Press.

Ericsson, K.A., Krampe, R.T., & Tesch-Römer, C. (1993). The role of deliberate practice in the acquisition of expert performance. *Psychological Review 100* (3), 363-406.

Ericsson, K.A., & Starkes, J.L. (2003). *Recent advances in research on sport expertise.* Champaign, IL: Human Kinetics.

Farrow, D., Pyne, D., & Gabbett, T. (2008). Skill and physiological demands of open and closed training drills in Australian football. *International Journal of Sports Science and Coaching, 3* (4), 485-495.

Farrow, D., & Raab, M. (2008). A recipe for expert decision making. In Farrow, D., Baker, J., & MacMahon, C. (Eds.), *Developing sport expertise. Researchers and coaches put theory into practice* (pp. 137-154). London: Routledge.

Gladwell, M. (2008). *Outliers.* London: Allen Lane.

Guadagnoli, M. (2007). *Practice to learn, play to win.* Cornwall, UK: Ecademy Press.

Kozar, B., Vaughn, R.E., Lord, R.H., & Whitfield, K.E. (1994). Basketball free-throw performance: Practice implications. *Journal of Sport Behavior, 18* (2), 123-129.

Masters, R. (2008). Skill learning the implicit way: Say no more! In Farrow, D., Baker, J., & MacMahon, C. (Eds.), *Developing sport expertise: Researchers and coaches put theory into practice* (pp. 89-103). London: Routledge.

Müller S., Abernethy, B., & Farrow, D. (2006). How do world-class cricket batsmen anticipate a bowler's intention? *The Quarterly Journal of Experimental Psychology, 59* (12), 2162-2186.

Patterson, J.T., & Lee, T.D. (2008). Organizing practice: The interaction of repetition and cognitive effort for skilled performance. In Farrow, D., Baker, J., & MacMahon, C. (Eds.), *Developing sport expertise: Researchers and coaches put theory into practice* (pp. 119-134). London: Routledge.

Schmidt, R.A., & Wrisberg, C.A. (2004). *Motor learning and performance: A problem-based learning approach* (3rd ed.). Champaign, IL: Human Kinetics.

Wulf, G. (2007). *Attention and motor skill learning.* Champaign, IL: Human Kinetics.

CHAPTER 13

Sharpening Mental Skills

Stephanie J. Hanrahan and Daniel F. Gucciardi

The best athletes are not only physically fit and technically sound, but also extremely mentally strong. In 2010 Justin Langer (former Australian international cricketer) echoed this line of reasoning: 'Being successful as an international cricketer transcends the ability to play an elegant cover drive, brutal pull shot or belligerent forward defence. The best players are not only physically fit and technically sound, they are also extremely mentally strong.'

Being confident in challenging and adverse situations is a hallmark of mentally tough athletes in all sports. Think of tennis players such as Federer, Nadal or Djokovic in the oppressive heat during a five-set match. They excel at maintaining their focus, effort and resolve despite the adverse conditions. Mentally tough athletes effectively manage their attention, persevere through difficult times, desire success, expect positive outcomes, effectively manage their emotions and understand their sport context (Gucciardi & Gordon, 2011). It is this constellation of key personal resources that enables mentally tough athletes to effectively negotiate the ups and downs of everyday life as well as acute (e.g., being dropped from a team) and chronic (e.g., long-term injury) stressors and adversities.

A useful exercise for athletes (and coaches) is to consider a list of factors that sometimes affect performance and then indicate those they believe can lead to inconsistent performances (see figure 13.1). They can then gather in small groups to discuss the factors they chose. Such discussions encourage reflection, let people know they are not alone in their concerns, help coaches determine which issues or skills might be useful to present in group workshops and result in participants recognising the importance of mental factors.

Mental skills training attempts to bolster the psychological skill arsenal of athletes, resulting in competitors who are better equipped to perform to their potential. This chapter details the components of that competitive mindset and suggests techniques to help athletes achieve it.

SELF-AWARENESS

What motivates you? What are your strengths? How often do you use your strengths? How do you typically respond to critical incidents or challenges (e.g., returning from injury)? The answers to these important questions help athletes become the object of their own attention or focus, and to identify, process and store information about themselves.

Acquiring such information through honest and accurate self-reflections is a fundamental building block for the development and application of mental skills. Armed with the knowledge of these issues, athletes can adjust or regulate their behaviour or other important processes to meet personally meaningful standards of performance. For example, conscious awareness of how they have successfully bounced back from competitive setbacks (e.g., losing to an opponent) can help athletes identify and practise strategies or processes that they can use to deal with other challenges in the future.

Figure 13.1 Factors Affecting Performance

Instructions: For each of the situations in the following list, place a tick mark if you believe it is something that sometimes contributes to inconsistent performance.

___ Thinking about work, relationships or study
___ Being distracted by someone in the stands
___ Worrying about losing (thinking about the outcome)
___ Doubting your own abilities
___ Worrying about the performances of others
___ Struggling with decisions
___ Having problems with a new technique or strategy early on in a competition
___ Having no plan
___ Being too anxious
___ Feeling too much pressure from others
___ Being overconfident
___ Thinking the competition is a lost cause while it is still going on
___ Thinking about the next round of competition (while still involved in the current round)
___ Worrying about what others might think
___ Thinking about what someone said or did to you before the competition
___ Skipping the normal precompetition routine
___ Wishing you were somewhere else
___ Feeling burned out
___ Having unrealistic expectations
___ Dwelling on mistakes
___ Having doubts about equipment or physical preparation
___ Falling in (or out of) love
___ Trying too hard
___ Being unable to concentrate or focus
___ Worrying about an injury or illness
___ Being self-conscious performing in front of others
___ Disagreeing with officials or administrators
___ Losing your temper
___ Thinking about what you do not want to do
___ Being distracted
___ Thinking about the venue, weather or conditions
___ Having no reason for being there
___ Realising the competition is running late (or early)
___ Doing unexpectedly well
___ Doing unexpectedly poorly
___ Thinking about what will happen after the competition is over
___ Swearing at yourself
___ Having ongoing arguments with others

___ _____ (add your own)

Adapted from L. Kidman and S.J. Hanrahan, 2011, *The coaching process: A practical guide to becoming an effective sports coach*, 3rd ed. (London: Routledge), 175-177.

MOTIVATION SOURCES

Motivation is one of the most central issues for individuals and organisations involved in mobilising others to act. *Motivation* is a term frequently mentioned in sport, but what is it? Motivation is the desire, or inner fire, that compels one to act and persist. To understand motivational orientations, coaches should consider three important components:

- Direction—whether a person prefers to seek out, approach or avoid certain situations or behaviours.
- Intensity—the amount of effort or energy one applies in a particular situation or to a particular behaviour.
- Persistence—the temporal stability of motivation. For example, two gymnasts like to seek out new information when learning a new apparatus, but Sarah takes a more casual, long-term approach than Jessica, who invests a significant amount of effort in a short period of time.

Excluding instances of amotivation (i.e., having no motivation), the reasons people engage in activities or behaviours can be classified according to five levels of self-determination. Coaches and athletes can use figure 13.2 to help determine what motivates them. It is common to agree with more than one statement because people can be motivated by more than one reason for a given activity or behaviour.

Figure 13.3 details how the questions relate to the motivation continuum. Those who strongly agree with the first statement are *intrinsically motivated* and driven by the pleasure and satisfaction derived from engaging in an activity or behaviour. Those who strongly agree with statement 5 are *externally regulated* and primarily driven by the desire to obtain external rewards or recognition from others. Located between these two ends of the motivational continuum are three other forms of extrinsic motivation ranging from being autonomous to being more controlled (i.e., progressing from statements 2 to 4).

Those who strongly agree with statement 2 typically view the activity or behaviour not only as important but also as congruent with their deeply held values and sense of self. This form of motivation is referred to as *integrated regulation*. Statement 3 refers to *identified regulation*. Those who strongly agree with this statement typically value and judge the outcomes of the activity or behaviour as being personally important. Finally, those who agree with statement 4 have partially internalised their desire for external rewards such that they typically engage in an activity or behaviour to avoid negative feelings (e.g., guilt, shame) or to enhance their egos and feelings of self-worth. This form of motivation is termed *introjected regulation*.

Autonomous forms of motivation (i.e., intrinsic, integrated and identified regulations) have primarily been associated with

Figure 13.2 Sources of Motivation

Consider the extent to which each of the following statements describes why you are currently practising your sport as an athlete or coach. Using a scale of 1 (strongly disagree) to 7 (strongly agree), choose the level at which you agree or disagree with each statement.

1. I engage in an activity or behaviour for enjoyment, learning or task accomplishment reasons. 1 2 3 4 5 6 7

2. I engage in an activity or behaviour because it reflects a valued aspect of my life or my core beliefs. 1 2 3 4 5 6 7

3. I engage in an activity or behaviour because I value its outcome(s). 1 2 3 4 5 6 7

4. I engage in an activity or behaviour to reduce uncomfortable feelings such as guilt, anxiety, external pressures or inadequacy. 1 2 3 4 5 6 7

5. I engage in an activity or behaviour to receive rewards or recognition or to demonstrate competence to others. 1 2 3 4 5 6 7

Low self-determination					High self-determination

Amotivation	Controlled extrinsic motivation		Autonomous extrinsic motivation		Intrinsic motivation
	External regulation	Introjected regulation	Identified regulation	Integrated regulation	
			What regulates the motivation?		
Non-intentional Non-valuing Incompetence Lack of control	Compliance External rewards and punishment	Self-control Ego involvement Internal rewards and punishment	Personal importance Conscious valuing	Congruence Awareness Synthesis with self	Interest Enjoyment Inherent satisfaction

Figure 13.3 Self-determination continuum of motivation.

Adapted, by permission, from R.M. Ryan and E.L. Deci, 2000, "Self-determination theory and the facilitation of intrinsic motivation, social development, and well-being," *American Psychologist* 55, 68-78. Published by American Psychological Association.

more favourable outcomes (e.g., better performance, better concentration, positive affect, persistence) than controlled motivational types have (i.e., external and introjected regulations). Coaches can help athletes focus less on external reinforcements (e.g., receiving prize money, having to do extra physical training as punishment) or engaging in or avoiding certain types of behaviours or activities and focus more on personally referenced desires (e.g., values, beliefs).

When presenting athletes with activities or behaviours that may not be inherently enjoyable, coaches can increase their motivation by providing rationales in a non-controlling way, while also acknowledging their feelings and providing some form of choice. For example, a football coach may say something like the following:

Today we're going to focus on video analysis because our opponents this weekend have been particularly effective at the counterattack, and we need to identify how we can reduce their effectiveness in such circumstances. I appreciate that this exercise may not be very enjoyable or challenging, so I'll let you decide when you want to stop for a break to mix things up.

The coach provides a rationale by stating that they are working to reduce the opponent's effectiveness on the counterattack. The coach then acknowledges the players' feelings by addressing the challenging nature of the exercise. Finally, the coach gives the players a choice of when to take a break.

Understanding what motivates athletes across a variety of situations (e.g., learning a new skill, injury rehabilitation) and contexts (e.g., in training and competition, or as a student or employee outside of sport) provides an important foundation on which coaches can set and adjust both short- and long-term goals that are personally meaningful. (Goal setting is discussed later in this chapter.)

STRENGTHS ASSESSMENT

What qualities do athletes possess that allow them to perform well or at their personal best? These characteristics can be considered personal strengths because they enable them to behave, think and feel in ways that facilitate optimal functioning and performance. An important distinction to be made here is between *possessing* and *using* strengths. For example, Rachel is highly curious but rarely makes use of this strength, whereas Erika consistently uses this attribute in a variety of situations including her sporting life (e.g., she regularly seeks advice from her teammates) and personal life (e.g., making new friends) to achieve her goals.

Coaches can work with athletes to identify and label personal strengths, as well as to explore how they currently use their strengths and how they might use them to address existing problems or facilitate positive functioning. It is important to note, however, that coaches and athletes should not ignore athletes' weaknesses; rather, they must identify, enable and develop strengths as well as work on managing the occurrence or the effects of weaknesses.

Identifying Strengths Coaches have a number of strategies available for exploring their own strengths and those of their athletes. Gordon and Gucciardi (2011) detailed an example of their strengths-based approach in the development of mental toughness in cricket. Their approach is built on the Realise 2 model by Capp (www.cappeu.com). Specifically, this model focuses on the following aspects:*

- Maximising unrealised strengths—characterised by high energy and high performance, but low use
- Marshalling realised strengths—characterised by high energy, high performance and high use
- Moderating learned behaviours—characterised by lower energy but high performance and variable use
- Minimising weaknesses— characterised by lower energy, lower performance and variable use

*Reproduced by kind permission of Capp. All rights reserved. Available: http://www.cappeu.com/Realise2/TheRealise24MModel.aspx

Prior to a practice session, the authors collaborated with coaches to assist players in identifying their strengths as batters, bowlers or fielders by having them answer the questions or complete the statements that follow.* Subsequent discussions focused on the implications of the players' responses for their self-regulated performance enhancement and training priorities.

- My strengths are . . .
- I feel strong when I am [doing this] . . .
- My best [shot, delivery, position] is . . .
- I get most of my [runs, wickets] by . . .
- I deliver my best and feel in my element when [doing these activities] . . .
- My favourite role(s) that I find most stimulating is/are . . .

- Things that I can do to build my batting/bowling/fielding strengths, or put myself into situations where I am in my element, are . . .

*Adapted from S. Gordon and D.F. Gucciardi, 2011, "A strengths-based approach to coaching mental toughness," *Journal of Sport Psychology in Action* 2: 143-155, adapted by permission of the publisher (Taylor & Francis Ltd, http://www.tandf.co.uk/journals).

A spin bowler commented that his strength is 'adapting my bowling style to the plan we [bowling pair] have set [for the batters] . . ., which could be tying down one end with tight bowling, or throwing up a couple of juicy ones to entice the batter into a poor shot'. He subsequently identified 'trying out different scenarios during training and developing strategies that can help me execute these plans effectively' as an avenue to help build his bowling strength. (Grordan and Gucciardi, 2010)

Other conversational techniques can be used in the strengths discovery process. What do strengths sound and look like? Coaches can ask their athletes to spend a couple of minutes talking about something they have recently been struggling with or about one of their weaknesses. Athletes can then spend a similar amount of time discussing one of their signature strengths, something they have recently done well, or do well when they are at their best.

While listening to athletes discussing their weaknesses and strengths, coaches should take notice of their tone, body language and other cues. More often than not, people are more energetic, engaged or relaxed, and the conversation flows more freely, when they are talking about their strengths when compared with their weaknesses. Cues to look for include rising inflection, rapid speech, better posture, wide eyes, raised eyebrows, smiling and laughing, increased hand gestures, increased use of metaphors and more fluent speech.

Identifying strengths can be a highly engaging activity for coaches and athletes. Although coaches can listen and look for instances of athletes' strengths in their conversations and their behaviours, these techniques are limited by their reliance on the strength being identified when it happens to come into play. Thus, it is also beneficial to work with athletes to look for strengths in themselves. Performance profiling (discussed later in this chapter) can be a useful and simple technique for coaches to implement with athletes. Additionally, the following questions can be used as a helpful framework or foundation on which to create dialogue around strengths:

- What are you good at? What do you enjoy doing?

- Tell me about the greatest experience you have had when you have been at your best. What enabled that to happen? How could you use this strength more? Where do you see opportunities to use this strength? How might you know when you should use this strength more and when you should use it less?

- What effect does using your strength have on others, and how does that feedback suggest you might better use your strength?

- What are some of the things from your past that you are most proud of? What energises you in the present? What are you looking forward to in the future?

The ability to identify one's strengths does not come naturally to all for various reasons (e.g., being self-critical, lacking introspection). Athletes who have difficulty naming their strengths can be encouraged to spot strengths in others by observing them, listening to them discuss their strengths and inquiring about the strengths of others. This process can help them develop an appreciation for this orientation, which provides a foundation for the identification of their own strengths.

Coaches can simply reword the preceding questions using another person, such as a teammate, as the subject (e.g., What is John good at? What does John enjoy doing?). Additionally, soliciting feedback from others, important in athletes' social networks (e.g., teammates, coaches, parents), often raises their awareness of their personal strengths.

Using Strengths Knowing their personal strengths is important, but if athletes never make use of them, they will be less likely to reach their full potential. Thus, having assisted athletes to identify their strengths, coaches can next work with them to explore how they might use these strengths to address existing problems or improve their performances. A formalised 'use of strengths' questionnaire has been developed (see Govindji & Linley, 2007). However, coaches who prefer to adopt more informal methods can simply integrate the following questions into their conversations with athletes:

- How often do you play to your strengths? How often have you played to your strengths this week?

- How easy is it for you to use your strengths in lots of different ways?

- Does using your strengths every day come naturally to you?

- How easy is it for you to use your strengths in lots of different situations?

Another useful starting point is to encourage athletes to consciously reflect on situations in which they used their strengths successfully and unsuccessfully. For example, although persistence can be extremely useful in one circumstance (e.g., learning a new skill), it can be detrimental in other situations (e.g., playing while injured). Identifying patterns in situations in which they were successful can help athletes understand when their strengths can be best used. An additional helpful exercise is to have athletes describe their top five signature strengths and then identify how they can make use of each strength in a new way every week or month.

SELF-CONFIDENCE

Some people think that self-confidence is the luck of the draw—great if you have it, bad luck if you don't. But self-confidence is a skill that can be developed. Confidence and anxiety tend to have an inverse relationship. In other words, it is rare to be confident and anxious at the same time. The goal is not to create egotistical monsters who think they are so good they don't need to train (overconfidence or false confidence), but instead to help athletes have a general faith in their abilities to perform. When self-doubt creeps in, the resultant decline in performance can instigate a downward spiral of decreasing performance and confidence.

Table 13.1 provides a number of confidence-boosting techniques that can, when combined with confirming performance, give athletes a greater sense of control. Indeed, a key concept in any mental skills training program is controlling the controllable. Too many athletes and coaches waste time and energy stressing out about things they cannot control. They are much better off putting their energy into things they can control. Also, reminding themselves about factors they can control helps athletes feel in control and therefore confident. Additionally, athletes can gain or sustain confidence by using the techniques for self-awareness, self-monitoring, self-regulation and self-preparation discussed in this chapter.

Table 13.1 Techniques for Enhancing Self-Confidence

Technique	Explanation or example
Focus on performance improvements.	When reflecting on past performances, be sure to remember positives.
Work on fitness and strength.	Feeling physically strong builds confidence.
Set short-term, challenging and realistic goals.	Achievement of goals leads to confidence in self, coach and training methods.
Verbally persuade each other.	Sincerity is a must.
Encourage positive self-talk (repeat affirmations).	Recording affirmations and playing them back is a useful exercise.
Discuss realistic expectations.	Avoid setting yourself up for failure.
Look at mistakes positively (reduces fear of failure).	If you never make mistakes, chances are you are not pushing yourself to try anything new.
Realise that confidence comes from hard work and practice.	Don't sit back and wait for confidence to find you.
Try to get informational as well as evaluative feedback.	You need information to know how to recreate positives or improve negatives.
Review videos of prior good performances.	Seeing is believing.
Use others as role models.	Others can model not only technique and strategy, but also confidence.
Act 'as if'.	Fake it 'til you make it. Act as if you are an animal or a machine (these never lack confidence).
Use imagery.	Rehearse previous achievements or image reaching goals.
Focus on reaching optimal arousal.	Arousal and activation are related to confidence.
Reduce anxiety through relaxation.	Anxiety and confidence rarely exist at the same time.
Reduce fear of anxiety by viewing it as a sign of readiness.	Replace 'OMG. I'm anxious!' with 'The adrenaline is pumping; I'm ready'.
Recognise that failure results from lack of effort or experience, or poor strategy.	Attribute failure to causes that are controllable (i.e., future success is possible).
Focus on internal and stable reasons for success.	Internal attributions for success underscore that the successes can be repeated.
Increase self-discipline.	Self-discipline in any area of life provides evidence of self-control.

SELF-MONITORING

Self-monitoring, which involves indentifying a specific aspect of behaviour or performance and recording the number of times it has occurred and the quality of these occurrences, is a relatively simple and versatile technique for increasing desirable and decreasing undesirable thoughts, feelings and behaviours. Many coaches and athletes may already engage in a fair amount of self-monitoring, but the focus is typically on physical, technical and tactical skills.

There are two components to self-monitoring. First is an observation component that involves ascertaining whether a given behaviour or process occurred. This component requires clarity as to the nature of the behaviour or process. Second is a recording component, which requires an assessment of whether the person engaged in or performed the desired behaviour or process in the intended manner. Self-monitoring tools and techniques can be used as a baseline against which future assessments can be compared to examine the degree of change accomplished in working towards increasing desirable and decreasing undesirable thoughts, feelings and behaviours.

PERFORMANCE PROFILING

Performance profiling is a useful technique for helping athletes raise their awareness of the important qualities (physical, technical, tactical and mental) required to perform at the highest level in their sports. This approach is considered a self-monitoring tool because it also provides an individualised profile that can be referred back to and amended when working towards increasing desirable and decreasing undesirable thoughts, feelings and behaviours.

Unlike traditional approaches in which the coach (or sport psychologist) imposes important qualities on athletes with little or no consultation, the performance profile is an athlete-centred assessment procedure that gives athletes an active role in determining the psychological skills or qualities that are important for performance in their sports. The performance profile technique follows three simple steps.

First, the coach introduces performance profiling by explaining to athletes how it will help them identify the attributes required to perform successfully in their sports. At this point the focus is on the athletes' self-perceived needs and strengths; there are no right or wrong answers. Coaches can outline some of the benefits of using the technique (e.g., enhanced self-awareness, intrinsic motivation and self-confidence, and the fact that it is an individualised monitoring tool) to encourage buy-in from athletes who are resistant to the process. Second, the coach helps athletes determine which attributes or characteristics are necessary for performing to their potential.

Finally, the athlete provides a self-assessment of the qualities obtained in the preceding step. Typically, athletes provide an assessment of their 'current self' (i.e., how they currently view themselves on each of the qualities or characteristics), as well as any number of alternative ratings (e.g., ratings from coaches or teammates, best-ever performance, ideal self). Figure 13.4 depicts an example of the outcome of this process from an elite swimmer. Although we have provided an example of the mental qualities required for successful performance, coaches can adapt this process to generate athletes' perspectives on the important technical, tactical, or physical qualities in their sports.

GOAL SETTING

Once they have completed performance profiles, athletes can select the two or three performance factors they would like to focus on and improve. The motivation to work on these factors can be increased or maintained through the use of goal setting. Goals are useful because they give direction, focus attention and effort and help foster new strategies, thereby enhancing persistence.

The goal-setting process also helps athletes see improvement. Athletes often compare their current performances to the performances they had yesterday or last week. Particularly at the elite end of the spectrum, notable

Figure 13.4 Elite Swimmer's Profile of Requisite Mental Skills

Date: _____

Athlete's name: _____

Coach's name: _____

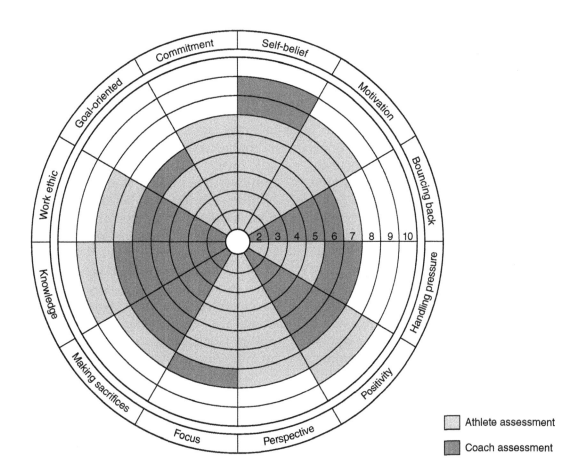

Athlete assessment
Coach assessment

Quality	Meaning	Quality	Meaning
1. Self-belief	Confidence in ability	**7. Focus**	Attention and concentration
2. Motivation	Desire to swim	**8. Making sacrifices**	Decisiveness
3. Bouncing back	Persistence	**9. Swimming knowledge**	Hungry for feedback
4. Handling pressure	Overcomes adversity	**10. Work ethic**	Trains harder and smarter
5. Positivity	Optimism	**11. Goal-oriented**	Guided by goals
6. Perspective	Faces adversity with optimism	**12. Commitment**	Dedication to swimming

improvements in performance are rarely made in a short time frame. A goal that is achieved, however, is obvious evidence of improvement. Not only does achieving a goal have a positive effect on motivation, but it also enhances confidence—in both the athlete's ability and the training process.

Many coaches have heard of the principle of SMART goals. To be effective, goals should be *specific, measurable, action-oriented, realistic* and *time based*. Table 13.2 provides questions that can be used to check whether goals meet these criteria. Three Ps (*positive, personal* and *process*) can be added to the acronym to make it SMART PPP.

In addition to the SMART criteria, goals should be *positive*. There is no point in focusing on what one does not want to do. For example, the only way to achieve the goal of not thinking about pink elephants is to have the positive goal of thinking about something else, such as pink cats or green elephants. Goals should also be *personal* (the second P). Athletes need to set their own goals. Although it may be quicker for coaches to set goals for their athletes rather than helping the athletes set their own goals, people are more invested when they set their own goals. People need to feel autonomous, that they have some say in what they are doing.

The final P is for *process*. Goals should focus on the process of improving technique, strategy, or particular behaviours. Almost all athletes and coaches want to win, but the focus, and therefore the goal, needs to be on what they are going to do to increase their chances of winning. A swimmer cannot control the outcome of a race. If Pedro is in lane 4, he can only control what happens in lane 4—that is, his own technique, strategy and behaviour. He cannot control what happens in the other lanes. If Pedro sets the goal of winning, he has no control over achieving it. It may be that the world champion is in town and competing in the same race. Outcome goals tend to lead to people giving up when they think they have no chance of winning or easing off when they think they have a competition won. It all goes back to the idea of controlling the controllable.

If winning is off limits as a goal, what are areas in which goals can be set? Goals can relate to fitness (agility, flexibility, endurance, power, strength), technique, tactics, mental skills (self-talk, imagery, anxiety control, precompetition routines), team issues (communication, trust, fulfilling specific roles), health (nutrition, hydration, sleep, injury rehab), or areas outside of sport (study, relationships, work).

The first step in the goal-setting process involves some self-reflection (e.g., Where am I now? Where do I want to be with my sport in two months, six months, two years?). Athletes should also reflect on their strengths and weaknesses. Goals often involve strengthening an area in which one is weak, but they can also focus on taking greater advantage of a strength.

The next step is selecting a specific area on which to focus, setting a long-term goal (usually six months to two years away), and then thinking of the first couple of short-term goals (to be achieved in one to two weeks) on a goal-setting staircase (i.e., the first step or two towards achieving the long-term goal). Athletes need

Table 13.2 Questions for Determining That Goals Are SMART PPP

Principle	Question to determine whether the principle has been met
Specific	Is the precise goal obvious?
Measurable	Is there an exact method of determining whether the goal has been achieved?
Action oriented	Will reaching the goal require effort?
Realistic	Is the goal achievable?
Time based	Is there a specific date by which the goal will be achieved?
Positive	Does the goal stipulate the desired behaviour?
Process	Does the goal relate to performance, technique or behaviour (rather than outcome)?
Personal	Has the goal been established by the person involved (and not imposed by someone else)?

to make sure that their first short-term goals are SMART PPP.

The third step (which is often skipped) is to brainstorm for strategies that could be used to achieve the goal. This stage is the one in which coaches can and should be most involved. Athletes should then select one or two of the strategies and specifically determine when they are going to do what, where, with whom and for how long.

The goal-setting process does not end here. Some coaches tend to tick goal setting off a list of things to do once goals have been set, but goals need to be regularly monitored and revisited. When athletes reach their goals, they (and their coaches) should enjoy the sense of achievement and then set the next goal. If they do not achieve a goal, they need to consider whether a different strategy is needed, the short-term goal was too challenging and needs to be modified, or laziness was the main culprit.

If the main issue appears to be lack of effort, then athletes could consider creating a contract. For those with good self-control, the contract can be with themselves and a reward (e.g., getting a massage, buying some new music) can be tied to achieving the goal. Athletes who are not particularly good at delayed gratification can set up a contract with someone else.

For example, athletes who know they should be doing strength and conditioning training in their own time but never seem to schedule it could give a trusted person $200. Any weeks in which the athlete completes a specified number of sessions, the athlete gets $20 back. But, any week in which the desired number of sessions is not completed, the $20 for that week gets sent as a donation to a rival club. The thought of their hard-earned money going to the opposition may motivate them to work towards their goals!

SELF-REGULATION

With an increased awareness of and appreciation for the important components of successful performance and development, combined with an understanding of processes to monitor progress, coaches can teach athletes strategies or techniques for attaining personal goals. This section focuses on techniques that can be used before, during, or after training or competition.

Coaches should encourage athletes to regularly return to the strategies and processes detailed in the previous sections of this chapter. For example, strength awareness discussions and goal setting can be used to help athletes before they engage in self-regulatory strategies, and the performance profile can provide a foundation from which to reflect on behavioural processes and outcomes after executing skills or performing.

ACTIVATION CONTROL

Athletes need to learn to control their levels of activation, or arousal. If they are underactivated (e.g., feeling lethargic) or overactivated, their performances will be less than optimal. The key is for athletes to determine their own ideal levels of activation. The optimal level of activation will depend on the sport or activity. Most people require a lower level of activation to putt well in golf than to successfully bench press. Even within the same sport, however, individual differences occur. Some athletes need to be calm, cool and collected when competing (i.e., have a relatively low level of activation), whereas others need to be pumped up and highly activated.

After athletes determine their zone of optimal functioning, they need to learn to regulate their level of activation so they are in that zone every time they perform. If activation levels are too low (more common at training than competition), they can increase them by listening to rowdy music, making noise, engaging in exercise, reminding themselves of their goals, or imaging scenes that energise them (e.g., picturing their rivals training hard). If activation levels are too high, athletes can lower them by listening to calming music, imaging peaceful scenes, or engaging in abdominal breathing (see figure 13.5).

The method of progressive muscle relaxation is more involved than others, but its benefits can be significant to athletes who 'play tight'. Releasing tension in the musculature allows effective, natural movement and eases the mind as the athlete gains a greater sense of control. The basic progressive muscle relaxation procedure presented in figure 13.6 is effective for many but can be tailored to address an athlete's individual needs.

Figure 13.5 Abdominal Breathing Procedure

1. Find a quiet and comfortable environment.
2. Lie down on your back and place a pillow under your knees, or place your feet on a chair if you have back problems.
3. Place your left hand on your abdomen just below your belly button and your right hand on your chest.
4. Breathe slowly and deeply so that your abdomen and left hand rise as you inhale and fall as you exhale.
5. Check that you are breathing deeply. Only your left hand should be moving, not your right.
6. Try to spend the same amount of time inhaling as you do exhaling.
7. Try to make the transition between inhaling and exhaling as natural as possible as if your breathing has a mind of its own.

Figure 13.6 Progressive Muscle Relaxation Procedure

1. Lie on your back with your arms at your sides and your legs out straight (uncrossed).
2. Close your eyes and focus on your breathing—abdomen up as you breathe in and abdomen down as you breathe out.
3. Now bring your attention to your hands. By spreading your fingers as wide as you can, gradually increase the tension in your hands. Hold for about seven seconds.
4. Stop and relax. Notice the difference between the feelings of tension and relaxation.
5. Use the same process of gradually increasing tension, holding the tension, releasing the tension and then reflecting on the feeling of relaxation for each of the following body parts in turn:
    1. Arms
    2. Feet
    3. Calves
    4. Quads/thighs
    5. Glutes/bum
    6. Abdominals
    7. Pecs/chest
    8. Upper back (squeezing shoulder blades together)
    9. Tongue and jaw (push your tongue up against the roof of your mouth)
    10. Face (scrunch up your eyes, nose and mouth)

Now scan your body for any signs of tension. If you are completely relaxed, enjoy that feeling of relaxation. If, however, you find a part of your body that still feels tense, increase the tension in that body part, hold it and then stop and relax.

Relaxation techniques must be practised to be effective, just as with any sport skill. After mastering the techniques in a fairly calm state, athletes must test them in stressful situations that elicit activation levels that closely approximate their preperformance anxiety.

ATTENTION AND CONCENTRATION

For athletes to perform well, they need to pay attention to what is important and ignore what is not. One way of considering attention is along two dimensions: width (broad or narrow) and direction (internal or external). This results in four general types of attention:

- Broad/external attention is used to assess a situation by considering multiple variables, such as positioning of teammates or opponents, wind direction and obstacles.
- Broad/internal attention is used to analyse and plan and is useful when strategising.
- Narrow/internal attention can be used to mentally rehearse a skill or control emotions (e.g., taking a breath to relax).
- Narrow/external attention is used to focus on one or two external cues (e.g., the ball).

In most sports, athletes need to be able to switch between various types of attention. Coaches can help athletes consider when they need each of the four types of attention as well as when each may be detrimental. This approach is far more effective than yelling at athletes to pay attention. The latter rarely proves helpful, and it does not answer the question, Pay attention to what?

Coaches can design activities to help athletes block out distractions. A generic activity is to have athletes try to maintain their balance while teammates do everything in their power (except touch them) to get them to lose it. A more sport-specific activity is to try to distract athletes while they are performing a skill. Coaches should keep in mind that being loud and obnoxious is not always the most effective distraction. Consider pistol shooters, who tend to be good at blocking out the boisterous behaviours of others during training. However,

AP Photo/John Donegan

During a serve, an experienced tennis player's attention can include assessing the wind and where the opponent is (broad/external), analysing where to serve (broad/internal), rehearsing the serve mentally (narrow/internal), and focusing on the ball (narrow/external).

when the distraction is limited to whispers, the shooters tend to be more distracted because they are straining to hear, particularly if they are the topic of the whispered conversation.

Drills can also help athletes broaden their focus of attention. For example, two people standing shoulder to shoulder and moving only their outside arms act as a mirror for a third person, who needs to reflect the arm movements of the pair. This mirror activity can be challenging if the third person uses only peripheral vision (i.e., does not flick the eyes back and forth). Difficulty can be increased by adding space between the pair.

A sport-specific example is a volleyball drill designed to make the setter more aware of what is happening on the other side of the net. After a ball is passed to the setter, but before the setter touches the ball, the setter needs to look to the other side of the net and call out the colour of a card the coach is holding. Later, the drill can be modified to have a blocker on the other side of the net shift slightly to the right or left just before the setter touches the ball; the setter needs to set the ball in the opposite direction to the movement of the blocker.

Another aspect of attention is whether athletes are in the past, present, or future. If athletes are not concerned about technique (e.g., swimming or running just to burn calories), then it does not matter too much whether they are thinking about the past, present, or future. If they are competing or training to develop skills, however, they need to be focused on the present. When athletes find that they are thinking about the past (e.g., an argument earlier in the day) or the future (e.g., what to have for dinner after training), they can use a four-step process to refocus on the present:

1. Recognise unwanted thoughts.
2. Use a signal to stop those thoughts (e.g., imaging a stop sign or screaming 'Stop' silently).
3. Inhale (from the abdomen).
4. Repeat a cue word or phrase when exhaling (e.g., *What's my next job? Focus. Be present*).

For thought stopping to be helpful in stressful situations, athletes need to practise it. To increase athletes' awareness of thoughts, coaches can yell 'Past, present, or future?' once or twice during each training session, at which time the athletes need to consider where their thoughts are. If they are in the present—great! If they are in the past or future, they need to refocus on the present.

IMAGERY

Imagery is a skill that involves the ability of a person to mentally recreate objects, persons, skills, movements, and situations when they are not present. Basically, the human brain can't tell the difference between perceptual and real stimuli. The more vivid the image (i.e., the more senses involved), the more the brain is going to think the image is reality. Imagery provides a mental and physical blueprint of the performance by developing muscle memory through neural firings.

Research has repeatedly demonstrated that people who combine physical practice with mental practice (i.e., imagery) learn skills faster and perform better than those who practise only physically or mentally. Imagery can also be used to control emotions, develop awareness and confidence, improve concentration and aid with healing and pain control.

Imagery is advantageous because it is not physically fatiguing, avoids the risk of injury or reinjury, can be used anywhere and anytime, uses a language understood by the body, accelerates the learning process and allows for slow-motion skill analysis or correction. Images need to be vivid and controlled to be effective. If imagery skills have not been developed, however, asking athletes to image may be counterproductive.

For example, there was a basketball player who could make free throws at training, but tended to choke when it came to competition. He decided to image himself making free throws in competition. Good in theory, but disastrous in practice. He had no control of his images. In his image, every time he went to dribble the ball before shooting, the ball would stick to the ground and he never got to shoot—making him even more anxious!

Imagery scripts that guide athletes through specific sporting skills can help both the vividness and control of images. Athletes should be relaxed but alert when imaging and also realistic and patient with the imagery. If a sprinter currently takes 14 seconds to run 100 metres, she cannot just press the fast forward button on her imagery and run the same distance in 8 seconds.

The analogy to video, however, can be useful. When athletes have a breakthrough with technique, coaches are well advised to take a couple of minutes of training time to ask the athletes to immediately stop and create an instant replay image of the skill. A precise image is less likely if they wait a week or even a day to create an image of the newly modified technique. Finally, athletes should always image good performances. Replaying execution errors in their minds is practising doing what they don't want to do.

SELF-PREPARATION

Armed with an enhanced awareness of the key mental skills and strategies for attaining and sustaining high levels of performance, athletes and coaches can work towards putting it all together to prepare for big performances (e.g., selection trials) or competitions. Preparation involves much more than just game day; it can involve days (e.g., a golfer preparing for a four-day tournament), weeks (e.g., a competition on every weekend for several months), months (e.g., a cricket team's tour of the subcontinent) and even years (e.g., Olympic cycles) of planning ahead. Coaches need to recognise that athletes have their own unique needs and demands, so a 'one size fits all' approach is not as effective as an individualised approach.

Athletes can develop and continually modify two broad types of routines to package their mental (and physical) preparation into a useful process that works best for them. Precompetition routines include strategies and processes that are implemented in the days leading up to a competition (e.g., visualising potential distractions and how to overcome them, rest and recovery from rigorous training schedules). In contrast, preperformance routines are implemented prior to executing a skill during a competition (e.g., golf putt, tennis serve, basketball free throw).

Routines enable athletes to control their anxiety-related symptoms and help them avoid being distracted by irrelevant cues. They help athletes feel settled and in control before competing so they will have a high level of confidence and an optimistic outlook for the imminent performance. The purpose of these routines is to help athletes begin the competition and initiate skill execution in their ideal performance states.

What is ideal will be different for different athletes. Some will need to be quiet and relaxed, and others will need to be pumped up and energised. Some will need to avoid thinking about the competition until right before it begins, and others will need to mentally prepare throughout the lead-up.

A routine can combine physical warm-up and stretching with mental and emotional preparation. Elements can include relaxation, cue words, music and imagery. Athletes should try a few variations before deciding on a routine to use regularly (i.e., before training as well as before competition).

SUMMARY

- Mental skills are integral to helping athletes maximise their performance.
- Coaches can use several techniques or strategies to help their athletes develop an awareness of their motivations and strengths, regulate or manage their behaviours and performances and monitor their progress towards a better mental game.
- Coaches should integrate mental skills training into their coaching practice.
- Mental skills training, like physical, technical and tactical skills training, is a continuous process that requires practice and works best when implemented proactively rather than reactively.

REFERENCES AND RESOURCES

Biswas-Diener, R. (2010). *Practicing positive psychology coaching: Assessment, activities, and strategies for success.* Hoboken, NJ: Wiley.

Gordon, S., & Gucciardi, D.F. (2010). Cricketer's feedback on a strengths-based approach to coaching mental toughness. Unpublished raw data.

Gordon, S., & Gucciardi, D.F. (2011). A strengths-based approach to coaching mental toughness. *Journal of Sport Psychology in Action, 2,* 143-155.

Govindji, R., & Linley, P. A. (2007). Strengths use, self-concordance and well-being: Implications for strengths coaching and coaching psychologists. *International Coaching Psychology Review, 2*, 143-153.

Gucciardi, D.F., & Gordon, S. (2009). Revisiting the performance profile technique: Theoretical underpinnings and application. *The Sport Psychologist, 23*, 93-117.

Gucciardi, D.F., & Gordon, S. (Eds.). (2011). *Mental toughness in sport: Developments in theory and research.* Abingdon, Oxon: Routledge.

Kidman, L., & Hanrahan, S.J. (2011). *The coaching process: A practical guide to becoming an effective sports coach* (3rd ed.). London: Routledge.

Langer, J. (2010 March 26). Mental toughness. [Web log post]. Retrieved from http://www.cricket.com.au/news-list/2010/3/26/justin-langer-blog-mental-toughness

Linley, P.A., & Burns, G.W. (2010). Strengths spotting. In G.W. Burns (Ed.), *Happiness, healing, enhancement: Your casebook collection for applying positive psychology in therapy* (pp. 3-14). Hoboken, NJ: Wiley.

Ryan, R.M., & Deci, E.L. (2000). Self-determination theory and the facilitation of intrinsic motivation, social development, and well-being. *American Psychologist, 55*, 68-78.

CHAPTER 14

Advocating Appropriate Nutrition

—— Kylie Andrew

Sports nutrition has come a long way over the past few years; most elite sporting teams now boast having their own dietitians to educate and advise team members. Many athletes, from recreational to elite and from junior to masters, consult sports dietitians to learn about how to fuel their bodies to get the most out of them and maximise their performance. Although optimal performance is a key goal of sports nutrition, two even more basic goals of a proper diet are to promote healthy development and functioning and to provide sufficient energy for the fullest participation.

Coaches need to understand sports nutrition principles. Although they may not directly educate their athletes about sound dietary practices or devise eating plans for training and competition, they should be able to grasp and support the advice provided by dietitians. Some nutritional knowledge will also help them identify issues of concern with athletes' diets and know when to refer them to a dietitian.

MACRONUTRIENTS

The macro-, or major, nutrients are those that provide the body with energy, in the form of kilojoules (calories). They include carbohydrate, protein and fat. Carbohydrate is the main source of energy for the body, whereas protein forms the building blocks of the body and is essential for growth, development and the repair of muscles and other tissues. Fat is also an essential macronutrient, providing the body with energy, supplying essential fatty acids and aiding in the body's use of fat-soluble vitamins.

CARBOHYDRATE

Carbohydrate is the best fuel for active muscles. It is also the sole source of energy for the brain. When carbohydrate-rich foods are eaten, they are broken down into glucose, which is absorbed into the bloodstream and carried to the muscles and brain where it can be used. Any carbohydrate that is not immediately used is stored with water in the muscles and liver. This store of carbohydrate and water is known as glycogen. When fuel is later required for a training session, glycogen is broken down to glucose.

Unless adequate carbohydrate is consumed on a daily basis between training sessions, muscle glycogen content gradually declines, resulting in fatigue and suboptimal performance. Carbohydrate-rich foods should contribute approximately 60 per cent of total energy intake. Put more simply, an athlete training at an intense level should consume 5 to 7 grams of carbohydrate per kilogram of body weight per day. (Divide body weight in pounds by 2.2 to obtain body weight in kilograms.)

Carbohydrate-rich foods include breads, breakfast cereals, rice, pasta, noodles and other grains; starchy vegetables such as potato,

CARBOHYDRATE LOADING

Carbohydrate loading is a technique whereby athletes can increase their glycogen stores. By significantly increasing carbohydrate intake, athletes can increase their muscle carbohydrate (glycogen), thereby providing more fuel to the muscles and allowing the body to exercise at a higher intensity for longer, delaying fatigue. This may be warranted in endurance sports and events lasting longer than 90 minutes in which carbohydrate stores may become depleted. It is not beneficial for weekly events such as football games or for shorter events such as track events or swimming races.

The current recommended strategy for carbohydrate loading includes increasing carbohydrate intake to 7 to 10 grams per kilogram of body weight per day for three days before the event and tapering exercise during this time. An athlete embarking on an endurance event and carbohydrate loading for the first time should speak with a sports dietitian for a personalised plan.

peas, sweet corn and pumpkin; fruit; milk and yoghurt; and sugar and foods containing sugar such as jam, honey, lollies, soft drinks and sports drinks.

Obviously, some of these foods are more nutritious than others and should be the focus of the diet. Sugar and foods containing sugar can help to meet total carbohydrate and energy needs. However, it must be remembered that these foods do not provide other vitamins and minerals and therefore should not displace the more nutritious carbohydrate-rich foods in the diet.

Carbohydrate-rich foods are no longer classified as complex and simple. They can be described as nutritious and non-nutritious or classified according to their glycaemic index. Glycaemic index (GI) is a ranking of the effect carbohydrate-rich foods have on blood glucose levels. Foods with a high GI are quickly digested and absorbed into the bloodstream resulting in a rapid and high rise in blood glucose levels. These foods are the best choice when energy is required quickly, such as during endurance exercise or afterwards for fast recovery. Foods with a low GI, on the other hand, are more slowly digested and absorbed into the bloodstream, resulting in a slower and sustained release of carbohydrate. See table 14.1 for the GI ranking of some carbohydrate-rich foods.

PROTEIN

Protein is made up of amino acids and is required for growth and development as well as tissue repair and maintenance. Athletes have increased protein requirements to allow for increased amino acid oxidation for energy and the repair of exercise-induced muscle damage. Although sedentary people require only 0.8

Table 14.1 Glycaemic Index (GI) of Some Carbohydrate-Rich Foods

Low GI	High GI
Wholegrain bread	White and wholemeal bread
Pasta	Rice
Sweet potato, peas and sweet corn	Potato
Most fruit	Tropical fruits, melons, pineapple, banana
Milk and yoghurt	Sugar, soft drinks, jelly beans
Legumes	

gram of protein per kilogram of body weight, strength training and endurance athletes require 1.2 to 1.7 grams per kilogram.

Protein-rich foods include lean meats (beef, lamb, pork), poultry (chicken and turkey), fish and seafood; eggs; dairy products such as milk, yoghurt and cheese; nuts and seeds; legumes (lentils, chick peas); and tofu. Animal sources of protein are the best quality, providing all of the essential amino acids required by the body. Plant sources of protein do not contain all of the essential amino acids, and so are considered a poorer-quality protein. A variety of these foods, together with plenty of breads and cereals, need to be eaten to provide all of the amino acids.

Athletes generally have little difficulty meeting their protein requirements; however, some athletes may be at risk of inadequate intake. These include vegetarians, vegans (especially), those on restrictive and low-energy diets, those following fad diets and those with excessive carbohydrate intakes.

Protein has become very popular in recent times, not just with bodybuilders and gym junkies, but also with the general community. Higher-protein diets are often touted as the key for weight control. Although protein and protein-rich foods certainly have some benefits, total energy intake and overall energy balance is the key to achieving changes in body weight. Protein supplements, including shakes and bars, have also become popular. These may provide a convenient option for meeting protein needs after a workout, but they contain no magical ingredients.

FAT

Low-fat diets are recommended for athletes for several reasons. The first is that a high fat intake results in weight or body fat gain, which is likely to hinder performance and is a health risk. Eating too many high-fat foods can also compromise carbohydrate intake because such food may be eaten at the expense of carbohydrate-rich foods. Athletes should therefore aim to consume less than 30 per cent of their energy as fat.

Although a low-fat diet is recommended, this does not mean a no-fat diet. Some fat is needed to provide fat-soluble vitamins and essential fatty acids. This should ideally come from the heart-healthy fats such as olive oil, avocado, nuts, seeds and fish. Athletes should be advised against taking low-fat recommendations to the extreme.

Omegas-3 is the latest in the list of good fats and is an important part of a balanced diet to maintain overall health. A type of polyunsaturated fat, omega-3 is important in reducing the risk of cardiovascular disease and useful in the management of inflammatory conditions. The best source of omega-3 is fish, but it can also be found in plant-based foods such as nuts, seeds and oils.

MICRONUTRIENTS

The micronutrients are vitamins and minerals; these don't provide energy per se, but they have numerous functions within the body. Table 14.2 provides a list of vitamins and minerals that are important for athletes and describes how each functions in the body. Food sources for the vitamins and minerals are also listed.

Two minerals of particular importance are calcium and iron. Calcium is known as the bone mineral because it is stored in bone and is essential in optimising bone mineral density. Calcium also has an important role to play in nerve and muscle function. A calcium deficiency is one cause of osteoporosis, or weakening of the bones. Bones are constantly breaking down and being rebuilt, so daily calcium intake is vital for maximal bone strength. The best dietary source of calcium is dairy products. Most population groups should aim to consume three or four serves of dairy daily.

Iron is another mineral essential to the body's health. It is the most common nutritional deficiency in athletes and can significantly affect performance. Iron is needed for the formation of haemoglobin in red blood cells. Haemoglobin is a protein that transports oxygen to the body's tissues, giving them energy. A reduction in iron leads to a reduction in haemoglobin, which in turn leads to a lowered oxygen supply to the muscles and thus impaired performance. Iron is present in foods in two forms: haem and non-haem. Lean red meat, offal (liver and kidney),

Table 14.2 Food Sources and Functions of Vitamins and Minerals

Vitamin or mineral	Food sources	Functions
Vitamin A	Butter and margarine Liver Full-cream dairy products Oily fish Green leafy vegetables Yellow-orange fruits and vegetables	Growth and development Vision Tissue repair Immunity
Vitamin B_1 (thiamin)	Wholegrain breads and cereals Meats, especially pork Nuts	Energy production Nervous system function
Vitamin B_2 (riboflavin)	Dairy products Liver and kidney Meat, fish, nuts	Energy production Growth and development Tissue repair
Vitamin B_3 (niacin)	Meat, fish, liver Wholegrain products, nuts	Energy metabolism
Vitamin B_6	Meat, poultry, fish Beans, nuts Wholegrain cereals	Protein metabolism Nerve and muscle function
Vitamin B_{12}	Animal foods—meat, poultry, fish, eggs, dairy products	Red blood cell production
Folate	Liver Green leafy vegetables Fortified breads and cereals	Cell growth and repair
Vitamin C	Citrus fruits, berries, tropical fruits, green leafy vegetables, tomato, capsicum	Tissue health Immunity
Vitamin D	Fish Dairy products Liver Egg	Calcium absorption
Vitamin E	Vegetable oils Wholegrain products Nuts and seeds	Antioxidant
Vitamin K	Green leafy vegetables Liver Soybeans	Blood clotting
Calcium	Dairy products Fish with edible bones Nuts and seeds Green leafy vegetables	Bone formation and strength Nerve and muscle function
Iron	Liver, kidney, red meat Green leafy vegetables Fortified breads and cereals Legumes	Oxygen carrier and energy Immunity
Magnesium	Green vegetables Cereals Legumes Meat, chicken and fish	Bone and teeth structure Energy metabolism
Zinc	Oysters Red meat, liver Legumes Wholegrain products Nuts and seeds	Growth and reproduction Wound healing

poultry and seafood contain haem iron, which is well absorbed. Non-haem iron, on the other hand, is poorly absorbed. It is found in legumes, cereals and vegetables, particularly dark green leafy ones.

ATHLETES' SPECIAL NUTRITION CONCERNS

In addition to basic macronutrient and micronutrient needs, coaches should be aware of situation- and athlete-specific dietary modifications that can prove beneficial in certain circumstances. Competition day is a particularly important time to ensure that nutritional requirements are met. A good training diet ensures that glycogen stores are high, but the foods that are eaten on competition day—before, during and after the event—can still have an impact on performance.

PRECOMPETITION NUTRITION

There is no one magical food to eat before an event to ensure a win or a personal best performance. However, the following guidelines can help to ensure that energy levels are high and avoid any stomach discomfort.

- Eat a meal or snack high in carbohydrate to top up energy levels.
- Choose foods that are low in fat because fat takes longer to digest, which may mean that the blood supply is diverted to the stomach during activity when ideally it should be going to the muscles.
- Avoid large protein serves, which also take longer to digest.
- Avoid excessive fibre, which can cause an upset stomach, especially if not used to it.

The real challenge in pre-event eating lies in determining when to eat the pre-event meal. Ideally, it should be approximately two hours before start time. However, extra carbohydrate can be consumed (e.g., a sip of a sports drink or a nibble of fruit) to top up blood sugar levels before exercise.

The most important rule with pre-event eating is to choose foods that are familiar and have been experimented with during training. Competition day is not the time for experimenting with new foods. The following foods are all low in fat and high in carbohydrate and are ideal pre-event meals (assuming athletes have tried these before and know they tolerate them well):

- Breakfast cereal with low-fat milk
- Toast, muffins or crumpets with jam or honey
- Spaghetti on toast
- Pasta with a tomato-based sauce
- Steamed rice and vegetables
- Roll or sandwich filled with banana and honey
- Roll or sandwich filled with salad
- Low-fat creamy rice pudding with fruit salad
- Low-fat milk smoothie

REFUELLING DURING EXERCISE

It may be necessary to consume some carbohydrate during exercise to top up energy levels and optimise performance, particularly during exercise lasting longer than 90 minutes, during which carbohydrate stores may become depleted. The amount of carbohydrate required is 30 to 60 grams (1 to 2 oz) per hour, although some ultra-endurance athletes may require as much as 90 grams (3 oz) per hour. The best foods to choose are carbohydrate-rich foods with a high glycaemic index.

Each of the following provides 50 grams (1.7 oz) of high GI carbohydrate and would be suitable to consume during exercise:

- 750 ml (25 fl oz) sports drink
- 50 g (3 oz) jelly beans or snakes
- 2 bananas
- 1 sports bar
- 2 sports gels

In a tournament situation with more than one game to play or more than one race in a day, fuel stores will need topping up between events. The foods and fluids chosen should meet the guidelines for the pre-event meal. Exactly which foods are chosen will largely depend on how much time is available and the athlete's preference. Table 14.3 provides some suggestions for how and what to eat between events.

Table 14.3 Eating Between Events

Time available	What to eat
Less than half an hour	Sports drink only
Half to one hour	Sports drink Select from banana, fruit bar or jelly beans
One to two hours	Sports drink Select from jam sandwich, banana sandwich, fruit or bars
More than two hours	Sports drink Select from pasta dish, rice dish or sandwiches

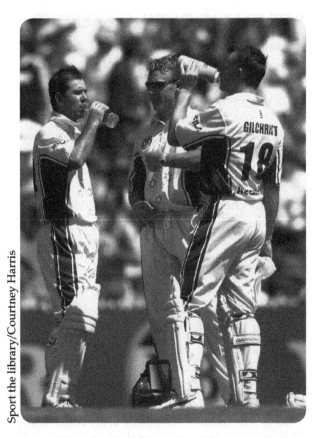

Consuming sports drinks is a good way to hydrate and replenish energy levels during competition.

RECOVERY

As well as rehydrating, refuelling is an important component to recovery. To refuel the muscle's energy stores (glycogen) after exercise, athletes should aim to consume 1 to 1.5 grams of carbohydrate per kilogram of body weight. High GI foods consumed during exercise are also good recovery foods. Other options include the following items, each of which provides 50 grams (1.7 oz) of carbohydrate:

- 1 1/2 jam or honey sandwiches
- 1 cup of rice
- 1 1/2 cups of jelly
- Large serve of tropical fruits
- 3 rice cakes with honey
- 500 ml (17 fl oz) soft drink

Protein also plays an important role in recovery. To stimulate muscle protein synthesis after strength training, athletes should aim to consume 20 grams (0.7 oz) of protein. This can be supplied by 500 millilitres (17 oz) of milk, 2 tubs of yoghurt, a 100-gram (3.5 oz) can of tuna or a large ham and cheese sandwich.

WEIGHT AND BODY COMPOSITION

For many athletes weight and body composition is very important. Some sports have weight categories that athletes must compete within; in others, leanness is desired for aesthetic reasons or to enhance performance. On the flip side of this are athletes who may benefit from gaining weight or 'bulking up' for their sports.

Several methods are available for monitoring weight and body composition. The obvious one is weighing on bathroom scales. Although this may be useful for athletes in weight-categorised sports, it does not differentiate among the components that make up body weight. Sports dietitians and sports scientists measure skinfolds using calipers to get a better idea of body fat levels. Similarly, a DEXA or BOD POD machine can be used to measure body composition and differentiate between body fat and fat free or lean body mass.

Athletes trying to reduce their weight or body fat levels need a sensible approach that provides enough energy to fuel training and promote recovery, but that creates an energy deficit to promote weight loss. It is beyond the scope of this chapter to detail all the issues involved in weight loss and the strategies available. A consultation with a sports dietitian can help athletes achieve their goals and gain a better understanding of how to safely reduce their weight without running into problems with eating disorders.

Athletes wanting to gain weight or 'bulk up' need to achieve positive energy balance, whereby their energy intake is greater than the energy they require. Of course, an adequate strength training program is also required, and good genetics help. To achieve positive energy balance, athletes should aim to eat three main meals per day with mini meals or large snacks in between that are based on a combination of both protein- and carbohydrate-rich foods. They should distribute food intake evenly across the day and have a recovery snack after training sessions that includes some good-quality protein.

SUPPLEMENTATION

A varied diet, including foods from each of the food groups, should meet all vitamin and mineral requirements without the need for supplementation for most athletes. Vitamin and mineral supplements may be required in certain situations. If a specific deficiency exists, a supplement may be required to correct this. A doctor or dietitian will be able to advise. Supplements may also be warranted when athletes are travelling for training and competition and for various reasons may not be able to consume the foods they normally would to meet their needs.

HYDRATION FOR SPORT

Meeting the body's fluid needs is important for health and also performance. Athletes have increased requirements for fluid to replace that lost via sweat. Sweating is the body's cooling mechanism. It is an effective way to dissipate heat, avoid the increase in core body temperature that occurs with exercise and minimise the risk of heat exhaustion. If fluid needs are not met, the consequence is dehydration, the effects of which can not only affect performance but can also be quite dangerous. The effects of dehydration include the following:

- Increased heart rate
- Increased body temperature

ACHIEVING ENERGY BALANCE

Sarah is a 14-year-old swimmer who has been struggling to get through training sessions lately and is constantly tired. Her times, which were improving, have been dropping off over the last few weeks. Her coach has been encouraging her to drink plenty of water during her training sessions and encouraging her to eat well, but is aware that several other factors could be causing her fatigue. He is particularly concerned that, as a female athlete, her iron levels could be an issue, so he suggests that she visit her doctor and a sports dietitian. A blood test shows good iron levels, and an assessment with the dietitian shows that she eats like a normal 14-year-old.

However, Sarah is an athlete, so she needs to eat much more than most teenagers. By starting her morning with a smoothie before training, taking a container of cereal to the pool to have immediately after training for rapid recovery, and increasing her snacks throughout the day, Sarah starts eating more like an athlete and starts to have lots more energy. More carbohydrate at dinner and a snack before bed help to refuel her body after her evening training sessions, so she has more energy in the morning. With better recovery and more energy, Sarah's training improves, her times get faster and she enjoys her swimming again.

- Increased perception of effort
- Decreased mental functioning and concentration
- Decreased motor performance skills
- Decreased muscular strength and power
- Premature fatigue
- Increased risk of gastrointestinal upsets
- Poorer performance

Water is obviously the best fluid to drink, although sports drinks can also be beneficial in some situations for replacing sweat losses. Energy drinks are not recommended because of their high sugar content and high levels of caffeine. The amount of fluid required varies considerably among athletes, depending on their sweat rates, fitness levels, intensity of exercise, acclimatisation and the environmental conditions on the day. Sweat rates in athletes may be as high as 0.5 to 1.5 litres per hour of exercise.

Several methods exist for assessing hydration status and fluid needs. Simply checking the urine can provide some valuable information. Urine that is dark in colour signals dehydration. Athletes should aim for light-coloured, less concentrated urine of a good volume. Sports dietitians and sports scientists can also perform other measurements on urine to determine hydration status. Athletes can calculate their own sweat rates to determine their own fluid needs. To do this, they can conduct a small fluid balance study. They can determine fluid (sweat) losses by weighing themselves before and after training or competition. Every kilogram lost represents one litre of fluid.

Coaches should be aware of the signs of dehydration so they can advise their athletes. Symptoms to watch out for include thirst, tiredness and fatigue, nausea, cramps, headaches and the effects of dehydration listed previously. The following hydration guidelines can help athletes maintain proper levels of hydration:

- Begin training and competitions in a hydrated state.
- Consume additional fluid in the lead-up to exercise.
- Include at least 2 cups of fluid at the pre-match meal.
- Commence drinking as early as possible during exercise. Do not wait until you are thirsty.
- Drink to a plan, based on your requirements, as determined by fluid balance studies.
- Drink at every opportunity during exercise, sipping small amounts frequently.
- Replace remaining fluid losses as soon as possible after exercise.

DRUG USE BY ATHLETES

The use of drugs in sport is always a controversial issue sparking much debate, discussion and media interest. Athletes have been using drugs for many years to improve their sporting performance, often with disastrous effects and even death. Today a collaborative worldwide campaign for doping-free sport is led by the World Anti-Doping Agency (WADA), which was established in 1999 as an international

SPORTS DRINKS

Sports drinks contain water with added carbohydrate and electrolytes. The carbohydrate (usually in the range of a 4 to 8 per cent concentration) provides extra energy during exercise and delays fatigue. This is particularly beneficial in high-intensity sports or exercise lasting longer than an hour. The sodium assists in fluid absorption and retention. On very hot days when fluid losses may be excessive, athletes would be wise to rehydrate with a sports drink, which will help them retain fluid better. Sports drinks also have the advantage of palatability. Studies have found that athletes consume more of a flavoured drink than of a non-flavoured one, which will help to keep them better hydrated.

independent agency. WADA's key activities are scientific research, education, development of anti-doping capacities and monitoring of the World Anti-Doping Code. WADA works towards a vision of a world in which all athletes compete in a doping-free sporting environment.

WADA is supported by regional and national anti-doping organisations (RADOs and NADOs). The Australian Sports Anti-Doping Authority (ASADA) is one such NADO. ASADA is a government statutory authority that is Australia's driving force for pure performance in sport. ASADA's mission is to protect Australia's sporting integrity through the elimination of doping. The use of drugs in sport is not confined to those used for performance enhancement. Drugs may also be used for medicinal purposes or for recreational reasons. The sections that follow examine more closely drugs that may be used by athletes.

CAFFEINE

Caffeine is probably the most widely known and used drug worldwide. Its effects in reducing fatigue and increasing wakefulness and alertness have been recognised for many years; it has been used by athletes and non-athletes the world over. In 1980 the use of excess caffeine in sport was banned because of concerns about its misuse. Of course, a cup of coffee or cola-type drink was not considered excessive and would not result in a positive test. However, at levels greater than 12 milligrams per millilitre, it was prohibited. In 2004 caffeine was removed from the WADA prohibited list, allowing athletes to consume caffeine, either as part of their normal diet or as an ergogenic aid, without fear of sanctions.

Caffeine has since been used widely by athletes as an ergogenic aid. Supplementation with caffeine has been found to enhance performance over a range of exercise protocols. Caffeine has numerous actions on various body tissues. It results in changes to muscle contractility, in improved alertness and reaction time (as a result of the release and activity of adrenaline) and in modifications to the central nervous system that alter the perception of effort or fatigue.

Traditional caffeine supplementing protocols have used high doses of caffeine such as 6 milligrams per kilogram of body mass taken one hour prior to the event, equating to approximately 300 to 500 milligrams of caffeine. More recent research in exercise lasting longer than 60 minutes has shown that a variety of protocols can enhance performance. Benefits have been seen with as little as 3 milligrams per kilogram of body mass taken before or during exercise (or both) or toward the end of exercise when the athlete is becoming fatigued. Performance benefits do not tend to increase with increases in caffeine dose above 3 milligrams per kilogram. In fact, although higher doses may benefit endurance performance, they may actually be detrimental to some athletes, particularly those in sports in which visual information processing is required, such as aiming for a target.

There are some things athletes should be aware of before considering caffeine use as an ergogenic aid. There is a lot of individual variability in the response to caffeine intake. Some people benefit from its use, whereas others may experience no effect from the same dose. At higher levels caffeine can cause side effects, including increased heart rate, impairment of fine motor control, overarousal and interference with sleep and recovery. The long-term intake of large amounts of caffeine (>500 milligrams per day) are generally discouraged by health authorities. Athletes who decide to use caffeine should experiment in training to find the lowest dose they need to achieve a performance enhancement.

TOBACCO

Tobacco smoking is the single most preventable cause of ill health and death. Smoking is a key risk factor for the three diseases that cause the most deaths in Australia: ischaemic heart disease, cerebrovascular disease and lung cancer.

In sport, some athletes use smoking as an aid to weight control. Although an increase in metabolic rate is associated with smoking, it is only slight and is certainly not a healthy way to control body weight. In athletes, smoking affects performance by causing a decrease in lung function and in oxygen transport to the muscles. Smoking may also lead to an increased risk of injury.

Passive, or involuntary, smoking (i.e., breathing air polluted by another person's tobacco smoke) is also dangerous to health and sporting performance. Many sporting organisations are now taking action by declaring smoke-free zones and banning smoking not only in competition areas, but also in spectator areas.

ALCOHOL

Alcohol is a widely used drug in our community today; it is consumed for social reasons, relaxation or simply enjoyment. In most instances it is consumed in moderate amounts that cause no adverse effects. However, in excess, whether acute or chronic, alcohol is often responsible for ill health, disease, death, injury and accidents.

The National Health and Medical Research Council's Australian Guidelines to Reduce Health Risks from Drinking Alcohol suggests that 'for healthy men and women, drinking no more than two standard drinks on any day reduces the lifetime risk of harm from alcohol related disease or injury' (National Health and Medical Research Council, 2009, p. 2) and 'for healthy men and women, drinking no more than four standard drinks on a single occasion reduces the risk of alcohol-related injury arising from that occasion' (p. 3).

In sport, alcohol is commonly used as a reward or to celebrate after sport. In days gone by, it was common practice for slabs of beer to be brought into teams' change rooms after games. However, with the increasing professionalism of sport, this is seen much less often at an elite level, although it may still occur at a recreational level. It is important for athletes to understand the effects that alcohol has not just on general health but also on sporting performance. Certainly we know that alcohol consumption negatively affects reaction time, balance, eye–hand coordination and decision making and can decrease strength, speed and power. Alcohol also affects hydration; being a diuretic, it promotes fluid loss. Because it can also affect recovery and increase swelling, athletes with soft tissue injury should avoid it.

In addition to tobacco smoking and alcohol, illicit drug use (including cannabis, ecstasy and cocaine) occurs in the athlete population. Although the use of these drugs may be less about performance enhancement and more for social or relaxation reasons, their use cannot be ignored. Australian studies reveal a low self-reported prevalence of drug use. However, one third of elite Australian athletes report having been offered or had the opportunity to use illicit drugs in the past year. Therefore, appropriate education concerning the use of illicit drugs is needed.

PROHIBITED SUBSTANCES AND METHODS

The WADA World Anti-Doping Code first came into force in 2004 and has since been reviewed and revised. The code harmonises regulations regarding anti-doping in sport across all sports and all countries. It provides a framework for anti-doping policies, rules and regulations for sport organisations and public authorities.

WADA is responsible for the preparation and publication of the prohibited list, which includes substances and methods prohibited in competition, out of competition and in particular sports. This list is updated annually and available for viewing at www.wada-ama.org. For a substance to be prohibited, it must meet two of the following three conditions:

- It has the potential to enhance or does enhance performance in sport.
- It has the potential to risk the athlete's health.
- It is deemed to violate the spirit of sport.

Because athletes are ultimately responsible and liable for any banned substance found in their bodies, they need to be familiar with the WADA code and the prohibited list. Athletes, coaches and medical and support personnel can also go online at ASADA (https://check-substances.asada.gov.au/) to find out whether their medications and substances are permitted or prohibited in sport.

The following substances are prohibited at all times: anabolic agents, peptide hormones, growth factors and related substances, beta-2 agonists, hormone antagonists and modulators and diuretics and other masking agents. These substances are prohibited in competition: stimulants, narcotics, cannabinoids and glucocorticosteroids. Alcohol and beta-blockers are prohibited in particular sports only. Additionally, the following methods are prohibited: enhancement of oxygen transfer, chemical and physical manipulation and gene doping. Table 14.4 provides information about the actions these prohibited substances take in the body as well as the side effects they may cause.

Table 14.4 Actions and Side Effects of Prohibited Substances

Substance	Examples	Medical or performance-enhancing action	Side effects
Anabolic agents	Stanozolol Nandrolone	Increase muscle bulk and strength	Hypertension Hypercholesterolaemia Decreased sperm production Aggressive behaviour
Peptide hormones, growth factors and related substances	Erythropoietin Human growth hormone Insulin	Clinically used to treat diabetes Accelerate growth Increase red blood cell production	Cardiac myopathy Hypertension Hypoglycaemia Thrombosis
Beta 2 agonists	Clenbuterol Salbutamol	Treat exercise-induced asthma May have anabolic effects	Tachycardia Tremor Palpitations
Hormone antagonists and modulators	Clomiphene	Clinically used to treat breast cancer and infertility To prevent steroid-induced gynaecomastia	Blurred vision Nausea Joint pain
Diuretics and other masking agents	Thiazides Furosemide	Treat hypertension and heart failure Decrease concentration of drugs in urine Cause rapid weight loss	Dehydration Electrolyte imbalance Muscle cramps
Stimulants	Cocaine Ephedrine Adrenalin	Mask fatigue Improve alertness	Increased anxiety Cardiac arrhythmia Muscle tremor
Narcotics Cannabinoids	Morphine Methadone	Reduce pain	Addictive Respiratory depression May be fatal
Glucocorticosteroids	Hydrocortisone Prednisolone	Anti-inflammatory	Sodium and water retention Decreased immune function Euphoria
Alcohol	Any alcoholic beverage	None	Adversely affects reaction time, coordination, balance
Beta-blockers	Any brand name of beta-blocker	Decrease blood pressure and heart rate	Tremor Anxiety
Blood doping	NA	Enhances oxygen transfer	Risks associated with transfusion (allergies, infection) Increased blood viscosity (blood clotting, hypertension)
Chemical and physical manipulation	NA	Reduces excretion of banned substances	Risks associated with method used (e.g., infection with IV infusion)
Gene doping	NA	Non-therapeutic use of genes or gene expression to enhance performance	Can be dangerous Risks involved include toxicities

SUPPLEMENTS

ASADA cannot provide information or advice to athletes about sport supplements specifically and whether they contain prohibited substances. Supplements can vary from batch to batch and may, either intentionally or unintentionally, contain banned substances. Athletes may not realise that if they return a positive test, they are liable, despite the fact that their ingestion of the substance may not have been deliberate.

An IOC investigation in 2001 obtained 634 nutritional supplements from 13 countries and 215 suppliers, from shops, on the Internet and by telephone order. Analyses revealed that almost 15 per cent of these supplements tested positive for banned substances. They contained prohormones (nandrolone or testosterone), which were not listed on the label. It is therefore essential that athletes be extremely careful with supplement use and use only products they know to be safe. Because substances are regulated and monitored differently overseas, athletes should use only Australian-made supplements from credible sources.

At times, athletes need to take substances that are banned for medical reasons. In such situations, they can apply to the Australian Sports Drug Medical Advisory Committee (ASDMAC) for a therapeutic use exemption (TUE). Coaches should refer athletes in this situation to their doctors, who can complete the relevant form and send it in.

DRUG TESTING IN AUSTRALIA

National anti-doping organisations (NADOs), such as ASADA, are responsible for testing national athletes in and out of competition, as well as athletes from other countries competing within that nation's borders. Once athletes are selected for drug tests, they are given an athlete privacy information notice and a doping control notification form, which they must sign. From this point on, they must remain in direct observation of the doping control officer or chaperone and report to the doping control station immediately. The athlete is then taken through the following procedure:

1. The athlete selects a sealed sample collection vessel, which must remain in the athlete's control at all times.

2. The chaperone then accompanies the athlete to the bathroom where the chaperone witnesses the actual passing of the urine. In the case of a blood sample, the athlete selects the blood collection equipment and the sample is collected in the presence of a doping control officer, chaperone and, if applicable, the athlete's representative.

3. The athlete then selects an individually sealed sample collection kit and confirms that the sample code numbers on the bottles or tubes, the lids and the containers all match and are recorded accurately. The athlete is then required to pour a measured amount of the urine into each of the A- and B-labelled bottles, and then secure the kits. In the case of blood samples, the athlete places and secures the blood samples in the relevant labelled containers and secures the kits.

4. Then, the final paperwork is completed, including personal details and information about prescription and non-prescription medications, vitamins, supplements and any other substances used in the last week.

5. The athlete, the doping control officer and the chaperone all sign the doping control test form. The samples are then sent to a WADA-accredited lab for analysis.

If ASADA is advised by the lab that a sample has recorded a positive result, which indicates the presence of a substance or doping method on the WADA prohibited list, the athlete is notified. ASADA can test the B sample, or the athlete has the right to request that the B sample be analysed to confirm the result.

It is then ASADA's role to present information to the independent anti-doping rule violation panel about a potential violation of the code. Members of the panel assess the information presented to them, including information provided by the athlete, and then decide whether to enter the athlete's details on the register of findings (a formal record of decisions on anti-doping rule violations and associated matters) and whether to recommend a sanction to the sport governing body. The athlete is then given the opportunity to have a hearing before a sport tribunal, and it is then up to the individual sport governing body to decide whether to sanction the athlete or support person. More information is available on the ASADA and WADA websites.

Although the athlete is ultimately responsible for any positive drug test, coaches are responsible for educating athletes and advising them appropriately. Coaches of athletes who are subject to drug testing can use the following guidelines to educate them:

- Be a good role model in eating healthfully and abstaining from drugs.
- Focus on performance enhancement via quality training and good nutrition.
- If athlete(s) wish to use caffeine as an ergogenic aid, ensure that they experiment in training to find the smallest dose required to elicit a benefit.

- Don't smoke around athletes and discourage smoking.
- Declare smoke-free zones.
- Discourage alcohol consumption and do not provide it to athletes.
- Educate athletes about the negative effect of alcohol on performance.
- Discourage recreational drug use.
- Conduct a drug information seminar for athletes
- Be aware that some over-the-counter preparations contain banned substances.
- Never administer drugs or medications to athletes.
- Encourage athletes to check with their medical doctor or ASADA regarding whether a substance or medication is permitted or prohibited.
- If providing supplements to athletes, be very careful and mindful of the quality and safety.

SUMMARY

- Athletes require a high-carbohydrate diet to fuel their bodies for training and competition.
- Protein is important for growth and development as well as recovery after exercise.
- A low-fat diet is recommended for athletes to ensure an adequate carbohydrate and protein intake and prevent unwanted weight gain.
- The competition diet requires careful consideration and planning to optimise performance.
- Water and sports drinks are best for replacing fluids lost in sweat and for rehydrating during and after exercise.
- Athletes should be aware that they are ultimately responsible for any banned substance found in their bodies and should be familiar with the WADA code and prohibited list.

The author of this chapter thanks Dr. Carmel Goodman for her assistance with the Drug Use by Athletes section of this chapter.

REFERENCES AND RESOURCES

Burke, L. (2007). *Practical sports nutrition.* Champaign, IL: Human Kinetics.

Burke, L., & G. Cox. (2010). *The complete guide to food for sports performance.* Sydney, NSW: Allen and Unwin.

Burke, L., & V. Deakin. (Eds.). (2010). *Clinical sports nutrition* (4th ed.). Sydney, NSW: McGraw-Hill. Cardwell, G. (2006). Gold medal nutrition (4th ed.). Champaign, IL: Human Kinetics.

Hawley, J., & Burke, L. (1998). *Peak performance.* St. Leonards, NSW: Allen & Unwin. Manore, M., Meyer, N., & Thompson, J. (2009). *Sports nutrition for health and performance* (2nd ed.). Champaign, IL: Human Kinetics.

National Health and Medical Research Council. (2009). *Australian guidelines to reduce health risks from drinking alcohol.* www.nhmrc.gov.au

Sports Dietitians Australia, www.sportsdietitians.com.au.

CHAPTER 15

Addressing Injuries and Illnesses

—— Carmel Goodman and Frank Pyke

Coaches are not expected to be medical experts, but they do play a vital role as part of the sports medicine team. The athlete's well-being is a coach's foremost concern. That is demonstrated by the use of effective injury and illness prevention measures. Many problems can be avoided with proper medical screening, off-season conditioning, and careful monitoring. Additionally, the following measures can reduce the occurrence of athletic injuries:

- Graduated increases in load (intensity, frequency, volume)
- Adequate recovery periods
- Recovery methods (ice baths and massage)
- Early injury recognition and management
- Protective and correct equipment, clothing, and footwear
- Taping and bracing of ankles, knees, and shoulders to prevent recurrent sprains or protect the area
- Modification of exercise according to environmental conditions and the athlete's health and fatigue levels
- Adequate warm-up, cool-down, and flexibility exercises

However, despite a coach's best efforts, not all injuries and medical conditions can be avoided. The force with which athletes move, the hours they spend training, and the collisions they sometimes have are bound to result in some injuries to some athletes. So coaches must be prepared to respond quickly and provide the first aid measures needed for the short-term management of athletes' ailments until qualified medical staff can be accessed.

Also, after injuries, coaches should insist that athletes adhere to appropriate rehabilitation programs before returning to practice. And they must encourage their athletes to inform them of any special health concerns from their history or recent competition and training.

ACUTE MUSCULOSKELETAL INJURIES

An acute injury may be either direct (caused by an external force) or indirect (no external objects involved). Direct injuries include trauma from the impact of an implement, such as a hockey stick or cricket or water polo ball, which may result in a fracture, bone or muscle bruising or a head injury. Trauma from a collision with an opposition player, such as contact with a knee or elbow in football or rugby, can similarly cause severe muscle bruising (cork) or joint injury. As players and the equipment used are usually travelling at high speed, these injuries involve great force and hence may result in significant injuries such as finger fractures and dislocations, shoulder dislocations and knee and ankle ligament injuries, which take weeks or months to heal.

Indirect injuries do not involve an external force and may be due to exercising on fatigued muscles, inadequate warm-up or stretching or simply bad luck. Examples include a hamstring strain in a sprinter or a footballer accelerating to get to the ball, an ankle ligament tear in a netball player landing awkwardly or a knee injury of the anterior cruciate ligament due to changing direction at speed in football or hockey.

JOINT AND LIGAMENT INJURY

A ligament injury is suspected if the affected joint is obviously dislocated (finger), movement of the joint causes pain, rapid swelling occurs or pain is experienced with weight bearing (ankle or knee). The coach should always be suspicious of an associated fracture if there is significant pain with moving or loading the joint, joint deformity is present or there is obvious, rapid swelling around the joint.

MUSCLE INJURY

When a muscle injury occurs, the athlete usually feels a sharp, stabbing pain at the moment of injury, and the pain can be reproduced by contracting the affected muscle (often the hamstring, quadriceps or calf). The athlete is likely to feel tenderness on palpation of the affected muscle, and the coach or the athlete may feel a defect in the area. Swelling and bruising usually occur after 24 to 48 hours. If no doctor or physiotherapist is present, the coach may have to make a diagnosis and decide whether the player can return to play. Once this decision has been made (whether the athlete returns to play now or later), appropriate initial management can significantly reduce recovery time.

ACUTE INJURY TREATMENT

Initial management of acute musculoskeletal injuries involves the tried-and-true RICE regime in the first 72 hours:

- **Rest.** Athletes should avoid any activity that causes pain to the injured muscle or joint. This may include not moving the affected joint at all, engaging in only non-weight-bearing activity, or simply modifying activity to within the pain threshold.

- **Ice.** Ice should be applied for 15 minutes every hour. Ice application decreases blood flow to the injured area and thus minimises swelling, further bleeding, pain and inflammation. To prevent ice burns, ice should be applied in a wet towel or plastic bag and not directly on the skin.

- **Compression.** Compression bandages, such as crepe or elastic bandages, should be comfortably tight and applied immediately. The compression minimises bleeding and thus prevents further oedema.

- **Elevation.** Keeping the injured area elevated causes the blood and fluid to drain away from the injury site and minimises oedema.

Heat, alcohol and massage should be avoided in the first 72 hours following injury because they increase blood flow and can thus cause further bleeding and swelling. If a fracture is suspected, the affected limb should be immobilised by strapping, splinting or bracing. The athlete should be transported as soon as possible to a doctor or hospital for examination and probable X-ray. After the initial 72 hours, the medical staff should have a good idea of the nature and extent of the injury, but if not will continue their investigation until conclusive results are found. Various physiotherapy modalities can then be employed to treat and heal the wound.

When deemed appropriate by the physician overseeing the athlete's care, a graduated strengthening, stretching and return-to-play program can be commenced. The coach should ensure that the athlete adheres to the rehabilitation plan. The coach can also recommend to the medical staff alternative forms of exercise the athlete can undertake while recovering from the injury. The medical staff, coach and athlete should jointly decide what alternative skills or cardiorespiratory exercise will enable the athlete to retain cardiorespiratory fitness and sport-specific skills while allowing optimal injury healing.

Muscle and ligament injuries usually take four to six weeks for full recovery (obviously, depending on the degree of damage). During that time rehabilitation involves regaining

ELITE-LEVEL GYMNAST

While training for upcoming major competitions, an elite-level gymnast landed awkwardly and felt immediate pain and swelling in her ankle. She was unable to bear weight on the ankle and had to be helped to the side of the gym. The coach immediately instituted a RICE regime. The next day, a sport physician examined her injury and found she had significant pain and swelling over the lateral malleolus and increased laxity of the lateral ligaments.

Physiotherapy management was commenced, including local treatment, and the athlete applied ice and compression for 20 minutes every few hours. Upper-body exercise was continued in the gym under the coach's supervision, and graduated lower limb rehabilitation exercise commenced as per instruction by the physiotherapist and sport physician. After a few weeks the ankle was not improving as expected, and an MRI revealed significant damage to all three lateral ligaments as well as to the anterior inferior tibiofibular ligament.

An orthopaedic opinion was sought and surgery recommended to repair the torn ankle ligaments, which would involve 12 to 16 weeks of recovery before return to gymnastics and would mean missing the world championships, the Commonwealth Games and potentially the Olympic Games.

In this situation the injury was such that there was a chance of healing without surgical intervention. The treating sport physician and coach decided to attempt an aggressive rehabilitation program, while modifying training and eliminating some routines. The gymnast had physiotherapy treatment twice a week; undertook rehabilitation exercises involving strengthening, stretching and proprioception on a daily basis; and spent a few hours in the gym daily working on aspects of the routine that involved no or minimal stress to the ankle. The gymnast went on to become world and Commonwealth champion and did not ultimately need surgery.

strength, proprioception, skills and range of motion, while maintaining cardiorespiratory fitness. If an athlete is allowed to return to training or competition before the injury is completely healed, there is a high risk of recurrent or chronic injury developing. In addition to medical and physiotherapy advice, the coach should make use of all the professional help available, including the services of a sport psychologist, exercise physiologist or strength and conditioning staff as necessary.

OVERUSE INJURIES

Overuse injuries include tendon and bone injuries that may occur in upper or lower limbs usually as a result of underlying anatomical and biomechanical factors or relative overload (increasing loads by too much, too soon). Common examples of overuse injuries in lower limbs are Achilles or patella tendinosis, which often occur in basketball or track and field, and tibial and navicular stress fractures, which can occur in any running athlete. In upper limbs,

overuse injuries include shoulder rotator cuff tendinosis, which happens in swimming and water polo; forearm tenosynovitis, which is common in tennis and rowing; and stress fractures of the ribs, which happen in rowing. Ideally, the coach should be able to recognise such an injury at an early stage and direct the athlete towards medical diagnosis and management.

TENDINOSIS AND TENOSYNOVITIS

In the early stages of a tendon injury, pain occurs before and after exercise, but not during exercise. As the condition worsens, pain is present during exercise as well. Recognising and treating tendon injuries at an early stage is crucial to keep them from becoming chronic and resistant to treatment. In tendinosis and tenosynovitis (inflammation of the synovial sheath), the tendon or tendon sheath is tender on palpation, and the athlete may feel crepitus or a creaking sensation. Pain may be experienced with resisted movement of the tendon or musculotendinous junction. Management includes early identification, ice massage, physiotherapy modalities and exercise within the pain threshold (no pain during exercise or within 24 hours postexercise).

STRESS FRACTURES

The presentation of stress fractures is extremely variable and, although a stress fracture usually presents as gradually worsening pain during exercise, it can have a sudden onset or present with intermittent pain. Common sites of stress fractures are the tibia (long-distance runners), the navicular or metatarsals in the foot (track and field, hockey and football athletes), the ribs (rowers) and the pars interarticularis in the lumbar spine (gymnasts, rowers and cricketers).

A stress fracture should be suspected in any athlete with progressive worsening or sudden onset of pain during exercise associated with an increase in training load, sustained high load or repetitive practise of a particular skill at training. Stress fractures are more common in female athletes, particularly those experiencing a disruption of the menstrual cycle. Any female athlete who has not had a menstrual period for six months is at risk for developing a stress fracture and must be referred for medical investigation and management.

DIAGNOSIS OF OVERUSE INJURY

Most overuse injuries have a classical presentation of progressive increase in pain during or after exercise or both. The coach should direct the athlete to seek immediate physiotherapy or medical examination. The diagnosis is then confirmed on radiological imaging such as a bone scan, CT or MRI scan. Early diagnosis is essential in the case of overuse injuries and can mean the difference between a few weeks and many months off training. The usual time for recovery from a stress fracture is six to eight weeks.

Once the diagnosis has been made, an appropriate rehabilitation and cross-training program can be planned, depending on the severity of the injury. This involves a team approach, including biomechanical analysis to correct any technique errors, physiotherapy,

strength and conditioning, medical management and graduated return to play. The coach has a vital role in supervising the athlete and should advise on sport-specific skills and alternative forms of cardiorespiratory and strengthening exercises during recovery from the injury. If an athlete is allowed to return to training before the injury has been adequately rehabilitated, the risk of chronic, ongoing injury is high. This is particularly common in athletes with recurrent hamstring and Achilles tendon injuries and often results in many months off training.

CHRONIC INJURIES

A number of athletes, particularly those who have been training and competing for many years, develop permanent injuries such as osteoarthritis of the hip, knee or back. In these situations, the athlete, coach and doctor need to decide whether the potential benefits of continued training and competition outweigh the potential for ongoing damage.

Team sport athletes, such as football and hockey players, may want to compete in one more Olympic Games or grand final, understanding the risks involved in ongoing exercise. The coach then has to decide whether the athlete is important enough to the team to accept training modifications and an individualised program. Once this decision has been made, the medical, fitness and strength and conditioning staff can create an appropriate management plan.

EMERGENCY SITUATIONS

It is extremely important that coaches are able to recognise the symptoms of and broadly assess the severity of brain and spinal cord injuries. They should also be able to institute basic first aid and make decisions as to when an athlete should be withdrawn from play.

CONCUSSION

Concussion can be defined as a disturbance in brain function that results from trauma to the brain. The changes are temporary, and the majority of players recover completely when

CHRONIC INJURIES AND OLYMPIC DREAMS

To achieve one more Olympics, many athletes are willing to take on specialized training and accept possible risks. For example a national hockey player who had competed in the Athens Olympics was desperate to compete in another Olympics before retiring. Two years out from the Beijing Olympics, she was experiencing increasing hip pain. The risks of continued play—namely, the progression of arthritis in the hip joint requiring early hip replacement—were explained to her, but she nevertheless chose to sign the informed consent form.

The coach believed that because she was one of the best players on the team, her contribution would help the team's medal chances. So, a program was devised to avoid all weight-bearing exercise apart from time spent on the hockey field. All cross-training was done on the bike or in the pool as opposed to running. She competed in the Olympics and was one of the best players in the team. She had a hip replacement after the Olympics and is adamant that she made the correct decision.

Another example was a rower, who had competed in two previous Olympic Games. The athlete presented with worsening lower back pain, consistent with significant multilevel disc pathology on MRI. The coach believed he was a valuable member of the crew (men's 8) training for the Sydney Olympics and would be competitive if he could complete all on-water training. The risks of ongoing training were explained to the athlete, and he chose to sign an informed consent form. His training was modified to minimise ergometer work. A very careful gym program was devised, balanced between strengthening and avoiding painful exercises, and he did extra fitness work on the bike. The crew won a medal at the Olympics, and the rower believes he made the correct decision.

managed correctly. Common symptoms of concussion are headache, blurred vision, nausea, balance problems, fatigue, feeling 'dinged' or 'dazed' and confusion. Loss of consciousness is seen in only 10 to 20 per cent of cases of concussion.

Complications are not common with concussions and usually occur only when the player is returned to play before fully recovered. It is thus essential that any player with suspected concussion be withdrawn from playing or training immediately and not return that day. Any player with symptoms of concussion needs an urgent medical assessment and should not be allowed to return to train or play until a formal medical clearance has been given.

MANAGEMENT OF AN UNCONSCIOUS ATHLETE

All coaches must have advanced first aid certificates because first aid principles should be employed when dealing with an unconscious athlete and CPR commenced immediately. Extreme care must be taken in the case of any suspected neck injury, and the spinal column must be completely immobilised as the player is removed from the field. The player should be carried by four people, avoiding any movement of the cervical spine, and remain immobilised while awaiting transfer to hospital. Indications of the need for urgent hospital referral include the following:

- Any concern regarding severe neck or head injury

- Any athlete with loss of consciousness or seizures

- Any player with persistent confusion

- Any player with worsening symptoms of headache, drowsiness and vomiting

- Any player with neck pain or spinal cord symptoms, such as numbness, tingling and weakness in the arms

- *If in any doubt, the coach must refer the player to the hospital urgently!*

For more information on the treatment of concussion, coaches should consult 'The

Management of Concussion in Australian Football' (see the References and Resources section at the end of the chapter), which is based on guidelines developed by the AFL Medical Officers Association and incorporates research funded by the AFL Research Board and published by the AFL in 2011.

SERIOUS MEDICAL CONDITIONS

Coaches need to know whether any of their athletes have pre-existing medical conditions, such as diabetes or asthma. They can then gather sufficient knowledge to manage these athletes in acute situations and make appropriate training modifications.

DIABETES

An athlete with diabetes is capable of training and competing at any level, and there are many examples of athletes with diabetes who have been extremely successful, including winning Olympic medals. A coach who has an athlete with diabetes in the squad needs to become familiar with the requirements of that athlete during exercise as well as any potential complications. The athlete must be allowed access at all times to fluids and foods that contain carbohydrate.

The coach must also be aware of the symptoms of hypoglycaemia (low blood glucose) and ensure that sugary fluid is given immediately when needed. Sweating, increased heart rate and tremor are early warning signs of hypoglycaemia and can mimic the effects of strenuous exercise. If these early signs are not recognised and treated immediately, more severe hypoglycaemia will result in poor coordination, confusion, convulsions and eventually coma. At the first indication of hypoglycaemia, the athlete must ingest carbohydrate in solid or liquid form.

Another, less common complication of diabetes is diabetic ketoacidosis, which is high blood sugar with ketones in the urine. Symptoms may include drowsiness, lack of concentration, nausea, dehydration and poor performance.

Athletes and coaches need to be aware of these symptoms, and athletes should not exercise until their blood glucose is under control.

EXERCISE-INDUCED ASTHMA (EIA)

Exercise-induced asthma (EIA), also known as exercise-induced bronchospasm (EIB), is defined as a transient increase in airway resistance (airway narrowing) as a result of vigorous exercise. EIA is a very common condition in athletes. The incidence ranges from 12 to 20 per cent, and screening studies have shown that up to 50 per cent of athletes with EIA are unaware of it.

In 2000, 21 per cent of the Australian Olympic team reported having EIA. The incidence of EIA is highest in athletes participating in endurance sports such as cycling, running, rowing and triathlons, and in winter sports such as cross-country skiing and ice skating; and less frequently in team sports such as basketball, soccer and rugby. Recent reports have demonstrated that the chlorine content in pools, particularly indoor pools, causes a chemical irritation in susceptible swimmers, resulting in bronchospasm.

The symptoms of EIA follow. Many of these symptoms are worse when exercising during the pollen season, indoors or in the cold air.

- Shortness of breath during or after exercise
- Persistent cough or dry cough postexercise
- Chest tightness
- Poor performance
- Wheezing
- Fatigue or dizziness

If an athlete is suspected of having EIA, medical referral for assessment and bronchial provocation testing must be organised as soon as possible. Appropriate treatment can then be commenced. In addition to inhaled beta 2 agonists and inhaled corticosteroids (which must be checked prior to use to ensure they are permitted by the IOC), other strategies that may aid in asthma management include the following:

- Environmental manipulation, such as exercising with a face mask in cold, dry air or using a humidifier when training indoors.
- Training modifications, such as a longer warm-up or repeated short sprints during the warm-up, induces a refractory period that may last up to four hours, during which further exercise results in significantly less EIB.

All athletes must use their prescribed inhalers on a regular basis, exactly as prescribed, and ensure they always have their rapidly acting inhaled beta agonist (e.g., Ventolin) readily available at every training and competition to rapidly reverse EIB if it occurs.

ENVIRONMENTAL AND CLIMATIC CONSIDERATIONS

The stress associated with training and competition is often intensified by harsh environments. High air temperatures and humidity can have a negative effect on endurance performance and, in extreme cases, cause progressive dehydration and collapse. Conversely, low air and water temperatures can create problems for winter sport athletes, open water swimmers and surfers. High altitude taxes the aerobic energy system and limits endurance performance. Air pollution makes breathing difficult and poses a potential health threat while travelling across time zones, particularly to unaccustomed climates; as a result, it can undo the benefits of the most carefully planned training program. Unless the circumstances prevailing in each of these environments are carefully managed, performances will suffer significantly.

HEAT

Depending on the level of activity involved, the body is protected against overheating by the dilation of blood vessels in the skin and the evaporation of sweat from the skin surface.

Triathletes need to be prepared to manage cool air and water temperatures.

AP Photo/Rick Rycroft

The effectiveness of sweating is reduced when the atmosphere is humid, which limits its evaporative potential. Furthermore, the capacity to sweat is dependent on the availability of body fluid. The core body temperature at rest is around 37 °C (98.6 °F) but can increase to over 40 °C (104 °F) during prolonged exercise in warm conditions. When this happens, heat illness can occur.

A number of environmental factors determine the level of heat stress encountered. These include radiation from both the sun and the surroundings, the movement of air and relative humidity. Collectively, these factors can be assessed by the wet bulb globe temperature (WBGT) index. This index weights humidity (wet bulb temperature × 0.7) ahead of radiation (black bulb or globe temperature × 0.2) and air temperature (dry bulb temperature × 0.1). Caution is needed when the index exceeds 25 °C (77 °F), and conditions are considered unsafe if it is higher than 28 °C (82.4 °F). There is a strong case for scheduling summer training and competitions in the early morning or evening hours rather than in midafternoon.

Heat Acclimatisation Heat acclimatisation is a necessity for athletes who are living and training in temperate conditions prior to competing in hotter regions of the world. Fortunately, the process of acclimatising to heat is a rapid one and can be achieved in 7 to 10 days with between one to one and a half hours of daily exercise in the specific conditions. This may take a little longer if the athlete is reducing the intensity of the training program prior to competition or is spending most of the time in air-conditioned premises.

The acclimatisation regime facilitates better heat dissipation by improving the rate of onset and capacity for sweating. This helps maintain the blood flow to the muscles and reduces the amount of lactic acid produced during prolonged exercise. Fluid balance must be maintained during this time to allow plasma volume and sweat rate to increase and the accompanying acclimatory adjustments to occur.

Heat Illness Heat-related cramps in the skeletal muscles result from heavy and prolonged sweating, inadequate salt intake or both.

Recovery requires rest in cool conditions with adequate fluid and salt replacement.

Heat syncope results from the dilation of peripheral blood vessels and the pooling of blood in the veins, which can lead to fainting and collapse. Treatment involves lying down in a cool environment, elevating the legs and replacing fluid.

Heat exhaustion is associated with dizziness, headache, nausea, rapid pulse, elevated core and skin temperatures and poor coordination. This condition requires urgent medical attention and the emergency administration of intravenous fluids, ice packs and sponges and cold sprays because it can progress to severe heat stroke characterised by fits and loss of consciousness.

Individual Differences Athletes with more linear, ectomorphic builds have a higher ratio of body surface area to mass. An ambient temperature below body temperature facilitates heat loss. The reverse is true when the ambient temperature exceeds the body temperature. On the other hand, those with a more endomorphic build and a high percentage of body fat have a lower ratio of body surface area to mass and are better able to store heat. The situation of storing heat is further exacerbated if an athlete also has a low level of cardiorespiratory fitness.

Differences in build generally explain the differences between age groups and genders. Children have a higher ratio of surface area to mass and a lower capacity for sweating than adults do. Combined with a high energy cost of movement, this makes children more prone to heat illness and requires them to be closely supervised during exercise in hot conditions. Younger men sweat more readily and are generally fitter than older men, making them more heat tolerant. Generally, women of comparable age to men are less tolerant of heat because of their lower aerobic fitness levels and sweat rates. These variations need to be factored into the safety guidelines associated with individual athletes exercising in the heat.

Fluid Replacement Regular replacement of fluid is essential in hot conditions to prevent dehydration and deterioration in endurance performance. The fluid should preferably be

HISTORIC CRICKET MATCH

Cricketer Dean Jones suffered a severe case of dehydration and heat exhaustion while batting during the historic tied Test against India in Chennai (Madras) in 1986. In oppressively hot (40 °C, or 104 °F) and humid (80 per cent relative humidity) conditions, he batted for almost eight and a half hours to score a double century in what was the third Test match that he played for his country. It was an epic performance and a defining moment in his career. His coach at the time, Bob Simpson, described the innings as the greatest ever played for Australia.

However, his efforts were not without medical consequences. During the latter stages of his innings, he was vomiting frequently, suffering from leg cramps, and having extreme difficulty standing at the crease and moving efficiently.

After his dismissal for 210 runs, he went straight to hospital and was placed on a saline drip. Such was the trauma that he experienced in this match. He has continued to experience similar physical effects whenever he is exposed to hot conditions.

There are some lessons to be learned from the Dean Jones story. The first is that extreme caution must be exercised when playing in the torrid conditions that he experienced. Frequent hydration and the use of ice towels are essential to ensure player health and safety. During major breaks in play, cold water immersion can be used to reduce core body temperature. Once a heat illness has been diagnosed, intravenous rehydration should be administered.

cold and contain low levels of carbohydrate and electrolytes to enhance its palatability, absorption and effectiveness. This is the formula used for sports drinks. However, in the absence of these additives, water taken alone at regular intervals is a viable alternative during the first hour of activity.

Depending on the intensity of the activity and the climatic conditions, fluid volumes of 300 to 500 millilitres (10 to 17 fl oz) should be taken prior to commencing, with 150 to 250 millilitres (5 to 8.5 fl oz) ingested at 15- to 20-minute intervals throughout. Participants should not rely on thirst to indicate a need to replace fluids. Daily weight checks should be performed to ensure that they have replaced at least 80 per cent of the fluid lost in the previous session. Alcohol should not be contained in replacement drinks because it acts as a diuretic and causes fluid loss.

Light Clothing The best clothing to wear in the heat is light-coloured clothing made from permeable, open-weave, natural fibres to maximise the evaporation of sweat. Wide-brimmed hats and long-sleeve garments provide protection from the sun and should be worn in sports such as golf and cricket in which long periods are spent outdoors. The rubber sweatsuits often

used in sports with weight divisions, such as weightlifting, rowing, and horse racing, are potentially dangerous because they induce heavy sweating with minimal evaporation and can cause overheating and chronic dehydration

COLD

If a person is inactive and the climate is cold, the body may not produce enough heat to prevent reductions in core body temperature to below 35 °C (95 °F), thus creating a condition known as hypothermia or exposure. Depending on the circumstances involved, the physiological responses to conserve body heat are the constriction of blood vessels in the skin and then shivering, which produces heat but has a negative effect on muscular coordination.

The movement of air across the surface of the body markedly increases the amount of heat lost by convection. This occurs if the air is cold and the wind is blowing strongly or the person is moving rapidly. This is referred to as the wind chill factor. It makes windproof overgarments essential for alpine skiers and road cyclists riding in cool climates. Because the thermal conductivity of water is more than 20 times higher than that of air, open water swimmers and surfers need to wear wetsuits to maintain their body temperatures while competing in lakes, rivers and oceans.

Cold Acclimatisation Generally, adjustments to cold conditions take longer than those required for the heat. At least 10 days are required to reduce the level of discomfort and lower the threshold for shivering. The process of elevating metabolism by hormonal means requires a much longer period.

Cold Injury Hypothermia is characterised by excessive shivering, loss of movement control, extreme fatigue, disorientation, and poor judgement and reasoning. Although seeking medical attention is important, to minimise further heat loss, the athlete should find shelter and dry clothing or wrap up in blankets or a preheated sleeping bag. Warm, sugared drinks should be administered, and the person should be kept awake.

Reserve or interchange players in team sports also need to be insulated against the cold, wind, and rain by having warm, dry clothing available while they sit on the sidelines. Body parts with a high ratio of surface area to mass, such as the hands, feet, nose, and ears, should be kept as warm as possible to avoid frostbite.

Individual Differences Other than wearing protective clothing, the best defence against the cold is the insulation provided by body fat. Thinner athletes, particularly preadolescent children who possess a high ratio of body surface area to mass, are susceptible to rapid cooling. This is of particular concern in unheated pools, where they need to be supervised carefully. Gender comparisons are complicated not only by body type and composition but also by the endurance fitness of the athlete and the intensity of effort being sustained.

Cold Weather Clothing Layers of insulating wool or wool blend clothing trap warm air close to the body and prevent heat loss by convection. Clothing thickness needs to vary with the intensity of exercise and the climatic conditions. An athlete who doubles the workload in 5 °C air temperatures can reduce insulated clothing by two thirds.

Heavy sweating in cold conditions must be avoided because it leads to rapid and excessive cooling when activity ceases. When this is not possible, such as in team sports played in cold conditions, warm and dry clothing must be provided between periods of play and as players come to the interchange bench.

The overall advice to coaches is to ensure that their athletes can adjust their clothing to suit the conditions and their level of activity. This involves having jackets that open down the front; drawstrings at the collar, waist, wrists, and ankles; and if necessary, drawback hoods. When athletes have to be still in cold air or water, they should adopt a curled position with knees to chest. This exposes less of the body surface area and reduces heat loss by radiation and convection.

ALTITUDE

As altitude increases, barometric pressure decreases and the air becomes less dense. This is an advantage for sprinters, jumpers, and throwers because the air offers less resistance to both them and their implements. However, the opposite is the case for endurance athletes, who have to overcome reduced oxygen pressure in the air, which lowers its pressure in the arterial blood and reduces the oxygen-carrying capacity of haemoglobin.

There has never been a better illustration of the effects of altitude on performance than at the 1968 Olympic Games held in Mexico City, located 2,300 metres (7,546 ft) above sea level. Several sprinters and jumpers broke world records, including long jumper Bob Beamon, who exceeded the existing mark by a phenomenal 55 centimetres (21.7 in.), a record that lasted for 23 years. By contrast, the winning times in distance track events were significantly slower than in the three previous Games.

A shortfall in oxygen transport is first experienced at altitudes above 1,500 metres (4,921 ft); approximately 3 per cent reductions in maximal oxygen uptake are experienced for each 300 metres (984 ft) upwards. This meant that unacclimatised endurance athletes competing at the Mexico City Olympic Games were performing with approximately a 10 per cent deficit in aerobic power.

Altitude Acclimatisation Increases in red blood cell count and haemoglobin concentration assist the oxygen-carrying capacity of the blood during altitude acclimatisation. Capillarisation and concentration of oxidative enzymes in the muscles also improve, but neither reaches sea level values. It takes three weeks to acclimatise to moderate altitude (2,300 to 2,700 metres, or 7,546 to 8,858 ft), but even then endurance performance and recovery values are still 6 to 7 per cent below those observed at sea level.

Because endurance training and altitude exposure produce similar benefits, training at altitude has been used to improve sea level performance. However, it has been shown that this is only possible when training occurs at 1,800 to 2,000 metres (5,905 to 6,561 ft) to facilitate the maintenance of the usual intensity of exercise. One alternative that has resulted in some success is 'live high, train low' programs in which athletes living at sea level spend 10 to 12 hours sleeping overnight in an altitude house or tent where the percentage of oxygen in inspired air is reduced to produce hypoxic conditions. They then train at their normal facilities during the day.

However, to perform at altitude, it is essential to train at altitude. During the first few days of such training, the work intensity needs to be low with long recovery periods. Plenty of fluid and a carbohydrate-rich diet are essential to offset dehydration and the hypoxic stress.

Altitude Illness During the first three days at altitudes above 2 000 metres (6,561 ft), athletes may experience the symptoms of mountain sickness, including headache, insomnia, dizziness, and nausea. These effects can be minimised with a slow ascent and increased fluid and carbohydrate in the diet. At high altitudes (3,500 to 4,000 metres, or 11,483 to 13,123 ft) medical emergencies such as pulmonary and cerebral oedema can occur and require oxygen therapy and evacuation.

AIR POLLUTION

Air pollution and smog are common in large, densely populated cities. Smog is formed as a result of carbon monoxide from car exhausts combining with sunshine to form ozone as well as sulfur dioxide from burning fossil fuels combining with water vapour to form sulfuric acid. Its intensity depends on the air temperature and humidity, wind speed and direction, and landscape. It particularly affects those who suffer from asthma, emphysema, and chronic bronchitis. Adding a heat or altitude factor can significantly add to the stress and affect the performance of the endurance athlete.

The presence of carbon monoxide reduces the oxygen-carrying capacity of the blood and the capacity to unload it from haemoglobin in the muscles. Sulfur dioxide increases airway resistance and creates breathing difficulties. Ozone irritates the throat and causes coughing spasms. The overall effect of pollution is the reduction of aerobic capacity, visual acuity, and mental functions. Polluted air is of greater concern among athletes with allergies, particularly asthmatics; these athletes must carry appropriate medication.

Athletes should avoid smog during training sessions and for three to four hours prior to competition. The preferred time for training is early morning or late evening. Above all, athletes should spend as little time as possible in smog because it is a long-term health risk.

TRAVEL

Athletes required to travel interstate and overseas by air can suffer serious disruptions in their internal or biological clocks as a result of alterations in their sleep/wake cycles. Many biological variables are affected when they experience jet lag, travel fatigue, and lifestyle changes. Travelling east is regarded as more taxing than travelling west because it shortens the day and intrudes into the time available for sleep. Athletes who must travel long distances by air should be regularly evaluated regarding their requirement for sleep, level of enthusiasm, and attention span, and the quality of their training and competitive performance.

Both biological and behavioural variables such as mood state, motivation, thought processes, and reaction time can be negatively affected during long-distance air travel.

Furthermore, the air in an aircraft is oxygen deficient compared to the air at sea level and can cause dehydration and lassitude. Prolonged sitting is not conducive to good circulation of blood, particularly when an athlete is nursing an injury.

A number of recommendations can result in less disruption to performance. Before travelling, athletes should adopt the sleep patterns in the time zone of their destination. Disruptions to sleep patterns can be minimised by travelling eastward in the morning and westward in the afternoon and, upon arrival, performing a light workout before sleeping. Athletes should drink plenty of fluid during the flight and avoid any that contain diuretics such as alcohol and caffeine. While in flight, athletes should flex their muscles and stretch regularly to avoid deep vein thrombosis and prevent stiffness and fluid accumulation. They can also wear stockings to minimise the risk of forming blood clots.

Traveller's Diarrhoea Traveller's diarrhoea is the most common infectious disease encountered when travelling; it affects 20 to 50 per cent of people travelling to Asia, Central America, Africa, and the Mediterranean. It is usually due to the ingestion of the E. coli bacteria, which may be present in tap water, ice cubes, raw vegetables, fresh fruit, and salads. The diarrhoea is usually mild and self-limiting, lasting three to four days. While afflicted, the athlete should have only clear fluids for 24 to 48 hours and avoid solid food, especially dairy products.

Anti-diarrhoeals, such as Imodium, may be taken if the diarrhoea is severe, but the most important management is maintaining adequate fluid and electrolyte intake in the form of soft drinks, fruit juice, sports drinks, and bland food such as dry biscuits. Persisting, severe or bloody diarrhoea requires medical intervention; appropriate treatment should be instituted immediately. High-risk sports include sailing

SAILING CASE STUDY

Two years before winning a gold medal in sailing at the 2008 Olympic Games in Beijing, Elise Rechichi had a debilitating experience when she slipped and fell into the water while launching her boat at the Olympics venue in Quingdao. As a result of ingesting some of the water, as well as possibly consuming other contaminated food and water at the venue, she developed ongoing gastroenteritis that did not respond to the usual medication. Although the condition was gradually brought under control when she returned to Perth, she became very dehydrated in the process, lost a lot of weight, and was unable to train regularly without becoming fatigued and feeling ill. She developed a form of chronic fatigue due to a combination of severe gastroenteritis and trying to resume training too soon.

Consequently, Rechichi, her coach, and her treating sport physician decided that she should take a few months completely off intensive training and competition. During this period she would need to maintain a baseline level of cardiorespiratory fitness and muscular strength before undertaking a graduated return to training. She was also required to follow a strict nutritional plan to ensure that her gastric symptoms were not aggravated and to gradually recover her muscle mass and energy levels and maintain a sustainable diet.

After a six-month period of slowly and progressively increasing the duration and intensity of training sessions, Rechichi returned to full training and limited racing, followed by a return to full competition. She and her sailing partner, Tessa Parkinson, then tackled the Quingdao course once again to win the Olympic test event in September 2007 and secure their place in the Australian Olympic team.

All athletes who went to the Beijing Olympics were given medication to prevent known causes of diarrhoea and instructed to eat and drink only beverages available at the Olympic village. Further education on health and hygiene issues was provided at their training and competition venues.

and rowing. To minimise the risk of contracting diarrhoea, athletes should be advised to wash their hands thoroughly before meals (using bottled water where necessary); drink bottled water only; eat only food that has been cooked; and avoid seafood, salads, unpasteurised milk products, and unpeeled fruit.

Upper Respiratory Tract Infections Upper respiratory tract infections (URTIs) are also common among travelling athletes. Moving from one environment to another exposes athletes to various strains of respiratory viruses. Air travel and accommodation in air-conditioned hotels also increase the risk of developing URTIs. URTIs are generally caused by viruses and are transmitted by direct contact, usually hand to nose, eyes or mouth, or airborne by coughing or sneezing into the air.

Cross infection among team members is a major concern, and research has shown that 30 to 70 per cent of teammates can be infected from one athlete. The incubation period is one to three days, and symptoms usually last three to seven days. Treatment of symptoms of nasal congestion, sore throat, cough, headache, and fatigue includes decongestants, throat or cough lozenges or syrup, and saline nasal irrigation. An athlete with a significant viral or bacterial infection should be isolated to minimise the risk of spread throughout the team. This requires that the infected athlete sleep in his or her own room and that the athlete ensures that no cross-contamination occurs by carefully handling towels and drink bottles.

Hygiene Travel Pack All athletes should travel with a pack aimed at reducing the risk of developing a viral infection and enabling early treatment of URTI or diarrhoea. The pack should contain the following items:

- **Waterless handwash gel.** This should be used before each meal and after each toilet visit.

- **Zinc/vitamin C tablets, Strepsils, and Betadine sore throat gargle.** The aim of this combination is to reduce the symptoms and severity of a URTI. It should be taken at the first sign of a sore throat and continued while symptoms are present.

- **Paracetamol and nasal decongestant spray.** This should be used if the sore throat is complicated by headache, runny nose or fever.

- **Imodium (loperamide).** Two tablets should be taken after each loose bowel movement.

- **Gastrolyte.** One sachet with water (as per instructions) for each loose bowel movement. If symptoms do not settle, a team doctor should be consulted.

SUMMARY

- Acute injuries of the muscles, ligaments, and joints should be managed initially with the RICE regime. After 72 hours under medical and physiotherapy treatment, a graduated program of muscle stretching and strengthening, cardiorespiratory fitness, and return to play can be commenced.

- Overuse injuries require early identification and management. Treatment involves the correction of technique errors, progressive muscle conditioning, and a graduated return to competition.

- Chronic injuries require considered medical decisions regarding whether athletes should continue in their sport and risk long-term body damage.

- Injury prevention strategies include ensuring that graduated training loads and warm-up and recovery regimes are followed, and that protective equipment and taping procedures are used wherever required.

- Emergency management procedures should be followed when athletes lose consciousness or experience medical problems such as diabetes and exercise-induced asthma.

- Heat illness can occur in hot or humid conditions, particularly in unacclimatised athletes with lower levels of cardiorespiratory fitness and a reduced capacity for sweating. Heat acclimatisation can be achieved in 7 to 10 days by improving the sensitivity and capacity of the sweating response.

- Regular fluid replacement and an awareness of symptoms of heat exhaustion must be a priority for coaches and medical staff working in hot and humid conditions.

- Insulative clothing is required to protect athletes against hypothermia resulting from exposure to cold air and water. Cold injury and illness require medical attention.

- High altitude has a negative effect on endurance performance but can induce acclimatory adjustments. Training and sleeping at moderate altitudes can enhance the capacity of the oxygen transport system and improve endurance at sea level.

- Polluted air reduces the oxygen-carrying capacity of the blood, creates breathing difficulties, and is a long-term health risk.

- Prolonged periods of sitting in aircraft and adjusting to new time zones can become significant problems. Athletes should also follow medical hygiene procedures to avoid infections when travelling internationally.

REFERENCES AND RESOURCES

Australian Football League. (2011). *The management of concussion in Australian football.* www.afl.com.au/portals/0/afl_docs/development/coaching/afl_concussion_management_booklet.pdf

Bloomfield, J., Fricker, P.A., & Fitch, K.D. (1995). *Science and medicine in sport* (2nd ed.). Melbourne: Blackwell Science.

Brukner, P., & Khan, K. (2007). *Clinical sports medicine* (3rd ed.). Sydney: McGraw-Hill.

Fields, K., & Fricker, P.A. (1997). *Medical problems in athletes.* Boston: Blackwell Science.

Peterson, L., & Renstrom, P. (2001). *Sports injuries: Their prevention and treatment.* London: Taylor and Francis.

Prentice, W.E. (2011). *Principles of athletic training.* New York: McGraw-Hill.

CHAPTER 16

Nurturing Life Skills

—— Deidre Anderson and Frank Pyke

Athletes require a range of personal skills and resilience to conquer the challenges and adjust to the changes they encounter during the course of their careers. Learning to steer their way through these transitions is an essential step in athletes' maturation and a tell-tale signal of their long-term potential in sport. A coach can help by fostering an environment that provides a proper balance between sport and life and broadens athletes' viewpoints so they can appreciate and seek opportunities for growth in other domains. When successful, a coach can look forward to resilient athletes who can stay engaged and committed and deal with transitions smoothly.

Adopting a balanced approach has other advantages as well. First, activities of the mind and the body complement each other. Long hours spent in any single activity, sporting or otherwise, create fatigue and inefficiency and ultimately stifle performance. Athletes involved in arduous physical training need time for activities of the mind. Conversely, those in busy workplaces need time for exercise.

Second, making progress in other areas of life is, in itself, fulfilling and places less reliance on sport for maintaining self-esteem and self-worth both during a career and when it is over. A balanced approach widens athletes' perspective on life, which helps them manage the transitions they face.

Third, time spent enjoying personal and family relationships and recreation activities and preparing for an alternative career provides some insurance for the future. Many champion athletes have obtained qualifications in professions and trades outside of sport and

gone on to establish significant careers within those areas. These athletes learned early on to handle their responsibilities in school and not let their studies slip despite their avid sport participation. Mature athletes demonstrate an ability to choose wisely between alternative career paths and pursue the professional development training needed to excel in their pursuits outside of sport.

A BALANCED PERSPECTIVE

Elite sport has become progressively more commercial and professional. This has brought considerable wealth to many professional athletes but often at a personal cost of a loss of identity, status and sense of belonging when they retire from sport. All too often, we become aware of poignant examples of athletes who suffer from gambling, alcohol or drug addictions; depression; or poor health later in their lives. Managing the transition following retirement from the adrenaline-charged environment of competitive sport and the accompanying media attention is difficult for any athlete, let alone one with no forward planning.

Similar problems exist for many young athletes who set their sights on a professional sporting career to the exclusion of all else and then fall short of their goals as a result of injury or lack of progress in performance. It can be a depressing experience. It is therefore vital that athletes in both professional and non-professional sports prepare themselves for life beyond sport by undertaking education and career development programs concurrently with their training and competition responsibilities. This requires commitment and discipline and the capacity to manage time effectively.

The philosophy underlying the need to adopt a balanced approach to athlete development formed the basis of the Athlete Career and Education (ACE) program, which has been administered within the institute and academy of sport network in Australia for many years. Developing a balanced perspective during the sport journey enables the athlete to take control of the important aspects of life and provides an even more intense ability to focus on the sporting dream. Furthermore, the transition into retirement from sport is often smoother for athletes with a balanced approach. This concept is still not fully understood by many coaches and sport administrators, despite the ongoing resources spent on helping athletes who are unable to manage the transition process.

Developing life skills gives athletes a greater level of self-awareness as they learn to explore their capabilities in a wider sphere of life. This creates a stronger base on which to operate and enables them to draw on a range of skills that will be needed throughout their sporting journey. The pillars that make up the self may include sport, personal development, family, friends, professional development and social connections. Creating a professional environment that builds on the overall life skills of the athlete is essential for developing resilience.

Athletes should set practical goals in all areas of life and have a level of self-knowledge that enables them to understand their personal strengths and weaknesses. Given that they will also be required to receive feedback from a range of people, including coaches, umpires, the media, spectators, team members, opponents, officials, family members, friends, peers and supporters, they need to develop effective communication skills. Practical skills such as these are necessary for managing both on- and off-field situations.

Once athletes have developed self-knowledge and effective communication skills, they can focus on developing other practical skills such as time management. Technological tools, including electronic calendars and planners, make this a much easier skill to develop. Most athletes

BALANCING LIFE AND SPORT SUCCESS

The life of rower James Tomkins is personified by the word *balance*. While competing in six Olympic Games between 1988 and 2008 and winning gold medals in 1992, 1996 and 2004, he completed a bachelor of business degree in economics and finance at RMIT in 1995 and has worked for several years in financial services, most recently as a senior account manager for BT Investment Management. During the time of his participation in the Olympic Games, he and his wife Bridget raised a family of three young girls. He has found the ideal balance among family, work and sport commitments.

When he was at Carey Baptist Grammar School in Melbourne, Tomkins played a number of sports, but rowing became his first choice after he turned 18. His first taste of success came as a member of the famous Oarsome Foursome, a coxless four crew that won world championships in 1990 and 1991. These victories were the first of seven world titles that saw him become the only rower in history to win world championships in every sweep oar event.

Tomkins' standing in Australian sport is such that in his final Olympic Games in Beijing in 2008, he was chosen as the Australian flag bearer. Presently, he is still contributing to sport as a member of the Australian Olympic Committee and the chair of its Athletes' Commission.

He regards obtaining qualifications as a personal achievement in areas other than sport and values work opportunities that add another layer to his life experiences. Tomkins strongly believes that his longevity in sport was related to having interests away from training and competition. He regards his family as his inspiration. His aim is to stay fit and healthy and belong to a happy and loving family. He was named the Victorian Father of the Year in 2008.

ELITE SPORTS AND LIFE SKILLS

Lauren Burns was introduced to the sport of taekwondo when she was 14 years old by her seven-year-old brother Michael, who was obsessed with it because he wanted to be a Ninja Turtle. Their father, lead singer Ronnie Burns, also attended classes with them. It became a family activity. Her love for the sport blossomed two years later when she became involved in competitions that progressed from the state to the national and then the international level. She went on to represent Australia in the sport for seven years, with the climax of her career coming at the Sydney Olympic Games in 2000 when she won the gold medal in the under-49-kilogram class.

From the very beginning, Burns saw the need to search for a broader meaning to her life. She has had a long-term interest in alternative health, and while pursing her sporting aspirations, she found naturopathy and completed a degree in health sciences, majoring in nutritional medicine, at the Endeavour College of Natural Health in Melbourne. Although this took her some years to complete, her knowledge as a nutritionist and herbalist is contained in her recently published cookbook: *Food From a Loving Home Cookbook*. (This book is her second. Her first is *Fighting Spirit: From a Charmed Childhood to the Olympics and Beyond*.)

Since her Olympic success, Burns has been heavily involved in motivational speaking and community work and is highly regarded in both spheres. Her involvement in the latter includes the Red Dust Role Models program that has been conducted in remote aboriginal communities. She is also an ambassador for the charitable organisation World Vision and contributes to sport as a member of the Athletes' Commission of the Australian Olympic Committee. Today, Burns is a wife and mother of two young children. Clearly, her experience as an elite athlete with other career aspirations continues to enable her to be well organised and manage her time effectively so that she can continue to make a valuable contribution to sport and the wider community.

do not acquire time management skills early enough in their sporting development. This is due, in part, to others controlling and structuring their time. As a result, independently managing their time is a struggle. The consequences for some athletes are that they do nothing during downtime and are always late, disorganised and disengaged. For these reasons, coaches should encourage the development of time management skills early in the athlete life cycle so that it becomes an integral part of self-management.

History tells us that not all athletes will earn a sustainable living from sport. Therefore, they need skills that will assist them in managing personal income and interacting with the public. The more opportunities athletes have to present to and interact with the public, the more networks they will gain that can help them build concurrent non-sporting careers. Leaving any of these skills underdeveloped can become a major source of stress, which can distract the athlete and affect performance. Good planning in these areas helps athletes take full advantage of opportunities to ensure that their future after sport is secure.

Just as athletes need to carefully choose their sport, they must also choose an education or career path that suits their unique skills and interests. Preparation for sport requires an individual training prescription and so does preparation for life. Although the circumstances may differ depending on age, the support available, access to training facilities and competition schedules, all athletes need to consider a concurrent educational and career pathway.

Very few claim that elite sport is a healthy environment; therefore, every athlete needs to develop a personal wellness plan that involves nutrition, recovery, sport psychology, injury prevention and drug awareness (both performance and social). An understanding of these issues can be the difference between success and failure.

Given their importance to athletes' success in sport and in life, coaches should encourage opportunities to develop life skills and to identify quickly any shortfalls they may have. Ignoring these areas may have no impact in the short term, but as their careers continue, weaknesses will be exposed that will affect performance.

SUPPORTING ROLES AND INFLUENCES

In the process of trying to maximise sporting talent, athletes become involved with many people and organisations, all of whom either have or want to have a stake in their development. The list of those who will be most affected by what they do ranges from family and friends, fellow athletes, coaches and support staff, teachers and employers to the personnel from sporting organisations, the government and corporate sector, the media and the wider general community.

In their own unique ways, these interested parties play significant roles in the development of athletes. It is essential that their respective influences be understood and that coaches manage these influences carefully. For example, parents need to be supportive rather than intrusive. Friends need to be aware of the demands imposed on high-performance athletes and their need to meet training and competition commitments and strict behavioural standards. Information sessions that cover these areas are very valuable in helping parents understand athletes' responsibilities. However, although all people in influential positions with athletes need to be supportive and understanding, unless athletes themselves take responsibility for their own development and performance, they will be unlikely to succeed, either in their sports or in their lives.

The head coach of a national training centre or professional club program should meet regularly with members of the athlete services team to review the progress of each athlete and plan the best way forward. The coaching and support staff must also emphasise regularly to members of the training squad the expectations they have of them, both in their sport and in other areas of their lives, within the high performance culture that has been established. These expectations should range from individual and team performance to ethical and behavioural standards. Many of these requirements are best enunciated at a meeting of the athletes when they are first inducted into the program.

Sporting organisations, employers and educators need to offer some flexibility in enabling athletes to fulfil their sport, work and study responsibilities. Discussion sessions between athletes and the various parties involved, aimed at improving mutual understanding, play an important role in this respect. For example, in some schools and tertiary institutions, athletes competing in international sport are offered some flexibility with examination and assignment submission schedules. The Elite Athlete Friendly University (EAFU) network has been established for this purpose. Short courses, open learning and distance education are also viable options for the high-performance athlete.

For interested parties and organisations to work together cooperatively, they need to have a high level of understanding of and respect for each other. All parties need to recognise mutual benefits in the relationship. For example, a sponsor receives publicity in return for financial support of a high-profile athlete or team, or a knowledge exchange is set up between a sporting organisation and a business to share common success factors. Such agreements need to be negotiated early in the relationship, and any conflicts should be resolved according to an agreed-upon process at stages throughout.

Relationships built on a shared vision and values, common goals and objectives and open communication and trust have a good chance of enduring. A long-term commitment involving regular evaluation of the agreed deliverables and a consultative, collaborative and cooperative mindset is essential in this process.

Building these types of strong relationships has direct relevance to any person or organisation taking on the role of managing a high-performance athlete. In addition to working with the athlete, coaches must work cooperatively with everyone else involved. This requires specialised knowledge and skills.

They must know their athletes well, including their performance backgrounds and training and competition commitments, but also the structure of the sport and the specific program in which the athletes are participating, including the personnel involved. Coaches must be aware of athletes' education and career options and employment opportunities, as well as have strong connections in media, marketing and sponsorship areas. Good business and financial management expertise and well-developed communication and negotiation skills are vital attributes for coaches as well.

TRANSITIONS IN SPORT

Transitions in sport are either voluntary or involuntary and may include moving from a junior to a senior level and coping with the respective changes in competition commitments, dealing with success and failure or coping with injury or poor performance, just to mention a few. The ability to move through and cope with any transition, which at times can be multiphased, depends on how well the situation can be normalised. Doing this requires an early understanding of the realities of elite sport and a capability to personally manage the environment.

The quality of the adjustment often depends on the following factors:

- **Socio-economic environment.** The athlete's physical, social and economic environment contributes to the ability to manage transitions. The breadth of family and other relationships and the ability to manage financial pressures can determine how athletes will deal with transitions. Coaches need to observe any changes in the behaviour of athletes and refer them to support if needed.

- **Nature of transitions.** Some transitions are voluntary, whereas others are not. For example, when an athlete has a serious injury that could be career-ending, it is involuntary, whereas an athlete who chooses to retire has made a conscious and voluntary decision to do so. When athletes are de-selected in squads, they

consider this an involuntary transition. Coaches can decide whether de-selected athletes need further support by observing whether they are exhibiting significant changes in behaviour and whether they are willing to communicate their reactions to the situation.

- **Athlete identity.** Struggles with identity occur when athletes measure their self-worth entirely based on their sport. The likely consequences are struggles exploring career and education options during their involvement in sport, and retirement-related difficulties afterwards. Having a limited set of life experiences can make transitions more stressful. In particular, injury, poor performance and changes within team structures can become escalated in the minds of athletes who have no balance in their lives between sport and other interests. Signs for coaches that this may be occurring include observing that the athlete talks only about sport, starts to opt out of challenges within the education or work environment and becomes isolated from family and non-sporting friends.

- **Athlete foreclosure.** An extreme case of athlete identity is athlete foreclosure, in which the athlete shuts out all non-sporting environments, relationships and personal development opportunities. The consequences include an inability to draw on a range of learning to problem solve and cope with transitions such as retirement, injury and poor performances. Athletes who foreclose often show signs of abnormal behaviours during difficult transitions and can be at risk of self-harm. Athletes who retire and want to go on to coaching professionally should first explore other career options and areas for personal growth outside sport before choosing a coaching career. Those who decide that coaching is for them should maintain balance in their lives by exploring new opportunities and skills. Additionally, coaching careers are like athletes' careers in that they can cease abruptly. Coaches should plan for that possibility.

- **Personal characteristics.** The capacity of athletes to cope with transitions often depends on personal characteristics, including the way they solve problems, measure their self-worth and cope with change and, ultimately, stress. Athletes who foreclose early in their sporting development ultimately struggle in managing transitions.

- **Personal development capabilities.** Focusing only on sport also limits the opportunity to develop the broad range of life skills necessary to create a healthy, well-rounded person who is able to cope with the many transitions required in sport and life.

The preceding factors contribute to how effectively athletes move through transitions and the subsequent actions they take. For example, if an athlete has never been injured and then sustains a serious problem that precludes her from competition for an extended period of time, has an impatient personality, lacks support and has no interests outside sport, recovery will be difficult. By comparison, an athlete who understands injury management; has a strong support network; and has other leisure, education or career pursuits in which to participate during recovery will find recovery easier.

TRANSITION STAGES

Regardless of their preparation and ability to handle transitions, athletes go through a number of stages before accepting transitions. Athletes with more resources, however, will likely move through the stages more quickly than athletes without those personal resources. The stages of transition often include the following:

1. Disbelief and denial that this has happened, causing a feeling of isolation and loneliness

2. Anger that, at times, will be projected towards the sporting system, the selectors, the coach, the sport, teammates, family and friends

3. Bargaining in any way to stay connected with the sport, to avoid a deep sense of

loss of control and identity because their sporting dream may not be realised

4. Depression and questioning whether all the effort was worth it, creating a sense of helplessness and despair that leads to frustration at watching others continue their campaigns

5. Acceptance and resignation and then moving through the transition with a renewed identity and sense of purpose

Not every athlete goes through each stage, nor do they all reach the acceptance stage. However, an athlete's reaction to the transition can elevate the risk from normal to caution to danger. It is important for coaches to observe athletes' reactions so they can assist or refer them for support. Coaches need to encourage all support staff and family members to be aware of signs of problems and to have a support plan in place if required. The behaviours to observe include the following:

- When the athlete is having a normal reaction to the transition, his thoughts are on the issue at hand and not on himself. The coach will see the athlete refocus on goals quickly.

- If the athlete is intensely disappointed and demonstrates marked changes in behaviour, then a degree of caution is required.

- If the athlete cannot separate from the issues and is having sleeping and eating disturbances, it might be worth encouraging further assistance.

- The real danger signs appear when the coach observes an intensely demoralised and depressed athlete who is showing a marked change in behaviour and may well be withdrawn or demonstrating significant mood swings. Further assistance should be sought as soon as possible.

COMMON TRANSITIONS FOR ATHLETES

Sport provides many forms of reinforcement, including fan acclamation, financial rewards, increased social status, media attention and other intrinsic and extrinsic factors, many of which can be withdrawn quickly. Figure 16.1 highlights most of the common transitions that athletes face at various stages. As mentioned earlier, athletes who develop a range of skills cope better with most of the issues they confront.

In the early stages, indicated on the dashed pathway, athletes need to learn how to balance a number of conflicting areas, including school and family expectations. Achieving this will avoid the athlete identity or athlete foreclosure challenge. The black pathway indicates the mid-career transitions in which perceived pressure and an inability to manage self and others can result in not achieving goals. The dotted pathway is when athletes can see success in their sights and may feel overly concerned by what this or failure may bring.

Coaches can assist athletes through all these transitions by normalising the experiences early in their development and by encouraging them to take personal control over important aspects of their lives. Ignoring the fact that athletes have to live in a broader context will only delay problems and ultimately detract from their ability to focus on their sport.

RETIREMENT FROM SPORT

Athletes are often blind to the fact that a sport career can be brief or unexpectedly terminated as a result of a range of mitigating circumstances. Hence, all athletes need an early intervention plan, which may result in less emotional and financial stress both during and after sport.

Retirement can be either voluntary or involuntary. Figure 16.2 shows the struggle that can occur when retirement is forced on an athlete as a result of injury, poor performance or non-selection. The stages of transition discussed earlier are extremely evident and can take considerable time for athletes to work through. Dealing with transitions following voluntary decisions is easier because the athlete may feel some sense of control, although the grieving process still occurs.

Retiring athletes have described the loss as so extreme that it feels like a death. Athletes who have maintained a balance between their sporting lives and their lives outside sport tend to deal with retirement far more effectively than those who have focused wholly on their sport.

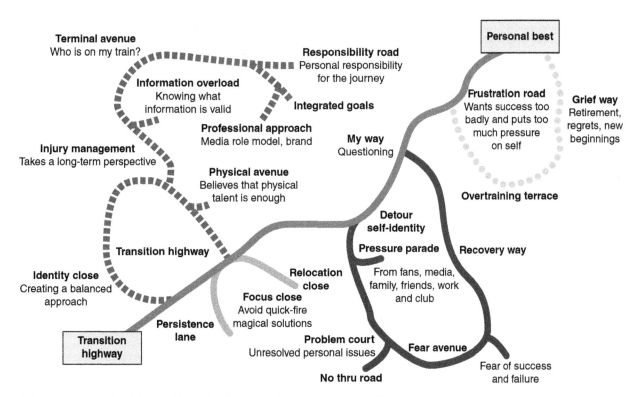

Figure 16.1 Navigating the journey to sporting excellence.

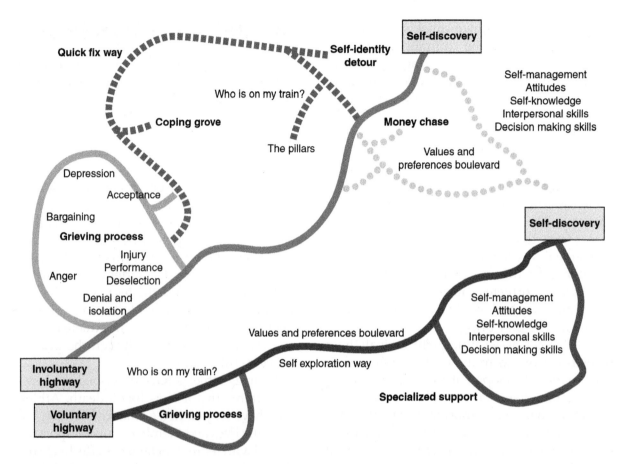

Figure 16.2 Retirement from sport.

ADVICE FOR COACHES

Irrespective of whether athletes have achieved all their hopes and dreams, retirement from sport will still require them to draw on all the physical and emotional attributes they have at their disposal.

Figure 16.2 shows the two pathways to retirement. The voluntary pathway is less demanding because it involves a degree of personal choice. The involuntary pathway is more complex because athletes have had the decision forced on them, which can result in a number of serious health conditions. Coaches can assist the process by developing and implementing a communication plan for athletes who are transitioning out of teams or squads for involuntary reasons, such as selection, injury or team balance. Although this is one of the most difficult things a coach must do, it is an essential skill in creating a professional environment.

A coach may have no formal requirement to foster the holistic development of their athletes, but they do have a moral and ethical obligation to do whatever it takes to create an environment in which all the people involved can perform at their best. This translates to creating a culture that promotes a balanced approach to excellence. Doing so helps both athletes and coaches process and adjust to a range of transitions.

The ultimate goal in sport should be to promote personal success through a balanced perspective that can be carried into all facets of future endeavours. The following guidelines can help coaches manage the sporting environment for themselves and for their athletes:

- **Stay balanced.** Athletes need measurable, realistic and achievable goals in at least two areas of their lives. While coaches are helping their athletes develop such goals, they should also be doing so for themselves. This will create an opportunity for both parties to measure self-worth according to more than just sport, and assist them with the ability to transition.

- **Integrate planning.** Coaches should provide workshops in time management and encourage athletes to develop their own diary systems. They should be forward thinking with athletes by outlining an annual plan that shows critical milestones and encourages them to incorporate their other demands, including career, study and other personal commitments. Once again, coaches should also undertake the exercise for themselves.

- **Schedule breaks.** Athletes need good friendships outside sport, and coaches can foster them by providing breaks so they can take time out to do things other than sport. Athletes need to avoid overtraining because being the best is not just about physical preparation. Sufficient time must always be allocated for rest, recovery and recreation so everyone on the team maintains a clear focus on wellness.

- **Stay accessible and aware.** Coaches can foster an open door policy enabling informal contact to be maintained with their athletes and support staff. They need to have good 'radar' on their athletes and support the introduction and implementation of a life skills program for them.

- **Encourage relationships.** Encouraging athletes to form working relationships with people who can assist them to be their best is crucial. This includes those within sport and their education and career partners. Leadership by the coach in this domain will be a powerful tool.

- **Manage transitions.** Transition management is a critical element for achieving success. Coaches should help athletes understand the transitions they may be required to manage and also support them during

Sven Simon/Imago/Icon SMI

Athletes need to prepare for their transitions out of competitive sport to find new and rewarding challenges. Cathy Freeman, for example, after winning Olympic gold now works to create educational opportunities for Indigenous children.

these phases. This will encourage athletes to take responsibility for their journeys.

- **Manage injuries.** Coaches should foster an environment that encourages the effective prevention and management of injuries. They can understand the pressures athletes are experiencing by observing and supporting them with psychological adjustment strategies.

- **Create a winning culture.** Coaches need to create an environment that enables the athlete to embrace change as a normal part of being an outstanding athlete. Developing and maintaining a competitive, professional attitude at all times creates a culture of success. Coaches should also take the time to honestly assess their own performance and progression.

- **Keep it fun.** Lastly, a commitment to sport is very time-consuming for everyone concerned, so where possible, coaches need to keep the journey fun. This helps create an enjoyable environment, strong relationships and a sense of belonging. Particularly in high-performance sport in which results are important, coaching can become a complicated juggling act. The gap between work and relaxation can cease to exist, health can become threatened and family relationships can become strained. Smart coaches survive by establishing priorities. Health and family are high on the list, and they make sure they have a life outside sport. They also become smarter in the workplace by delegating some responsibilities to others, knowing that they cannot be everything to everyone.

SUMMARY

- The responsibility of the coach is to encourage athletes to find a balance of time and effort between their sport and other areas of their lives.
- Pursuing career opportunities for life beyond sport and enjoying time spent in leisure, family and personal development activities should all be given high priority. These activities not only benefit performance in sport, but also are an investment for the future.
- The involvement of all the parties interested in an athlete's program must be carefully managed in the best interests of all.
- Having well-developed life skills will assist the process of managing the transitions that inevitably occur throughout a sporting career and when it is over.
- Coaches need to understand the stages in the transition process. Some athletes can navigate the stages of transition relatively easily. Others may require special assistance.
- Coaches have a responsibility to create a culture that fosters a balanced approach to excellence in their athletes.
- Coaches need to ensure that they allow sufficient time for rest and recovery in their own lives and clearly recognise health and family as priorities.

REFERENCES AND RESOURCES

Anderson, D.K. (1998). Life skill intervention and elite performances. Unpublished master's thesis, Victoria University of Technology.

Baillie P.H.F. (1993). Understanding retirement from sports: Therapeutic ideas for helping athletes in transition. *The Counseling Psychologist,21,* 399-410.

Baillie P.H.F., & Danish S.J. (1992). Understanding the career transition of athletes. *The Sport Psychologist, 6,* 77-98.

Lauren, L. (2003). *Fighting spirit: From a charmed childhood to the Olympics and beyond.* Camberwell, VIC: Penguin Books.

Lauren, L. (2010). *Food from a loving home: A collection of vegetarian recipes.* Lauren Burns.

Lavallee, D., & Wylleman, P. (2000). *Career transitions in sport.* Morgantown, WV: Fitness Information Technology.

INDEX

Note: The italicised *f* and *t* following page numbers refer to figures and tables, respectively.

A

abdominal breathing 195, 196*f*
Abdul-Jabbar, Kareem 35-36
absolute strength 136
abstract random thinkers 21
abstract sequential thinkers 21
acceleration principles
 Newton's Laws 154
 semi-universal 158, 159
acceleration speed 131, 133*t*
acceleration sprints 133
acclimatisation
 altitude 225
 cold 224
 heat 222
ACE program 230
Achilles tendinosis 217, 218
acronyms, for core values 63
ACSM 143
action force 154
activation control 195-197, 196*f*
active foot strike 154
active listening 80-81. See also listening skills
adaptability
 athletes 34
 coaches 25, 33, 35, 36
 contingency plans 56
 as leadership trait 78
 team culture 60
adaptation 111, 112*f*, 113
administration details 26
administrators, working with 82-83
adolescents
 athlete testing 101, 103-104
 coaching approaches 16-17
 physical development 100-101, 100*f*
adults 17-18. See also masters athletes
aerobic capacity ($\dot{V}O_2$max) 125, 128-129
AFL 106
age considerations
 athlete testing 103-104
 coaching approaches 15-18
 endurance abilities 125
 heat tolerance 222
agility speed 133*t*
'ahead of the game' 24
AI 66-69, 68*t*
air pollution 225
air travel 225-226
AIS swimming program 102

alcohol use
 air travel and 226
 drinking culture 31
 effects of 117, 210
 with injuries or illness 216, 223
 as prohibited substance 211, 211*t*
allergies 225
altitude and altitude sickness 224-225
American College of Sports Medicine (ACSM) 143
amino acids 203
anabolic agents 210, 211*t*
anaerobic threshold 125-126, 128, 128*f*
analogies, for instruction 183
angular motion 154
annual plans
 periodisation 48-51, 50*t*, 52*t*, 53*t*, 117-123, 120*t*-121*t*, 122*t*
 sample plans 54*t*-55*t*, 118*t*-119*t*
 training principles 51, 53*t*, 111-117, 112*f*
anticipation 178-181
Appleby, Chris 38
appreciative inquiry (AI) 66-69, 68*t*
artefacts 60, 64
ASADA 209, 210
ASA theory 66
ASDMAC 212
assertiveness 79-80
assessment. See athlete testing
assistant coaches. See support staff
asthma 220-221, 225
Athlete Career and Education (ACE) program 230
athlete development
 adult athletes 18
 as coaching goal 4-5
 influences on 232-233
 leadership styles and 14, 15
 long-term plans and 48, 49*t*
 in PRIDE acronym 123
athlete foreclosure 233
athlete identity 233
athletes. See also Olympic athletes
 beginners 5-6, 175
 bonding between 38
 career paths 231, 233
 coach relationships with 33, 40
 educational goals 75-77, 231
 life balance 46, 77, 229-232
 in program planning 46
 retirement 235-236, 236*f*
 stars 34
 transition management 233-235, 235*f*, 237

athlete testing
    ASI swimming program 102
    attributes and performance 102-106
    functional fitness 120
    junior athletes 101, 103-104
    program development 101-102
    program management 106-108
    purposes 99-100
    results 106-108, 108*f*
    skill learning versus performance 171-173
attack (offence) 37
attention (mental skill) 197-198
attention to detail 25-26, 34
attitudes, in team culture change process 64
attraction-selection-attrition (ASA) theory 66
auditory learners 20
augmented feedback 181-182
Australian and New Zealand Standards for Risk Management 87, 88
Australian Football League (AFL) 106
Australian Institute of Sport (AIS) swimming program 102
Australian National Coach Accreditation Scheme (NCAS) 3
Australian Sports Anti-Doping Authority (ASADA) 209, 210
Australian Sports Commission 7
Australian Sports Drug Medical Advisory Committee (ASDMAC) 212
Australian Wheelchair Rugby team 84
authoritarian leadership 13-14
autonomous motivation 187-188, 188*f*
axes, of movement 151, 151*f*, 151*t*

B
balance (physical) 152-153, 159. See also life balance
ballistic stretching 143
base of support 152
Beamon, Bob 224
beginner athletes 5-6, 175
behavioural values 64, 64*t*
Bellamy, Craig 93
belonging, sense of 4-5
beta agonists (beta-blockers) 211, 211*t*, 220, 221
Betadine throat gargle 227
biomechanics. See also movement analysis
    in expert performance 156
    force and motion principles 152-156
    movement and direction terms 149, 149*t*-150*t*
    movement planes and axes 151, 151*f*, 151*t*
    musculoskeletal system 148-149
    value of understanding 147
bionegative surface 166
biopositive surface 166
blocked practice 174-176
blood doping 211*t*
blood sugar levels 220
board members, working with 82-83
bodily (kinaesthetic) learners 20

body composition 125, 206-207
body fat, in cold tolerance 224
body motion 154-155
body position, in maximal heart rate 126
body weight 203, 206-207, 209
body weight exercises 141
bones
    calcium for 203
    defined 148
    injuries to 217-218
brain injuries 218-220
brainstorming, in goal-setting process 195
breathing exercise 195, 196*f*
broad attention 197
Brown, Joyce 38-39
Buchanan, John 32-34
burnout, avoiding 10
Burns, Lauren 231

C
caffeine 209, 226
calcium 203
Camplin, Alisa 78
cannabinoids 210, 211*t*
cannabis 210
capabilities, in CCOT analysis 47
carbohydrate 201-202, 205-206
carbohydrate loading 202
career paths, of athletes 231, 233
caring (compassion) 5, 39
cartilage 148
cartilaginous joints 148
cause-and-effect observation 24
CBS-S 10
CCOT analysis 47, 57
centre of gravity 152, 155
challenges, in CCOT analysis 47
change, initiating 32-33
change-of-direction speed 131
character development, in athletes 5
Charlesworth, Richard 29, 36-37
Chetkovich, Liz 57
child abuse 91-92
children
    coaching approaches 15-16
    heat and cold tolerance 222, 224
    laws regarding 89-90, 92
chronic injuries 218
circuit training 141
Cirque du Soleil 167
climatic considerations
    air pollution 225
    altitude 224-225
    cold 223-224
    heat 221-223
clothing, for heat or cold 223-224
The Coach: Managing for Success (Charlesworth) 37
coaching
    as athlete career choice 233

forms of 5-6
goals of 4-5
philosophy of 6-8, 36, 72-74
professionalisation of 3, 8-10
Coaching Behaviour Scale for Sport (CBS-S) 10
coaching process 4, 13
cocaine 210
codes of conduct. See also ethics
    coaching philosophy and 7-8
    harassment 92
    spectator behaviour 75
coefficient of friction 166
cold climates 223-224
cold water immersion 114
commitment
    of athletes 46, 75-77
    as leadership trait 78
communication
    with administrators and board members 82-83
    as athlete life skill 230
    as coaching quality 32, 34
    with educational institutions 75-77
    with female athletes 18-19
    with parents 71-75
    with sponsors 81-82
    with support staff 77-81
community contexts 6
compassion 5, 39
competence, in athletes 4
competition (in-season) phase 49-51, 52t, 121, 122t
competitions
    nutrition 205-206, 206t
    problems 23
    self-preparation 199
competitive contexts 6
competitiveness, in male athletes 19
compliance, of sport surface 167
compression, for injury treatment 216
concentration 197-198
concentric internal force 152
concrete random thinkers 21
concrete sequential thinkers 20-21
concussions 218-220
confidence. See self-confidence
conflict resolution 81
confusion, from injury 219
connection (sense of belonging) 4-5
conservation of momentum 155
contingency plans 56
contract–relax (PNF) stretching 143, 144
contracts, in goal-setting process 195
controlled motivation 188, 188f
Cook Brian 61
Cooper, Jacqui 78
core stability 138, 157, 158f
core values. See values
corticosteroids 220
Costas, Bob 35
CPR 219

criminal acts 91
crisis management 35-36
cross-training 115, 117, 123
Crum, Denny 35

D
Dahlhaus, Luke 73-74
Davey, Colin 38
deception 180-181
decision making
    as coaching quality 30, 39
    perceptual, in players 176-178
deep vein thrombosis 226
defamation 92-93
dehydration
    alcohol use and 210
    altitude and 225
    effects of 207-208
    heat exposure and 222-223
delegation 26-27
deliberate practice theory 173-174
democratic leadership 14-15
demonstrations (coaching method) 22
detail orientation 25-26, 34
deterministic models 160, 161, 161f
development coaches, defined 6
Devery, Keeley 38
diabetes 220
diabetic ketoacidosis 220
diagrams 22
diarrhoea 226-227
diligence 37
direction, in motivation 187
direction terms 149, 149t
direct musculoskeletal injuries 215
Disability Discrimination Act 91
disabled athletes 90, 104
discrimination 90-91
disguise 180-181
disrepute 93-94
distractions 197, 199
diuretics 210, 211t
Donaldson, Noel 40
drag suits 141
drills 23, 30, 32
drinking culture 31. See also alcohol use
drug testing 212-213
drug use. See also specific substances
    alcohol 210
        anti-doping organisations 208-209
        caffeine 209, 226
        effect on maximal heart rate 126
        prohibited substances 210-211, 211t
        supplements 212
        therapeutic use exemptions 212
        tobacco 209-210
dual-task testing 173
Dubberley, Brad 84
dumbbells 141

duty, in risk management 89-90
dynamic stretching 143-144

E
E. coli bacteria 226
EAFU network 232
eccentric internal force 152
eccentric training 137-138
economy of movement 126, 157
ecstasy (drug) 210
education, in PRIDE acronym 123
educational goals, of athletes 75-77, 231
educational institutions 75-77, 232
effort 36
EIA 220-221, 225
EIB 220-221, 225
electromyography 164, 165f
elevation, for injury treatment 216
Elite Athlete Friendly University (EAFU) network 232
elite sporting contexts 6
Elliott, Bruce 151
emergency situations 218-220
endurance, defined 125
endurance training
    ability determinants 125
    concurrent strength and speed training 129-130, 130t
    heart rate monitoring 126-127
    trainable physiological characteristics 125-126
    training zones 127-129, 127t
energy balance 207
energy drinks 208
environment and facilities
    as competition problem 23
    illnesses related to 221-225
    individualisation and 117
    as risk management issue 90
equipment
    evaluating 100
    importance of 166
    as risk management issue 90
    running shoes 168-169
ergogenic aids 209, 212
Ericsson, Anders 173-174
ethics 7-8, 88, 94. See also codes of conduct
evaluation. See athlete testing; program evaluation
exclusion clauses 95-96
exercise, eating during 205
exercise-induced asthma (EIA) 220-221, 225
exercise-induced bronchospasm (EIB) 220-221, 225
expectations, in induction process 72-74
exposure 223-224
external attention 182-183, 197
external regulation 187
extraneous movements 157
extrinsic motivation 187, 188f
'eyes in the back of your head' 24

F
facilities. See environment and facilities
fad diets 203

fair play 31
fat, dietary 201, 203, 205
fatigue, and nutrition 201
fatigue resistance 126
feedback
    from coaches 23, 24, 162-163, 181-183
    to coaches 9-10, 37, 56, 77
female athletes
    athlete testing 104
    coaching approaches 18-19, 38
    endurance abilities 125
female athlete triad 104
Ferguson, Alex 30-32
fibre 205
first aid certification 219
Fischer, Peter 181
Fitballs 141
flexibility (character trait). See adaptability
flexibility, defined 142
flexibility training 132, 142-144
fluid balance 208, 222
focus
    in athletes 182-183, 198
    as coaching quality 38
foot motion, in running shoes 168-169, 168f
force 152, 154
force platforms 164
force reduction 167
forearm tenosynovitis 217
four Cs 4-5
fractures 216
free body diagrams 159, 161
free weights 141
friction, on sport surface 166-167
fuel usage 126
fun 238
functional fitness 120
functional flexibility 143-144
functional variability 174
future, focusing on 198

G
game analysis 99-100
game sense 177
gastroenteritis 226
Gastrolyte 227
Gaze, Andrew 75
Geelong Cats Football Club 61
Geelong Cricket Club 63
gender differences
    athlete testing 104
    coaching approaches 18-20, 38
    endurance abilities 125
    heat or cold tolerance 222, 224
gene doping 211, 211t
general motion 154-155
genetics, in endurance abilities 125
George, Martine 57
GI 202, 202t
glucocorticosteroids 211, 211t

glucose 201
glycaemic index (GI) 202, 202*t*
glycogen stores 126, 201, 206
goals
    coaching 4-5
    program planning 46-47
    in self-monitoring 192-195, 194*t*
    support staff relationships and 79
    in team culture change process 65, 65*t*
    ultimate 236
Good Samaritan provision 90
governing bodies 7-8
Greaves, Aaron 72-74, 77
growth factors 210, 211*t*
Guadagnoli, Mark 176

H
haemoglobin 203
hamstring injuries 218
hand sanitiser 227
harassment 91-92
hardness, of sport surface 167
harnesses 134
Hawkes, Rechelle 37
head coaches, and support staff
    communication 77-81
    delegation 26-27
    successful relationships 79, 84
head injuries 219-220
heart rate monitoring 126-127
heat and heat illness 221-223
heat exhaustion 222
heat syncope 222
heat treatment 216
high-performance coaches, defined 6
hollow sprints 134
honesty 37
Hood, Paul 73
hormone antagonists or modulators 210, 211*t*
hormones 210, 211*t*
hot climates 221-223
humour 80
'hurt but hold' pace 125-126, 128, 128*f*
hydration
    alcohol use and 210
    altitude and 225
    heat exposure and 222-223
    as nutrition component 207-208
hygiene travel packs 227
hypertrophy training 137, 138, 139*t*
hypoglycaemia 220
hypothermia 223-224
hypoxic stress 225

I
ice, for injury treatment 216
identified regulation 187
If Better Is Possible (Buchanan) 32-34
illicit drugs 210
illnesses. See injuries and illnesses

imagery 16, 198-199
Imodium 227
impartiality 78
impulse generation and absorption 158-159
inclusion, of all players 33, 72
incorporation 94
indirect musculoskeletal injuries 216
individual differences
    in activation levels 195
    in heat or cold tolerance 222, 224
individualisation
    based on testing 102
    in program planning and design 51, 53*t*, 117
    value of biomechanics in 147
individual sports
    athlete testing in 103
    coaching qualities for 39-40
induction process, in junior sports 72-74
inertia, minimisation of 158
infectious diseases 91
influence
    of coaches 3, 4
    management of 232-233
inhalers, for asthma 221
injuries and illnesses
    acute musculoskeletal injuries 215-217
    biomechanics in 151-152, 159
    chronic injuries 218
    diabetes 220
    emergency situations 218-220
    environmental issues 221-225
    exercise-induced asthma 220-221
    individualisation and 117
    musculoskeletal testing in 100
    overuse injuries 217-218
    prevention and management 215, 237
    in PRIDE acronym 123
    reversibility due to 116
    as risk management issue 88-90, 91
    school absences due to 76
    sport surfaces and 167-168
    travel-related 225-227
innovation, as coaching quality 34, 78
in-season (competition) phase 49-51, 52*t*, 121, 122*t*
instruction
    internal or external focus in 182-183
    modes of 21-24
instructors, defined 5-6
insurance 95
integrated regulation 187
integrity, in athletes 5
intensity, in motivation 187
intensity of training
    overload principle 111-113
    volume and 51
    in Wooden's practice sessions 34
interceptive skill training 178-181
internal attention 182-183, 197
interval training 128
intrinsic feedback 182

intrinsic motivation 187, 188*f*
introjected regulation 187
iron (nutrient) 203
isometric training 137

J
joints
  defined 148
  injuries to 216
Jones, Dean 223
junior sports
  athlete testing 101, 103-104
  balancing with education 75-77
  parents and 71-75
  physical development and 100-101, 100*f*

K
kettlebells 142
Kilderry, Rob 159
kinaesthetic learners 20
kinematic concepts 154-155
kinematic measurement systems 163-164
kinetic chain 158
kinetic measurement systems 163-164
knowledge, as coaching quality 37

L
Langer, Justin 34, 185
Lapchine, Nikolai 57
Lassila, Lydia 78
laws of motion 154
leadership
  athlete development and 4
  role in team culture 60-61
  styles of 13-15
  traits of positive 77-80
leadership behaviour 60
learning
  as coaching quality 37, 39
  coaching sources of 8
  versus skill performance 171-173, 174, 177
learning styles 20
legacies 32-33
legal issues 88-90, 92
liability insurance 95
life balance
  athletes 46, 77, 229-232
  coaches 10
  ultimate goal 236-237
life skills
  balance 46, 77, 229-232
  relationships influencing 232-233
  retirement from sport 235-236, 236*f*
  transition management 233-235, 235*f*, 237
lifestyle intervention testing 100
ligaments
  defined 148
  injuries to 216
linear motion 154
Lipshut, Geoff 78

liquid crystal occlusion goggles 178, 180*f*
listening skills 35, 36-37, 80-81
'live high, train low' 225
load. See intensity of training; repetition maximum
logistics, in program planning 47-48
longevity in coaching 10
long-slow distance (LSD) training 127
long-term athlete development (LTAD) model 101
long-term goals 47
long-term plans 48, 49*t*
LSD 127
LTAD model 101
lumbar spine stress fractures 218

M
macrocycles 49, 117, 120*t*-121*t*, 121, 122*t*
macronutrients 201-203
male athletes, coaching approaches for 19-20
management behaviour 60
Managing My Life (Ferguson) 30-32
massage 216
masters athletes 104. See also age considerations
maximal heart rate 126-127
maximal oxygen uptake ($\dot{V}O_2$max) 125, 128-129
maximal speed 130, 133*t*
maximal strength training 137
maximisation of acceleration path 159
McIntosh, Jill 39
media relations 92-94
Mediballs 141
medicine balls 142
Member Protection Policies 92
menstrual cycle issues 104, 218
mental skills and issues
  consultants in 38-39
  factors affecting performance 185, 186*f*
  as problem 23
  self-awareness 185-190, 186*f*, 187*f*, 188*f*, 230
  self-confidence 4, 38, 190-191, 191*t*
  self-monitoring 192-195, 193*f*
  self-preparation 199
  self-regulation 195-199, 196*f*
mentors 27
mesocycles 49, 117
metatarsal stress fractures 218
microcyles 49, 118
micronutrients 203-205, 204*t*
minerals 203-205, 204*t*, 207, 227
minimisation of inertia 158
mirror activity 197-198
mission, defined 60
mission statements
  defined 60
  leadership role in 60-61
  in strategic plan 25
  in team culture change process 65-66
mistakes
  learning from 30, 33
  responsibility for 78-79

Mitchell, Lauren 57
'mixed action' 151
momentum 155
moral character development, in athletes 5
motion, laws of 154
motivation
    four Cs and 4-5
    sources and types 187-188, 187f, 188f
movement analysis
    biomechanical principles 148-156, 153f
    example 159
    feedback from 162-163
    methods 159-161
    planes and axes 151, 151f, 151t
    principles 156-159, 158f
    process 161-163
    technology 163-164
    terminology 149, 149t-150t
movement phases 159, 160, 160f
muscles. See also strength training
    aspects of development 138
    defined 148
    injuries to 216
    in maximal heart rate 126
musculoskeletal injuries 215-217
musculoskeletal system 148-149
musculoskeletal testing 100

N
NACE 77
narcotics 210, 211t
narrow attention 197
nasal decongestant sprays 227
National Athlete Career and Education (NACE) program
    77
National Health and Medical Research Council's Aus-
    tralian Guidelines to Reduce Health Risks from
    Drinking Alcohol 210
navicular stress fractures 217, 218
NCAS 3
neck injuries 219
negligence 88-90
networking 9
Newton's laws of motion 154
No Limits: Joyce Brown (Smithers, Appleby) 38-40
nutrition. See also hydration
    competition days 205-206, 206t
    energy balance 207
    hydration 207-208
    individualisation and 117
    macronutrients 201-203
    micronutrients 203-205, 204t
    recovery 114, 206
    supplements 203, 207
    weight and body composition 206-207

O
O'Brien 78
observation

in movement analysis 162
in SPORT acronym 24
offence (attack) 37
off-season (transition) phase 51, 53t, 117, 123
Olympic athletes
    chronic injuries 219
    gastroenteritis case study 226
    life skills 230, 231
    performing at altitude 224
    talent transfer programs 78, 107
    training program sold to 95
omega-3 fatty acids 203
Open Space Technology (OST) 66
opportunities, in CCOT analysis 47
opposition analysis
    as coaching quality 34, 38
    as problem 23
oral contraceptives 104
oral instructions 21
organisational culture. See team culture
organisational socialisation 66
organisation skills 24-27
OST 66
osteoarthritis 218
osteoporosis 203
overload 111-113
overreaching 111
overspeed training 132, 133
overtraining 112, 237
overuse injuries 217-218
Owne, Harrison 66

P
paddles, for strength training 141-142
Paracetamol 227
parachutes 134
parents
    behaviour 74-75
    in induction process 72-74
    influence 232
    player rotation and 71-72
Parkin, David 78
Parkinson, Tessa 226
participation coaches, defined 6
passive smoking 210
past, focusing on 198
patella tendinosis 217
peak cycles 49
peak height velocity 100, 100f
perceptual–decision-making skills
    versus fundamental skills 176-178
    training methods for 178-181, 180f, 181f
performance
    age-related reductions 104
    expert 156
    four Cs and 4-5
    mental factors affecting 185, 186f
    versus skill learning 171-173, 174, 177
    testing 102-106

performance coaches, defined 6
performance details 25-26
performance goals
    goal-setting process 192-195
    in team culture change process 65, 65*t*
performance profiling 192, 193*f*
periodisation phases
    in annual plan 48-49
    competition phase 49-51, 52*t*, 121, 122*t*
    macro- and microcycles 49, 117, 118, 120*t*-121*t*, 121, 122*t*
    preparation phase 49, 50*t*, 118, 120*t*-121*t*
    transition phase 51, 53*t*, 117, 123
persistence 31-32, 187
personal strength assessment 188-190
philosophy of coaching
    as coaching quality 36
    developing 6-8
    in induction process 72-74
physical demands, on athletes 75-76
plan–do–review 45, 46*f*
planes, of movement 151, 151*f*, 151*t*
planning skills. See also program planning and design;
    strategic planning
    adages 111
    in coaches 24-27, 33, 35
    as life skill 237
playbooks 22
player rotation 71-72
players. See athlete development; athletes
player welfare manager 77
plyometrics 132, 134-136, 135*t*, 138
PNF stretching 143, 144
positive reinforcement
    for children 16
    as coaching quality 30
    as instruction 23
    in SPORT acronym 24
power, defined 136
power endurance 137, 138, 141, 141*t*
power-to-weight ratio 137
power training 132, 138, 140*t*
practical wisdom 24
practice
    challenge point in 175-176, 176*t*
    deliberate practice theory 173-174
    performance versus learning in 172-173, 174, 177
    tactical skills 177-178
    variability in 174-175, 176*t*
Practice to Learn, Play to Win (Guadagnoli) 176
practise, in SPORT acronym 24
praise, of support staff 79
precompetition nutrition 205
precompetition routines 199
precompetitive subphase 121
preparation
    as coaching quality 36
    as mental skill 199
preparation (preseason) phase 49, 50*t*, 118, 120*t*-121*t*
preperformance routines 199

preseason (preparation) phase 49, 50*t*, 118, 120*t*-121*t*
present focus 198
pressure measurements 164
PRIDE acronym 123
problem solving 22-23, 30
process goals 65, 65*t*
professional development 8
professional indemnity insurance 95
professionalisation of coaching 3, 8-10
program evaluation 48, 56-57
program planning and design. See also planning skills
    annual plans 48-56, 50*t*, 52*t*, 53*t*, 54*t*-55*t*, 117-123, 118*t*-
        119*t*, 120*t*-121*t*, 122*t*
    contingency plans 56
    example 57
    key considerations 45-48, 123
    long-term plans 48, 49*t*
    planning and evaluation cycle 45, 46*f*, 56-57
progressive muscle relaxation 195, 196*f*
projectile motion 155
proprioceptive neuromuscular facilitation (PNF) stretch-
    ing 143, 144
protein 201, 202-203, 205, 206
protein supplements 203
psychological demands, on athletes 75-76
public liability insurance 95
Pyramid for Success 36

R
random practice 174-176
rapport
    with athletes 33
    with support staff 80
reaction force 154
Realise 2 model 189
Rechichi, Elise 226
recovery
    nutrition for 114, 206
    in speed training 131
    stressing importance of 38
    as training principle 113-114, 114*f*, 115*t*
recreational contexts
    coaching form in 6
    testing in 103-104
recruitment 66
redundancy, of coaches 33
refueling 205-206, 206*t*
regret 33
rehabilitation, for injuries 216-217
reinforcement. See positive reinforcement
relationships
    administrators and board members 82-83
    athletes 33, 38, 40, 237
    educational institutions 75-77
    in influence management 232-233
    parents 71-75
    proactive approaches to 84
    sponsors 81-82
    support staff 77-81

relationship values 64, 64*t*
relative strength 136
relaxation techniques 195-197, 196*f*
repetition, in training
    balance in 32
    as coaching quality 30, 34
    skill transfer and 175
repetition maximum (RM) 136, 137
repetition sprints 134
resilience, of sport surface 167
resistance aids 142
resistance to change of direction 154, 155
resisted sport movements 141
resources, in program planning 47-48
respect, of coaches 29
respect for authority, in adolescents 16-17
responsibility, in PRIDE acronym 123
rest, for injury treatment 216
results, in team culture change process 65
retention testing 172-173
retirement from sport 235-236, 236*f*
reversibility 116-117
rib stress fractures 217, 218
RICE 216
Rice, Stephanie 116
Richards, Joanne 57
risk management
    defined 87
    ethical issues 88, 94
    legal issues 88
    primary risks 88-92
    process of 88
    risk minimisation 94-96
risk-taking, in adolescents 17
risk warnings 95-96
RM 136, 137
Rodionenko, Andrei 57
role models, coaches as 4, 35, 74
Rollason, Shannon 104
rotator cuff tendinosis 217
routines 199
running economy 157
running shoes 168-169

S
safety. See risk management
Safety Guidelines for Children and Young People in Sport
    and Recreation 90
Sampras, Pete 181
sand running 134
Schipper, Jessica 95
scouting, of opposition 34, 38
self-awareness 185-190, 186*f*, 187*f*, 188*f*, 230
self-confidence
    athletes 4, 38
    coaches 79-80
    enhancing 190-191, 191*t*
self-evaluation 8-9
self-monitoring 192-195, 193*f*

self-preparation 199
self-reflection
    in athlete goal-setting 194
    by coaches 8-9
self-regulation 195-199, 196*f*
self-worth 233
sequential muscle sequencing 158
'Sexual Harassment and Abuse in Sport' 92
sexual misconduct 91-92
short-term goals 47
show, in SPORT acronym 24
Simpson, Bob 223
simulation training 180-181, 181*f*
situational analysis 24-25
skeleton training, talent transfer in 107
skill learning. See learning
skill performance. See performance
skill transfer
    from practice to competition 175, 177
    in retention testing 172-173
Slater, Allana 57
sleep 114, 225-226
SMART goals 46, 47, 194
Smartplay program 90
SMART PPP goals 194, 194*f*
Smith, Cam 93
Smith, Jenny 57
Smithers, Edie 38
smog 225
smoking 209-210
SOAR strategic planning 66-67, 67*f*
socialisation, organisational 66
socio-economic environment 233
specificity
    in muscle endurance training 138
    principle 114-116
    in speed training 131, 132, 135
    in training children 15-16
    training zones and 128
spectator behaviour 74-75
speed
    defined 130
    in laws of motion 154
    types 130-131, 131*t*
speed endurance 131, 132, 133*t*, 134
speed training
    concurrent endurance training 129-130, 130*t*
    guidelines 131-132
    methods 132-136, 135*t*
    print resources 132, 133
    six-step progressive model 132
    variables 133*t*
speed work (training zone) 129
spinal cord injuries 218-220
sponsors 81-82, 232
SPORT acronym 24
sport loading training 132, 133-134
sports culture, defined 59
sports drinks 208, 223

sports teachers, defined 5-6
sport surfaces 164, 166-169
sprint-assisted (overspeed) training 132, 133
sprint-resisted (sport loading) training 132, 133-134
sprint training 130, 132, 134, 135*t*
stability 152-153, 153*f*, 159
stair climbs 134
stakeholders, feedback from 37, 56. See also relationships
standard of care 89-90
standards, upholding 37
star athletes 34
static stretching 143
step test, for maximal heart rate 126
Stewart, Anthony 38-39
stimulants 210, 211*t*
Stosur, Samantha 159
strategic planning
    as coaching skill 25
    strength-based 66-69, 67*f*, 68*t*
strategic values 64, 64*t*
strength, defined 136. See also personal strength assessment
strength endurance 136, 138, 140*t*
strength training
    aids 141-142
    concurrent endurance training 129-130, 130*t*
    methods 137-138, 139*t*, 140*t*
    in speed training 132, 134
    sport performance benefits 136
Strepsils 227
stress 10. See also relaxation techniques
stress fractures 217, 218
stretch cords 141
stretching. See flexibility training
stretch-shortening cycle 156-157
student-athletes 75-77
subcultures 60
submissive leadership 15
success 31, 237-238
sugar 202
summation of force 152, 158
supervision 90
supplements
    protein 203
    sports supplements 212
    for URTIs 227
    vitamin and mineral 207
support staff
    communication with 77-81
    delegation to 26-27
    successful relationship examples 79, 84
sweat rates 208
Swiss balls 141
synovial joints 148

T
tactical skill practice 177-178
talent identification (TID) programs 99, 105-106
talent transfer 78, 105-106, 107

tapers 51, 114
teachers, communicating with 75-77
team culture
    coach's role in changing 31, 60-66
    functions 59
    recruitment and socialisation in 66
    strengths-based strategic planning in 66-69, 67*f*, 68*t*
    terminology 59-60
'team first' attitude 78-79
team sports
    athlete testing 99, 103
    diagrams 22
    endurance training 129-130, 130*t*
technique. See also movement analysis
    difficulties in 23
    evaluating and correcting 147-148
    in expert performance 156
    refinement of 30
    in speed training 131
    surfaces and equipment and 164-169
technology
    data management 108
    evaluating 100
    for evaluating technique 147-148, 162, 163-164
    feedback from 181-183
    simulation training 180-181, 181*f*
    temporal occlusion 178-179, 179*f*, 180*f*
Telfer, Michelle 57
temporal measurement systems 163
temporal occlusion 178-179, 179*f*, 180*f*
tendinosis 217-218
tendon injuries 217-218
tendons, defined 149
tenosynovitis 217-218
testing. See athlete testing
tethers 141
therapeutic use exemptions (TUE) 212
thinking styles 20-21
thirst 223
thought stopping 198
threats, in CCOT analysis 47
throat gargle 227
tibial stress fractures 217, 218
TID programs 99, 105-106
time, in SPORT acronym 24
time commitments, of athletes 46, 75-77
time management 230-231, 237
tobacco 209-210
Tomkins, James 40, 230
traction, on sport surface 166
training analysis 99-100
training principles
    overload 111-113
    recovery 38, 113-114, 114*f*, 115*t*
    reversibility 116-117
    specificity 15-16, 114-116, 128, 131, 132, 135, 138
training session evaluation 56-57
training zones 127-129, 127*t*
transfer of angular momentum 158

transformational leadership 60
transition management 233-235, 235f, 237
transition (off-season) phase 51, 53t, 117, 123
travel
    hygiene packs 227
    illnesses from 225-227
    school absences and 76
traveller's diarrhoea 226-227
TUE 212
Turner, Michael 73

U
ultrasonography 164
unconsciousness 219-220
unpredictable circumstances 25. See also adaptability
uphill sprinting 134
upper respiratory tract infections (URTIs) 227
urine colour 208
URTIs 227

V
values
    in coaching philosophy 6-8
    defined 60
    identifying core values 61-63, 63f
    leadership role in 60
    matching behaviours and attitudes to 64
values-based behaviours 60
values-based cultural change
    defined 60
    steps in 61-66, 62f
values enactment 60
variety
    in drills 23, 30, 32
    in speed training 131
vegans 203
vegetarians 117, 203
velocity, in laws of motion 154
verbal cues 21
vicarious liability 91
Victoria State women's team 63
video
    camera selection and operation 163-164
    use of 147-148, 162
vilification 91
vision
    as coaching skill 32
    defined 60
    leadership role in 60-61
    steps in creating 61-66, 62f
    in working with support staff 77
vision statement 60, 66
visualisation 30-31
visual learners 20, 22
vitamins 203-205, 204t, 207, 227
volume of training 51, 132
volunteer coaches 29, 89
V̇O$_2$max 125, 128-129

W
WACA 68-69
WADA 208-209, 210
WAIS women's gymnastics program 57
Waldron, Brian 93
Walton, Bill 34
warm-ups 131, 144
water pressure, in maximal heart rate 126
WBGT index 222
weaknesses, personal 189
weight control 203, 206-207, 209
weighted sleds 134
weighted vests 134
weight monitoring, for hydration status 223
weight training. See strength training
wellness plans 231
Western Australian Cricket Association (WACA) 68-69
Western Australian Institute of Sport (WAIS). See WAIS women's gymnastics program
wet bulb globe temperature (WBGT) index 222
whiteboards 22
whole body motion 155
Wilson, Vicki 39
wind chill factor 223
winning culture 237-238
women's skeleton event 107
Wood, Graeme 68
Wood, Ken 95
Wooden: A Lifetime of Observations. . . (Wooden, Jamison) 34-36
Wooden, John 34-36
workers' compensation 95
World Anti-Doping Agency (WADA) 208-209, 210
written instructions 21-22

Z
Z-score charts 107, 108f

ABOUT THE EDITOR

Frank Pyke (deceased November 2011) played a leadership role in sport science, coach education and sport administration in Australia for more than 30 years. From 1972 to 1990 he taught at the University of Western Australia, the Canberra College of Advanced Education and the Universities of Wollongong and Queensland, the latter as professor and head of the department of human movement studies. After that, he became the inaugural executive director of the Victorian Institute of Sport (VIS), a position he held until his retirement from full-time work in 2006.

Pyke's academic qualifications include bachelor's and master's degrees in physical education from the University of Western Australia and a PhD in exercise physiology and human performance from Indiana University, USA. He has authored or edited 11 books on scientific training, coach education and elite athlete development and published many articles in scientific journals and magazines. He was the editor of all three editions of the textbooks used in the National Coaching Education Program in Australia in 1980, 1991 and 2001. He also co-authored *Cutting Edge Cricket* and was the editor for *Better Coaching Advanced Manual*, both published by Human Kinetics.

He was awarded an Australian Sports Medal in 2000 and a Life Membership of the Australian Council for Health, Physical Education and Recreation in 2002. Pyke was inducted into the Sport Australia Hall of Fame in 2003 and received the Mobley International Distinguished Alumni Award from Indiana University in 2010.

ABOUT THE CONTRIBUTORS

Deidre Anderson, MA, is the deputy vice chancellor, students and registrar, at Macquarie University in Sydney. She obtained a bachelor's and a master's degree in arts and a graduate diploma in athlete counselling at Victoria University and is currently completing a PhD at Macquarie University.

Anderson has held senior management positions at the national level of sport both in Australia and the United Kingdom. Her lifelong commitment has been to support the development of young people both in sport and other areas of their lives. She is also an accredited coach in basketball and softball and still actively involved with coaching in these sports.

Kylie Andrew, MS, is the nutrition coordinator at the Victorian Institute of Sport. She has completed a bachelor of science degree at Monash University and a master's degree in nutrition and dietetics at Deakin University.

Andrew has worked as a sports dietitian for over 15 years with a variety of elite athletes and sports. She consults with the Richmond Football Club and is currently coordinating the athlete nutrition program at the Victorian Institute of Sport working with gymnastics, diving, aerial skiing, sailing, cycling, netball and track and field programs. Andrew regularly lectures to athletes, coaches and other dietitians.

Elizabeth Bradshaw, PhD, is a senior lecturer in the School of Exercise Science at the Australian Catholic University, Melbourne Campus. She has a bachelor of education (physical education), a bachelor of applied science (human movement) with honours and a PhD from Deakin University in Melbourne.

Bradshaw is an accredited women's gymnastics coach and a fellow of the International Society of Biomechanics in Sport. She worked at the New Zealand Academy of Sport in Auckland as the biomechanics program director for three years and is now the sports science advisor for Gymnastics Australia. Although her specialties are gymnastics and track and field athletics, she has also worked with athletes in netball, equestrian, triathlon, badminton, squash, basketball, cycling and softball.

Ken Davis, PhD, is a consultant in sport psychology and coach education. He has completed both a bachelor's and a master's degree in physical education at the University of Western Australia and a PhD in sports psychology at Florida State University.

Davis taught human movement and physical education at Deakin University in Geelong for many years and has played and coached cricket at first grade level as well as coached the Victorian women's team, Vic Spirit. He is presently a sports science consultant with Cricket Victoria. He has co-authored two books on cricket and is currently the editor and a contributing writer of *Coaching Edge*—a publication for accredited coaches in AFL football. He has also worked as a sport psychologist at the Geelong and Richmond Football Clubs and with the AFL Umpires Panel.

Brian Dawson, PhD, is a professor in exercise and sports physiology in the School of Sport Science, Exercise and Health at the University of Western Australia. He completed bachelor's and master's degrees in physical education and a PhD at the University of Western Australia.

Dawson has had extensive experience in coaching Australian football, having been the fitness coach for the West Coast Eagles in the Australian Football League from 1988 to 2000 and then research coordinator and sports science adviser since 2001. He has also been an assistant and senior coach at the Swan Districts Football Club in the Western Australian Football League, winning a league premiership in 2010. He was the state team coach in 2011.

Brian Douge, PhD, is the football services manager with AFL Queensland. His qualifications include bachelor's and master's degrees in physical education from the University of Western Australia, a graduate diploma of teaching from Deakin University and a PhD from Ohio State University.

Douge has taught physical education in primary and secondary schools and at the university level and has been a youth coach in cross-country, rowing, rugby union, cricket and basketball and a professional Australian football coach with the West Coast Eagles, Brisbane Bears and Subiaco Clubs. In the latter sport he has also played a coordinating role as director of coaching and football with the Western Australian Football League and the West Coast Eagles, respectively. He is the head of teacher/coach education at the University of Queensland, the deputy head of boarding and director of sport at the Anglican Church Grammar School, and the chairman of Western Australian and Queensland Junior Sport Committees.

Damian Farrow, PhD, holds a joint appointment as a professor of Sports Science with the Institute of Sport, Exercise and Active Living at Victoria University and within Movement Science at the Australian Institute of Sport. He has completed both a bachelor's degree in physical education and a master's degree in applied science (skill acquisition) at Deakin University and a PhD (in sport expertise) at the University of Queensland.

Farrow has been involved in a wide range of Australian Institute of Sport and national programs, including Australian football, rugby union, netball, cricket, tennis and swimming. He is responsible for the provision of evidence-based sport science support to coaches seeking to improve the design of skill practice and in turn the perceptual-motor expertise of their athletes.

Carmel Goodman, MD, is the chief medical officer at the Western Australian Institute of Sport. She obtained her medical degree at the University of Witwatersrand in South Africa. As the chief medical officer at the Western Australian Institute of Sport, Goodman is responsible for diagnosing and treating injuries and illnesses in athletes from a wide range of individual and team sports.

She is also currently the principal medical officer/team doctor for the National Women's Hockey Team and the National Rowing Team. She spent 15 years as a lecturer in exercise physiology in the School of Sport Science, Exercise and Health at the University of Western Australia and is a fellow of the Australasian College of Sports Physicians.

Sandy Gordon, PhD, is a professor of sport and exercise psychology in the School of Sport Science, Exercise and Health at the University of Western Australia. His undergraduate training included a diploma of physical education at Jordanhill College in Glasgow, which preceded a postgraduate diploma and master of education degree at the University of Aberdeen and master of arts and PhD degrees in sport psychology at the University of Alberta in Edmonton, Canada.

Gordon has played and coached soccer, volleyball, sailing, squash, golf and cricket and, as a sport psychologist, has contributed to athlete and coach education programs in over 10 countries. He has also consulted with the cricket boards and national teams of Australia, India, Sri Lanka and Zimbabwe.

Daniel F. Gucciardi, PhD, is a postdoctoral research fellow in the School of Human Movement Studies at the University of Queensland. He has a bachelor of science degree with honours and a PhD in sport psychology from the University of Western Australia.

Gucciardi has consulted with athletes in both individual sports (e.g., golf, archery) and team sports (e.g., football, cricket) and currently coordinates a course in performance psychology for the postgraduate programs in sports coaching at the University of Queensland.

Stephanie J. Hanrahan, PhD, is an associate professor in the Schools of Human Movement Studies and Psychology at the University of Queensland. She has a bachelor of arts degree from the University of California at Santa Barbara, a master of science from the University of Illinois at Urbana–Champaign and a PhD from the University of Western Australia.

Hanrahan is a certified coach in swimming and volleyball and has worked as a sport psychologist with athletes and coaches in over 30 sports. She is currently managing programs that combine games and mental skills training to enhance the life satisfaction and self worth of marginalised youth.

Sue Hooper, PhD, is the director of the Centre of Excellence for Applied Sport Science Research at the Queensland Academy of Sport. She completed a bachelor's degree (with honours), a master's degree in human movement studies (biomechanics) and a PhD crossing elite sport physiology, biomechanics and psychology at the University of Queensland.

Hooper is an Olympian who turned to swim coaching at developmental and elite levels as an important focus of her life for over 25 years. She taught at the University of Queensland for nearly 30 years before moving to her present position, which allows her to contribute to building knowledge and skills in a variety of sports and at all levels across the athlete pathway.

Paul Jonson, PhD, is an associate professor and head of events in leisure, sport, tourism and arts management programs, Management Discipline Group, Business School, University of Technology, Sydney. He has bachelor's degrees in arts (with honours) and law from the University of Sydney, a graduate diploma in leisure studies from Kuring-gai College of Advanced Education and a PhD from the University of Technology, Sydney.

Jonson has been both the honorary solicitor and the president of the New South Wales and Australian Touch Associations and is currently the president of the Sport Management Association of Australia and New Zealand (SMAANZ) and of the World Association for Sport Management (WASM). He was the deputy CEO and director of academic programs of Sport Knowledge Australia from 2005 to 2009.

Paul Kiteley, Graduate Diploma (ACC), is the performance services manager at the Victorian Institute of Sport. He commenced a career in teaching after finishing a bachelor of education degree with major studies in physical education at Victoria College, Rusden. He then completed a graduate diploma in accounting at the Swinburne Institute of Technology and has been working in sports administration and management since 1985.

Kiteley undertook roles in sports administration at Swinburne University, Badminton Victoria and the Australian Masters Games before joining the Victorian Institute of Sport in 1995 and has progressed within that organisation to become the performance services manager. This role involves coordinating the key areas of sports science, sports medicine, physical preparation, sports nutrition and athlete career and education.

Cliff Mallett, PhD, is an associate professor of sport psychology and coaching in the School of Human Movement Studies at the University of Queensland. His qualifications include a bachelor's degree in education (physical education) from the Queensland University of Technology and a bachelor's degree in arts (with honours in psychology) and a PhD in sport psychology from the University of Queensland.

Mallett is an experienced international coach in athletics, having represented Australia at the Olympic and Commonwealth Games and world championships. He has consulted with many national and international sporting federations and organisations and professional and Olympic coaches and athletes in sport psychology, high performance coaching and coach development. He coordinates the postgraduate programs in sports coaching at the University of Queensland.

David Pyne, PhD, is a physiologist at the Australian Institute of Sport in Canberra. His qualifications include bachelor's and master's degrees in applied science from the Canberra College of Advanced Education and a PhD from the Australian National University.

Pyne has had 20 years' experience as a sports physiologist at the Australian Institute of Sport, working with athletes and coaches in its programs as well as in several national programs, primarily including swimming, Australian football, basketball, rugby union, rugby league and cricket. During this time he has focused on the areas of fitness testing and coach education and has extensive experience in biomedical research related to exercise, training and the human immune system.

Peter Reaburn, PhD, is an associate professor in exercise and sports science at Central Queensland University in Rockhampton. He graduated from the University of Queensland with an honours degree in human movement studies and a PhD before completing a graduate certificate in flexible learning at Central Queensland University.

Reaburn has been involved in many sports both as an athlete and a coach. He is a masters athlete who competes in cycling, running, swimming and triathlon, and he won the national ironman triathlon championship in 2005. He was a premiership coach in club rugby and junior netball, a representative and current A-grade netball coach and a former state coaching director (Queensland) and member of the National Coaching Panel for Masters Swimming.

Find more outstanding resources at

www.HumanKinetics.com

In the **U.S.** call 1-800-747-4457
Canada 1-800-465-7301
U.K./Europe +44 (0) 113 255 5665
International 1-217-351-5076

eBook
available at
HumanKinetics.com

HUMAN KINETICS